DALIT STUDIES

A Bibliographical Handbook

DALIT STUDIES
A BIBLIOGRAPHICAL HANDBOOK

CHINNA RAO YAGATI

KANISHKA PUBLISHERS, DISTRIBUTORS
NEW DELHI-110 002

KANISHKA PUBLISHERS, DISTRIBUTORS
4697/5-21A, Ansari Road, Daryaganj
New Delhi -110 002
Phones: 2327 0497, 2328 8285
Fax: 011-2328 8285
E-mail: kanishka_publishing@yahoo.co.in

Dalit Studies :
A Bibliographical Handbook
First Published 2003
Edition 2018

ISBN: 978-81-7391-580-6

PRINTED IN INDIA

Published by Madan Sachdeva for Kanishka Publishers, Distributors, 4697/5-21A, Ansari Road, Daryaganj, New Delhi-110 002, Typeset by Sunshine Graphics, Delhi, and Printed at Rajdhani Printers, Delhi.

Foreword

Dalit studies burgeoned in the last few decades and yet an essential research aid, a basic bibliography as a guide to researchers, has not been available. Dr. Chinna Rao Yagati is to be congratulated on the work he has accomplished in providing a comprehensive bibliography on Dalit studies. Prior to this work a few bibliographies were compiled – one in 1961 and another in 1972—but the merit of the present work is that it has a wider coverage and, of course, it encompasses all the major studies published in the last three decades.

'Dalit' as a concept entered the lexicon of social sciences recently, perhaps as a late as the 1970's. But there is a substantial corpus of writings pre-dating the emergence of the concept, writings on the history, economic position, social status or identity politics of the people later identified as 'Dalit'. Dr. Yagati has chosen a wide enough definition of 'Dalit Studies' to include such writings. Thus in the search for relevant literature and sources this work traces a complex path through the shifting categorization of the Dalits as 'Untouchables', 'Outcastes', 'Backward Castes', 'Depressed Classes', 'Harijans', 'Scheduled Castes', 'Weaker Sections', and other similar concepts current in the domains of ethnography, legislation, social science analysis, and politics. This was necessary in order to cover the entire gamut of the discourse on Dalit through history.

While the majority of the items enlisted in this

bibliography are contemporary products, mainly of the period since the 1970's, the historical depth in Dr. Yagati's collection is revealed in the inclusion of many rare publications of the late nineteenth and the early twentieth century. The careful reader will notice that Christian missionary writings occupy a lot of space, a lot more than what one is led to believe in works of history which emphasize exclusively the role of Hindu social reformers. Dr. Yagati has had access, during his research trip to Edinburgh, to a mass of missionary tracts and journals which addressed the problems of the so-called "outcastes" in the late nineteenth and early twentieth centuries. Such rare publications include those published by the Foreign Mission Committee of the Church of Scotland, the Mission Study Council of the United Free Church of Scotland, the Church Missionary Society of London, the Society for the Propagation of the Gospel etc. More attention to this category of writings may help correct some imbalances in the perspective on Dalit history.

Another set of source books now no longer generally available to researchers, being out of print for decades, are the ethnographic and demographic reports by various agencies of the Indian government from the 1880's onwards. Not only were there the classic works Risley, Crooke, Thurston, Enthoven, Russel, Anantha Krishna Iyer *et al.* but important information are available in the series of census reports since 1881 (culminating in the last exhaustive report of this kind in 1931) as well as the reports of committees on franchise and representation in the Legislatures. Some of these sources, e.g. the report of the Southborough Commission, escaped the attention of historians. Dr. Yagati has rendered a valuable service in itemizing these sources in this bibliography. That also applies to the section in this volume which covers articles published in journals, many of them difficult to trace.

Finally, another merit of this bibliography is that it includes unpublished research dissertations. Possibly a more exhaustive enumeration of much dissertations remains to be done but this is a preliminary attempt of great value.

For all these reasons this volume can be recommended to readers as an essential research guide in Dalit studies.

Sabyasachi Bhattacharya
Professor of History
Centre for Historical Studies
School of Social Sciences
Jawaharlal Nehru University
New Delhi–110 0067.

Preface

I registered for my Ph.D programme at Centre for Historical Studies, Jawaharlal Nehru University to work on Dalits in the early years of 1990's. As a first step, my Supervisor asked me to collect a list of secondary works on the subject. After visiting half a dozen libraries/institutions in Delhi and spending nearly three months I could manage to collect a bibliographical list of fifty pages. That was the beginning of my collection. The only systematically compiled bibliography I could get was Professor Eleanor Zelliot's compilation in Michael Mahar's volume (1972). The available sources on Dalits are centered around either on Maharashtra or on Ambedkar. Rests of the works are on socio-economic aspects of Dalits of post-colonial or contemporary society. Untill 1997-98, my purpose of collection was for my personal research. But as this collection seemed to be increasing day by day, then I thought of bringing it out as a volume. Works on historical aspects of lesser known, though vibrant, regions like Punjab, Andhra, Tamil Nadu were not very well known. Ambedkar's birth centenary year (1991-92) witnessed numerous seminar, collection of works and the proliferation of articles. Within this one decade (since the centenary year), literature on various aspects, rather newer aspects on Dalits, produced was as much as that of all the previous years put together.

In 2002, I got an opportunity to visit U.K. on Charles Wallace Visiting Fellowship, where I was exposed to treasure of sources on Dalits especially related to Christian missionary activities. More particularly at National Library of Scotland, Edinburgh University Library, New College Library and many other missionary collections at Edinburgh; British Library, SOAS library and CMS archives in London were of great help in this collection. In India, the one and only place where I could get all the possible list of published books and monographs was at Gautam Publishers and Distributors.

I express my deep feeling of gratitude to Professor Sabyasachi Bhattacharya, who has been guiding spirit throughout and kindly accepted my request of writing a 'Foreword' to this volume. I am thankful to Dr. Ambrose Pinto, S.J., Professors Eleanor Zelliot, Ghanshyam Shah and S.K. Thorat for their help in this regard. Finally I thank my wife Dr. Priyadarshini Vijaisri for being 'goading' as and when I was postponing or taking long pauses in completing this work.

It is hoped that this volume will help the researcher as a reference book, more particularly, younger scholars those who intend to work on Dalits to save the trails I went through. In this volume only published books/monographs, articles and reports in English are included, except very few articles/books of non-English are included only on the basis of either they are no more available/accessible or not known at all. I do not claim that this is a complete list of writings on Dalits. There may be more, perhaps important ones as well. Since it is an individual endeavour, readers may excuse me for ominious they may notice. If the reader notices any source relating to this subject, I would request them to bring to the knowledge of the Editor, or Publisher so that we can include them in the next edition.

Shortcomings and errors of any kind, I alone am responsible.

Chinna Rao Yagati

Contents

Introduction

The issue of identity of untouchables has been a recurrent theme especially during the colonial and post-colonial period. Frequent change in the nomenclature or identity is characteristic of "untouchables" history than any other community in India and intertwined with the intellectual developments in the wider milieu. In addition to their caste or sub-caste (or *jati*) identity, homogeneous categories expressing generic identity of untouchables cutting across regional and intra untouchable distinctions have been deployed by various agencies during the colonial period. For instance, they have been categorized as Depressed Classes, Harijans, and Scheduled Castes serving multifarious contexts, ranging from official documentation necessitated by the colonial structure to the cultural movements of the caste Hindu and untouchable communities. The following section seeks to understand in a historical context as to how these multiple identities/nomenclatures evolved from time to time.

Changing Process of Dalit Identity: A Historical Note

The identification of Dalits and their struggles with those of African Americans, Vietnamese, Cambodians and Africans indicates the internal identity of the oppressed, which is more explicitly stated in their respective manifestos. The only difference of Dalits from those of other oppressed lot of the world is the problem of untouchability, a peculiar

Indian phenomenon. The basic characteristic features of the Dalits in India are: they are stigmatized people and poverty is their constant companion. Segregated by the society, marginalized by the polity, oppressed by the power mongerers. Acts of brutality and terror continue to be part of the atrocities perpetuated on Dalits, the more they become conscious of their rights and begin asserting themselves. But when one looks at their history, probably they are the only lot in the India society who have been abused than any other sections. Throughout Indian history the Dalits were labeled by others and interestingly, these labels changed from time to time and place to place depending upon their purpose they served. But deconstructing these articulated labels; Dalits reconstructed their own identity with a collective conscience. Their conscious liberation, quest for identity continues to be integral to Dalit activism. The road that struggle takes will invariably have important consequences that extends far beyond the untouchable minority. Despite of twentieth century changes and 50 years of Indian Independence the Dalits are still concentrated at the bottom of the two hierarchies i.e., caste and class, that define so much of Indian life. In the following section an attempt made to study the concepts or labels of the varied terms arouses a curiosity as to how and when the system of untouchability came into existence and what were the factors that helped its continuation, yet this will not be the focus as there has been much specialized work under progress.

The constructions of a label or a nomenclature to identify the Indian untouchables have under gone many changes and each time it appears with new nomenclature with a salient dimension to their identity. The Hindu doctrine of creation exemplified in the *Chaturvarna* scheme of social stratification does not clearly account for the origin of untouchables, because all those who belong to the four varnas are above the pollution line. However by implication those who are below the Pollution line are fifth *varna,* hence called panchamas. The identity of the Dalits was defined in the context of the doctrine of creation and its context was essentially religious. Legitimized by the theory of *karma* and reincarnation, the *panchamas* deserved to be untouchables.[1] These nomenclatures were crystallized and transformed invariably multi dimensionally in particular contexts and given times.

Untouchability with its manifold manifestations is rooted in the notions of purity, pollution, which is believed to have developed in the later vedic period, when the Brahminic literature emerged in the form of *smritis, samhitas,* and the *upanishads.* The Rigveda shows no acquaintance with people, with whom contact was even remotely tabooed. In later vedic period texts refers the *chandala*[2] and the *poulkasa*[3] are manifest objects of contempt and exist at the lowest ritual and social level, however they are not treated as untouchables. According to Baudayana Dharma Sutra, *Chandala* is an offspring of Sudra father and Brahmin mother.[4] The notion of pollution becomes a potent reality and is seen in full play with respect to *chandala.* All though Brahminical texts are not unanimous on the origin of *chandala* but are represented as an instrument of derivative pollution as a well transmitting contagion through contact. Further the references to infection from the *chanadala* through sight, speech and proximity occur. These forbears of several castes subsequently treated as untouchables are met with. These are *Nisada,* the *Kaivartha,* the *Dasa* the *Bidalakari,* the *Malaga,* etc. Shadow not regarded polluting then was a later development. The commensal and connubial taboos in relation to the *chandala* appear extremely severe and absolute.

These *chandalas* does not denote one single homogeneous class, but offspring of five different varieties. Those are: the offspring of a Sudra father and a Brahmin mother; child of an unmarried woman; offspring of Brahmins union with sagotra woman; offspring of ascetic turns back to the house hold life and an offspring of barber father and Brahmin mother.[5] Segregation was the natural corollary to the ardently preached and widely shared belief in pollution and several terms such as *antya* (the last or at the end), *bahya* (outside, pale of Chaturvarna hence became out-caste), *antyaja* (born at the end, *antavasin* (those who lives in the end) testify to the current practice. Perhaps all this meant a conscious perpetuation of an old state of affairs and created a definite barrier to free mixing in future. Most often, these generic terms developed into a specific caste name, as it happened in the case of *Nishada* (an offspring of Brahmin father and Sudra mother),[6] *Antyavasin* etc. Thus, use of words *Antyaja* and *Antyavasin*, is significance. Firstly it shows that they were living in separate quarters and secondly they were pushed to the corner by the victorious invaders. This was even recorded by the Chinese pilgrim Fahien, contemporary of Chandra Gupta - II, who lived in India between 405 AD and 411 AD. He stated that *Chandalas* live apart from others... i.e., "in separate quarters".[7] The next Chinese traveler Yuan Chaung, who visited in 629 AD reiterated that "these people were forced to live outside the city..."[8] *Purusha Sukta,* which is a part of the Rigveda states that from the face of *Virat Purusha* were born the Brahmins (Thinkers), from his hands the *Kshatriyas* (Kings) from his things the Vaishyas (Trader) and from his feet the Sudras (Servants),[9] looks mythical and unbelievable lie. This hymn reveals although irrational and unscientific, about the genesis of the chatarvarna. However, none of the *Vedas* has references to the untouchability. But there are references to Asuras, *dasas* and or *Dasyas* and *raksasas* with hatred and contempt. The concept *panchamas* referred in the *Narada smriti,* which speaks of the slaves as the fifth class or fifth order. The value givers and norm setters of the time, namely Brahmins, struck this label on them.

By the time of medieval period, it is witnessed the clear-cut growth and practice of untouchability. In the beginning of the eleventh century Alberuni visited India and left some valuable accounts, said that Sudras followed by a section of people, Antyaja or outcaste (outside the *Chaturvarna*), who were engaged in eight varieties of crafts and guides.[10] Those were sailor, fisherman, Juggler, basket maker, weaver, shoe-maker and hunter of birds and wild animals. Nevertheless, it is considered that prior to Muslim invasions of the thirteenth century was a determining period for the status and occupational duties of untouchables.[11]

The bhakti movement that swept India south to north from the eighth to the eighteenth century untouchables were honoured as saints and poets. Nandanar (700-900), a shaivate saint from Tamil Nandu and his contemporary Tiruppan, became one of the twelve Vaishnavite Alvars. The first expression of the concern for the Dalits comes from the Bhakti period in the fourteenth and fifteenth centuries in the form of religious reform. Ramananda, a Hindu reformer, preached equality and chose disciples even from among the untouchables. One of his twelve disciples was Rai Das, a chamar from Banaras. He found a sect/ association of chamars known as Raidasis or Ravidasis, followed the teachings of Ramandanda. The Bhakti movement also gave rise to the poet saints of Maharashtra among whom was Chokhamela and his entire family, Mahars of fourteenth century, inveighed against untouchability. The Bhakti tradition rejected the authority of Vedas, Brahmin priest hood and ritual practices, but failed to recover the lost identity. It was continued in various forms till the eighteenth century. However each of revolting group was reabsorbed into Hindu fold when the reform and reiteration of Hindu identity was taking place, as a sect, denomination of or as caste group. Perhaps the last saint poet in this stream was a Narsi Mehta, a Gujarati, who coined the term Harijan. The term Harijan literally means children of the god. There is unconformity as to in what sense he used and to whom to meant. In fact the term initially was used only to refer to the children of *Devadasis*, the female temple dancers. Symbolically speaking they were children of god. In that *Devadasis* (deva means god and *dasi* means servant) were dedicated to the services of god/goddess and the sexual union between the agents (priests and nobility of the village) and the servants of the god was mystified and even invested with an aura of divinity. However, the children of Devadasis had a stigmatise identity among the general population because of their ambiguous paternal identity.[12] But this term Harijan surfaced again when M.K. Gandhi picked it up popularized the term as synonym to the untouchables. But it was totally rejected by conscious untouchables and wondered why they had been sighed out as children of god? If not, whose children were they (caste Hindu) after all? In this terminology Dalits perceived another attempt to subtle segregation from the rest of society.[13]

In the modern period European visitors to India noted the existence of despised groups, and the Tamil word *Pariah* caste lent its name to the English vocabulary as a synonym for an out caste from society. For them, Pariah means a person of low caste, or of no caste or socially out-caste.[14] The Tamil Pariah is derived from Tamil Paraiyar, plural of paraiyan meaning hereditary drummer, but in common usages refers to a low caste of southern India below the Sudra rank (?). The word Pariah occurs for the first time in a poem of Mangudi Kilar, a poet of second century A.D. It is not found either in any earlier Tamil literature or in any ancient inscription. Towards the close of nineteenth century Gopalkrishna Ghokhale often used the expression to describe the state of Indian people as pariahs of the Empire.[15] In course of time it acquired so much pejorative connotation that it began to convey the opposite of all that is holy and respectable.[16] Even the first association of the untouchables was formed in 1892, the suggestion to designate it as Paraiya Mahajana Sabha was chosen. However the same association, in a memorandum presented to Lord Chelmsford and B.S. Montagu in 1917, requested to help them in their efforts to attain social elevation by issuing orders that thereafter in all government communications they should be designated as Adi-Dravidas, or the original Dravidians. Accordingly government designated as Adi-Dravidas to use as substitute for pariahs.[17]

With advent of British in modern times, their policies though originally not intended to uplift the Dalits, but benefited them like a bliss in disguise. The benefits themselves should be attributed to what some extent have called unintended positive effects of a policy that was not specifically geared to that purpose. Simultaneously, enumeration of numbers i.e., census reports, the efforts of British colonial government to collect systematic information about the many aspects of the natives and society, this gave an opportunity to Dalits not just to know about themselves but also about their counter parts of the various corners in India.

1920s witnessed major changes and challenges by the Dalits, which gave again a new set of self-conscious identities, with a more assertive manner by the Dalit radicals with a claim that they were the original inhabitants of the land, claimed that they were the sons of the soil. This culminated with on *Adi* (means original) ideology and prefixed to their regional identity *Adi*. Those were from Telugu speaking areas of Madras presidency, claimed themselves as Adi-Andras, Tamil speaking Dalits claimed themselves as Adi-Dravidas, from Canarese Adi-Kannadas. In Hyderabad, Telugu speaking Dalits called themselves as Adi-Hindus but a large section of them gave to this a militant, anti-Brahmin interpretation. For them Hindu is a not a religion. As early as in 1917, the first provincial Adi-Andhra Mahasabha claimed that the so called *Panchamas* were the original sons of the soil and they were the rulers of the country.[18] U.P. too, began to organize the Dalits on the basis of an Adi-Hindu identity under the leadership of an untouchable ascetic, Acchatananda, who argued that the untouchables are in fact adi-Hindu, i.e., the original or autochthonous Nagas or Dasas of north and the Dravidas of the South of the subcontinent and they are the undisputed, heavenly owners of Bharat. And all others are immigrants to the land, including the Aryans, who conquered the original populations.[19] Similar argument also can be seen among Punjab Dalits, who organized themselves into Adi-Dharm movement.

During 1930s emerged a new set of British official euphemisms for Dalits, such as Depressed Classes, Exterior Castes, Scheduled Castes. In 1930, the Indian Statutory Commission defined that in origin, these castes seem to be partly functional comprising those who followed occupations held to be unclean or degrading. Such as scavenging, leather working and partly tribal i.e., aboriginal tribes absorbed into Hindu fold and transformed into an impose caste.[20] The term "exterior castes" appeared for the first time in the census of India, 1931. This term for the Hindu castes hitherto known as Depressed was originally suggested by C.S. Mullan, the Census Superintendent for Assam and has been adopted in the census report 1931 as the most satisfactory alternative to the unfortunate and since the label depressed class is so depressing. It has been criticized as being the same term as out caste only of five instead of two syllables, and it must be admitted that exterior is but old out writ large. At the same time it is here submitted that out caste, with an *e* has not unnaturally attracted to its connotation the implications of the quite differently derived out caste, with no *e*. Out caste correctly interpreted seems to mean no more than one who is outside the caste system and is therefore not admitted to Hindu society. But since in practice the exterior castes also contained those who had been cast out from the Hindu social body for some breach of caste rules out caste and outcast were in some cases synonymous and the derogatory implications of obliquity attaching to the latter term have unjustly coloured the former, a taint which is not conveyed by the substitution of the word exterior, which may cannot exclusion but not extrusion.

The instructions of the government of India for the taking of this Census (1931) concluded with a rejoinder saying that, the Government of India also desire that attention should be paid to the collection of information conductive to a better knowledge of the backward and depressed classes and of the problem involved in their present and future welfare, and they also have explained that the "depressed castes as castes, contact with whom entails purification on the part of high caste Hindus. It is not intended that the term should have any reference to occupation as such but to these castes which by reason of their traditional position in Hindu society are denied access to temples, for instance, or have to use separate wells or not allowed to sit inside a school building but have to remained outside or which suffer similar social disabilities. These disabilities vary in different parts of India being much more severe in the south of India than elsewhere. At the same time the castes which belong to this class are generally known as and can in most parts of India be listed for a definite area, though perhaps the lists for India as a whole will not coincide".[21]

The question of the preparation of lists for each province was discussed at a meeting of the Superintendents of Census operations in January 1931 before the census took place. It was decided that each province should make a list of castes who suffered disability on account of their low social position and on account of being debarred from temples, schools or wells. No specific definition of depressed castes was framed and no more precise instructions were issued to the Superintendents of Census Operations because it was realized that conditions varied so much from province to Province and from district to district, even within some Provinces, and it would be unwise to tie down the Superintendents of Census Operations with too meticulous instruction. The general method of proceeding prescribed was that of local enquiry into what castes were held to be depressed and why and the framing of a list accordingly.

The census of India, 1931 has played an important role, at least in case of Dalit history for more than one reason. All Census Reports preceding to 1931 suffered greatly and were termed as estimations. Every new estimate either increased their number or added to the conflicting statements. For instance commissioner in 1921 gave what he described as *minimum* number of the Depressed Classes in various provinces making a total of 52,680,000.[22] This figure he states must be taken as low estimate, since it does not include all those who should have been included, and he says, we may confidently place the numbers of these depressed classes all of whom are considered impure, at something between 55 and 60 millions in India proper. Of the 52.6 millions for which the Census Commissioner gave actual figures, less than 43.5 million were to be found in British-India. This figure agrees fairly with the 42 million add given as the figures of depressed classes by the Franchise Committee of 1919. It is also not greatly at variance with 44.5 million estimated by the Nair Central Committee of 1929 as the figure of depressed classes in British - India, but it varies considerably from the Hartog Committees figure of approximate 30 million. These governmental agencies estimated these numbers for various purposes. For instance, the data prescribed by the Seventh Quin-Quinnial Review was meant for the educational upliftment of Dalits, the data ascertained by the Home department was intended for partial implementation of the resolution moved in the

Imperial Legislative Council regarding the amelioration conditions of the Dalits. All those numbers remained as approximate figures but not accurate. So, 1931 census decided to procure some more definite figures to be obtained than the estimations hitherto employed. However, they found it difficult to arrive at a determine numbers of Dalits. To face this they introduced the following tests to be consider a person as member of Depressed Class, such as: (1) Whether the caste or class in question can be served by the barbers, water carriers tailors, etc., who serve the caste-Hindus; (2) Whether the caste or class in question can be served by clean Brahmin or not; (3) Whether the caste in question pollutes a high caste Hindu by contact or by proximity; (4) Whether the caste or class in question is one from whose hands a caste Hindu can take water; (5) Whether the caste or class in question is debarred from using public conveniences, such as roads, ferries, wells or schools; (6) Whether the caste or class in question is debarred from the use of Hindu temples; (7) Whether in ordinary social inter-course a well educated member of the caste or class in question as an equal by high caste; (8) Whether the caste or class in question is merely depressed on account of its own ignorance, illiteracy or poverty and but for that would be subject to no social disability and (9) Whether it is depressed on the account of the occupation followed and whether but for that occupation it would be subject to no social disability.

The above mentioned tests were implemented by the Census operators to find out and obtain the exact number. Though these tests are not altogether free of difficulty, however, they clearly point to the incidence of disability as the crucial test. It is at least clear that the above mentioned forms of backwardness were not intended to enter into the definition process. The insufficiency of any single test to identify the untouchables provoked a variety of responses on the Franchise (Lothian) Committee.[23] However, the majority of the Committee, adhering to denial of access to temples and causing pollution by touch or approach as generally accepted tests of untouchability reiterated its conviction that the depressed class should include only untouchables and not those Hindus who are only economically poor and in other ways backward but are not regarded as "untouchables".[24] Finally all those untouchable groups were listed (i.e., scheduled) in 1936 for the purposes of giving effect to the provisions for special electoral representations in the Government of India Act, 1935. These scheduled groups of communities, later known as Scheduled Castes, adopted by the Indian Constitution, which legalized the term to use its all official purposes.

The concept Dalit is comparatively more recent appearance, although is not very recent coinage as some of the scholars suggests.[25] But the recent theological research shows that the concepts such as *Dalit, dal, dalah* etc., have been extensively used in the Hebrew Language.[26] But in Indian case, the concept *Dalit* came into vogue in 1972 in Maharashtra with the formation of Dalit Panthers movement. For them, Dalit is a symbol of change and revolution who believes in humanism, rejects the existence of God, rebirth, soul, sacred books that teach discrimination, fate and heaven. Because these have made him slave and a Dalit represents the exploited in the country.[27] Dalit literally means trampled, squeezed crushed or broken, or reduced in to pieces.[28] Therefore Dalit is the most secular identity than any others. Originally it denotes a class, than a caste, but now a days it is being increasingly used as synonym for untouchables. Initially it was used only to a particular community called Mahar, later it spread to all Scheduled Castes, became popular. Later on Namadeo Dhosal, a Mahar himself, a powerful poet and one of the founders of Dalit Panther movement, widened its scope to include all Scheduled Castes, Tribes, and landless labourers and the economically exploited. But again, it is applied only to the Scheduled Castes, as distinct from Tribal and OBCs.[29] In the background of Dalit Panthers movement, the Dalit sahitya movement emerged and the term was legitimized and reinforced. But this literary expression of Dalit souls emerged enough from the regions such of Andhra and Maharashtra but from the other corners of India is yet to come. This whole gamut of Dalit identity is the product of a long historical process, which rooted in a collective conscience specific to them in consolidating identity. Dalit can act as a collective actor ignoring political differences to bring about the desired incremental revolution, the democratic revolution. However, the contradictions of internal and external are not letting them to do so. The internal contradictions are to Dalits, who emerged, as the Dalit bourgeoisie is prone to capture and monopolize all the advantage of protective discrimination. The other, external forces are either accommodating the Dalit intelligentsia and political leadership by the caste Hindu political parties or creating conflicts (divide and rule) within the strong radical Dalit movement where ever it is seen emerging.

Review of Literature: A Brief Sketch

The Dalit problem is at once an old question and a new challenge. It has been with us as an existential social reality, but the magnitude of the crisis assured by it is relatively a new occurrence. Several social reformers and concerned intelligentsia, both Dalit and non-Dalit, have tried their best to eradicate untouchability from the social fabric.

The study of Dalits has been often been left to anthropologists and sociologists. They do valuable studies, but the historical point of view is often incomplete and incoherent. Dalit history has not yet become a part of Indian historiography, even though the study is of immense importance with regard to its inherent radical democratic identity and its inter-relation with the contemporary movements. Available studies on Dalit history in India suffer from lack of historical and written documentation, providing scope for ambiguity. Mainstream historical works suffer from apathy to the Dalit consciousness and maneourings in different parts of the country during the colonial period. Many works dealing with the stratification of Indian society, do give a chapter or a section on Dalits of a particular region or of a country as a whole as historical antecedents. As there are not many studies till recently on the historic movement of Dalits. Yet again, this is not to rule out the immense significance of few analytical and comparative studies on the subject. The saga of the outcaste from the

Pariah, an "untouchable" whose very shadow was considered polluting, to the present day defiant Dalit, has been long, troubled, and painful. For the different communities, juridically encapsulated within the official category of Scheduled Castes, receiving recognition as equal citizens of a democratic republic is a project still waiting to be actualized.

Owing to their extremely dehumanized and degraded position in Indian society, Dalits have always been a subject of interest for missionaries, social historians and social anthropologists, studies on Dalits started as early as the late nineteenth century, though at the early stage they were sporadic and fragmentary in nature. They mostly emerged as the outcome of missionaries' travel records and personal accounts,[30] official papers, district Gazetteers, ethnographic notes, census reports and such sources. These sources provide some account of the conditions of these communities. Some early writings of officials, including Risley,[31] Crooke,[32] Enthoven,[33] Sherring,[34] Thurston,[35] Rose,[36] Russell,[37] and Iyer,[38] have contributed in furnishing a very rich account of the ethnic background, occupation pattern, and customary habits and practices of almost all important communities belonging to different regions of India of the late nineteenth and early part of the twentieth centuries.

Perhaps what is interesting is that, most authorities on caste in colonial India were at some level or the other related to census operations. Regular estimations of Dalit populations in selected regions of the country by various governmental agencies provided some account of life and conditions of the Dalit populace. These census reports provide very useful notes on the customs, practices and organization of various communities later deemed as Scheduled Castes. After a detailed caste and tribe wise denotation of the population of India in the1931 census, with a considerable variation in their detailed tabulation and form, there was a gap of studies on Dalits in the colonial period. The post-colonial period witnessed the emergence of problem-oriented studies on Dalits. These studies were concerned about certain vital issues like: Dalit social structure; socio-economic and other disabilities of

Dalits; the impact of a deliberate development strategy of protective discrimination for their upliftment; and caste conflict.

Perhaps the earliest exhaustive and systematic work on any Dalit caste was by G.W.Briggs.[39] Drawing from variety of sources he examined in detail the socio-economic and religious life while also focusing on the private or what he terms the 'domestic' sphere of *Chamars,* the leather-workers in United Provinces. Another early work that followed Briggs was by William Hunt.[40] Writing with missionary zeal, he provides a vivid account of the life of India's Untouchables as they were in the early decades of this century. Their conversion to Christianity and their firm belief and determination to continue to be Christians were elaborately described.[41] Until Fuchs's anthropological work[42] on Nimar Balahis in Madhya Pradesh, there was a big vacuum on Dalit studies. By studying the social structure and culture of 'untouchables', Fuchs sought to fill the lacuna of anthropological literature on the marginalized sections of Indian society. Being an anthropologist he believed that for a sound understanding and true interpretation of Indian religion, culture and history, a detailed study of Indian non-Aryan "low castes" was crucial. He also believed that it is from these pre-Aryan races that the Hindu castes, in the course of centuries must have assimilated many customs and usages, which are today regarded as 'genuine Hindu traditions'.

Among the works on Dalit social structure as a part of problem oriented studies, Issacs[43] and Desai[44] and Lakshmanna[45] are important. Harold Issacs based his work on interviews with fifty educated Dalits from different professional backgrounds, and Desai on his fieldwork in 69 Gujarati villages have separately located many areas where Dalits were seriously discriminated against, including the minimum human right as basic as drawing water. While the former concludes that at the root of many social disabilities lies the problem of acute poverty among Dalits, the later highlights as many as nine different forms of discrimination, which the Dalits of his sample area suffered from. Similarly Lakshmanna has splendidly explained the extent of discrimination in a sample of twenty Andhra villages, ranging from the matter of drawing drinking water from the wells to interaction among women folk.

Among those who have visualized the problem of Dalits in the perspective of social change, some attempted their works in rural areas while others based their studies on urban dwellers. While some of them located Dalit mobility upward in the traditionally established social hierarchy due to their own initiatives and under the impact of many modern forces, constitutional, legal, and political, while others have seen them in the light of on going urbanization and industrialization. Most of them have visualized social mobility in the context of changes in the occupational pattern, customary practices, behaviour and levels of aspiration among Dalit society. But Srinivas noted that the Sankritization process is never applicable to Dalits in the sense that they can never rise up as a group.

Other significant contributions to studies on social change are works of Epstien,[46] Beteille,[47] Alexander,[48] Lynch,[49] and Zelliot[50]. They have described the impact of social change among Dalits. While Esptein shows the impact of economic development in the overall political structure in two Mysore villages, Beteille describes the process of Sanskritization among Dalits that resulted in renounciation of their traditional occupations. Alexander analyzes the multi-faceted impacts of economic independence, modern education and various public welfare programmes on the *Pulayas*, an important Dalit community of Kerala. Similarly Lynch describes the process of social mobility among the Jatavs of Agra (U.P.), Zelliot depicts the process of Dalit utilization of emerging political changes in Maharashtra.

Michael Mahar's edited volume[51] on Dalits is one of the best collections of articles by eminent specialists. Though the title suggests it, dealing with "contemporary" issues, but the authors have assessed change since the time of Gandhi and Ambedkar. Eleanor Zelliot gave a very elaborative account of the different approaches of these two leaders to bring change.[52] Lelah Dushin, while examining the role of public welfare measures in bringing about change, rightly concluded that they have so far been unable to provide a suitable means of integration to Dalits in the societal mainstream.[53] This has been justified in part by the projection of their image as dependent and their competence as suspect on the grounds that they come through special privileges.

Saberwal,[54] Patwardhan[55] and many more have seen the positive impact of urbanization and modernization on the Dalits in their individual studies; while Patwardhan undertakes the case of those who migrated to Pune (Maharashtra), Saberwal's work is about industrial townships of Punjab. In the case study of Pune, consequent changes occurring within the family structure, kinship organization and customs among Dalits have been highlighted. The author has also highlighted the non-homogenous character of the class of individuals lumped together for all legal purposes under the wider umbrella of the term Scheduled Castes; subsequently she examined the comparative aspects of purity and pollution among the various untouchable groups viz., Mahars, Mangs, Chambers, Holars and Dhors thus creating a sub-system of caste within the broader cluster of Scheduled Castes. Saberwal, in a similar attempt, explored many underlying social processes involved in the transformation of closed status group (i.e. caste) into an open unbounded system in which any person of a group can take part according to their achieved role and described how political processes led the Dalits to a higher level of consciousness of their rights and how the former relation between caste and occupation was being eroded leading many of them to join the high status network. Thus the processes of social mobility and change, has been explained in the context of the only variable, industrialization. However, Sengupta highlights an opposite casethrough his study of the *Bauri* community living in the industrial agglomerates of Bokaro (Bihar).[56] Making a detailed analysis of economic social and political conditions of these people, he focused on the reasons they were left behind in the development of the region at large. Similarly, D'Souza[57] cited the case of Amritsar (Punjab) where Dalits were segregated (in spite of the growth of industrialization and urbanization) in a separate locality at the periphery of the city.

Many studies in the era of post colonial societal development concentrated primarily on assessing the impact of constitutional safeguards and various public welfare measures and programmes to bring about change in the position of Dalits, need specific mention. Locating change in his specific context Oommen[58] perceives that they have so far served a negative purpose of creating 'caste consciousness', Ramaswamy[59] concludes that they led to the establishment of a separate identity as helpless, dependent and destitute community rather than integrating them into the rest of the society. She argues that provisions like reservations and educational facilities have benefited only the urban and semi-urban dwellers while the lots of rural Dalits remain the same as centuries ago. Agrawal and Ashraf[60] have similar opinions in their studying of Haryana, and concluding that the over all impact of the public measures is too mild to make any purposeful assessment. While analyzing the socio-economic and cultural life of Dalits in the face of developmental measures Singh[61] realizes that most of the programmes fail to attain absolute success mainly due to the relative failure of their implementation.

A section of sociological and social anthropological works by both Indians and foreign scholars have attempted to study the intercaste conflict and the state of crisis arising out of it. Perhaps the first work of this kind is by Murphy,[62] who tried to study the social tension in India and highlighted differences between the castes as well as within caste at family and kinship level. Silverton[63] focused on the existing relations among various castes, primarily between the Dalits and caste-Hindus in Tanjore villages. He admits that although, mainly due to unavoidable political circumstances, some changes had taken place in Dalits' status, their relation with caste-Hindus remained unchanged, as the caste Hindus still avoided association with them. These studies were followed by Orenstein,[64] who highlighted the situation of Maharashtra. Aiyappan[65] depicted the Iravas's agitation against the discriminations they suffered in Kerala.

None of the above studies mentioned are, however, concerned about the Dalit movement. Dalits were often categorized either as marginal people without a history of their own or as objects, rather than subjects of the history of India as a whole. The Dalit movement has not fared much better in the histories of modern India by Indian historians, who generally relegate Dalits to chapters on social reform and portray them as passive victims, recipients and beneficiaries rather than active participants in their own struggles.[66] This brief survey would seem to strongly suggest that there was no such thing as a Dalit movement, particularly during the colonial period.

Thompson and Garrett[67] did refer to the Dalit movement at several points but failed to describe it. Percival Spear, in his revision of the modern section,[68] refers to Gandhi as the leader of a movement for the upliftment of the Depressed Classes, but acknowledges Ambedkar merely as a 'Harijan leader' of outstanding courage and ability. But in his own volume,[69] neither the Dalits nor Ambedkar found any place for themselves. Amongst the British historians on Modern India, though O'Malley devoted a section on the Dalit movement, portrays it as "movement for the upliftment of the untouchables" initiated and sustained by others.[70] A later addition to the literature on modern Indian history by a western scholar is by Judith Brown, who does monitor the condition of Dalits at several points to their history but makes no reference to any organized efforts or Dalits initiatives to improve their own lot.[71]

The Indian historians by and large do not acknowledge the positive role of the Dalits either in their own movements or in anti-colonial struggles. The only paragraph that Mazumdar[72] devoted to Dalits describes them as objects of philanthropic and social work conducted by others. In his later work[73] Mazumdar refers to Ambedkar and Dalits as mere political bargainers of the 1930s and 40s struggles which ultimately led to independence. However, his long depiction of Dalits, portrayed social reformers, Congress and Gandhi as the primer movers, while Ambedkar is cast in the role of perceptive critic.[74] R.R.Sethi refers to Dalits only in connection with the communal Award of 1932 and as objects of 'uplift' work.[75] Bipan Chandra confines his treatment of Dalits to a three page section on 'the struggle against caste' in his textbook,[76] but he gives them a more activist role than his predecessors. However, this cannot be said of his recent work,[77] which is concerned only with Gandhi's "Harijan uplift movement". Finally Sumit Sarkar reluctantly includes a brief treatment of the Mahar movement, but in his discussion of the 1930s only the Gandhian Harijan campaign is highlighted.[78]

Virtually, all the above mentioned historians, Dalits were not significant and even if they were referred to, Dalits were not seen as acting on their own but in the wake of socially concerned members of the dominant castes. Dalit maneovering and consciousness was perceived as mundane or at most selfish and negative. Such interpretations of Dalit as passive indicate a failure of these scholars to get into the intricacies of Dalit perspective. This kind of historicization of Dalits is elitist and often patronizing. Metaphorically speaking, nationalist historians and caste Hindu sociologists visited the village and saw the 'upper' caste houses and wrote about village India, while the Marxist and subaltern historians visited Dalit huts and wrote about their history. But reality of the Dalit history is yet to come.

Beginning with the pioneering efforts of Eleanor Zelliot,[79] a growing number of historical monographs have recently offered a necessary corrective. These provide ample evidence of a Dalit movement prior to the enactment of the 1919 constitutional reforms which grew in proportion and political significance throughout the 1920s and 1930s. Dalits may not have had a single organization parallel to the Muslim League or the Hindu Mahasabha, but they did have strong grassroot organizations, common demand for political recognition for their own political representation as well as for dignity, equality and justice, and a recognized leadership, pre-eminent among whom was Babasaheb Ambedkar.

The Dalit struggles in colonial India, understood in the simplest possible terms, is the organizational or institutional efforts made by Dalit leaders for the liberation of Untouchables.[80] At a time when profound economic and political changes are opening new critical perspectives to review the situation of various movements for the empowerment of Dalits, not many works are available by the Indian intelligentsia. The available sources reveal the fact that the positive roles of Dalits in their movements, especially during colonial times, were acknowledged only by western scholars and Dalits themselves. One of the common denominators of this new reality is the Dalit assertion that the time has come to delineate social, economic and political realities from a Dalit perspective. The assumption is that the dominant discourse continues to be highly Brahminical both in its approach to social sciences as well as in the formulation of various state policies. It is therefore, a question of projecting a new Dalit vision capable of providing a new and more realistic understanding of tradition, history and culture.

To begin with the assumption of Eleanor Zelliot,[81] 'the year (1890) saw the beginning of articulate protest among Mahars. She concludes with an assessment of condition of Dalits following Ambedkar's death in 1956. While describing the history of Dalit movement, Zelliot moves back and forth between developments within the mahar caste on the one hand and on the other the mahars' involvement with the changing political context of the nationalist movement to which the British responded by progressively democratizing the political process. Both as the acknowledged leader of the Mahars and a recognized spokesperson of the Dalits, Ambedkar provides a continuing meeting point of these two developments. While Zelliot centered on the mahar movement in her descriptive analysis, J.R. Kamble's work[82] presents 'the saga of [how] people suffering from social, economic and political discrimination from times immemorial... have achieved their emancipation'.[83] In this narrative account, the necessary conditions for the Dalit movement were provided by British rule while the caste-Hindu reformers changed their attitudes. Much of the history is devoted to Dalit efforts to gain political representation in the legislatures between the Montagu Declaration (1917) and the Poona Pact (1932).

The first monograph on the Dalit movement to appear in the 1980s is Mark Juergensmeyar's work on Ad-Dharma Movement,[84] which is somewhat similar to Zelliot's in that he traces the history of the Ad-Dharma movement from its origins in the 1920s to its demise in 1946 and its revival in 1970. However his major concern is not with the history of one particular movement but with the role of religion in the 'lower caste' struggles for social change. Following Juergensmeyar, three studies sequentially starting from mid 80s aimed at providing a more comprehensive view of the Dalit movement in India.

The purpose of S.K. Gupta's study[85] was to present a detailed and analytical account of the multi-faceted struggle of the Scheduled Caste, the odyssey of the transformation occurring between the last quarter of the nineteenth century and the Government of India Act of 1935, the precursor for Dalits of the Constitution of India in the post colonial era. He analyzes with painstaking data to prove his point that this transformation passed through three stages. The Dalits' initiation into politics by 1916; their establishing a political identity by 1927; and a marked change in their political status secured by the 1935 Act. A.C. Pradhan[86] tells essentially the same story, but with a different frame work. Pradhan considers the developments prior to 1917 to be preparatory and treats them in a very summary form, but he then extends his period beyond 1935 to 1947. Another significance of his framework is the manner in which he organized his account less around the various British initiated announcements, missions and commissions than around the three key parties to the emergence of Depressed Classes as a social reality and a political force to be taken increasingly serious by these parties were: the British policy-makers; the Congress, Gandhi and caste-Hindu religious organizations; and the Depressed Classes' leaders and their organizations.

In his work, Trilok Nath[87] aims to throw some light on the socio-political conditions which necessitated the evolution of policies which facilitated the Dalits' participation in political arena. He concentrates primarily upon the decade from 1927 to 1937, although his treatment of history from the nineteenth century grows increasingly detailed as he approaches 1927. Like Gupta, he sees the communal struggle for power following the Aga Khan deputation and the 1909 reforms as providing Dalits an opportunity for political participation. Also, like Gupta and Pradhan, Trilok Nath, not only concentrates upon politics at the All India level, which he considers to have been crucial for Dalits but also provides considerable information on Dalit political activities aimed at influencing policy at the Centre. In his treatment of the 1927-1937 period, his narrative on the constitutional development stops with the Poona Pact.

Later on, the Birth Centenary year of Babasaheb Ambedkar (1991) has seen a plethora of publications, adding to the growing literature on Ambedkar on the one hand and Dalit politics and Dalit movement on the other. Though the number of monographs written on the Dalit movement in the1990s is small in quantitative terms, it gives us much more in qualitative terms. The whole decade of 1990s saw more of micro-level studies on various aspects of Dalit life. Often they are either related to the post colonial era Dalits in general or centered around Ambedkar.

Nevertheless by the1990s, it had become apparent that there are major differences of approach to this subject which have implications for the proper understanding of the Dalit movement. Interpreting the Dalit movement in "class" terms, marxists have been able to see it as basically progressive due to its working class and agricultural labourer base. In the colonial period, however, all Marxists along with most nationalists saw it as basically "divisive" and dangerously pro-British. This was due to the belief that the "main contradiction" was that of the oppressed Indian nationality and imperialism. The nationalist movement is perceived at the centre of the broad democratic movement in India, and the Indian National Congress was the core of this, with other major movements including working class and peasant movements having a complex relation to the Congress and only "communal and castiest movements "forming" an alternative stream of politics not nationalist or anti-imperialist but (with) loyalist pro-colonial tendencies".[88] Within this perspective Dalit movements, naturally, are condemned as diversionary. Because the Marxists in India have veered between a rather pure class perspective[89] and a pro-Congress nationalism,[90] analysis of the Dalit movement has suffered from both interpretations. It has been seen as diversionary either from the economic class struggle because of its argument for the necessity of a struggle against social oppression or in terms of the needs of a national struggle because of its insistence on putting the needs of the most oppressed or exploited group first and because of its willingness to treat the Indian elite, not foreign power, as the prime enemy.[91]

A holistic interpretation is offered by Gail Omvedt, who locates the Dalit movement in the frame work of Immanuel Wallerstein,[92] as "anti systemic", which in the language of functionalist sociological theory indicates a "value oriented movement"[93] as opposed to "norm oriented movements". Among sociologists it is possible to discern a dominant ideological current that has bearing on the study of Dalit movements. There is a "Liberal" trend among a group of scholars, who believe that it is the ancient Hindu reactionary traditions and the deep-rooted prejudice against Dalit by the caste-Hindu that has led to the protest from the Dalits. This trend views Dalit protest as a necessary outcome of an obscurantist Hindu tradition. This liberal view also has a strong tendency to assume that the Dalit movement is limited to achieving the partial advance that it has in the socio-economic, civic and political fields within the existing social order, without any thought regarding its radical transformation in other respects. It is due to this ideological position that concepts like "social mobility", "reference group" and "relative deprivation" figure so prominently in their writings on Dalit movement,[94] becoming a major frame of reference for studying Dalit movement.

While analyzing the typology of Dalit movements, Ghanshyam Shah[95] classifies them into (a) reformative and (b) alternative movements. The former tries to reform the caste system to solve the problem of untouchability and the alternative movement attempts to create an alternative socio-cultural structure by conversion to other religions or by acquiring education, economic status and political power. Both types of movements use political means to attain their objectives. The reformative movements further divided into:

(a) bhakti movements; *(b)* neo-vedantic movements; and *(c)* sanskritization movements. The alternative movements are divided into: *(a)* conversion movements, and *(b)* religious or secular movements.

In spite of various approaches and hypothetical frame works used to locate the Dalit Movement during colonial times, it would be most appropriate to perceive it in the frame work of Wallerstein's anti-systemic movements". This signifies the revolutionary ideology of the anti-caste movements that "challenged and sought to transform the basic structure of Indian social system, replacing caste and accompanying social oppression economic exploitation and political domination by egalitarian society."[96] The simplistic classification of the Dalit movement as "reformist", "castiest" or "divisive" movements is an inadequate frame work for a crucial movement which strove to establish an egalitarian society.

During the decade of the1980s and major the part of the1990s, a new trend of historiography has emerged, popularly identified as the "subaltern" school,[97] which dismisses previous historical writing as "elite" historiography, but has little to offer by way of an understanding of the comprehensive history of the people.

Two major themes that have emerged in the writings of the scholars writing under the subaltern banner are (a) peasant resistance and peasant consciousness in colonial India and (b) the relationship between the peasantry and the national movement. The term "subaltern" categorizes under its fold "the lesser rural gentry, impoverished landlords, rich peasants, and upper-middle peasants".[98] The socially oppressed, economically exploited, politically marginalised, land less agricultural labourer, Dalit does not fall within the ambit of their ideological construction. Consequently the "subaltern" sections of Indian society constitute rural gentry and impoverished landlords, the direct oppressors and exploiters of Dalit masses. marxists being limited to a class perspective, could not reach out to caste, to visualize the Indian social reality. Neo Marxists or subalterns could speak only of intermediary classes of Indian social setting. Dalitist or Dalit perspectives of Indian history can be invariably distinguished from the subaltern. I prefer to call this trend as the sub-subaltern, which is, of course, yet to emerge as a major discourse in historiography.

As the dominant historiographies find no place to locate the Dalits in historical writings, it is high time for the Dalits to articulate and reconstruct their own past. The sub-subaltern perspective calls for a Dalit interpretation of history, with a dual purpose. Firstly, to deconstruct the Dalits' passive identity throughout the historical writings and, secondly, to construct a Dalit positive identity and Dalits' appropriate place in Indian historiography.

References

1. T.K. Oommen, "Panchams to Dalits: The context and Content of Identity", *Times of India*, 11 May 1994.
2. *Vajasaneyi Samhita*, XXX. 21; *Taitreya Brahmana*, III. 4.7; *Chandogya Upanishad*, V. 10.7; V. 24.4; cited in Vivekananda Jha, "Stages in History of Untouchability", *Indian Historical Review*, Vol. II, No.1 (July) 1975, pp. 28-31.
3. *Brahadaranyaka Upanishad*, IV, 3.22; For details see Vivekananda Jha, *Early History of Untouchables in India*, (unpublished Doctoral Dissertation submitted to Patna University), 1972.
4. *Baudhayana Dharma Sutra*, Kashi Sanskrit Series, No. 104, (Benaras: 1934), pp. 6-14.
5. Vanamali Chakarvarti, "A Short Note on the Hinduisation of the Aboriginals: The Swelling of the Chandala Caste", *Indian Antiquity*, Vol. XLI, 1921, pp. 75-76; Vivekananda Jha, "Candala and the Origin of Untouchability", *The Indian Historical Review*, Vol. XIII, Nos. 1-2 (July 1986 and January 1987) pp. 1-36; also see B.R. Ambedkar, *The Untouchables: Who were they and why did they became Untouchable*? (Sravasti: 1969), (First published in 1948).
6. T. Ganapati Sastri, *The Arthasastra of Kautilya*, (Trivandrum: 1925) Vol. III, p.7; also see Vivekananda Jha, "From Tribe to Untouchable: The case of Nisadas" in R.S. Sharma and V. Jha (eds.), *Indian Society: Historical Probings* (New Delhi: 1974) pp. 67-71; S.J. Tambiah, "From Varna to Caste Through Mixed Unions" in Jack Goody (ed.) *Character of Kinship* (Cambridge: 1973), pp. 204-205.
7. James Legge, *The Travels of Fa-Hein*, (Delhi: 1971) (First published in 1886) p. 43.

8. For details see T. Waters, *On Yuan-Chaungs Travels in India*, 2 Vols. (London: 1904-05).
9. R.T. H. Griffith, *Hymns of the Rigveda*, (Delhi: 1976), p. 603.
10. Qeyamuddin Ahmed (ed.) *India by Alberuni*, (New Delhi: 1993), Second edition, pp. 44-47; also see E.C. Sachau (Tr.) *Alberunis India*, (London: 1914), pp. 101-102.
11. Eleanor Zelliot, "Untouchability", in Ainslie T. Embreee (ed.), *Encyclopaedia of Asian History*, (New York: 1988), pp. 169-171.
12. For a Similar Views of Untouchable Voices, see Horald R. Issacs, *India's Ex-Untouchables*, (New York: 1964).
13. Chinna Rao Yagati, "Education and Identity Formation Among Dalits in Colonial Andhra", in Sabyasachi Bhattacharya (ed.), *Education and the Disprivileged: Nineteenth and Twentieth Century India*, (New Delhi: 2002), pp. 84-120.
14. A.S. Hornby, *Oxford Advanced Learners Dictionary of Current English*, (Delhi: 1985), (8th impression), p. 608.
15. Cited in Trilok Nath, *Politics of the Depressed Classes*, (Delhi: 1987), p. 5.
16. M.C. Rajah, *The Oppressed Hindu*, (Madras: 1925) p. 30.
17. For details see Madras Legislative Council Proceedings, 1921-22, Vol. IV, pp. 2047-2052.
18. For details see M.B. Gautam, *Bhagyodayam: Maadari Bhagyareddy Varma, Life Sketch and Mission*, (Hyderabad: 1991).
19. R.S. Khare, *The Untouchable as Himself: Ideology, Identity and Pragmatism among the Lucknow Charnars*, (London: 1984), p.85.
20. *Indian Statutory Commission, Report*, Vol. I, (Calcutta: 1930), p. 37.
21. For details see *Census of India*, 1931, Vol. I - India, Part I-Report, (Delhi: 1933). In this volume Appendices were of a particularly informative, by J.H. Hutton, "Exterior Castes", pp. 471-501.
22. *Census of India, 1921*, Vol. I, Part - I, Paragraph 193.
23. For details see, *Indian Franchise Committee, 1932*, Volume I (London: 1932).
24. *The Government of India, (Scheduled Castes) Order, 1936.*
25. T.K. Oommen, "Panchamas to Dalits", op. cit.
26. See, James Massey, *Towards Dalit Hermeneutics: Re-reading the text, the history and the Literature*, (Delhi: 1994), Despite of many disagreements one might have with the way in which author argued, still it is a thought provoking work.
27. Gangadhar Pantawane, "Evolving a New Identity: The Development of Dalit Culture", in Barbara R. Joshi (ed.) *Untouchables! Voices of Dalit Liberation Movement*, (New Delhi, 1986), pp. 79-87.

28. See Molesworth's *Marathi English Dictionary*, 1975, (Reprint of 1831 edition).
29. Eleanor Zelliot, "Dalit -New Cultural context for an Old Marathi Word", in her *From Untouchable to Dalit: Essays on the Ambedkarite Movement*, (New Delhi, 1992 reprint), pp. 267-292.
30. Perhaps first in its kind was of Abbe J.A. Dubois, a French Missionary's experiences of early decades of 19th century of Indian people, society and culture. In Chapter five of his work contains one of the earliest documented description of Dalits. This was originally written in 1815, translated by Henry K. Beauchamps. See *Hindu Manners, Customs and Ceremonies*, (London: 1953), (third edition, 1906).
31. Herbert Hope Risley, *The Tribes and Castes of Bengal*, 4 vols., (Calcutta: 1891), also see his, *The Peoples of India*, (Calcutta: 1909).
32. William Crooke, "Chamars" in *Census of India*, vol. 1, *India: Ethnographic Appendices*, edited by H.H. Risely, (Calcutta: 1903), pp.167-175 and also see his, *The Tribes and Castes of the North-Western Provinces and Oudh* 4 vols., (Calcutta: 1906).
33. Reginald Edward Enthoven, *The Tribes and Castes of Bombay*, 3 vols., (Bombay: 1920-22).
34. Mathew Atmore Sherring, *Hindu Tribes and Castes as Represented in Benaras*, 3 vols., (Calcutta: 1872-1881); *The Tribes and Castes of the Madras presidency*, (London: 1909).
35. Edgar Thurston, *Castes and Tribes of Southern India*, 7 vols., (Madras: 1909).
36. Horace Arthur Rose, *A Glossary of the Tribes and Castes of the Punjab and North-West Frontier of Provinces*, 3 vols., (London: 1911-1919).
37. Robert Vane Russel, *The Tribes and Castes of Central Provinces of India*, 4 vols, (London: 1916).
38. L. Anantha Krishna Iyer, *The Cochin Tribes and Castes*, 2 vols, (Madras: 1909-12); *The Mysore Tribes and Castes*, 4 vols, (Mysore: 1928-36); and *The Travancore Tribes and Castes*, 3 vols, (Trivandrum: 1933-41).
39. George Weston Briggs, *The Chamars*, (London: 1920).
40. William Hunt, *Indian's Outcastes: A New Era*, (London: 1924).
41. Many of the illustrative cases he described were of Dornakal region of Andhra. His materials were drawn mostly from information given by Christian Missionaries and his personal observations.
42. Stephen Fuchs, *The Children of Hari: A Study of Nimar Balahis in Madhya Pradesh, India*, (Ahmadabad: 1966), (first published in 1951).

43. Harold R. Issacs, *India's Ex-untouchables,* (Bombay: 1976).
44. I.P. Desai, *Untouchability in Rural Gujarat* (Bombay: 1976).
45. Chintamani Lakshmanna, *Caste-Dynamics in Village India,* (Bombay: 1973), also see *Harijans and the Social Discrimination* (A study of some Telangana Villages), (Hyderabad: 1977).
46. G. Scarlett Epstein, *Economic Development and Social Change in South India,* (Manchester: 1962).
47. Andre Beteille, "The future of the backward classes: The competing demands of status and power" in Philip Mason, (ed.), *India and Ceylone: Unity and Diversity,* (London: 1965), pp. 83-120.
48. K.C. Alexander, "Changing status of Pulaya Harijans of Kerala", *Economic and Political Weekly,* Vol. III, July, 1968 (Special Number), pp. 1071-74.
49. Owen M. Lynch, *The Politics of Untouchability: Social Mobility and Social Change in a City of India,* (New York: 1969).
50. Eleanor Zelliot, "Learning the Use of Political Means: The Mahars of Maharashtra" in Rajni Kothari (ed.), *Caste in Indian Politics,* (New Delhi: 1970), pp. 29-69.
51. J. Michael Mahar, (ed.), *The Untouchables in Contemporary India,* Tuseson, (Arizona: 1972).
52. *Ibid.,* pp. 69-95.
53. *Ibid.,* pp. 165-226.
54. Satish Saberwal, "Status, Mobility and Networks in Punjabi Industrial Town" in S. Saberwal, (ed.), *Beyond the Village: Sociological Explorations,* (Shimla: 1972), pp. 111-84. also see his, *Mobile Men: Limits of Social Change in Urban Punjab,* (Shimla: 1976).
55. Sunanda Patwardhan, *Change Among Indian Harijans* (Maharashtra – A Case Study, (Delhi: 1973).
56. N. Sengupta, *Destitute and Development: A Study of Bauri Community in Bokaro Region,* (New Delhi: 1979).
57. V. D'Souza, "Scheduled Castes and Urbanization in Punjab: An Explanation", *Sociological Bulletin,* vol.35, no.1, March, 1975, pp.1-12; "Does Urbanism Desegregate Scheduled Castes: Evidence from District of Punjab", *Contribution to Indian Sociology,* (N.S.) vol. II, no. 1, 1977.
58. T.K. Oommen, "Strategy for Social Change (A study of untouchability)", *Economic and Political Weekly,* vol. III, no.25, 1968, pp.1959-1964.
59. Uma Ramaswamy, "Scheduled Castes in Andhra: Some Aspects of Social Change", *Economic and Political Weekly,* vol. 9, no. 29, 1974, pp. 1153-1158; "Self-Identity Among Scheduled

Castes: Study of Andhra", *Economic and Political Weekly*, vol. 9, no. 47, 1974, pp. 1959-1964.

60. Pratap Agrawal and C. Ashraf Md. S., *Equality through Privileges: A Study of Special Privileges of Scheduled Castes in Haryana*, (Delhi: 1976).
61. S. Singh, "The Scheduled Castes and New Dimension of Social Change", *Indian Journal of Comparative Sociology*, vol. III, No. 1, February 1977, pp. 28-38.
62. Gardener Murphy, *In the Minds of Men: The Study of Human Behaviour and Social Tensions in India*, (New York: 1953).
63. D. Silverton, *When Caste Barrier Fall: A Study of Socio-Economic Change in South Indian Village*, 1963.
64. H. Orenstein, *Goan: Conflicts and Cohesion in an Indian Village*, (Princeton: 1965).
65. Ayinipalli Aiyappan, *Social Revolution in a Kerala Village*, (Madras: 1966).
66. John, C.B. Webster, "Understanding the Modern Dalit Movement", *Sociological Bulletin*, vol.45, no.2, (September 1996), pp.189-204.
67. Edward Thompson and G.T. Gerrett, *Rise and Fulfillment of British Rule in India*, (Allahabad: 1962), (first published in 1934) pp. 623, 631 and 651.
68. P.E. Roberts, *History of British India under the Company and the Crown* (third edition by T.G.P. Spear), (London: 1958), pp. 652-653; and Vincent A. Smith, *The Oxford History of India*, 3rd edn. (edited by Percival spear) (Oxford: 1961), p. 851.
69. Percival Spear, *A History of India*, vol. II, (Harmons Worth: 1973).
70. L.S.S. O'Malley, "The Hindu Social Systems" in L.S.S. O'Malley, (ed.), *Modern India and the West: A Study of the Interaction of their Civilization*, (London: 1968), (first published in 1941), pp. 374-381.
71. See Judith M. Brown, *Modern India: The Origins of an Asian Democracy*, (Oxford: 1974), (second edition).
72. R.C. Mazumdar et.al., *An Advanced History of India: Modern India*. part III, (London: 1958), pp. 959-960.
73. R.C. Mazumdar, *The History and Culture of the Indian People: Struggle for Freedom*, (Bombay: 1969), pp. 479, 494, 521, 696, 731.
74. *Ibid.*, pp. 523-525 and 1000-1012.
75. R.R. Sethi, "The Last Phase: 1919-1947" in H.H. Dodwell, *The Indian Empire, 1858-1918*, vol. VI, (Delhi: 1958), pp. 630-31, 685-686.

76. Bipan Chandra, *Modern India: A Text book of History for Secondary Schools*, (New Delhi: 1971), pp. 231-233.
77. Bipan Chandra, et.al. *India's Struggle for Independence*, op.cit.
78. Sumit Sarkar, *Modern India, 1885-1947*, (Delhi: 1983), pp. 56, 243, 328-330.
79. Elearnor Zelliot's Doctoral Dissertation on *Dr. B.R. Ambedkar and the Mahar Movement*, submitted to the University of Pennsylvania, (Philadelphia: 1969) has not yet been published, but has provided the basis for many of her oft cited collection of articles in Eleanor Zelliot, *From Untouchable to Dalit: Essays on the Ambedkar Movement*, (New Delhi: 1992), (second ed. 1996).
80. R.K. Kshirsagar, *Dalit Movement in India and its Leaders, 1857-1956*, (New Delhi: 1974), pp. 4-5.
81. Eleanor Zelliot, *Dr. Ambedkar and the Mahar Movement*, *op.cit.*, p. 2.
82. J.R. Kamble, *Rise and Awakening of Depressed Classes in India*, (New Delhi: 1979).
83. Ibid., p. xvii.
84. Mark Juergensmeyer, *Religion as Social Vision: The Movement Against Untouchability in 20th Century Punjab*, (Berkeley: 1982).
85. S.K. Gupta, *the Scheduled Castes in Modern Indian Politics: Their Emergence as Political Power*, (Delhi: 1985).
86. A.C. Pradhan, *The Emergence of the Depressed Classes*, (Bhubaneswar: 1986).
87. Trilok Nath, *Politics of the Depressed Classes*, (Delhi: 1987).
88. Bipan Chandra, "Introduction", in Bipan Chandra et.al, *India's Struggle for Independence*, op. cit., p. 28.
89. This was represented by B.T. Ranadive and the Communist Party of India (CPI) in its "Class Sectarianism" period cited in Gail Omvedt, *Dalit and the Democratic Revolutions: Dr. Ambedkar and the Dalit Movement in Colonial India*, (New Delhi: 1994), p. 14.
90. This is represented by the CPI in other periods, and also later followed by the new Marxian academicians.
91. Gail Omvedt, *Dalits and the Democratic Revolution*, op.cit., p. 14.
92. Immanuel Wallerstein, "Anti-Systematic Movements and he Three Worlds", *Lanka Guardian*, 1 June, 1985, cited in Gail Omvedt, *Ibid.*, p. 10.
93. For details see Neil Smelser, *A Theory of Collective Behaviour*, (New York: 1963).
94. Among those notable scholars who fall into this liberal category is M.S.A. Rao, who has used similar concepts for

understanding the emergence of the protest movements among Dalits and Backwards. See M.S.A. Rao, *Social Movements in India,* (Delhi: 1982), Vol. I, p. 4.

95. Ghanshyam Shah, "Anti-Untouchability Movements", in Vimal Shah, (ed.), *Removal of Untouchability,* (Ahmedabad: 1980).
96. Gail Omvedt, *Dalit and the Democratic Revolution, op.cit.,* pp. 12-16.
97. These trend setting volumes were edited by Ranajit Guha under the title of *Subaltern Studies: Writing on South Asian History and Society,* (Delhi: from 1984 on wards) are an obvious part of what goes by the name of the "Subaltern School".
98. Ranajit Guha, "On Some Aspects of the Historiography of Colonial India" in Ranajit Guha, (ed.), *Subaltern Studies,* Vol. I, *op.cit.,* p. 8.

1

Published Books and Monographs

Abbasayalu, Y.B., *Emergence of Political Leadership among Scheduled Castes: A Sociological Study of Scheduled Caste Legislators in Andhra Pradesh*, (Hyderabad: Centre for Harijan Studies, Osmania University, 1978).

Abbasayalu, Y.B., *Scheduled Caste Elite: A Study of Scheduled Caste Elite in Andhra Pradesh*, (Hyderabad: Department of Sociology, Osmania University, 1978).

Abbasayalu, Y.B., *Impact of Higher Education on Scheduled Castes and Scheduled Tribes and Backward Classes Students within the Jurisdiction of the Osmania University*, (Hyderabad: Osmania University, 1978), [Mimeo].

Abbasayalu, Y.B., *Sociology of Depressed Groups*, (Hyderabad: Centre for Harijan Studies, Osmania University, 1979).

Abbasayalu, Y.B. and T. Tirupati Rao, "Harijan Movement", in B.A.V. Sharma and K. Madhusudhan Reddy (eds.), *Reservation Policy in India*, (New Delhi: Light and Life Publishers, 1979).

Abraham, P., *Ambedkar's Contribution for Economic Planning and Development*, (New Delhi: Kanishka, 2002).

Adhicary, Radica Mohan, *The Suppressed Classes of India*, (Dacca: A.C. Roy Chowdhury, 1922).

Adiseshiah, M.S., *Social Stratification and Trends in Income Earnings and Distribution of Harijan Communities in Tamil Nadu*, (Madras: Madras Institute of Development Studies, 1973).

Adiseshiah, M.S. and S. Ramanathan, "Educational Problems of Scheduled Castes and Scheduled Tribes in Tamil Nadu", (Madras: Madras Institute of Development Studies, 1974), [A research monograph, out of a project financed by the ICSSR].

Agarwal, C.B., *The Harijans in Rebellion*, (Bombay: Taraporevala and Sons, 1934), [A liberal caste Hindu view point, primarily concerning Maharashtra].

Agarwal, P., "Pariahs in a Non-Hindu Village", in Harjinder Singh (ed.), *Caste Among the Non-Hindus in India*, (New Delhi: National Publishing House, 1977).

Agarwal, Pratap C., *Equality Through Privileges: A Study of Special Privileges granted to Scheduled Castes in Haryana*, (New Delhi: Indian Council for Social Science Research, 1977).

Agarwal, Pratap, *Halfway to Freedom*, (New Delhi: Manohar, 1983).

Agarwal, Sudarshan (ed.), *Dr. B.R. Ambedkar: The Man and His Message: A Commemorative Volume*, (New Delhi: Prentice Hall of India, 1991).

Agarwala, S.K., "Protective Discrimination for Backward Classes in India", in M. Imam (ed.), *Minorities and the Law*, (New Delhi: Indian Law Institute, 1972).

Aggarwal, Y.P., "A Study of Locus of Control and General Intelligence among Scheduled and Non-Scheduled Caste Students", (Kurukshetra: Department of Education, Kurukshetra University, 1975), [A research monograph, out of a project financed by the University Grants Commission].

Aggarwal, Yash, Sarika Sibou and Ashok Kumar, "Educating Scheduled Castes", (New Delhi: National Institute of Educational Planning and Administration, 1992), [A research monograph].

Aggarwala, P.C. and Md. S Ashraf, *Equality Through Privileges: A Study of Special Privileges of Scheduled Castes in Haryana*, (New Delhi: Sri Ram Centre for Industrial Relations and Human Resources, 1976).

Agnihotri, Sheo Prakash, "Harijans and the Concept of Untouchability", in R.B. Rao (ed.), *Bharat-Ratna Dr. Ambedkar*, (Allahabad: Chugh Publications, 1993).

Agrawal, Binod C., "Mediating Through Media for Equality: Is There any Hope", in Vimal P. Shah and Binod C. Agrawal (eds.), *Reservation Policy, Programmes and Issues*, (Jaipur: Rawat Publications, 1986).

Aherwar, S.P., *Caste Based Discrimination and Durban Conference*, (New Delhi: Samyak Prakashan, 2001).

Ahir, D.C., *Babasaheb's Message*, (Delhi: Institute of Buddhist Thought, 1962).

Ahir, D.C., *Buddhism and Ambedkar*, (New Delhi: Ajay, 1968).

Ahir, D.C., *Gandhi and Ambedkar*, (Jullunder: Study Circle, 1979).

Ahir, D.C., Dr. *Ambedkar on Buddhism*, (Bombay: Siddharth Publication, 1982).

Ahir, D.C., *Life of Dr. Ambedkar*, (Delhi: B.R. Publishing Corporation, 1990).

Ahir, D.C., "Ambedkar Conversion and its Impact", in Sanghasen Singh and Priyasen Singh (eds.), *Ambedkar on Buddhist Conversion and Its Impact*, (Delhi: Eastern Book Linkers, 1990).

Ahir, D.C., *The Legacy of Dr. Ambedkar (Bharat Ratna)*, (Delhi: B.R. Publishing Corporation, 1990).

Ahir, D.C., *Dr. Ambedkar and Punjab*, (New Delhi: B.R. Publishing Corporation, 1992).

Ahir, D.C., "Dr. Ambedkar: A Modern Bodhisattva", in *Ambedkar and Social Justice*, Vol. II, (New Delhi: Director, Publications Division, Ministry of Information and Broadcasting, 1992), [on behalf of Baba Saheb Dr. B.R. Ambedkar Birth Centenary Celebrations Committee, Ministry of Welfare, Government of India].

Ahir, D.C., "Dr. Ambedkar's The Buddha and His Dhamma: An Assessment", in K.N. Kadam (ed.), *Dr. B.R. Ambedkar: The Emancipator of the Oppressed*, (Bombay: Popular Prakashan, 1993).

Ahir, D.C., *Gandhi and Ambedkar: A Comparative Study*, (New Delhi: Blumoon, 1995), 3rd edition.

Ahir, D.C., "Ambedkar – A Modern Bodhisattva", in V.T. Patil (ed.), *Studies in Ambedkar*, (Delhi: Devika Publications, 1995).

Ahir, D.C., *Dr. Ambedkar on Indian History*, (New Delhi: Blumoon, 1996).

Ahir, D.C., *Dr. Ambedkar on Islam*, (New Delhi: Blumoon, 1996).

Ahir, D.C., *Dr. B.R. Ambedkar: Buddhist Revolution and Counter Revolution in Ancient India*, (New Delhi: B.R. Publishing Corporation, 1996).

Ahir, D.C., *Dr. Ambedkar on Christianity in India*, (New Delhi: Blumoon, 1997).

Ahir, D.C. (ed.), *Dr. Ambedkar on the British Raj*, (New Delhi: Blumoon, 1997).

Ahir, D.C. (ed.), *Selected Speeches of Dr. Ambedkar*, (New Delhi: Blumoon, 1997).

Ahir, D.C., "The Great Conversion: Dr. Ambedkar's Pilgrimage to Buddhism", in M.L. Ranga (ed.), *B.R. Ambedkar: His Life, Work and Relevance*, (New Delhi: Manohar, 2000).

Ahir, D.C., *Selected Speeches of Dr. B.R. Ambedkar*, (New Delhi: Blumoon, 2000).

Ahir, D.C., *Ambedkar the Great*, (New Delhi: Blumoon, 2000).

Ahluwalia, B.K. and Shashi Ahluwalia (eds.), *B.R. Ambedkar and Human Rights*, (New Delhi: Vivek Publishing Company, 1981).

Ahluwalia, B.K., "Ambedkar and Gandhi", in B.K. Ahluwalia and Shashi Ahluwalia (eds.), *B.R. Ambedkar and Human Rights*, (New Delhi: Vivek Publishing Company, 1981).

Ahluwalia, Sashi, "Ambedkar Profile", in B.K. Ahluwalia and Shashi Ahluwalia (eds.), *B.R. Ambedkar and Human Rights*, (New Delhi: Vivek Publishing Company, 1981).

Ahmad, Karuna, "Sponsored Social Change and Positive Discrimination: The Case of the Scheduled Castes", in Vimal P. Shah and Binod C. Agrawal (eds.), *Reservation Policy, Programmes and Issues*, (Jaipur: Rawat Publications, 1986).

Ahmad, S.H. and J. Sreenath, *All India Anthropometric Survey: South Zone: Tamil Nadu*, (Calcutta: Anthropological Survey of India, 1991), [Anthropmetric aspect of many *untouchable* communities can be found in these series].

Aikara, Jacob, *Scheduled Castes and Higher Education: A Study of College Students in Bombay*, (Poona: Distane Ramachandra, 1980).

Ainapur, L.S., "Abolition of Caste: Ambedkar's Perspective", in *Ambedkar and Social Justice*, Vol. I, (New Delhi: Director, Publications Division, Ministry of Information and Broadcasting, 1992), [on behalf of Baba Saheb Dr. B.R. Ambedkar Birth Centenary Celebrations Committee, Ministry of Welfare, Government of India].

Aiyappan, A., *Social and Physical Anthropology of the Nayadis of Malabar*, (Madras: Madras Museum Publications, 1937).

Aiyappan, A., *Iravas and Culture Change*, (Madras: Superintendent, Government Press, 1944), Originally published as *Madras Museum Bulletin*, New Series, Vol. V, No. 1, (1943). [Ira also spelled Iluva, Ezhava, initially they were part of the generic term "Depressed Class" until 1931, but later on not listed as Scheduled Caste, but now they became one of the most powerful community in Kerala].

Aiyappan, A., *Report on the Socio-Economic Conditions of the Tribes and Backward Castes of Madras Province*, (Madras: 1948).

Aiyappan, A., *Social Revolution in a Kerala Village: A Study in Cultural Change*, (New York: Asia Publishing House, 1965).

Aiyar, T.S., *Problems of Depressed Classes*, (Madras: M. Subrahmanya, 1923).

Ajnat, Surendra, *Ambedkar on Islam*, (Jalandhar: Buddhist Publishing House, 1986), [Pamphlet].

Ajnat, Surendra (ed.), *Letters of Ambedkar*, (Jalandhar: Bheem Patrika Publications, 1993).

Ajnat, Surendra, "Dr. Ambedkar: A Humanist Perspective", in Bhajan Kaur (ed.), *The Philosophy of Dr. B.R. Ambedkar*, (Chandigarh: Dr. Ambedkar Study Circle, 1999).

Ajnat, Surendra, "Neo-Buddhism: A Quest for Identity", in G.S. Bal (ed.), *Understanding Ambedkar*, (Delhi: Ajanta Books, 2000).

Akhtar, Saleem, "Dr. B.R. Ambedkar's Contribution as an Eminent Constitutionalist", in Nazeer H. Khan (ed.), *B.R. Ambedkar on Federalism, Ethnicity and Gender Justice*, (New Delhi: Deep & Deep, 2001).

Alam, Javed and B.N. Sahay, "Halalkhore: A Muslim Untouchable Community of Ranchi (Bihar)", in Makhan Jha (ed.), *Scheduled Castes Today*, (New Delhi: M.D. Publications, 1997).

Alam, Md. Rafique, "Quality of Life of Scheduled Caste and High Caste Youths", in N. Hasnain (ed.), *Weaker Sections: The Psycho-Social Perspective*, (New Delhi: Gyan, 1998).

Alexander, K.C., "The Neo-Christians of Kerala", in J. M. Mahar (ed.), The *Untouchables in Contemporary India*, (Tucson: University of Arizona Press, 1972).

All-India Federation of Scheduled Castes, Scheduled Tribes and Other Backward Classes, *Memorandum for the Implementation of the Report of the Backward Classes Commission, Government of India*, (New Delhi: S.M. Kaushik, 1964).

All-India Scheduled Castes Pratinidhi Sabha (held at Nanded), *The Four Immediate Needs of Twelve Crore Suppressed Human Beings in India (Resolutions Passes Unanimously)*, (Hyderabad: B.Sham Sunder, 1965).

Alone, Y.S., "Excellent Career", in *Souvenir of Oriental Insurance SC/ST Employees' Association*, (Pune: 1996).

Alone, Y.S., "Dr. Ambedkar's Historicism: Confrontations and Enquiries", in S.K. Thorat (ed.), *Ambedkar in Retrospect: Reflection on Contributions*, (Delhi: Manohar, forthcoming).

Alte, I.D., *Rural Employment of Scheduled Castes*, (New Delhi: Deep & Deep, 1992).

Alva, J., *Man and Superman of Hindusthan*, (Bombay: Thacker and Co., 1943).

Ambaikar, B.M., "Contribution of Dr. B.R. Ambedkar to the Evolution of Jural Postulates in India", in K.N. Kadam (ed.), *Dr. B.R. Ambedkar: The Emancipator of the Oppressed*, (Bombay: Popular Prakashan, 1993).

Ambedkar, Dr. B.R., *The Evolution of Provincial Finance in British India*, (London: P.S. King and Son, 1923).

Ambedkar, Dr. B.R., "Prantik Bahiskrit Parishad, Adhiveshan Dusre", *Presidential Address* delivered at the Second Session of the District Conference of the Depressed Classes held in Barshi, Solapur District, (May 10-12, 1924), [A handwritten manuscript in Marathi].

Ambedkar, Dr. B.R., *Presidential Address to the All-India Depressed Classes Congress*, (Bombay: Bharat Bhushan Printing Press, 1930), [delivered on 8 August 1930 at Nagpur].

Ambedkar, Dr. B.R. and R. Srinivasan, "Supplementary Memorandum on Claims of the Depressed Classes for Social Representation", Appendix 7 in the *Indian Round Table Conference (Second Session) 7th September 1931 – 1st December 1931, Proceedings of Federal Structure Committee and Minorities Committee*, Vol. 3, (Calcutta: Government of India, 1932).

Ambedkar, Dr. B.R., *Annihilation of Caste, With a Reply to Mahatma Gandhi*, (Bombay: Bharat Bhusan Press, 1936).

Ambedkar, Dr. B.R., *Mukhti Kon Pathe* [Which Way Freedom?], (Bombay: Bharat Bhushan Press, (1936), [A pamphlet in Marathi].

Ambedkar, Dr. B.R., *Federation Vs. Freedom*, (Poona: Gokhale Institute of Economics and Political Science, 1939), [originally it was Kale Memorial Lecture delivered on 29 January 1939].

Ambedkar, Dr. B.R., *Grievances of the Scheduled Castes: Memorandum Submitted to His Excellency the Governor General on the 29th October*, (New Delhi: Government of India, 1942).

Ambedkar, Dr. B.R., *Thoughts on Pakistan*, (Bombay: Thacker and Co., 1941).

Ambedkar, Dr. B.R., *What Congress and Gandhi Have Done to the Untouchables*, (Bombay: Thacker and Co., 1946), (2nd edition), (first published in 1943).

Ambedkar, Dr. B.R., *Ranade, Gandhi and Jinnah*, (Bombay: Thacker, 1943), (Reprinted by Bheem Patrika Publication, Jullundhur City, 1964), [Address delivered on 10th Birth Anniversary of M.G. Ranade, in Gokhale Memorial Hall, Poona, in 1943].

Ambedkar, Dr. B.R., *Annihilation of Caste*, (Amritsar: Ambedkar School of Thoughts, Katra Jaman Singh, 1944).

Ambedkar, Dr. B.R., *Commercial Deadlock and A Way to Solve it*, (Delhi: F and O Printing, 1945), [originally it was Address to the All-India Scheduled Castes Federation, delivered on 6 May 1945].

Ambedkar, Dr. B.R., *Mr. Gandhi and the Emancipation of the Untouchables*, (Bombay: Thacker and Co., 1946).

Ambedkar, Dr. B.R., *History of Indian Currency and Banking*, (Bombay: Thacker and Co., 1946).

Ambedkar, Dr. B.R., *Pakistan or the Partition of India*, (Bombay: Thacker and Co., 1946).

Ambedkar, Dr. B.R., *Who were the Shudras and How they came to be the Fourth Varna in Indo-Aryan Society*, (Bombay: Thaker and Co., 1946).

Ambedkar, Dr. B.R., *States and Minorities: What are their Rights and How to Secure them in the Constitution of Free India*, (Bombay: Thacker and Co., 1947).

Ambedkar, Dr. B.R., *The Untouchables: Who were They? And Why They Became Untouchables?*, (New Delhi: Amrit Books Co., 1948).

Ambedkar, Dr. B.R., *Maharashtra as a Linguistic Province*, (Bombay: Thacker and Co., 1948).

Ambedkar, Dr. B.R., *Case for the Hindu Code*, (New Delhi: Beacon Information and Publications, 1949).

Ambedkar, Dr. B.R., *Conditions Precedent to the Success of Parliamentary Democracy in India*, (Poona: V.B. Gogate, Honorary Secretary, Poona District Law Library, 1953].

Ambedkar, Dr. B.R., *Thoughts on Linguistic States*, (Bombay: Ram Krishna Printing Press, 1955).

Ambedkar, Dr. B.R., *Buddha and Karl Marx*, (Kathmandu: Conference of World Fellowship of Buddhists, 1956), [Speech delivered on 20 November 1956 in the Conference].

Ambedkar, Dr. B.R., *The Buddha and His Dhamma*, (Bombay: Siddharth College Publications, 1957).

Ambedkar, Dr. B.R., *Thus Spoke Ambedkar: Selected Speeches*, (Compiled by Bhagwan Das), (Jullundhur City: Bheem Patrika Publications, 1963).

Ambedkar, Dr. B.R., "Buddhism and Communism", *National Seminar on Marx, Ambedkar and Polarization of Oppressed and Exploited Classes in India*, (New Delhi: Sanjivayya Institute of Socio-Economic Studies, 1991).

Ambedkar, Dr. B.R., *The Cabinet Mission and the Untouchables*, (Bombay: Privately printed, no date).

Ambedkar, Dr. B.R., *Dr. Babasaheb Ambedkar: Writings and Speeches*, (Edited by Vasant Moon), (Bombay: Department of Education, Government of Maharashtra, 2000), 17 Volumes.

Ambedkar, Dr. B.R., "In an Unjust World: The Meaning of Being a Dalit", in K.C. Yadav (ed.), *Beyond the Mud Walls: Indian Social Realities*, (Gurgaon, Haryana: Hope India Publications, 2001).

Ambedkar and Social Justice, 2 Vols., (New Delhi: Director, Publications Division, Ministry of Information and Broadcasting, 1992), [on behalf of Baba Saheb Dr. B.R. Ambedkar Birth Centenary Celebrations Committee, Ministry of Welfare, Government of India].

Ambedkar Buddhist Mission, *Constitution of the Ambedkar Buddhist Mission*, (Jullundur: Ambedkar Buddhist Mission, 1966), (mimeo).

Dr. B.R. Ambedkar: A Centenary Tribute: An Anthology of Papers Placed and Speeches Delivered (Including Hindi) at the Seminar on B.R. Ambedkar's Birth Centenary, (Calcutta: Department of Information and Cultural Affairs, Government of West Bengal, 1993).

Ambedkar, R.M., "Role of Development Schemes for Scheduled Castes and Tribes: Do They Work?", in Barbara R. Joshi (ed.), *Untouchable! Voices of the Dalit Liberation Movement*, (London: The Minority Rights Groups Ltd. and Zed Books Ltd., 1986).

Ambulgekar, Kailash G., "Varna and Oppression", in Ambrose Pinto (ed.), *Dalit Assertion for Identity*, (New Delhi: Indian Social Institute, 1999), [Proceedings of the National Seminar of Dalit Postgraduate and Research Students held on 23-25 January 1999 in the Indian Social Institute].

Anand, C.L., *Equality, Justice and Reverse Discrimination*, (New Delhi: Mittal, 1987).

Anand, Mulk Raj, *Untouchable*, (New Delhi: Arnold Associates, 1981), (First Published in 1935).

Anand, Mulk Raj and Eleanor Zelliot (eds.), *An Anthology of Dalit Literature (Poetry)*, (New Delhi: Gyan, 1992).

Anandan, K., "The Influence of Dr. Ambedkar", in *Ambedkar and Social Justice*, Vol. II, (New Delhi: Director, Publications Division, Ministry of Information and Broadcasting, 1992), [on behalf of Baba Saheb Dr. B.R. Ambedkar Birth Centenary Celebrations Committee, Ministry of Welfare, Government of India].

Anandhi, S., *Contending Identities: Dalits and Secular Politics in Madras Slums*, (New Delhi: Indian Social Institute, 1995).

Anant, Santokh Singh, "Changing caste Hindu attitudes towards Harijans: A Follow-up after Four Years", in G.R.Gupta (ed), *Cohesion and Conflict in Modern India*, (New Delhi: Vikas, 1978)

Andhra Pradesh Civil Liberties Committee, 1991, *The Chundur Carnage*, Vijayawada, APCLC.

Anil Singh, C.B., "Religion and Identity", in Ambrose Pinto (ed.), *Dalit Assertion for Identity*, (New Delhi: Indian Social Institute, 1999), [Proceedings of the National Seminar of Dalit Postgraduate and Research Students held on 23-25 January 1999 in the Indian Social Institute].

Anjaneyulu, D., "Manu of Modern India", in B.K. Ahluwalia and Shashi Ahluwalia (eds.), *B.R. Ambedkar and Human Rights*, (New Delhi: Vivek Publishing Company, 1981).

Anonymous, "The Greatest Social Reformer and Educationist of this Era", in *Babasaheb Dr. Ambedkar Jayanti Sandesh*, (Agra: Ambedkar Bhavan, 1966).

Anonymous, *Gandhi or Ambedkar*, (Madras: Gandhi Era Publications, 1945), [Forewarded byRadhakrishnan].

Anonymous, *The Depressed Classes: A Chronological Documentation*, Part I, (Ranchi: Rev. Fr. Jans, S.J., Catholic Press, 1935), Part II–XI, (Kurseong: St. Mary's College, 1935–37), [This was a review of the conversion movement and its consequences of 1930s].

Anonymous, *The Depressed Classes: An Enquiry into Their Condition and Suggestions for Their Uplift*, (Madras: G.A. Natesan, 1912).

Anonymous, *Traffic in Women: Socio-Economic Condition of Koltas and Bajgis of Jaunsar Bawar*, (Lucknow: Tribal Research Centre, 1973).

Anonymous, *Rightful Place for Harijans*, (New Delhi: DVAP, 1976).

Anonymous, "Ambedkar on Ambedkar: What does it mean to be a Dalit", in K.C. Yadav, (ed.), *From Periphery to Centre Stage: Ambedkar, Ambedkarism and Dalit Future*, (New Delhi: Manohar, 2000).

Anthoni Raj, Thumma, *Springs From the Subalterns: Patterns and Perspectives in People's Theology*, (Delhi: ISPCK, 1999).

Anthoni Raj, Thumma, *Dalit Liberation Theology: Ambedkarian Perspective*, (Delhi: ISPCK, 2000).

Antony, M.J., *Dalit Rights: Landmark Judgements on SC/ST/ Backward Classes*, (New Delhi: Indian Social Institute, 1997).

Appa Rao, V. (ed.), *Facilities to Scheduled Castes and Scheduled Tribes in Universities and Colleges: Analysis on the Position of Actual Admission and Employment of Scheduled Castes and Scheduled Tribes in Universities and Colleges During 1977-78)*, (New Delhi: University Grants Commission, 1982).

Appavoo, James Theophilius, "Dalit Religion", in James Massey (ed.), *Indigenous People: Dalits. Dalit Issues in Today's Theological Debate*, (Delhi: ISPCK, 1998), (First Published in 1994).

Arakeri, Siddharth, S., "Ambedkar and Reservation Policy", in A.M. Rajasekharaiah (ed.) *The Socio-Economic Transformation of India—Dr. Ambedkar's Vision*, (Dharwad: Karnatak University, 1983).

Arnold, David, 'Land and Labour in Late Eighteenth Century South India: The Golden Age of the Pariah?', in Peter Robb (ed), *Dalit Movement and the Meanings of Labour in India*, (New Delhi, Oxford University Press, 1996), (First Published in 1993).

Arokiasamy, S., "Sarvodaya Through Antyodaya: Liberation of the Dalits in the Contextualisation of Morals", in James Massey (ed.), *Indigenous People, Dalits: Dalit Issues in Today's Theological Debate*, (Delhi: ISPCK, 1998), (First Published in1994).

Arora, P.N. and Dileep Kapoor, "Self-Disclosure of Martially Adjusted and Unadjusted Scheduled Caste Women", in N. Hasnain (ed.), *Weaker Sections: The Psycho-Social Perspective*, (New Delhi: Gyan, 1998).

Arputharaj, S., "Christian Minority in India", in V. Devasahayam (ed.), *Dalits and Women: Quest for Humanity*, (Madras: The Gurukul Summer Institute, 1992).

Arulraja, M.R., *Jesus the Dalit: Liberation Tehology by Victims of Untouchability, An Indian Version of Apartheid*, (Hyderabad: Arulraja Volunteer Centre, 1996).

Arunajyothi, K.P., "Historiographical Critique on the Dalit Movement", in Ambrose Pinto (ed.), *Dalit Assertion for Identity*, (New Delhi: Indian Social Institute, 1999), [Proceedings of the National Seminar of Dalit Postgraduate and Research Students held on 23-25 January 1999 in the Indian Social Institute].

Ashirvad, N., "Dr. Ambedkar and Social Justice", in *National Seminar on Marx, Ambedkar and Polarization of Oppressed and Exploited Classes in India*, (New Delhi: Sanjivayya Institute of Socio-Economic Studies, 1991).

Ashraf, Mohd., "Dr. Ambedkar and His Concept of Social Justice: An Analysis", in Nazeer H. Khan (ed.), *B.R. Ambedkar on Federalism, Ethnicity and Gender Justice*, (New Delhi: Deep & Deep, 2001).

Assayag, Jackie, "Modern Devadasis: Devotees of Goddess Yellamma in Karnataka", in Gabriella Elchinger and Ferro Luzzi (eds.), *Rites and Beliefs in Modern India*, (Delhi: Manohar, 1990).

Augustine, P.A., *Social Equality in Indian Society*, (New Delhi: Concept, 1991).

Awasthi, A.B.L., "Dr. Bhim Rao Ambedkar–An Assessment", in R.B. Rao (ed.), *Bharat-Ratna Dr. Ambedkar*, (Allahabad: Chugh Publications, 1993).

Awaya, Toshie, "Some Aspects of the Tiyyas' 'Caste' Movement with Special Reference to British Malabar", in H. Kotani (ed.), *Caste System, Untouchability and the Depressed*, (New Delhi: Manohar, 1997).

Ayrookuziel, A.M.A., "The Religious Resources of the Dalits in the Context of their struggle", in S.K. Chatterji (ed.), *Essays in Celebration of the CISRS Silver Jubilee*, (Madras: Christian Institute for the Study of Religion and Society, 1983).

Ayrookuzhiel, A.M.A., *Swami Anand Thirth, Untouchability: Gandhian Solution on Trial*, (Delhi: ISPCK, 1987).

Ayrookuzhiel, A.M.A. (ed.), *The Dalit Desiyata: The Kerala Experience in Development and Class Struggle*, (Delhi: ISPCK, 1990), [published for the Christian Institute for the Study of Religion and Society, Banglore.].

Ayrookuzhiel, A.M.A., "The Ideological Nature of the Emerging Dalit Consciousness", in Arvind P. Nirmal (ed.), *Toward a Common Dalit Ideology*, (Madras: Gurukul Lutheran Theological College and Research Institute, 1990), [Papers presented at the National Seminar on Dalit Ideology organized by the Department of Dalit Theology, Gugukul Lutheran Theological College and Research Institute].

Ayrookuzhiel, A.M.A., "Dalits Move Towards the Ideology of Nationality", in Arvind P. Nirmal (ed.), *A Reader in Dalit Theology*, (Madras: Gurukul, 1992).

Ayrookuzhiel, A.M.A., "Dalit Theology: A Movement of Counter-Culture", in James Massey (ed.), *Indigenous People, Dalits: Dalit Issues in Today's Theological Debate*, (Delhi: ISPCK, 1998), (First Published in1994).

Ayrookuzhiel, A.M.A., "Chinna Pulayan: The Dalit Teacher of Sankaracharya", in Walter Fernandes (ed.), *The Emerging Dalit Identity: The Reassertion of Subalterns*, (New Delhi: Indian Social Institute, 1996).

Ayrookuzhiel, A.M.A., "The Religious Factor in Dalit Liberation: Some Reflections", in S.K. Chatterjee and H.P. Mabry (eds.), *Culture, Religion and Society*, (Banglore: Christian Institute for the Study of Religion and Society, 1996).

Ayyangar, A., "Adi Dravidas", in the *Report of the Criminal Tribes Act Enquiry Committee, 1949-50.*

Ayyar, S.V., *A Study of Opinion Regarding the Various Ameliorative Measures to Improve the Conditions of Backward and Scheduled Castes*, (Annamalainagar: Annamalai University, 1965).

Azariah, M., "The Church's Healing Ministry to the Dalits", in James Massey (ed.), *Indigenous People, Dalits: Dalit Issues in Today's Theological Debate*, (Delhi: ISPCK, 1998), (First Published in1994).

Azariah, M., *Christ and Dalit Liberation*, (Madras: Christian Literature Society, n.d.).

Azariah, M., *The Un-Christian Side of the Indian Church: The Plight of the Untouchable Converts*, (Bangalore: 1985).

Azariah, Masilamani, *A Pastor's Search for Dalit Theology*, (Delhi: ISPCK, 2000).

Azmi, S.S.H., "Dr. Ambedkar as Pioneer for the Upliftment of Status of Women", in Nazeer H. Khan (ed.), *B.R. Ambedkar on Federalism, Ethnicity and Gender Justice*, (New Delhi: Deep & Deep, 2001).

Babasaheb Dr. Ambedkar Commemorative Souvenir, (New Delhi: Dr. B.R. Ambedkar Vichar Manch, 1989).

Babasaheb Ambedkar Portrait Unveiling Ceremony Commemorative Souvenir, (New Delhi: Dr. B.R. Ambedkar Vichar Manch, 1990).

Babb, Lawrence A., "The Satnamis – Political Involvement of a Religious Movement", in J. Michael Mahar (ed.), *The Untouchables in Contemporary India*, (Tucson: University of Arizona Press, 1972).

Bag, Dulal Chandra, *Impact of Education on Some Backward Communities of West Bengal: Study Based on West Dinajpur*, (Calcutta: OPS Publications, 1984).

Bagale, V.N., *No Violence, No Liberation*, (Nagpur: Author, 1993).

Bagale, V.N., *Manusmruti and Neo Brahmanism*, (Nagpur: Author, 1998).

Bagale, V.N., *For Indians to Think*, (Nagpur: Author, 1999).

Bahadur, K.P., *Castes and Tribes in India,* (New Delhi: Ess Ess Publications, 1977).

Bahadur, Virendra, "Dr. Bhim Rao Ambedkar and Indian Caste System", in R.B. Rao (ed.), *Bharat-Ratna Dr. Ambedkar,* (Allahabad: Chugh Publications, 1993).

Bahuguna, S.D. and D.N. Majumdar, "The Material Culture of the Rawattas of Rawari", *Proceedings of the Indian Science Congress,* (Hyderabad: 24th Session, 1937).

Bailey, F.G., "The Boad Outcastes", in *Caste and the Economic Frontier,* (Manchester: Manchester University Press, 1957).

Bailey, F.G., *Caste and Economic Frontier: A Village in Highland Orissa,* (Bombay: OUP, 1958).

Bailey, F.G., *Tribe, Caste and Nation,* (Manchester: Manchester University Press, 1960).

Bains, P.S., *Socio-Economic Problems and Rights of Scheduled Castes/Scheduled Tribes and Other Backward Castes,* (Dehradun: P.S. Bains, 1990).

Bains, Ravinder Singh, *Reservation Policy and Anti-Reservationists,* (New Delhi: B.R. Publishing Corporation, 1994).

Baisanthy, D.K., *Dr. Ambedkar: A Pioneer of Labour Welfare,* (Jalandhar: Buddhist Publishing House, 1982), [Pamphlet].

Baisanthy, D.K., *Ambedkar: The Total Revolution,* (New Delhi: Segment, 1991).

Bajpai, Amar Nath, "Dr. Ambedkar and Upliftment of Down-Trodden", in R.B. Rao (ed.), *Bharat-Ratna Dr. Ambedkar,* (Allahabad: Chugh Publications, 1993).

Bakshi, S.R., *Gandhi and the Status of the Harijans,* (New Delhi: Deep and Deep Publications, 1987).

Bakshi, S.R., *Jagjivan Ram: the Harijan Leader,* (New Delhi: Anmol, 1992).

Bakshi, S.R. (ed.), *B.R. Ambedkar: His Political and Social Ideology,* 2 vols., (New Delhi: Deep and Deep, 2000).

Bal, G.S., "Dr. Ambedkar's Concept of Democratic System", in Bhajan Kaur (ed.), *The Philosophy of Dr. B.R. Ambedkar*, (Chandigarh: Dr. Ambedkar Study Circle, 1999).

Bal, G.S. (ed.), *Understanding Ambedkar*, (Delhi: Ajanta Books, 2000).

Bal, Gian Singh, "Ambedkar-Gandhi Controversy", in G.S. Bal (ed.), *Understanding Ambedkar*, (Delhi: Ajanta Books, 2000).

Balasundaram, Franklyn J., *Dalits and Christian Mission*, (Bangalore: Asia Trading Corporation, 1997).

Balawant, Damodar, *Dr. B.R. Ambedkar and Revolutionary Thoughts*, (Bangalore: K. Shanta, n.d.).

Ballav, Rebati, *Dalit: A Sub Human*, (New Delhi: Ashish, 1994).

Balley, L.R., "India Needs a Cultural Revolution", in Barbara R. Joshi (ed.), *Untouchable!: Voices of the Dalit Liberation Movement*, (London: Zed Books, 1986).

Balraj and Rameshwar Das, "Dr. Ambedkar's Vision on Socio-Economic Justice", in Bhajan Kaur (ed.), *The Philosophy of Dr. B.R. Ambedkar*, (Chandigarh: Dr. Ambedkar Study Circle, 1999).

Bamfield, J.A.M. et. al., *Thoughts on Dr. Ambedkar*, (Jalandhar: Bheem Patrika Publications, 1972).

Banarjee, B.N., *Struggle for Justice to Dalit Christians*, (New Delhi: New Age International Publishers, 1997).

Bandhu, K.P.R., "B.R. Ambedkar and His Contribution to Buddhism", in Sanghasen Singh and Priyasen Singh (eds.), *Ambedkar on Buddhist Conversion and Its Impact*, (Delhi: Eastern Book Linkers, 1990).

Bandopadhyay, Sekhar, "Social Protest or Politics of Backwardness?: The Namasudra Movement in Bengal, 1872–1911", in Basudeb Chattopadhyay, H.S. Vasudevan and Rajat K. Ray (eds.), *Dissent and Consensus: Social Protest in Pre-Industrial Societies*, (Calcutta: 1989).

Bandopadhyay, Sekhar, "Caste, Class and Politics in Colonial Bengal: A Case Study of the Namasudra movement of 1872-1937", in K.L. Sharma (ed.), *Caste and Class in India*, (Jaipur: Rawat Publications, 1994).

Bandopadhyay, Sekhar, "Development, Differentiation and Caste: The Namasudra Movement in Bengal, 1872–1947", in Sekhar Bandopadhyay, Abhijit Dasgupta and Willem Van Schendel (eds.), *Bengal: Communities, Development and States*, (New Delhi: Manohar, 1994).

Bandopadhyay, Sekhar, *Caste, Protest and Identity in Colonial India: The Namasudras of Bengal, 1872 – 1947*, (London: Curzon, 1997).

Bandyopadhyaya, J., M. Sachidananda, Rafiq Khan and S.S. Singh, *The Harijans*, (Varanasi: Gandhian Institute of Studies, 1978), [collection of essays by the various authors].

Bardan, Kalpana, *Of Women, Outcastes, Peasants and Rebels*, (Berkeley: 1990).

Bansode, Kranti, "Experiences of Discrimination", in Ambrose Pinto (ed.), *Dalit Assertion for Identity*, (New Delhi: Indian Social Institute, 1999), [Proceedings of the National Seminar of Dalit Postgraduate and Research Students held on 23-25 January 1999 in the Indian Social Institute].

Baranwal, Keshava Prasad, "Dr. Bhim Rao Ambedkar – A Creative Writer and an Educationist", in R.B. Rao (ed.), *Bharat-Ratna Dr. Ambedkar*, (Allahabad: Chugh Publications, 1993).

Barve, S.G., *Dr. B.R. Ambedkar – A Symbol of Social Revolt*, (Bombay: Maharashtra Information Centre, 1967).

Basavalingappa, B., *The Emancipation of Scheduled Castes: The Ambedkar Path*, (Banglore: Nagesena Vidyalaya, 1991), [Pamphlet].

Basham, Ardythe, *Untouchable Soldiers: The Mahars and the Mazhbis*, (edited by Bhagwan Das), (Bangalore: Ambedkar Sahitya Prakashana, 1980).

Basu, Sunil Kumar and S. Bhattacharya, *Crafting Practising Scheduled Castes*, (Calcutta: Cultural Research Institute, 1987).

Baxi, Upendra, "Emancipation of Justice: Babasaheb Ambedkar's Legacy and Vision", in *Ambedkar and Social Justice,* Vol. I, (New Delhi: Director, Publications Division, Ministry of Information and Broadcasting, 1992), [on behalf of Baba Saheb Dr. B.R. Ambedkar Birth Centenary Celebrations Committee, Ministry of Welfare, Government of India].

Baxi, Upendra, "Emancipation of Justice: Babasaheb Ambedkar's Legacy and Vision", in V.T. Patil (ed.), *Studies in Ambedkar,* (Delhi: Devika Publications, 1995).

Baxi, Upendra, "Emancipation as Justice: Legacy and Vision of Dr. Ambedkar", in K.C. Yadav, (ed.), *From Periphery to Centre Stage: Ambedkar, Ambedkarism and Dalit Future,* (New Delhi: Manohar, 2000).

Behar, S.C., "Reservation: An Insufficient Condition for Social Transformation", in Ghanshyam Shah (ed.), *Dalits and the State,* (New Delhi: Concept Publishing Company, 2002), [Published for Centre for Rural Studies, Lal Bahadur Shastri National Academy of Administration, Mussoorie].

Behera, Sanjeeb K. (Comp.), *Database on Scheduled Castes Literacy in India,* (New Delhi: Indian Social Institute, 1999).

Behera, Sanjeeb K. (ed.), *Dalits and Land Reforms in India,* (New Delhi: Indian Social Institute, 2000).

Benjamin, Joseph, *Scheduled Castes in Indian Politics and Society,* (New Delhi: Ess Ess Publications, 1989).

Berreman, Gerald D., *Hindus of the Himalayas,* (Berkeley: University of California Press, 1963). [This work provides excellent information on the Pahari Dom Castes].

Berreman, Gerald D., *Caste and Other Inequalities: Essays on Inequality,* (Delhi: Manohar, 1979).

Berwa, Laxmi N., *A Warning of Our Times: United We Stand, Divided We Fall,* (New Delhi: Centre for Alternative Dalit Media, 1999).

Berwa, Laxmi N., *Asian Dalit Solidarity*, (Delhi: ISPCK, 1999). [This contains the speeches and writings of Dr. Laxmi N. Berwa, a Dalit organic intellectual, press clippings of events in which Dr. Berwa was involved on behalf of Dalit cause between 1981–1999].

Beteille, Andre, "The Future of the Backward Classes: The Competing Demands of Status and Power", in Philip Mason (ed.), *India and Ceylon: Unity and Diversity*, (London, New York and Bombay: Oxford University Press, 1967).

Beteille, Andre and M.N. Srinivas, "The Harijans of India", in Andre Beteille (ed.), *Castes Old and New*, (Bombay: Asia Publishing House, 1969).

Beteille, Andre, "Pollution and Poverty", in J.M. Mahar (ed.), *The Untouchables in Contemporary India*, (Tucson: University of Arizona Press, 1972).

Beteille, Andre, *Backward Classes and the New Social Order*, (New Delhi: OUP, 1981).

Bhadra, Samanta, "Recent Race Mixture in Kerala: Some Social Aspects", in Bala Ratnam (ed.), *Anthropology on the March*, (ed.), (Madras: The Book Centre, 1963).

Bhadra, V. Shanti, "Bodhisattva Ambedkar", in *Dr. Babasaheb Ambedkar Amrat Mahotsab Visesanka*, (Nagpur: Dr. Ambedkar Adhyayan Man Mandal, 1966).

Bhagat, M.G., *The Untouchable Classes of Maharashtra*, (Bombay: Karnatak Publishing House, 1936), [Originally published in the *Journal of University of Bombay*, Vol. 4, part I, July, 1935].

Bhagat, M.G., *The Untouchable Classes of the Janjira State*, (Bombay: Karnatak Publishing House, 1938), [Originally published in the *Journal of University of Bombay*, Vol. 7, part I, July, 1938].

Bhagvan, K.S., *Violence in Hinduism*, (Banglore: Dalit Sahitya Academy, 1986).

Bhagwat, Vidyut, "Dalit Women: Issues and Perspectives – Some Critical Reflections", in P.G. Jogdand (ed.), *Dalit*

Women in India: Issues and Perspectives, (New Delhi: Gyan Publishing House, in collaboration with University of Poona, Pune, 1995).

Bhai, P. Nirmal, *Harijan Women in Independent India*, (Delhi: B.R. Publishing Corporation, 1986).

Bhalla, V.K., "Special Tables for Scheduled Castes", in *Census of India, 1981*, Series 28, Part 9, (Delhi: Controller of Publications, 1988).

Bhandare, Murlidhar C., "Ambedkar and the Political Rights of the Scheduled Castes", in Rabi Ray (ed.), *Dr. B.R. Ambedkar*, (New Delhi: Lok Sabha Secretariat, 1991), [Eminent Parliamentarians Monograph Series 12].

Bhandari, C.S. and S.R. Ramaswamy, *Dr. Bhim Rao Ambedkar: An Outstanding Patriot*, (New Delhi: Suruchi Prakashan, 1991).

Bhandari, R.K. and G.A. Khurana, *Study of Administrative Setup in States for Educational Programmes of Scheduled Castes and Scheduled Tribes*, (New Delhi: Ministry of Education and Social Welfare, Planning, Monitoring and Statistics Division, 1978).

Bhanusree, B.V.S., "The Buddhist Ambedkar", in K.S. Chalam (ed.), *The Relevance of Ambedkarism in India*, (Jaipur: Rawat, 1993).

Bharadwaj, A.N., *The Problems of Scheduled Castes and Scheduled Tribes in India*, (New Delhi: Light and Life Publishers, 1979).

Bharadwaj, Anil, *Welfare of Scheduled Castes in India*, (New Delhi: Deep and Deep, 2002).

Bharadwaj, O.P., "Special Tables for Scheduled Castes, Haryana", in *Census of India, 1981*, Series 6, Part 9 (1), (Delhi: Controller of Publications, 1988).

Bharat Dalit Sevak Sangh, *Report of the Seminar and Shibir on the Problems of Scheduled Castes and Scheduled Tribes*, (Poona: The Sangh, 1955).

Bharathi, K.S., *Foundations of Ambedkar's Thought*, (Nagpur: Datt Sons, 1990).

Bharathi, T., "Ambedkar and Uplift of Women", in *Ambedkar and Social Justice*, Vol. II, (New Delhi: Director, Publications Division, Ministry of Information and Broadcasting, 1992), [on behalf of Baba Saheb Dr. B.R. Ambedkar Birth Centenary Celebrations Committee, Ministry of Welfare, Government of India].

Bharathi, Vizia, "Hindu Epics: Portrayal of Dalit Women", in P.G. Jogdand (ed.), *Dalit Women in India: Issues and Perspectives*, (New Delhi: Gyan Publishing House, in collaboration with University of Poona, Pune, 1995).

Bharatiya Adimajati Sevak Sangh, *Acts and Orders of Government of India and other Important Information Relation to Scheduled Castes and Scheduled Tribes, and OBC and Anglo-Indians*, (New Delhi: n.d.).

Bhargava, G.S. and R.M. Pal (eds.), *Human Rights of Dalits: Societal Violation*, (New Delhi: Gyan Publishing House, 1999).

Bhargava, S.M. and S.C. Mittal, "Sample Survey of Educational Facilities for Scheduled Castes and Scheduled Tribes in Rajasthan", (New Delhi: NCERT, n.d.), [A research Monograph].

Bharill, Chandra, *Social and Political Ideas of B.R. Ambedkar (A Study of His Life, Services, Social and Political Ideas)*, (Jaipur: Aalekh Publishers, 1977).

Bharill, Chandra, "The Emancipator", in B.K. Ahluwalia and Shashi Ahluwalia (eds.), *B.R. Ambedkar and Human Rights*, (New Delhi: Vivek Publishing Company, 1981).

Bhatia, K.L., *Dr. B.R. Ambedkar: Social Justice and the Indian Constitution*, (New Delhi: Deep and Deep, 1994).

Bhatia, K.L., Hari Om and Rekha Chowdhary, *Social Justice of Dr. B.R. Ambedkar*, (New Delhi: Deep and Deep, 1995).

Bhatia, S.C., *Education and Socio-Cultural Disadvantage*, (Delhi: Xerxed Publications, 1982).

Bhatia, Suman, H.C. Hasit and B.K. Roy Burman, *Study of Customary Rights and Living and Working Conditions of Scavengers in Two Towns*, Vol. I, Part II-D, Census of

India, 1961 Monograph Series, (Delhi: Manager of Publications, 1966).

Bhatt, G.S., "Trends and Measures of Status Mobility Among the Chamars of Dehradun", in K.S. Mathur and B.C. Agarwal (eds.), *Tribe, Caste and Peasantry*, (Lucknow: Ethnographic and Folk Culture Society, 1974).

Bhatt, K.N., "Politics in Protective Discrimination: A Case Study of Uttaranchal", in A.K. Lal (ed.), *Protective Discrimination: Ideology and Praxis*, (New Delhi: Concept, 2002), [Published for B.G. Pant Social Science Institute, Allahabad].

Bhatt, Vanamrai A., *The Harijans of Maharashtra*, (Delhi: All India Harijan Sevak Sangh, 1941).

Bhattacharya, Jogendranath, *Hindu Castes and Sects*, (Calcutta: Thacker, Spink, 1908).

Bhave, Sumitra, *Pan on Fire: Eight Dalit Women Tell Their Story*, (Tr. by Gauri Deshpande), (New Delhi: Indian Social Institute, 1988).

Bhole, R.R., *An Untouchable Speaks*, (London: Britain Publishing Company, 1944).

Bhole, R.R., "A Soldier in Babasaheb's Struggle", in K.N. Kadam (ed.), *Dr. B.R. Ambedkar: The Emancipator of the Oppressed*, (Bombay: Popular Prakashan, 1993).

Bhowmik, K.L. (ed.), *Development of Scheduled Communities*, (New Delhi: Inter-India Publications, 1988).

Bhowmik, K.L., *Social Structure of the Dule-Bouri Community*, (Calcutta: Calcutta University, Department of Anthropology, 1968).

Bhoyar, Ashok, *My Encounter with Dronacharya*, (Pune: Sugava Prakashan, 2001).

Bhoyar, Ashok, *Soul-Searching of an Educated Dalit*, (Nagpur: Sugawa, 2002).

Bhushan, Shashi, "Reflections on the Material Condition of the Musahars", in Hemant Joshi and Sanjay Kumar (eds.), *Asserting Voices: Changing Culture, Identity and*

Livelihood of the Musahars in the Gangetic Plains, (Delhi: Deshkal Publications, 2002).

Biswas, A.R., "Dr. B.R. Ambedkar: The Jurist of the Modern India", in K.N. Kadam (ed.), *Dr. B.R. Ambedkar: The Emancipator of the Oppressed*, (Bombay: Popular Prakashan, 1993).

Biswas, Manohar, "The Contemporary Literature and the Dalit Writers", in Bojja Tharakam (ed.), *The First All India Dalit Writers Conference: A Commemorative Volume and Who's Who*, (Hyderabad: Dr. B.R. Ambedkar Memorial Trust, 1994).

Biswas, Oneil (Compiler), *Thus Spake Dr. Ambedkar*, (New Delhi: Blumoon Books, 1998).

Biswas, Oneil, *A Phenomenon Named Ambedkar*, (New Delhi: Blumoon, 1998).

Biswas, Oneil, *Dalits after Partition (Reservations and Constitutional Review)*, (New Delhi: Blumoon Books, 2001).

Biswas, S., "Ideas Afflicting the Dalits", in Radhakant Nayak (ed.), *The Fourth World: Appraisal and Aspirations*, (New Delhi: Manohar, 1997).

Biswas, Samudra, "Dalit Identity in the Ambedkar Era", in Ambrose Pinto (ed.), *Dalit Assertion for Identity*, (New Delhi: Indian Social Institute, 1999), [Proceedings of the National Seminar of Dalit Postgraduate and Research Students held on 23-25 January 1999 in the Indian Social Institute].

Biswas, S.K., "Dr. Ambedkar, Science and Society", in *Ambedkar and Social Justice*, Vol. I, (New Delhi: Director, Publications Division, Ministry of Information and Broadcasting, 1992), [on behalf of Baba Saheb Dr. B.R. Ambedkar Birth Centenary Celebrations Committee, Ministry of Welfare, Government of India].

Biswas, S.K., "Autochthon of India and the Aryan Intrusion" in M. Gopinath and Fr. Lazer (eds.), *The Emergence of Indigenous Peoples: Collection of Papers Presented at the First All India Conference of Indigenous Peoples of India*, (24-25 December), (Bangalore: Sarani, 1993).

Biswas, S.K., "Reinterpreting History for the Dalit-Bahujan", in Ashish Ghosh (ed.), *Dalits and Peasants: The Emerging Caste-Class Dynamics*, (Delhi: Gyan Sagar Publications, 1999).

Biswas, S.K., "Socialism: The Ambedkarite Approach", in G.S. Bal (ed.), *Understanding Ambedkar*, (Delhi: Ajanta Books, 2000).

Biswas, S.K., *Constitution-Review and Disempowerment of the Dalit Bahujan*, (Delhi: Tulsi Ram on behalf of Dalit Bahujan Intellectual Forum of India, 2000).

Biswas, Sasikumar Badoi, *Namasudra Dwijatattva*, (in Bengali), (Barisal: 1911).

Biswas, Swapan Kumar, *Gods, False-Gods and the Untouchables*, (Delhi: Orion, 1998).

Blakiston, Hillary, *But Little Dust: Life amongst the Ex-Untouchables of Maharashtra*, (Cambridge: 1990).

The Board of Economic Enquiry, Government of Punjab, *Tanning Industry in Punjab*, (Lahore: 1939).

Bombay Presidency, *Report of the Depressed Classes and Aboriginal Tribes Committee*, (Bombay: Government Central Press, 1930).

Bombay State, Government of, *Privileges Provided by Bombay Government for the Backward Classes*, (2nd edition, revised up to 30th September, 1949), there is also a later edition available, corrected up to 31st March, 1954.

Bondurant, J. (ed.), *Harijan: A Journal of Applied Journalism, 1933-35*, 19 vols. (New York: Garland, 1973).

Bora, Neeta, "Free Legal Aid in the Ray of Hope to the Scheduled Castes and Scheduled Tribes", in M.P. Dube and Neeta Bora (eds.), *Social Justice and Women in India*, (Delhi: Swaraj Prakashan, 1999).

Borale, P.T., *Segregation and Desegregation in India: A Socio-legal Study*, [India compared with USA], (Bombay: Manaktalas, 1968).

Borale, P.T., "Dr. Ambedkar and Constitution of India", in K.K. Kavlekar and A.S. Chausalkar (eds.), *Political Ideas and Leadership of Dr. B.R. Ambedkar*, (Pune: Vishwanil Publications, 1989).

Bose, Anil Baran, *Economic and Living Conditions of Harijans in Uttar Pradesh*, J.K. Institute Monograph, 5, (Lucknow: J.K. Institute of Sociology and Human Relations, Lucknow University, 1957).

Bose, Nirmal Kumar (ed.), *Data on Caste: Orissa*, (Calcutta: Anthropological Survey of India, (1960).

Brahmchary, O.P. and Krishna Roy, *Employment Planning for Rural Poor, Scheduled Castes and Tribes*, (New Delhi: Deep and Deep, 1993).

Brander, H.R., *32nd Sikh Pioneers: Regimental History*, (Calcutta: Thacker & Spink, 1906).

Brar, Gurbir, "Socio-Religious Reform Movements and Untouchables in Northern India", in Prakash Pimpley and Satish Sharma (eds.), *Struggle for Status*, (Delhi: B.R. Publishing Corporation, 1985).

Briggs, George Weston, *The Chamars*, (New Delhi: D.K. Publishers, 1997), (first published in 1920).

Briggs, George Weston, *The Doms and Their Relations*, (Mysore: Wesley Press, 1953), (first published in 1916).

Brochure on Reservation for Scheduled Castes and Scheduled Tribes in Services, (New Delhi: Department of Personal and Training, Ministry of Personal Public Grievances and Pensions, Government of India, 1987).

Burditt, J.F., *Work Among the Depressed Classes and the Masses*, (Bombay: Education Society's Steam Press, 1893).

Burman, B.K. Roy (ed.), *Social Mobility Movement Among Scheduled Castes and Tribes of India*, (New Delhi: Registrar General of India, Ministry of Home Affairs, 1970).

Callewaert, Winand M. and Peter G. Friedlander, *The Life and Works of Raidas*, (New Delhi: Manohar, 1992).

Carr, Dhyanchand, "A Biblical Basis for Dalit Theology", in James Massey (ed.), *Indigenous People: Dalits, Dalit Issues in Today's Theological Debate*, (Delhi: ISPCK, 1998), (First Published in1994).

Carr, Dhyandchand, "Dalit Theology is Biblical and It makes the Gospel Relevant", in Arvind P. Nirmal (ed.), *A Reader in Dalit Theology,* (Madras: 1991).

Cartwright, Mrs., *How We Teach the Paraiya,* (Madras: 1906), 3rd edition.

Carvalho, A.A., *Dalit People: A Socio-Political Study of the Caste Oppressed,* (Baroda: Shreyans Publications, 1975).

Cavey, William, *A Garo Jungle Book (of the Mission to the Garos of Assam),* (Philadelphia, Boston: The Indson Press, 1919).

Cederlof, Gunnel, *Bonds Lost: Subordination, Conflict and Mobilisation in Rural South India c.1900-1970,* (New Delhi: Manohar, 1997), [This work analyses the changing agrarian and social relations and mobilization among Scheduled Caste agricultural labourers in the highlands in western Tamil Nadu].

Central Government Scheduled Castes and Scheduled Tribes Employees Welfare Association, *Memorandum on Reservation of Posts in Government Services for the Scheduled Castes and Scheduled Tribes,* (New Delhi: 1966).

Centre for Social Studies, Surat (ed.) *Caste, Caste Conflict and Reservation,* (Delhi: Ajanta, 1985).

Chahal, S.K., *Dalits Patronized: The Indian National Congress and Untouchables of India, 1921-1947,* (Delhi: Shubhi Publications, 2002).

Chakladhar, H.C., "Problems of the Racial Composition of Indian Peoples", Presidential Address, Section on Anthropology and Archaeology, *Proceedings of the Indian Science Congress,* Part II, (23rd Session, 1936).

Chakravarti, Satis Chandra and Serojendra Nath Ray (eds.), *Brahmo Samaj, The Depressed and Untouchability,* (Calcutta: Sadharan Brahmo Samaj, 1933).

Chalam, K.S., *Education and Weaker Sections,* (New Delhi: Inter-India Publications, 1987).

Chalam, K.S. (ed.), *The Relevance of Ambedkarism in India,* (Jaipur: Rawat, 1993).

Chalam, K.S., "Ambedkar and Democratic Socialism in India", in K.S. Chalam (ed.), *The Relevance of Ambedkarism in India*, (Jaipur: Rawat, 1993).

Chalam, K.S., "Ambedkar's Contribution to the Demolition of Tradition in India", in K.S. Chalam (ed.), *The Relevance of Ambedkarism in India*, (Jaipur: Rawat, 1993).

Chamberlain, Jacob, *In the Tiger Jungle: And other Stories of Missionary work among the Telugus of India*, (Edinburgh and London: Oliphant Anderson and Ferrier, 1897).

Chanchreek, K.L., *Dr. B.R. Ambedkar*, (New Delhi: Gian, 1990).

Chanchreek, K.L., S. Prasad, and R. Kumar (eds.), *Dr. Ambedkar: Social Justice and Political Safeguards for Depressed Classes*, (New Delhi: Shree, 1991).

Chanchreek, K.L., Saroj Prasad, and R. Kumar (eds.), *Dr. Ambedkar (1891–1956) Economic Writings*, 3 Vols., (Delhi: H.K. Publishers, 1992).

Chanchreek, K.L., Saroj Prasad, and R. Kumar (eds.), *Dr. Ambedkar: Patriot, Philosopher and Statesman*, (Delhi: H.K. Publishers, 1992).

Chanchreek, K.L. and Saroj Prasad (eds.), *Dr. B.R. Ambedkar: Social Justice and Political Safeguards for Depressed Classes*, (New Delhi: Shri Publishers, 1995).

Chand, Ram, "Relevance of Philosophy of Dr. Ambedkar for Human Rights", in *Ambedkar and Social Justice*, Vol. II, (New Delhi: Director, Publications Division, Ministry of Information and Broadcasting, 1992), [on behalf of Baba Saheb Dr. B.R. Ambedkar Birth Centenary Celebrations Committee, Ministry of Welfare, Government of India].

Chand, Ram, "Ambedkar and Human Rights", in V.T. Patil (ed.), *Studies in Ambedkar*, (Delhi: Devika Publications, 1995).

Chand, Ram, "Dr. Ambedkar and Socio-Economic Development", in Bhajan Kaur (ed.), *The Philosophy of Dr. B.R. Ambedkar*, (Chandigarh: Dr. Ambedkar Study Circle, 1999).

Chandar, Krishan, "Kalu Bhangi", in K. Natwar Singh (ed.), *Tales from Modern India*, (New York: Macmillan, 1966).

Chandel, M.P.S., *A Social Force in Politics: Study of Scheduled Castes of UP*, (New Delhi: Mittal, 1990).

Chandra Mowli, V., *B.R. Ambedkar: Man and His Vision*, (New Delhi: Sterling, 1990).

Chandra Mowli, V., *'Jogin': Girl-Child Labour Studies*, (New Delhi: Sterling, 1992).

Chandra, A.V. Satish, "Annihilation of Caste: The Unfinished Task of Dr. Ambedkar", in *Ambedkar and Social Justice*, Vol. I, (New Delhi: Director, Publications Division, Ministry of Information and Broadcasting, 1992), [on behalf of Baba Saheb Dr. B.R. Ambedkar Birth Centenary Celebrations Committee, Ministry of Welfare, Government of India].

Chandra, A.V. Satish, "The Annihilation of Caste: The Unfinished Task of Ambedkar", in V.T. Patil (ed.), *Studies in Ambedkar*, (Delhi: Devika Publications, 1995).

Chandra, R. and Chanchreek, K.L., *Dalit Identity, History and Tradition: Rigveda period to New Millennium*, (New Delhi: Ocean Books, 2002).

Chandra, R. and Sangh Mittra (eds.), *Dalit Identity in the Millennium*, (New Delhi: Commonwealth, 2002).

Chandra, Ramesh (ed.), *Dr. Ambedkar: Science and Society*, (New Delhi: Shree Publications, 2000).

Chandra, R.C., *Population Geography of Scheduled Castes in India (A Project sponsored by the University Grants Commission): Report*, (Chandigarh: Punjab University, Department of Geography, 1985).

Chandra, R.C., *Spatial Dimensions of Scheduled Castes in India*, (New Delhi: Intellectual Publishing House, 1989).

Chandra, R.N.L., "Monograph of Tanning and Working in Leather in the Province of Bengal", in *Art in Industry Through the Ages*, (New Delhi: Navrang Publishers, 1975), (reprint).

Chandra, Snehalatha, *Marginal Communities and Social Development*, (New Delhi: Kanishka, 1998).

Chandra, Sudhir, "Metaphor of Suffering", in Bojja Tharakam (ed.), *The First All India Dalit Writers Conference: A Commemorative Volume and Who's Who*, (Hyderabad: Dr. B.R. Ambedkar Memorial Trust, 1994).

Chandra, V., *Handbook on Scheduled Castes and Scheduled Tribes*, (New Delhi: Office of the Commissioner for SC&ST, 1968).

Chandra, Vimal, *Lists of Scheduled Castes and Scheduled Tribes with Clarifications*, (New Delhi: The Author, 1981).

Chandraiah, B.N., *A Descriptive Grammer of Harijan Dialect*, (Mysore: Sharat Prakashana, 1987).

Chandraiah, K, 'The Awakening of Adi-Hindus of Hyderabad as Part of the National Movement For Freedom', *Souvenir*, (Hyderabad: Dr. Ambedkar People's Educational Society, 1992).

Chandrasekharaiah, K., "Educational Problems of Scheduled Castes", (Dharward: Department of Sociology, Karnataka University, 1969), [[A research monograph, out of a project financed by NCERT].

Chandrika, R., *Plan for Harijans and other Backward Classes*, (New Delhi: Bharatiya Depressed Classes League, 1951).

Chaplin, Susan E., "Scavengers: Still Marginalised", in Ghanshyam Shah (ed.), *Dalits and the State*, (New Delhi: Concept Publishing Company, 2002), [Published for Centre for Rural Studies, Lal Bahadur Shastri National Academy of Administration, Mussoorie].

Chari, R.B., *Census of India: Scheduled Castes and Tribes*, Series-1, paper-1 of 1973, (New Delhi: Government of India, 1971).

Charsley, Simon R. and G.K. Karanth, *Challenging Untouchability: Dalit Initiative and Experience from Karnataka*, (New Delhi: Sage, 1998), [Cultural Subordination and the Dalit Challenge, Vol. 1].

Chatterjee, H., "School Dropout among Harijan Children: Causes and Cure", (New Delhi: Central Institute of

Research and Training in Public Cooperation, 1975), [A research Monograph, covered a total of seventeen villages in the Ballia and Azamgarh districts of eastern Uttar Pradesh].

Chatterji, Saral K., "Some Aspects of Dalit Ideology", in Arvind P. Nirmal (ed.), *Toward a Common Dalit Ideology*, (Madras: Gurukul Lutheran Theological College and Research Institute, 1990), [Papers presented at the National Seminar on Dalit Ideology organized by the Department of Dalit Theology, Gugukul Lutheran Theological College and Research Institute].

Chatterji, Saral K., "Why Dalit Theology?", in Arvind P. Nirmal (ed.), *A Reader in Dalit Theology*, (Madras: Gurukul, 1992).

Chatterji, Saral K., "Why Dalit Theology", in James Massey (ed.), *Indigenous People, Dalits: Dalit Issues in Today's Theological Debate*, (Delhi: ISPCK, 1998), (First Published in1994).

Chatterjee, Sarajit Kumar, *The Scheduled Castes in India*, 4 vols., (New Delhi: Gyan, 1996), [Compendium of official material by Anthropologist retired from Police].

Chatterjee, S.K., *Educational Development of Scheduled Castes: Looking Ahead*, (New Delhi: Gyan, 2000).

Chatterson, A., *Monograph on Tanning and Working in Leather in the Madras Presidency*, (Madras: Government Press, 1904).

Chaudhary, Pratima, "Problems of Female Scavengers of Patna", in S.N. Chaudhary (ed.), *Changing Status of Depressed Castes in Contemporary India: Essays in Honour of Professor S.C. Dube*, (Delhi: Daya Publishing House, 1988).

Chaudhary, P.K., "Problems of the Chamars of Patratu Village under Chanho Block, Ranchi: A Sociological Study", in Makhan Jha (ed.), *Scheduled Castes Today*, (New Delhi: M.D. Publications, 1997).

Chaudhary, Ram Naresh, "The Relevance of Babasaheb Dr. Bhim Rao Ambedkar", in R.B. Rao (ed.), *Bharat-Ratna Dr. Ambedkar*, (Allahabad: Chugh Publications, 1993).

Chaudhary, S.N. (ed.), *Changing Status of Depressed Castes in Contemporary India: Essays in Honour of Professor S.C. Dube,* (Delhi: Daya Publishing House, 1988).

Chaudhary, S.N., "Harijan Atrocities in India: A Case Study of Bihar", in S.N. Chaudhary (ed.), *Changing Status of Depressed Castes in Contemporary India: Essays in Honour of Professor S.C. Dube,* (Delhi: Daya Publishing House, 1988).

Chaudhary, S.N., "Ambedkar, Caste and Hindu Religion: An Analysis", in *Ambedkar and Social Justice,* Vol. I, (New Delhi: Director, Publications Division, Ministry of Information and Broadcasting, 1992), [on behalf of Baba Saheb Dr. B.R. Ambedkar Birth Centenary Celebrations Committee, Ministry of Welfare, Government of India].

Chaudhary, S.N., *Occupationally Mobile Scavengers,* (New Delhi: Har-Anand, 2000).

Chauhan, B.R., "Special Problems of Education of the Scheduled Castes", in M.S. Gore, I.P. Desai (eds.), *Papers in Sociology of Education in India,* (New Delhi: N.C.E.R.T., 1967).

Chauhan, Brijraj, G. Narayana and T.R. Singh, *Scheduled Castes and Education,* (Meerut: Anupam Publications, 1975).

Chauhan, R.K., "Sudras in the Vedas: A Critical Exposition by Ambedkar", in K.S. Chalam (ed.), *The Relevance of Ambedkarism in India,* (Jaipur: Rawat, 1993).

Chauhan, S.S., "A Comparative Study of the Achievement Motivation of Scheduled Tribe and Scheduled Caste Studets of Himachal Pradesh in Relation to their Intelligence and Socio-Economic Status", (Chandigarh: Department of Education, Himachal Pradesh University, 1984), [A research monograph, out of a project financed by University Grants Commission].

Chaurasia, B.P., "Dr. Baba Saheb Bhim Rao Ambedkar and the Down-Trodden Society in India", in R.B. Rao (ed.), *Bharat-Ratna Dr. Ambedkar,* (Allahabad: Chugh Publications, 1993).

Chavan, Sheshrao (ed.), *Bharat Ratna Dr. Babasaheb Ambedkar,* (Aurangabad: 1990).

Chavan, Sheshrao, *Gandhi and Ambedkar: Saviours of Untouchables,* (New Delhi: Authors Press, 2001), [in association with Bharatiya Vidya Bhavan, Mumbai].

Chentharasserty, T.H.P., "Dalit Literature in Malayalam", in Bojja Tharakam (ed.), *The First All India Dalit Writers Conference: A Commemorative Volume and Who's Who,* (Hyderabad: Dr. B.R. Ambedkar Memorial Trust, 1994).

Chentharasserty, T.H.P., *Ambedkar on Indian History,* (Jaipur: Rawat, 2000).

Chetty, V.B. Krishnaiah, *Scheduled Castes and Development Programmes in India,* (Allahabad: Vohra Publications, 1991).

Chikhalikar, Y.K., "Ambedkar: A Devotee of Freedom", in *Ambedkar and Social Justice,* Vol. II, (New Delhi: Director, Publications Division, Ministry of Information and Broadcasting, 1992), [on behalf of Baba Saheb Dr. B.R. Ambedkar Birth Centenary Celebrations Committee, Ministry of Welfare, Government of India].

Chinchunsure, B., *Rights, Social Equality and Riots: A Study with reference to the recent Riots in Marathwada,* (Bombay: Maharashtra Sarvodaya Mandal, 1978).

Chinna Rao, Yagati, "The World of Untouchables in Medieval Telugu Literature: A Study of Vemana", in R. Soma Reddy, M. Radhakrishna Sharma and A. Satyanarayana (eds.), *Social Evils in Andhra Desa: 17th and 18th Centuries AD,* (Proceedings of the Seminar), (Hyderabad, Department of History, Osmania University, 1999).

Chinna Rao, Yagati, "Change in Nomenclature: A Historical Note", in Ambrose Pinto (ed.), *Dalit Assertion for Identity,* (New Delhi: Indian Social Institute, 1999), [Proceedings of the National Seminar of Dalit Postgraduate and Research Students held on 23-25 January 1999 in the Indian Social Institute].

Chinna Rao, Yagati, "Education and Identity Formation Among Dalits in Colonial Andhra", in S. Bhattacharya (ed.), *Education and the Disprevileged: Nineteenth and Twentieth Century India,* (New Delhi: Orient Longman, 2002).

Chinna Rao, Yagati, *Dalits' Struggle for Identity: Andhra and Hyderabad, 1900-1950,* (New Delhi: Kanishka, 2003).

Chinnaiah, E.V., "The Impact of Dr. Ambedkar's The Buddha and His Dhamma", in K.N. Kadam (ed.), *Dr. B.R. Ambedkar: The Emancipator of the Oppressed,* (Bombay: Popular Prakashan, 1993).

Chitkara, M.G., *Dr. Ambedkar: Towards Buddhism,* (New Delhi: A.P.H. Publishing Corporation, 1997).

Chitkara, M.G., *Dr. Ambedkar and Social Justice,* (New Delhi: A.P.H. Publishing Corporation, 2002).

Chitnis, M.B., "An Educational, Social and Economic Survey of Milind College Students", in Barbara R. Joshi (ed.), *Untouchable! Voices of the Dalit Liberation Movement,* (London: Zed Books Ltd., 1986).

Chitnis, Suma, *Literacy and Educational Enrolment among the Scheduled Castes of Maharashtra,* (Bombay: Tata Institute of Social Sciences, 1974), [TISS series: 31].

Chitnis, Suma, "Problems of the Scheduled Caste College Students of Bombay", (Bombay: Tata Institute of Social Sciences, 1976), [A research monograph].

Chitnis, Suma, "Education of the Scheduled Castes and Scheduled Tribes in Maharashtra", in A.B. Shah (ed.), *The Social Context of Education: Essays in Honour of J.P. Naik,* (New Delhi: Allied Publishers, 1978).

Chitnis, Suma, *A Long Way to Go: Report on a Survey of Scheduled Caste High School and College Students in 15 States of India,* (New Delhi: Allied, 1981).

Chitnis, Suma, "Identity of Scheduled Caste Students", (Bombay: Tata Institute of Social Sciences, 1981), [A research monograph, out of a project financed by the ICSSR].

Chitnis, Suma, "Measuring upto Reserved Admissions", in Vimal P. Shah and Binod C. Agrawal (eds.), *Reservation Policy, Programmes and Issues,* (Jaipur: Rawat Publications, 1986).

Chitnis, Suma, "Definition of the Terms Scheduled Castes and Scheduled Tribes: A Crisis of Ambivalence", in

V.A. Pai Panandiker (ed.), *The Politics of Backwardness: Reservation Policy in India*, (New Delhi: Konark Publishers, 1997), [Under the auspices of Centre for Policy Research, New Delhi].

Chokhamela Abhang Gatha, (Collection of Chokhamela's Abhangas), (Bombay: Balkrishna Lakshman Pathak, 1950).

Choondawat, P.S., "Untouchability and the Untouchable Youths: A Study in Urban Context", in R.G. Singh (ed.), *The Depressed Classes of India: Problems and Prospects*, (New Delhi: B.R. Publishing Corporation, 1986).

Chopra, Vipla, "Economic Development of Scheduled Castes in Punjab: An Assessment", in V.S. Mahajan and B.S. Mann (eds.), *Economic Development of Scheduled Castes*, (New Delhi: Anmol, 1997).

Chousalkar, A.S., "Dr. Ambedkar's Theory of Political Resistance", in K.K. Kavlekar and A.S. Chausalkar (eds.), *Political Ideas and Leadership of Dr. B.R. Ambedkar*, (Pune: Vishwanil Publications, 1989).

Chousolkar, Ashok S., *Indian Idea of Political Resistance: Aurobindo, Tilak, Gandhi and Ambedkar*, (Delhi: Ajanta, 1990).

Chousalkar, Ashok S., "Ambedkar on Linguistics – A Critical Study", in V.T. Patil (ed.), *Studies in Ambedkar*, (Delhi: Devika Publications, 1995).

Chowdhury, J.N., *A Comparative Study of Adi Religion*, (Shillong: North-East Frontier Agency, 1971).

CIRTPC, *School Drop-outs among Harijan Children – Causes and Cure*, (New Delhi: Central Institute of Research and Training, 1975).

CLRI, *Development and Export Potential of India's Leather and Allied Industries*, part I, (Chennai: 1985).

Clark, Sathianathan, *Dalits and Christianity: Subaltern Religions and Liberation Theology in India*, (New Delhi: OUP, 1998).

Clarke, C.R., *The Outcastes: Being a Brief Account of the Magahiya Doms*, (Calcutta: 1903).

Clayton, A.C., *Gangai's Piligrimage*, (London: Culley, 1909), [A fascinating little book, giving the reader a very fascinating and vivid impression of Dalit life of south India].

Clough, John E., *Social Christianity in the Orient*, (New York: Macmillan, 1914), [This books deals with the missionary work among the Outcastes of coastal Andhra of late nineteenth century].

Cohn, Bernard S., "Changing Traditions of a Low Caste", in Milton B. Singer (ed.), *Traditional India: Structure and Change*, (Philadelphia: American Folklore Society, 1959).

Cohn, Bernard S., "The Changing Status of a Depressed Caste" in McKim Marriott (ed.), *Village India: Studies in the Little Community*, (Chicago: University of Chicago Press, 1955). This was later on reproduced in Bernard S. Cohn, *An Anthropologist Among the Historian and Other Essays*, (Delhi: Oxford University Press, 1987).

Cohn, Bernard S., 'Chamar Family in A North Indian Village: A Structural Contingent' in his *An Anthropologist Among the Historians and Other Essays*, (Delhi, Oxford University Press, 1992), (First Published in 1987).

Commissioner for Scheduled Castes and Scheduled Tribes, *Agenda and Notes on Welfare of Scheduled Castes*, (Hyderabad: Social Welfare Department, Government of Andhra Pradesh, 1981).

Cone, James H., *God of the Oppressed*, (San Francisco: Harper and Row, 1975).

Constitution of the Harijan Sevak Sangh (including complanatory Notes and Bye-Laws), (Delhi: Harijan Industrial Home, 1935).

Craig, John, *Forty Years Among the Telugus: A History of the Mission of the Baptists of Ontario and Quebed, Canada, to the Telugus, South India 1867-1907*, (Toronto: Author, 1908).

Crooke, W., *The Tribes and Castes of North-Western Provinces and Oudh*, 4 vols., (Calcutta: Office of the Superintendent of Government Press, 1896).

Crooke, W., "Chamar" in *Census of India, 1901*, Vol. I, *India: Ethnographic Appendices*, edited by H.H. Risley, (Calcutta: Superintendent of Government Printing, 1903).

Crooke, W., *The Tribes and Castes of Northern India*, 2 vols., (Delhi: Cosmos, 1974), (Reprint).

Crowley, Eileen, *Champion of the Outcaste: Lester Hooper of Travancore*, (London: Highway Press, 1941).

D'Souza, Paul, "Dalit Identity in Gujarat", in Fernando Franco (ed.), *Pain and Awakening: The Dynamics of Dalit Identity in Bihar, Gujarat and Uttar Pradesh*, (New Delhi: Indian Social Institute, 2002).

D'Souza, Victor S., "Does Urbanism Desegregate Scheduled Castes?: Evidence from a District in Punjab", in Satish Saberwal (ed.), *Process and Institutions in Urban India*, (New Delhi: Vikas, 1978).

D'Souza, Victor S., *Educational Inequalities Among Scheduled Castes: A Case Study in Punjab*, (Chandigarh: Department of Sociology, Punjab University, 1980), [This was originally a research project financed by the ICSSR].

D'Souza, Victor S., *Development Planning and Structural Inequalities: The Response of the Under-Privileged*, (New Delhi: Sage, 1990).

Dahiwale, S.M., *Emerging Entrepreneurship among the Scheduled Castes of Contemporary India: A Study of Kolhapur City*, (New Delhi: Concept, 1989).

Dahiwale, S.M., "The Continuity of Disabilities of Scheduled Castes in India", in R.S. Tripathi and P.D. Tiwari (eds.), *Dimensions of Scheduled Caste Development in India: Problems and Prospects*, (New Delhi: Uppal, 1991).

Daiya, K.C., "Judiciary in India", in *Ambedkar and Social Justice*, Vol. I, (New Delhi: Director, Publications Division, Ministry of Information and Broadcasting, 1992), [on behalf of Baba Saheb Dr. B.R. Ambedkar Birth Centenary Celebrations Committee, Ministry of Welfare, Government of India].

The Dalit Struggle for Freedom in Pondicherry Diocese, (Madras: Dalit Christian Movement, 1990).

Dalit Vikas Samiti, *Dalit Organisations: A Directory*, (New Delhi: Indian Social Institute, 1990).

Dalton, Dennis, "The Gandhian View of Caste and Caste After Gandhi", in Philip Mason (ed.), *India and Ceylon: Unity and Diversity*, (New York: Oxford University Press, 1967).

Damle, Y.B. and I. Karve, "Note on the Position of Scheduled Castes and Their Position in the Villages", in *Group Relations in a Village Community*, (Poona: Post-Graduate & Research Institute, Deccan College, 1963).

Damle, Y.B. and R.N. Kulhali, "Changing status of Scheduled Castesin Maharashtra as revealed by Census data", *Indian Census Centenary Seminar*, (New Delhi: Office of the Registrar General, 1972).

Danda, A.K., *Weaker Sections in Indian Villages*, 2 vols. (New Delhi: Inter-India, 1993).

Dandavate, Madhu, "The Dreamer", in B.K. Ahluwalia and Shashi Ahluwalia (eds.), *B.R. Ambedkar and Human Rights*, (New Delhi: Vivek Publishing Company, 1981).

Dangle, Arjun (ed.), *Poisoned Bread: Translations from Modern Marathi Dalit Literature*, (Hyderabad and Bombay: Orient Longman, 1992).

Dangle, Arjun (ed.), *No Entry for the New Sun: Translations from Modern Marathi Dalit Poetry*, (Hyderabad: Orient Longman, 1992), [A selection from the famour anthology *Poisoned Bread*].

Dangle, Arjun (ed.), *Homeless in my Land: Translations from Modern Marathi Dalit Short Stories*, (Hyderabad: Orient Longman, 1992), [A selection from the famour anthology *Poisoned Bread*].

Dangle, Arjun (ed.), *A Corpse in the Well: Translations from Modern Marathi Dalit Autobiography*, (Hyderabad: Orient Longman, 1992), [A selection from the famous anthology *Poisoned Bread*].

Darshankar, A.Y., "Dr. Babasaheb Ambedkar's View on Public Services", in K.K. Kavlekar and A.S. Chausalkar (eds.), *Political Ideas and Leadership of Dr. B.R. Ambedkar*, (Pune: Vishwanil Publications, 1989).

Das, Amal Kumar, Bidyit Kumar Roy Chowdhury and Manis Kumar Raha, *Handbook on Scheduled Castes and Scheduled Tribes of West Bengal*, (Calcutta: Tribal Welfare Department, Government of West Bengal, 1966), [Bulletin of the Cultural Research Institute, special series no. 8].

Das, Bhagwan (Comp.), *Selected Speeches of Dr. Babasaheb B.R. Ambedkar*, (Jullundhur City: The Bheem Patrika Publications, 1963).

Das, Bhagwan (ed.), *Thus Spoke Ambedkar: Selected Speeches*, Vol. 2, (Jallundar: Bheem Patrika Publications, 1969).

Das, Bhagwan (ed.), *Untouchable Soldiers: The Mahars and the Mazhbis*, (Banglore: Ambedkar Sahitya Prakashan, 1980), [This is a portion of Ardythe Basham's Ph.D. thesis from the University of British Columbia].

Das, Bhagwan (Comp.), *Selected Speeches of Dr. Babasaheb B.R. Ambedkar*, (Banglore: Ambedkar Sahitya Prakashana and Ambedkar Memorial Society, 1980).

Das, Bhagwan, "Ambedkar's Journey to Mass Conversion", in Devendra Swaroop (ed.), *Politics of Conversion*, (Delhi: 1986).

Das, Bhagwan, "Buddhist Mass Conversion 1956", in Sanghasen Singh and Priyasen Singh (eds.), *Ambedkar on Buddhist Conversion and Its Impact*, (Delhi: Eastern Book Linkers, 1990).

Das, Bhagwan, "The Significance of Dr. Ambedkar Writings and Speeches on Buddhism", in K.N. Kadam (ed.), *Dr. B.R. Ambedkar: The Emancipator of the Oppressed*, (Bombay: Popular Prakashan, 1993).

Das, Bhagwan, "Dalits and the Caste System", in James Massey (ed.), *Indigenous People: Dalits. Dalit Issues in Today's Theological Debate*, (Delhi: ISPCK, 1998), (First Published in 1994).

Das, Bhagwan and James Massey, *Dalit Solidarity*, (Delhi: The Indian Society for Promoting Christian Knowledge, 1995).

Das, Bhagwan, "Reservations Today and Tomorrow", in Walter Fernandes (ed.), *The Emerging Dalit Identity: The Reassertion of Subalterns*, (New Delhi: Indian Social Institute, 1996).

Das, Bhagwan, "Ambedkar and the Fourth World", in Radhakant Nayak (ed.), *The Fourth World: Appraisal and Aspirations*, (New Delhi: Manohar, 1997).

Das, Bhakta, *A Glimpse of Scheduled Castes and Their Socio-Economic Development in Assam*, (New Delhi: Omsons Publications, 1968).

Das, Debi Prasad, *The Untouchable Story*, (New Delhi: Allied Publishers, 1985).

Das, Ganga, *Who Worship False Gods: A Rejoinder to Arun Shourie's Worshipping False Gods*, (New Delhi: S.K. Associates, 1997).

Das, Mahabir, *National Penitence: Removal of Untouchability*, (New Delhi: Publication Division, Government of India, 1976).

Das, Naresh Chandra, *Namasudra Sampraday O Bangladesh*, (in Bengali), (Calcutta: 1368 B.S).

Das, Sudhir Ranjan, "Liberation of the Oppressed – Ambedkarism is the Solution", in *National Seminar on Marx, Ambedkar and Polarization of Oppressed and Exploited Classes in India*, (New Delhi: Sanjivayya Institute of Socio-Economic Studies, 1991).

Dasan, M., "Dalits and Human Rights Protection: A Case Study of Kerala", in R.M. Pal (ed.), *Protection of Human Rights: A Critique (With Special Reference to SC/STs, the Girl Child/Women belonging to SC/STs, marginalized Section and the Minorities*, (New Delhi: Indian Social Institute, 1999), [Proceedings of the National Seminar held on 13 and 14 November 1998 at the Indian Social Institute].

Dayal, Virendra, "Religious and Social Practices and Human Rights of Dalits", in G.S. Bhargava and R.M. Pal (eds.), Human Rights of Dalits: Societal Violation, (New Delhi: Gyan Publishing House, 1999).

De Vos, G. and H. Wagatsuma (eds.), *Japan's Invisible Race: Caste in Culture and Personality*, (Berkeley, CA: University of California Press, 1967).

Debi, Sailabala, "Inequality of Access to Elementary Education in Orissa: An inter- and intra spatial Analysis", in A. Vaidyanathan and P.R. Gopinathan Nair (eds.), *Elementary Education Rural India: A Grassroots View*, (New Delhi: Sage, 2001).

Degaonkar, C.K., "Dr. Ambedkar on Indian Monetary System", in J.S. Narayana Rao, A. Somasekhar and K. Audiseshaiah (eds.), *B.R. Ambedkar: His Relevance Today*, (New Delhi: Gyan Publishing House, 1994).

Deliege, Robert, "Caste without a System: A Study of South Indian Harijans", in M. Searle-Chatterjee and U. Sharma (eds.), *Contextualising Caste: Post-Dumontian Approaches*, (Oxford: Blackwell/Sociological Review, 1994).

Deliege, Robert, "At the Threshold of Untouchability: Pallars and Valaiyars in a Tamil Village", in C. Fuller (ed.), *Caste Today*, (Delhi: Oxford University, 1996).

Deliege, Robert, *The World of the "Untouchables": Paraiyars of Tamil Nadu*, (Tr. from the French by David Phillips), (Delhi: Oxford University Press, 1997).

Deliege, Robert, *The Untouchables of India*, (Tr. from the French by Nora Scott), (New York and Oxford: Berg, 1999).

Deming, Wilbur S., *Ramdas and the Ramdasis*, (Calcutta: Association Press, 1928).

Denning, Margaret B., *Mosaics from India*, (Oliphant: Anderson and Ferrier, 1902), [A brightly written book covering a good range of subjects connected with Christian Missions work in India. Chapter X and XI are one of the earliest descriptions of Dalit Women and famines].

Depressed Class Awakenings: News and Views of the All-India Depressed Conference, (Lucknow: C.O. Forsgren, June 24, 1936).

DeReuck, Anthony and Julie Knight, *Caste and Race: Comparative Approaches*, (London: J and A Churchill Ltd., 1967).

Desai, Govindbhai Hathibhai, *A Glossary of Castes, Tribes and Races in the Baroda State*, (Baroda: Census Office, 1912).

Desai, Haribhai and D.A. Uchat, "Self-Concept of Harijan Students and Attitude of Other Students Towards Them", (1981), [A research study on students of the Sourashtra University affiliated colleges].

Desai, Harshad and Chandu Maheria, "Dalit Assertion for Self-Esteem: From Sambarda to Swamannagar", in Ghanshyam Shah, Mario Rutten and Hein Streefkerk (eds.), *Development and Deprivation in Gujarat*, (New Delhi: Sage, 2002).

Desai, I.P., *Water Facilities for the Untouchable in Rural Gujarat*, (New Delhi: ICSSR, 1973).

Desai, I.P. and G.A. Pandor, *The Scheduled Caste and Tribe High School Students in Gujarat*, (Surat: Centre for Regional Development Studies, 1974), [A research monograph, out of a project financed by the ICSSR].

Desai, I.P., *Untouchability in Rural Gujarat*, (Bombay: Popular Prakashan, 1976).

Desai, I.P., "Education of the Scheduled Castes and Scheduled Tribes in Gujarat", in A.B. Shah (ed.), *The Social Context of Education: Essays in Honour of J.P. Naik*, (New Delhi: Allied Publishers, 1978).

Desai, I.P. et. al., *Caste, Caste-Conflict and Reservation*, (Delhi: Ajanta, 1985).

Desai, Mahadev, *The Diary of Mahadeo Desai*, (Translated from the Gujarati and Edited by Valji Govinji Desai), (Ahmedabad: Navajivan, 1953), [Record of Gandhi's life between March 10, 1932 – September 4, 1932, the period of intensive concern with untouchability].

Desai, Mahadev, *The Epic of Travancore,* (Ahmedabad: Navjivan, 1937).

Desai, V.H., "Relevance of Dr. Ambedkar Today", in J.S. Narayana Rao, A. Somasekhar and K. Audiseshaiah (eds.), *B.R. Ambedkar: His Relevance Today,* (New Delhi: Gyan Publishing House, 1994).

Desai, Valji G., *The Shastras on Untouchability,* (Ahmedabad: Navajivan, n.d.).

Deshmukh, Sharad Rao, "Distinct Awareness in Dalit Poetry", in Bojja Tharakam (ed.), *The First All India Dalit Writers Conference: A Commemorative Volume and Who's Who,* (Hyderabad: Dr. B.R. Ambedkar Memorial Trust, 1994).

Deshpande, Sudha, "Structural Adjustment and its Impact on Poverty and Female Work among Scheduled Castes and Scheduled Tribes", in P.G. Jogdand (ed.), *New Economic Policy and Dalits,* (Jaipur: Rawat, 2000).

Deshpande, V.V., "Educational Planning: Some Aspects of Protective Discrimination", in G.S. Sharma (ed.), *Educational Planning: Its Legal and Constitutional Implications in India,* (Bombay: N.M. Tripathi, 1967).

Deshpande, Vasant, *Towards Social Integration: Problems of Adjustment of Scheduled Caste Elite,* (Pune: Shubhada-Saraswat, 1978).

Deshpande, Vasant, *The Mhaisal Untouchables,* (Pune: Dastane Ramchandra, 1983), [Struggle of the Deprived for Development – I].

Deva, Shanti and C.M. Wagh, *Dr. Ambedkar and Conversion,* (Hyderabad: Dr. Ambedkar Publications Society, 1965), [Pamphlet].

Devasahayam, V. (ed.), *Dalits and Women: Quest for Humanity,* (Madras: The Gurukul Summer Institute, 1992).

Devdurg, Mariyappa, "The Politics of Conversion: A Discussion with Special Reference to the Scheduled Castes", in V.T. Patil (ed.), *Studies in Ambedkar,* (Delhi: Devika Publications, 1995).

Devgan, Vipin Kumar, "Entrepreneurship and Economic Development of Scheduled Castes in Punjab", in V.S. Mahajan and B.S. Mann (eds.), *Economic Development of Scheduled Castes*, (New Delhi: Anmol, 1997).

Devi, Bhagwati, "Our Whole Existence is Burning", in Hemant Joshi and Sanjay Kumar (eds.), *Asserting Voices: Changing Culture, Identity and Livelihood of the Musahars in the Gangetic Plains*, (Delhi: Deshkal Publications, 2002).

Devisingh, Ashok, "The Conversion Movement: A Proud Legacy of Ambedkar", in Sanghasen Singh and Priyasen Singh (eds.), *Ambedkar on Buddhist Conversion and Its Impact*, (Delhi: Eastern Book Linkers, 1990).

Dewan, Ram Prakash, *How to Erase Untouchability?*, (New Delhi: R.P. Bookwala and Co., 1979).

Dhanda, J.R., "A Study of Attitudes of College Teachers Towards Education of Scheduled Caste Students in Aurangabad District", (Pune: Indian Institute of Education, 1985), [A research monograph].

Dharmalingam, A.M., "Ambedkar's Idea of Secularism", in A.M. Rajasekharaiah (ed.) *The Socio-Economic Transformation of India—Dr. Ambedkar's Vision* (Dharwad: Karnatak University, 1983).

Dharmalingam, A.M., *B.R. Ambedkar and Secularism*, (Banglore: Dalit Sahitya Academy, 1985).

Dharmanand, "Acharya Ambedkar: As a Dharmarakshaka", in G.S. Bal (ed.), *Understanding Ambedkar*, (Delhi: Ajanta Books, 2000).

Dhiwal, Dilip M., "Dr. Ambedkar: The Architect of India's Labour Policy (1942-46)", in K.N. Kadam (ed.), *Dr. B.R. Ambedkar: The Emancipator of the Oppressed*, (Bombay: Popular Prakashan, 1993).

Dias, Charence J., *The Quest for Equality: Protective Discrimination or Compensatory Justice, Ethical Dilemmas of Development in Asia*, (Lexington: D.C. Heath, 1983).

Dietrich, Gabriele, "Dalit Movements and Women's Movement", in *Reflections on the Women's Movements in*

India: Religion, Ecology and Development, (New Delhi: Horizon India Books, 1992).

Dietrich, Gabriele, "Dalit Movements and Women's Movements", in Gabriele Dietrich, *Reflections on the Women's Movement in India: Religion, Ecology, Development*, (New Delhi: Horizon India Books, 1992).

Din, Mata, "Ambedkar: The Architect of Constitution", in *Ambedkar and Social Justice*, Vol. I, (New Delhi: Director, Publications Division, Ministry of Information and Broadcasting, 1992), [on behalf of Baba Saheb Dr. B.R. Ambedkar Birth Centenary Celebrations Committee, Ministry of Welfare, Government of India].

Diwakar, D.M., "Dalit Question of Distributive Justice and Mobilization", in D.M. Diwakar (ed.), *Distributive Justice Through Social Mobilization*, (New Delhi: Manak, 1998).

Dixit, M.R., "Ambedkar's Contribution and Relevance", in *Ambedkar and Social Justice*, Vol. II, (New Delhi: Director, Publications Division, Ministry of Information and Broadcasting, 1992), [on behalf of Baba Saheb Dr. B.R. Ambedkar Birth Centenary Celebrations Committee, Ministry of Welfare, Government of India].

Dolas, Avinash, "Dalit Theatrical Movement", in Bojja Tharakam (ed.), *The First All India Dalit Writers Conference: A Commemorative Volume and Who's Who*, (Hyderabad: Dr. B.R. Ambedkar Memorial Trust, 1994).

Dolas, Avinash, "Dalit Women and the Women's Movement in India", in P.G. Jogdand (ed.), *Dalit Women in India: Issues and Perspectives*, (New Delhi: Gyan Publishing House, in collaboration with University of Poona, Pune, 1995).

Dongre, M.K., *Economic Thought of Dr. B.R. Ambedkar*, (Nagpur: Ambedkar Samaj, 1974).

Donogue, J.R., *Pariah Persistence in Changing Japan: A Case Study*, (Washington, D.C.: University Press of America, 1978).

Doraiswamy Iyengar, N.A., *A Pillar of Swaraj: Being a Collection of Three Short Stories on Untouchability*, (Madras: Everyman Publishers, 1922).

Doshi, H.C., *Untouchability in Surat City*, (Surat: Department of Sociology, South Gujarat University, 1977).

Doshi, Harish, "Gandhi and Ambedkar on the Removal of Untouchability", in Vimal P. Shah and Binod C. Agrawal (eds.), *Reservation Policy, Programmes and Issues*, (Jaipur: Rawat Publications, 1986).

Doshi, R.R., "Can the New Economic Policy Do Anything for the Scheduled Castes and Scheduled Tribes", in Yeswant Khillare (ed.), *Present Status of Backward Classes in India*, (Aurangabad: Centre for Studies on SCs/STs, 1997).

Downie, David, *The Lone Star: The History of the Telugu Mission*, (Philadelphia: American Baptist Publication Society, 1892), [This deals with the detailed description of earliest of attempt of missionary work among the Dalits of Andhra].

Dube, M.P., "Protection of the Scheduled Castes' and Tribes' Human Rights", in C.P. Barthwal (ed.), *Social Justice in India*, (Lucknow: Bharat Book Centre, 1998).

Dube, M.P., "Protection of the Scheduled Castes' and Tribes' Human Rights", in M.P. Dube and Neeta Bora (eds.), *Social Justice and Women in India*, (Delhi: Swaraj Prakashan, 1999).

Dube, S.C., *Indian Village*, (London: Routledge, 1955), [Heavily deals with Madigas of Andhra Pradesh].

Dube, Saurabh, "Myths, Symbols and Community: Satnampanth of Chhattisgarh", in Parth Chatterjee and Gyanendra Pandey (eds.), *Subaltern Studies VII: Writings on South Asian History and Society*, (New Delhi: OUP, 1993).

Dube, Saurabh, *Caste and Sect in Village Life: Satnamis of Chhattisgarh, 1900-50*, (Shimla: Indian Institute of Advanced Studies, 1993).

Dube, Saurabh, *Untouchable Pasts: Religion, Identity and Power among a Central Indian Community, 1780-1950*, (New York: State University of New York, 1998).

Dube, Siddarth, *In the Land of Poverty: Memoirs of an Indian Family, 1947-1997*, (London: Zed Books, 1998).

Dubey, Abhay Kumar, "Anatomy of a Dalit Power Player: A Study of Kanshi Ram", in Ghanshyam Shah (ed.), *Dalit Identity and Politics*, (New Delhi: Sage Publications, 2001), [Cultural Subordination and the Dalit Challenge, Vol. 2 of Sage series].

Dubey, S.M., "Study of Scheduled Caste and Scheduled Tribe College Students in Assam", (Dibrugarh: Department of Sociology, Dibrugarh University, 1974), [A research monograph, out of a project financed by the ICSSR].

Dubey, S.N., *Administration of Social Welfare Programmes in India*, (Bombay: Somaiya Publications, 1973).

Dubois, Abbe J.A., *Hindu Manners, Customs and Ceremonies*, (Translated by Henry K. Beauchamps), (Oxford: Clarendon Press, 1959), (3rd edition). [This was originally written in 1815, the fifth Chapter contains one of the earliest descriptions of 'untouchables' noted by a missionary].

Dumont, L., *A South Indian Subcaste: Social Organisation and Religion of the Pamalai Kallar*, (Delhi: OUP, 1986), (First edition 1957).

Dundes, Alan, *Two Tales of Crow and Sparrow: A Freudian Folkloristic Essay on Caste and Untouchability*, (Lanham, Maryland: Rowman & Littlefield, 1997).

Dushkin, Lelah, "Scheduled Caste Politics", in Michael J. Mahar (ed.), *The Untouchables in Contemporary India*, (Tucson: University of Arizona Press, 1972).

Dutt, Krishna, "Women's Work and Employment belonging to Special Categories (SC and ST)", in Devaki Jain and Nirmala Banerjee (eds.), *Tyranny of the Household: Investigative Essays on Women's Work*, (Delhi: Shakti Books, 1985).

Dutta, Nalinikant, *An X-Ray on Reservation Provisions*, (Delhi: Anmol Publishers, 1991).

Dwivedi, R.G., "On the Problems of Scheduled Castes Observations Harijan Elite", in R.S. Tripathi and P.D. Tiwari (eds.), *Dimensions of Scheduled Caste Development in India: Problems and Prospects*, (New Delhi: Uppal, 1991).

Ekbote, Gopal Rao, "Dr. Ambedkar: National Integration", in *Dr. B.R. Ambedkar Memorial Lectures*, (Hyderabad: Dr. B.R. Ambedkar Memorial Trust, 1993), [This Lecture was originally delivered on 6 December 1992].

Elliot, H.M., *The Races of the North-Western Provinces of India*, Vol. I, (London: 1869).

Elst, Koernraad, *Indigenous Indians: Agastya to Ambedkar*, (New Delhi: Voice of India, 1993).

Elst, Koernraad, *Dr. Ambedkar: A True Aryan*, (New Delhi: Voice of India, 1993).

Elwin, V., *Agariya: Myths of Middle India*, (Bombay: 1946).

Elwin, V., *Chok Agaria: Myths of Middle India*, (Bombay: 1946).

Elwin, V., *The Agaria*, (London: Oxford University Press, Indian Branch, 1942).

Emmett, P.B. et. al., *The Malas and Madigas*, (Calcutta: Association Press, n.d.), [Religious Life of India Series].

Enthoven, R., *The Tribes and Castes of Bombay*, 3 vols., (Bombay: Government Central Press, 1920-22).

Farquhar, John N., "Help for the Depressed Classes", in his *Modern Religious Movements in India*, (London, New York: Macmillan, 1917), (Reprinted in Delhi: Munshiram Manoharlal, 1967).

Fazal-ud-din, Joshua, *Tragedy of the Untouchables*, (Lahore: Civil and Military Gazette, 1934).

Fernandes, Walter, *Caste and Conversion Movements: Religion and Human Rights*, (New Delhi: Indian Social Institute, 1981).

Fernandes, Walter, *Dalit Christians in Tamil Nadu*, (New Delhi: Indian Social Institute, 1994).

Fernandes, Walter (ed.), *The Emerging Dalit Identity (The Reassertion of Subalterns)*, (New Delhi: Indian Social Institute, 1996).

Fernandes, Walter, "The Emerging Dalit Identity: An Introduction", Walter Fernandes (ed.), *The Emerging Dalit Identity (The Reassertion of Subalterns)*, (New Delhi: Indian Social Institute, 1996).

Fernandes, Walter, "Conversion to Christianity, Caste Tension and Search for a New Identity in Tamil Nadu", in Walter Fernandes (ed.), *The Emerging Dalit Identity: The Reassertion of Subalterns*, (New Delhi: Indian Social Institute, 1996).

Fernandes, Walter, "Reservation as a Tool of Social Change", in A.K. Lal (ed.), *Protective Discrimination: Ideology and Praxis*, (New Delhi: Concept, 2002), [Published for B.G. Pant Social Science Institute, Allahabad].

Fisher, F.B., *Touching the Untouchables: India's Silent Revolution*, (New York: Macmillan, 1920).

Fishman, Alvin Texas, *Culture Change and Underprivileged: A Study of Madigas in South India under Christian Guidance*, (Madras: The Christian Literature Society for India, 1941).

Fiske, Adele M., "The Understanding of 'Religion' and 'Buddhism' among India's New Buddhists", in T.S. Wilkinson and M.M. Thomas (eds.), *Ambedkar and the Neo-Buddhist Movement*, (Madras: 1972).

Fiske, Adele, "Scheduled Caste Buddhist Organizations", in J.M. Mahar (ed.), *The Untouchables in Contemporary India*, (Tucson: The University of Arizona Press, 1972).

Fitzgerald, Timothy, "Ambedkar, Buddhism and the Concept of Religion", in S.M. Michael (ed.), *Dalits in Modern India: Vision and Values*, (New Delhi: Vistaar Publications, (1999).

Forrester, Duncan B., "The Depressed Classes and Conversion to Christianity: 1860 – 1960", in G.A. Oddie (ed.), *Religion in South Asia: Religious Conversion and Revivalist*

Movements in South Asia in Medieval and Modern Times, (New Delhi: Manohar, 1991), [First Published in 1977].

Francis, D., "Dalit Rights as Human Rights", in Chandu Subba Rao and D. Francis (eds.), *Development of Weaker Sections (Essays in Honour of Prof. K.S. Chalam)*, (Jaipur: Rawat, 2000).

Francis, W., "Adiyan", *Census of India, 1901, Vol. XV, Madras, Part I: Report*, (Madras: 1902).

Franco, Fernando and Vijay Parmar, "Dalit Organisations: Reconstituting Reality", in Walter Fernandes (ed.), *The Emerging Dalit Identity: The Reassertion of Subalterns*, (New Delhi: Indian Social Institute, 1996).

Franco, Fernando, Jyotsna Macwan and Suguna Ramanathan, *The Silken Swing: The Cultural Universe of Dalit Women*, (Calcutta: Stree, 2000).

Franco, Fernando (ed.), *Pain and Awakening: The Dynamics of Dalit Identity in Bihar, Gujarat and Uttar Pradesh*, (New Delhi: Indian Social Institute, 2002).

Franco, Fernando and Archana Sinha, "Dalit Identity in Uttar Pradesh", in Fernando Franco (ed.), *Pain and Awakening: The Dynamics of Dalit Identity in Bihar, Gujarat and Uttar Pradesh*, (New Delhi: Indian Social Institute, 200[illegible]).

Freeman, James M., "The Consciousness of Freedom among India's Untouchables", in D. Basu and R. Sissions (eds.), *Social and Economic Development in India*, (New Delhi: Sage Publications, 1987).

Freeman, James M., *Untouchable: An Indian Life History*, (Stanford, CA: Stanford University Press, 1979).

Friske, A., "Scheduled Castes Buddhist Organizations", in Michael J. Mahar (ed.), *The Untouchables in Contemporary India*, (Tucson: University of Arizona Press, 1972).

Friske, A., "The Understanding of 'Religion' and 'Buddhism' among India's New Buddhists", in T. Wilkinson and M. Thomas (eds.), *Ambedkar and the Neo-Buddhist Movement*, (Madras: The Christian Literature Society, 1972).

Fuchs, Stephen, "Clan god myth and worship among the Nimar Balahis", in J.P. Mill et.al. (eds.), *Essays in Anthropology: Presented to S.C.Roy*, (Lucknow: Maxwell and Co., 1942).

Fuchs, Stephen, *Children of Hari: A Study of the Nimar Balahis in the Central Provinces of India*, (Vienna: Verlag Herold, 1950 and New York: F.A. Prager, 1951).

Fuchs, Stephen, *Rebellious Prophets*, (Bombay: Asia Publishing House, 1965).

Fuchs, Stephen, "The Satnami Movement of the Chamars", in *Rebellious Prophets*, (Bombay, London: Asia Publishing House, 1965).

Fuchs, Stephen, *At the Bottom of Indian Society: The Harijan and Other Low Castes*, (Delhi: Munshiram Manoharlal, 1981).

Furquhar, H.N., "The Tiyas", in *Modern Religious Movements in India*, (London, New York: Macmillan, 19170, (Reprinted by Delhi: Munshiram Manoharlal, 1967).

Gadekar, D.R., "Socio-Economic Thoughts of B.R. Ambedkar", in Shyam Lal and K.S. Saxena (eds.), *Ambedkar and Nation-Building*, (Jaipur: Rawat, 1998).

Gafoor, Syed Khaja Abdul, *Social Service Among the Tribes and Backward Classes in Hyderabad*, (Hyderabad: Government Printing Press, 1952).

Gaikwad, D.S., "The Impact of Dr. Babasaheb Ambedkar on the Education of the Weaker Sections of India", in K.N. Kadam (ed.), *Dr. B.R. Ambedkar: The Emancipator of the Oppressed*, (Bombay: Popular Prakashan, 1993).

Gaikwad, Jaideo, "The Dalit Women's Dual Fight: Fight for Caste Eradication and Fight for Women's Liberation", in P.G. Jogdand (ed.), *Dalit Women in India: Issues and Perspectives*, (New Delhi: Gyan Publishing House, in collaboration with University of Poona, Pune, 1995).

Gaikwad, Shankar L., *Protective Discrimination Policy and Social Change: An Analytical Study of State Action on Scheduled Castes in Aurangabad City*, (Jaipur: Rawat, 1999).

Gaikwad, Shankar L., "In the Wake of New Economic Policy: Responses of Scheduled Caste/Scheduled Tribe Associations to Privatization", in P.G. Jogdand (ed.), *New Economic Policy and Dalits*, (Jaipur: Rawat, 2000).

Gaidwad, Vijay B., *The Lampoons by Arun Shourie*, (Ulhasnagar, Thane: Vaibhav Prakashan, 1997).

Gaidwad, Vijay B., *Dr. Ambedkar Foreign Policy and Its Relevance*, (Ulhasnagar, Thane: Vaibhav Prakashan, 1999).

Gaikwar of Baroda, His Highness the, *The Depressed Classes*, (Madras: G.A. Natesan, n.d.).

Gajbhiye, Anil, "Trends in Marathi Dalit Story", in Bojja Tharakam (ed.), *The First All India Dalit Writers Conference: A Commemorative Volume and Who's Who*, (Hyderabad: Dr. B.R. Ambedkar Memorial Trust, 1994).

Gajendragad, V.N., "Minority and Backward Community", in *Ambedkar and Social Justice*, Vol. I, (New Delhi: Director, Publications Division, Ministry of Information and Broadcasting, 1992), [on behalf of Baba Saheb Dr. B.R. Ambedkar Birth Centenary Celebrations Committee, Ministry of Welfare, Government of India].

Galanter, Marc, "The Religious Aspects of Caste: A Legal View", in Donald E. Smith (ed.), *South Asian Religion and Politics*, (Princeton, N.J.: Princeton University Press, 1966).

Galanter, Marc, "Changing Legal Conceptions of Caste", in Milton Singer and Bernard S. Cohn (eds.), *Structure and Change in Indian Society*, (Chicago: Aldine Publishing Company, 1968).

Galanter, Marc, "The Abolition of Disabilities – Untouchability and the Law", in J.M. Mahar (ed.), *The Untouchables in Contemporary India*, (Tucson: The University of Arizona Press, 1972).

Galanter, Marc, "Untouchability and the Law" in A.W. Murphy et al. (eds.), *Law and Poverty*, (Bombay: N.M. Tripathy, 1973).

Galanter, Marc, "Pursuing Equality: An Assessment of India's Policy of Compensatory Discrimination for

Disadvantaged Groups", in Dilip K. Basu and Richard Sission (eds.), *Social and Economic Development in India,* (New Delhi: Sage, 1986).

Galanter, Marc, *Competing Equalities: Law and the Backward Classes in India,* (Delhi: OUP, 1984).

Gandhi, M.K., *My Soul's Agony: Being Gandhiji's Statements from Yeravada Prison on the Removal of Untouchability among Hindus,* (Ahmedabad: Navajivan, 1932).

Gandhi, M.K., *The Bleeding Wound! Being a most up-to-date Collection of Gandhiji's Speeches, Writings and Statements on Untouchability,* (Compiled and edited by Shri Ramnath Suman, Introduction by C.Y. Chintamani, Foreword by G.D. Birla), (Benares: Shyam Lal, 1932).

Gandhi, M.K., *Untouchability,* (Lahore: Gandhi Publications' League, 1944).

Gandhi, M.K., *For Workers Against Untouchability,* (Ahmedabad: Navjivan Publishing House, 1954).

Gandhi, M.K., *The Removal of Untouchability,* (Ahmedabad: Navjivan Publishing House, 1954).

Gandhi, M.K., *All Are Equal in the Eyes of God: Selections from Mahatma Gandhi,* (Delhi: Government of India, Publications Division, 1964).

Gandhi, M.K., *Caste Must Go and the Sin of Untouchability,* (Compiled by R. K. Prabhu), (Ahmedabad: Navajivan, 1964).

Gandhi, M.K., *My Varnashrama Dharma,* (Edited by Anand T. Hingorani), (Bombay: Bharatiya Vidya Bhavan, 1965).

Gandhi, M.K., *None High: None Low,* (Edited by Anand T. Hingorani), (Bombay: Bharatiya Vidya Bhavan, 1965).

Ganesan, L., *Relevance of Reservation,* (Madras: Valentina, 1991).

Gangawane, Kamalakar, 'Social Awareness in Dalit Literature' in Bojja Tharakam, (ed), *The First All India Dalit Writers Conference,* (Hyderabad, Dr B R Ambedkar Memorial Trust, 1994).

Gangrade, K.D., *Educational Problems of the Scheduled Castes in Haryana (College Students),* (Delhi: Delhi School of

Social Work, 1974), [Originally a research project financed by the ICSSR].

Gangrade, K.D., "Educational Problems of the Scheduled Castes in Haryana (School Students", (Delhi: Delhi School of Social Work, Delhi University, 1974), [A research monograph, out of a project financed by the ICSSR].

Ganguli, B.N., "The Democrat", in B.K. Ahluwalia and Shashi Ahluwalia (eds.), *B.R. Ambedkar and Human Rights*, (New Delhi: Vivek Publishing Company, 1981).

Ganguly-scrase, Ruchira, *Global Issues, Local Contexts: The Rabi Das of West Bengal*, (New Delhi: Orient Longman, 2001).

Gannasambandan, D., "Belated Recognition and Present Relevance", in *Ambedkar and Social Justice*, Vol. II, (New Delhi: Director, Publications Division, Ministry of Information and Broadcasting, 1992), [on behalf of Baba Saheb Dr. B.R. Ambedkar Birth Centenary Celebrations Committee, Ministry of Welfare, Government of India].

Ganni, Raju G., *The Life of Dr. B.R. Ambedkar*, (Hyderabad: Babasaheb Dr. Ambedkar Memorial Society, 1979).

Gatwood, Lynn, *Devi and the Spouse Goddess: Women's Sexuality and Marriage in India*, (Delhi: Manohar, 1985).

Gaur, J.S., C.M. Thukral, V.K. Jain, J.P. Malik, Papiya Ghosh, Narinder Kaur and Sunita Sharma, "Psychological Basis of Educational and Vocational Development of Scheduled Caste Students", (New Delhi: Department of Educational Psychology, Counseling and Guidance, NCERT, 1987), [A research monograph].

Gaur, J.S., C.M. Thukral, V.K. Jain and Sunita Sharma, "Values and Career Maturity of Scheduled and Non-Scheduled Caste High School Boys", (New Delhi: NCERT, 1989), [A research monograph].

Gaur, K.K., *Role of Agricultural Credit in the Prosperity of Scheduled Castes*, (New Delhi: Manak, 1999).

Gautam, M.B., *Bhagyodayam: Maadari Bhagya Reddy Varma, Life Sketch and Mission*, (Hyderabad, Adi-Hindu Social Service League, 1991).

Gautam, Munshilal, *Dr. B.R. Ambedkar on National Unity Integration*, (Aligarh: Siddharth Gautam Shikshan and Sanskriti Samiti, 1993).

Gavai, R.S., *The Caste War Over Reservations: A Case Before the People's Bar*, (Bombay: W.K. Ganar, President and Bajirao Kamble, General Secretary Maharashtra State Republican Party, 1981).

Gavane, Sudhir, "Deniel from Bottom: Scheduled Castes and Scheduled Tribes in Higher Education", in Yeswant Khillare (ed.), *Present Status of Backward Classes in India*, (Aurangabad: Centre for Studies in SCs/STs, 1997).

Gawali, Chandrashekhar S., "Psycho-Social Dimensions of Dalit Identity", in Ambrose Pinto (ed.), *Dalit Assertion for Identity*, (New Delhi: Indian Social Institute, 1999), [Proceedings of the National Seminar of Dalit Postgraduate and Research Students held on 23-25 January 1999 in the Indian Social Institute].

Geeta, V. and S.V. Rajdurai, *Towards a Non-Brahmin Millennium: From Iyotheee Thass to Periyar*, (Calcutta: Samya, 1998), [in association with the Book Review Literary Trust].

George, E.I., "Educational Problems of the Scheduled Caste and Scheduled Tribe College Students in Kerala", (Department of Psychology, Kerala University, 1975), [A research monograph, out of a project financed by the ICSSR].

George Victor, P., "Ambedkar's Life: A Search for Social Justice", in K.S. Chalam (ed.), *The Relevance of Ambedkarism in India*, (Jaipur: Rawat, 1993).

Ghatak, B.K. (ed.), *Dr. Ambedkar's Thought*, (New Delhi: A.P.H. Publishing Corporation, 1996).

Ghatak, B.K., *Autobiography of Dr. B.R. Ambedkar*, (New Delhi: Runa Printing House, 2000).

Ghospade, A.K., *Dr. Baba Saheb Ambedkar*, (Poona: Thokal Prakashan, 1940).

Ghosh, Ashish (ed.), *Dalits and Peasants: The Emerging Caste-Class Dynamics*, (Delhi: Gyan Sagar Publications, 1999).

Ghosh, Kunal, "Buddha, Vivekananda and Ambedkar: Progression in Indian Thought", in G.S.Bal (ed.), *Understanding Ambedkar*, (Delhi: Ajanta Books, 2000).

Ghosh, S.K., *Protection of Minorities and Scheduled Castes*, (New Delhi: Ashish Publishing House, 1980).

Ghouse, Mohammad, "Ambedkar and Federalism: Ambedkar as Architect of the Constitution", in Nazeer H. Khan (ed.), *B.R. Ambedkar on Federalism, Ethnicity and Gender Justice*, (New Delhi: Deep & Deep, 2001).

Ghurye, G.S., *Caste and Race in India*, (Bombay: Popular Prakashan, 1959), 5th edn. [One chapter on Scheduled Caste].

Gill, H.S., "The Dalit Discourse", in Harish Narang (ed.), *Writing Black Writing Dalit: Essays in Black African and Dalit Indian Writings*, (Shimla: Indian Institute of Advanced Studies, 2002).

Ginwalla, Persis and Suguna Ramanathan, "Dalit Women as Receivers and Modifiers of Discourse", in Walter Fernandes (ed.), *The Emerging Dalit Identity: The Reassertion of Subalterns*, (New Delhi: Indian Social Institute, 1996).

Giri, V.V., "Ambedkar: A Dedicated Life", in B.K. Ahluwalia and Shashi Ahluwalia (eds.), *B.R. Ambedkar and Human Rights*, (New Delhi: Vivek Publishing Company, 1981).

Glasenapp, H. Von, *Brahman et Boudha*, (Paris: Payot, 1937).

Glen, M. and Sipra Bose Johnson, "Social Mobility Among Untouchables", in G.R. Gupta (ed.), *Cohesion and Conflict in Modern India*, (New Delhi: Vikas, 1978).

Gnanadason, Aruna, "Dalit Women: The Dalit of the Dalit", in Arvind P. Nirmal (ed.), *Toward a Common Dalit Ideology*, (Madras: Gurukul Lutheran Theological College and Research Institute, 1990), [Papers presented at the National Seminar on Dalit Ideology organized by the Department of Dalit Theology, Gugukul Lutheran Theological College and Research Institute].

Gnanadason, Aruna, "Dalit Women: The Dalit of the Dalit", in James Massey (ed.), *Indigenous People, Dalits: Dalit*

Issues in Today's Theological Debate, (Delhi: ISPCK, 1998), (First Published in1994), [This article initially published in A.P. Nirmal (ed.), *Towards A Common Dalit Ideology*, (Madras: Gurukul Lutheran Theological College and Research Institute, 1990)].

Gobind, K.B., *Reformative Law and Social Justice in Indian Society: A Sociological Study with Special Reference to Weaker Classes of Bhagalpur*, (New Delhi: Regency, 1995).

Goel, Dharmendra, "B.R. Ambedkar's Critique of Panchayats and their Historical Role (from the Subaltern Perspective)", in G.S. Bal (ed.), *Understanding Ambedkar*, (Delhi: Ajanta Books, 2000).

Goel, M.M., "Economic Ideas of Dr. Ambedkar and their Relevance Today", in M.L. Ranga (ed.), *B.R. Ambedkar: His Life, Work and Relevance*, (New Delhi: Manohar, 2000).

Goel, Veena and Jasbir Singh, "A Socio-Economic Analysis of Scheduled Caste Families in Bhai Ladhu Village of Amritsar District", in V.S. Mahajan and B.S. Mann (eds.), *Economic Development of Scheduled Castes*, (New Delhi: Anmol, 1997).

Goffin, H.J., *At Grips: Talks with the Telugus of South India*, (London: London Missionary Society, 1913).

Gogate, S.B., "A Critical Study of the Availability of Scholarships and Other financial Facilities to Scheduled Caste Students in Marathwada", (Pune: Indian Institute of Education, 1985), [A research monograph].

Gokhale, B.D., "Dr. Bhimrao Ramji Ambedkar: Rebel Against Hindu Tradition", in Bradwell Smith (ed.), *Religion and Social Conflict in South Asia*, (Leiden: E.J. Brill, 1976).

Gokhale, Gopal Krishna, "The Depressed Classes", in Rajendra Singh Vatsa (ed.), *The Depressed Classes in India*, (New Delhi: Gitanjali Prakashan, 1977), This piece was also reprinted in D.G. Kaine and D.V. Ambedkar (eds.), *Speeches and Writings of Gopal Krishna Gokhale*, Vol. III, (Poona: Servants of India Society, in collaboration with Asia Publishing House of Bombay, 1903), [Originally it was a speech delivered at the Dharwar Social Conference held on 27 April, 1903].

Gokhale, Gopal Krishna, *Treatment of Indians by the Boers and Treatment of the Low Castes in India by Their Own Countrymen*, (London: Christian Literature Society for India, 1903).

Gokhale-Turner, Jayshree B., "Bhakti or Vidroha: Continuity and Change in Dalit Sahitya", in Jayant Lele (ed.), *Tradition and Modernity in Bhakti Movements*, (Leiden: E.J. Brill, 1981).

Gokhale, Jayashree B., "The Evolution of a Counter Ideology: Dalit Consciousness in Maharashtra", in Frankel Francine R. and M.S.A. Rao (eds.), *Dominance and State Power in India, Vol. II Decline of a Social Order*, (Delhi: OUP, 1990).

Gokhale, Jayashree B., *From Concessions to Confrontation: The Politics of an Indian Untouchable Community*, (Bombay: Popular Prakashan, 1993).

Gomongo, Giridhar, *Constitutional Provisions for the Scheduled Castes and Scheduled Tribes*, (Bombay: Himalaya Publishing House, 1992).

Gooptu, Nandini, 'Caste and Labour: Untouchable Social Movements in Urban UP in the Early Twentieth Century' in Peter Robb (ed), *Dalit Movements and Meanings of Labour in India*, (Delhi, Oxford University Press, 1996), (First Published in 1993).

Gopal, B., "Emancipation of Scheduled Castes/Scheduled Tribes: Facts and Fallacies", in J.S. Narayana Rao, A. Somasekhar and K. Audiseshaiah (eds.), *B.R. Ambedkar: His Relevance Today*, (New Delhi: Gyan Publishing House, 1994).

Gopal, Jaya, "Dr. Ambedkar on Annihilation of Caste", in G.S. Bal (ed.), *Understanding Ambedkar*, (Delhi: Ajanta Books, 2000).

Gopala Jeevaratnam, Avula, *Political Implications of Untouchability*, (Hyderabad: Kondaveedu Press, 1973).

Gopinath, M., *Dalit Self-Determination*, (Banglore: A Dalit Voice Publication, 1992), [Pamphlet].

Gopinath, M. and Lazer, Fr., (eds.), *The Emergence of Indigenous Peoples: Collections of Papers Presented at the First All India Conference of Indigenous Peoples of India*, (Bangalore: Council of Indigenous People-India and Indian Social Institute, 1993).

Gore, M.S., *The Social Context of an Ideology: Ambedkar's Political and Social Thought*, (New Delhi: Sage Publications, 1993).

Gorhe, Neelam, "Social Development and Dalit Women", in P.G. Jogdand (ed.), *Dalit Women in India: Issues and Perspectives*, (New Delhi: Gyan Publishing House, in collaboration with University of Poona, Pune, 1995).

Gosal, G.S. and A.B. Mukherjee, "Scheduled Caste Population in India", in A. Chandrasekhar (ed.), *Economic and Socio-Cultural Dimensions of Rationalization, Census of India, 1971*, (New Delhi: 1972), [Monograph No. 7].

Goswami, B., *Constitutional Safeguards for Scheduled Castes and Scheduled Tribes*, (Jaipur: Rawat, 2003).

Goswami, Bonomali, *Untouchables: A Novel*, (New Delhi: Mittal Publications, 1994).

Gough, K., "Harijans in Thanjavur", in K. Gough and H. Sharma (eds.), *Imperialism and Revolution in South Asia*, (New York and London: Monthly Review Press, 1973).

Government of India, Central Advisory Board for Harijan Welfare, Ministry of Home Affairs, *Report of the Scavenging Conditions Enquiry Committee*, (New Delhi: 1961).

Government of India, Department of Education, *Education of Scheduled Castes and Scheduled Tribes 1988-89*, (New Delhi: 1993).

Government of India, *The Depressed Classes*, (New Delhi: 1928).

Government of India, *Harijans Today*, (New Delhi: Ministry of Information and Broadcasting, 1955).

Government of India, Home Department, *Proceedings in the Home Department*, Nos 130-1, July 1916 [Local government reports on depressed class conditions, and proposals.] *Proceedings of the Home Department*, Nos. 329-

4, August 1920 [Local government reports on depressed class conditions, and proposals].

Government of India, Ministry of Education, *Educational Facilities to Scheduled Castes and Scheduled Tribes,* (New Delhi: Planning Monitoring and Statistics Division, Scheduled Castes and Scheduled Tribes Cell, Ministry of Education, 1985).

Government of India, Ministry of Education and Culture, *Development of Scheduled Castes and Scheduled Tribes in India, 1967-68 to 1977-78,* (New Delhi: 1983).

Government of India, Ministry of Information and Broadcasting, *Harijans Today,* (Delhi: Ministry of Information and Broadcasting, 1952).

Government of India, Ministry of Law, *The Untouchability (Offences) Act, (22 of 1955),* (Delhi: 1955). [Pamphlet].

Government of India, Office of the Registrar General, *A Preliminary Appraisal of the Scheduled Castes of India,* (Compiled by H.L. Harit, Supervised by B.K. Roy Burman, (New Delhi: 1969). [Mimeographed].

Government of India, Planning Commission, Programme Evaluation Division, *Study of Post-Matric Scholarship Scheme for Scheduled Castes and Scheduled Tribes: Report Survey (July-August 1980),* (New Delhi: Planning Commission, 1982).

Government of India, Publications Division, *Ambedkar and Social Justice,* 2 vols., (New Delhi: Publications Division, 1993).

Government of India, *Selected Statistics on Scheduled Castes,* (New Delhi: Ministry of Home Affairs, 1984).

Government of India, *Social Mobility Among Scheduled Castes and Scheduled Tribes,* (Delhi: Manager of Publications, 1970).

Government of India, *Social Mobility Movements among Scheduled Castes and Scheduled Tribes of India,* (New Delhi: Registrar General, 1969).

Government of India, *The Scheduled Castes and Tribes List's Modification Order*, (Delhi: Manager, Government of India Press, 1957).

Government of India, *State-Wise Information on Education of Scheduled Scheduled Castes and Scheduled Tribes*, (New Delhi: Ministry of Education, SC & ST Cell, 1985).

Government of Karnataka, *Welfare Measures for Scheduled Castes and Tribes in Karnataka*, (Bangalore: Ministry of Rural Development and Social Welfare, 1976).

Government of Rajasthan, *Progress of Education of Scheduled Caste and Scheduled Tribes in Rajasthan, 1977-78*, (Bikaner: Directorate of Primary and Secondary Education, 1979), [Studies in Educational Statistics, 1979].

Government of Tripura, Department of Welfare, *Socio-Economic Survey of the Cobbler Communities of Agartala's Municipality and its Adjacent Areas*, (Agartala: Department of Welfare, Scheduled Castes and Scheduled Tribes, 1980).

Govind, Bal, "Experiences of Atrocities", in Ambrose Pinto (ed.), *Dalit Assertion for Identity*, (New Delhi: Indian Social Institute, 1999), [Proceedings of the National Seminar of Dalit Postgraduate and Research Students held on 23-25 January 1999 in the Indian Social Institute].

Goyal, B.R., *Educating Harijans* (Gurgaon, Haryana: Academic, 1981), [This work deals with general history of the Scheduled Castes from educational point of view].

Goyal, S.K., "The Study of Scheduled Caste Students of Colleges in East Uttar Pradesh", (Varanasi: Department of Sociology, Banaras Hindu University, 1974), [A research monograph].

Goyal, S.R., "Ambedkar and Buddhism", in *Ambedkar and Social Justice*, Vol. II, (New Delhi: Director, Publications Division, Ministry of Information and Broadcasting, 1992), [on behalf of Baba Saheb Dr. B.R. Ambedkar Birth Centenary Celebrations Committee, Ministry of Welfare, Government of India].

Great Britain, East India (Constitutional Reforms), *Addresses Presented in India to His Excellency the Viceroy and the Right Honourable, the Secretary of State for India,* (London: H.M.S.O. Cmd. 9178, 1918). [This includes lists of the Depressed Classes and excerpts from their representations].

Greeven, R., *Knights of the Broom: An Attempt to Collect Some of the Ceremonies of Sweepers in the Benares Division,* (Benares: 1894).

Grierson, G.A., "Rai Dasis", in James Hastings (ed.), *Encyclopaedia of Religion and Ethics,* Vol. 10, (New York: 1919).

Grigson, Wilfred Vernon, *The Challenge of Backwardness: Some Notes and Papers on Tribal and Depressed Classes Policy with Special Reference to Hyderabad State,* (Hyderabad: Government Publications Press, 1947).

Grover, Virender (ed.), *B.R. Ambedkar,* (New Delhi: 1993).

Gupta, B.P. Mahesh Chandra, "Bharat Ratna Dr. B.R. Ambedkar", in *Ambedkar and Social Justice,* Vol. II, (New Delhi: Director, Publications Division, Ministry of Information and Broadcasting, 1992), [on behalf of Baba Saheb Dr. B.R. Ambedkar Birth Centenary Celebrations Committee, Ministry of Welfare, Government of India].

Gupta, B.P. Mahesh Chandra, "Ambedkar and Journalism", in V.T. Patil (ed.), *Studies in Ambedkar,* (Delhi: Devika Publications, 1995).

Gupta, Dauji, *Gandhi and Ambedkar: Great Emancipators,* (Lucknow: Inter-Globe Publications, 1993).

Gupta, Dipankar (ed.), *Social Stratification,* (New Delhi: OUP, 1991), [One can draw a good theoretical models for caste studies, and the contributions are from the experts of their respective fields].

Gupta, K., "Economic Deprivation of Socially Deprived in Uttar Pradesh", in K.L. Bhowmik (ed.), *Development of Scheduled Communities,* (New Delhi: Inter-India Publications, 1988).

Gupta, M.R., *The Untouchable*, (Delhi: Rajkamal Publications, 1948), [A Play].

Gupta, P.K., *Commentaries on the Scheduled Castes and Scheduled Tribes (Prevention of Atrocities) Act, 1989*, (Lucknow: Eastern, 1992).

Gupta, Ram Lakhan Prasad, *Reservation: Why Necessary?*, (Munghyr: Author, 1978).

Gupta, Shandi Swarup, *Varna, Castes and Scheduled Castes: A Documentation in Historical Perspective with a Classification Index to Scholarly Writings in Indian Journals, 1890-1990)*, (New Delhi: Concept, 1991).

Gupta, Shiv Bhushan, "Dr. Bhim Rao Ambedkar as an Economist", in R.B. Rao (ed.), *Bharat-Ratna Dr. Ambedkar*, (Allahabad: Chugh Publications, 1993).

Gupta, Shiv K., *Leadership Structures in Harijan Community*, (Allahabad: G.B. Panth Social Science Institute, 1982), [Project Report. 5].

Gupta, S.K., *The Scheduled Castes in Modern Indian Politics: Their Emergence as a Political Power*, (New Delhi: Munshiram Manoharlal, 1985).

Gupta, S.K., "Dr. Ambedkar's Perception of Indian Society and his Egalitarian Vision", in K.C. Yadav, (ed.), *From Periphery to Centre Stage: Ambedkar, Ambedkarism and Dalit Future*, (New Delhi: Manohar, 2000).

Gupta, S.K., "Indian Society and Dr. Ambedkar's Idea of Equality", in M.L. Ranga (ed.), *B.R. Ambedkar: His Life, Work and Relevance*, (New Delhi: Manohar, 2000).

Gupta, V.P. and Mohini Gupta (ed.), *Bhimrao Ramji Ambedkar*, (Delhi: Ambe Books, 1998), [Makers of Modern India Series, II].

Guru, Gopal, "Political Reservations for the Scheduled Castes: A Politics of Reformism", in R.G. Singh (ed.), *The Depressed Classes of India: Problems and Prospects*, (New Delhi: B.R. Publishing Corporation, 1986).

Guru, Gopal, "Dr. Ambedkar on Political Reservations", in K.K. Kavlekar and A.S. Chausalkar (eds.), *Political Ideas and Leadership of Dr. B.R. Ambedkar*, (Pune: Vishwanil Publications, 1989).

Guru, Gopal, "Dr. Ambedkar's Concept of Political Power and The Question of Dalit Movement", in *Dr. B.R. Ambedkar Memorial Lectures*, (Hyderabad: Dr. B.R. Ambedkar Memorial Trust, 1993), [This Lecture was originally delivered on 6 December 1991].

Guru, Gopal, "Dalit Movement in Mainstream Sociology", in Sandeep Pendse (ed.), *Dalit Movement Today*, (Bombay: Vikas Adhyayana Kendra, 1994), [Vikas Adhyayan Kendra, Bombay, *Perspectives* 1].

Guru, Gopal, *Dalit Cultural Movement and Dialectics of Dalit Politics in Maharashtra*, (Mumbai: Vikas Adhyayan Kendra, 1997).

Guru, Gopal, "Human Rights and the Dalits", in G.S. Bhargava and R.M. Pal (eds.), Human Rights of Dalits: Societal Violation, (New Delhi: Gyan Publishing House, 1999).

Guru, Gopal, "Dalits in Pursuit of Modernity", in Romila Thaper (ed.), *India's Another Millennium?*, (New Delhi: Penguin India, 2000).

Guru, Gopal, "The Man who thought Differently: An Inquiry into Political Thinking of Dr. Ambedkar", in K.C. Yadava, (ed.), *From Periphery to Centre Stage: Ambedkar, Ambedkarism and Dalit Future*, (New Delhi: Manohar, 2000).

Guru, Gopal, "The Language of Dalit-Bahujan Political Discourse", in Ghanshyam Shah (ed.), *Dalit Identity and Politics*, (New Delhi: Sage Publications, 2001), [Cultural Subordination and the Dalit Challenge, Vol. 2 of Sage series].

Guru, Gopal, "The Interface Between Ambedkar and the Dalit Cultural Movement in Maharashtra", in Ghanshyam Shah (ed.), *Dalit Identity and Politics*, (New

Delhi: Sage Publications, 2001), [Cultural Subordination and the Dalit Challenge, Vol. 2 of Sage series].

Guru, Gopal, "Ambedkar's Idea of Social Justice", in Ghanshyam Shah (ed.), *Dalits and the State,* (New Delhi: Concept Publishing Company, 2002), [Published for Centre for Rural Studies, Lal Bahadur Shastri National Academy of Administration, Mussoorie].

Haimendorf, Christopher Von Furer, 'Foreward', to Fuchs, Stephen, *The Children of Hari: A Study of the Nimar Balahis in Madhya Pradesh, India,* (Bombay: Thacker and Co, 1946).

Halbar, B.G., *Lamani Economy and Society in Change,* (Delhi: Mittal Publications, 1986).

Hamilpurkar, J.S., "The Protagonist of the Depressed Classes", in *Ambedkar and Social Justice,* Vol. I, (New Delhi: Director, Publications Division, Ministry of Information and Broadcasting, 1992), [on behalf of Baba Saheb Dr. B.R. Ambedkar Birth Centenary Celebrations Committee, Ministry of Welfare, Government of India].

Hanumantha Rao, G., *Caste and Poverty: A Case Study of Scheduled Castes in a Delta Village,* (Malikipuram: Savithri, 1977).

Hanumanthan, K.R., *Untouchabiiity: A Historical Study upto 1500 A.D. with Special Reference to Tamil Nadu,* (Madurai: Koodal Publishers, 1979).

Haragopal, G., "Dr. B.R. Ambedkar's Perspective of Indian Women", in *Dr. B.R. Ambedkar Memorial Lectures,* (Hyderabad: Dr. B.R. Ambedkar Memorial Trust, 1993), [This Lecture was originally delivered on 6 December 1990].

A Harijan (psued), *Gandhi or Ambedkar,* (Foreword by Radhakrishan), (Madras: Gandhi Era Publications, 1945).

Hari, H.L., "Marx, Ambedkar and Polarization of Oppressed and Exploited Classes in India", in *National Seminar on Marx, Ambedkar and Polarization of Oppressed and*

Exploited Classes in India, (New Delhi: Sanjivayya Institute of Socio-Economic Studies, 1991).

Harijans Today, (New Delhi: Publications Division, Ministry of Information and Broadcasting, Government of India, 1952).

Hariprasanna, A., "Ambedkar and Upliftment of the Status of Women", in *Ambedkar and Social Justice*, Vol. I, (New Delhi: Director, Publications Division, Ministry of Information and Broadcasting, 1992), [on behalf of Baba Saheb Dr. B.R. Ambedkar Birth Centenary Celebrations Committee, Ministry of Welfare, Government of India].

Harper, Edward B., "A Comparative Analysis of Caste: The United States and India", in Milton Singer and Bernard S. Cohn (eds.), *Structure and Change in Indian Society*, (Chicago: Aldine, 1968).

Harper, Edward B., "Social Consequences of an 'unsuccessful' Low Caste Movement", in James Silverberg (ed.), *Social Mobility in the Caste System in India: An Inter-disciplinary Symposium*, Comparative Studies in Society and History Supplement III, (The Hague: Mouton Press, 1968).

Harris, Nigel, *The New Untouchables: Immigration and the New Worker*, (London: I.B. Taurish Publisers, 1995).

Hasan, Suraj-Ul, *The Caste and Tribes of H.E.H. the Nizam's Dominion*, 2 vols., (Bombay: The Times Press, 1920).

Hasan, Zaheer, *Gandhi and the Harijans*, (New Delhi: Shree Publishing House, 1986).

Havinghurst, R.J., "Who are the Socially Disadvantaged", in S.W. Webster (ed.), *The Disadvantaged Learner*, (Sanfranscisco: Chandler, 1966).

Hayat, Qaisar, "Ambedkar on Ethnic Relations: National Unity", in Nazeer H. Khan (ed.), *B.R. Ambedkar on Federalism, Ethnicity and Gender Justice*, (New Delhi: Deep & Deep, 2001).

Hayat, Qaisar, "Revocation of Dalit Act: A Retrograde Step to Mow the Concept of Social Justice", in Nazeer H. Khan (ed.), *B.R. Ambedkar on Federalism, Ethnicity and Gender Justice*, (New Delhi: Deep & Deep, 2001).

Hazari, (pseud. of Marcus Abraham Malik), *An Indian Outcaste*, (London: Bannisdale, 1951), [reprinted as *I Was an Outcaste* by the Hindustan Times, New Delhi, 1957, again reprinted as *Untouchable: The Autobiography of an Indian Outcast*, (New York: Fredrick A. Praeger Co., 1969), (Originally published by Pall Mall Press, London, 1951)].

Heggade, Odeyar D., "Ambedkar's Social Theory of Labour Exploitation", in *Ambedkar and Social Justice*, Vol. II, (New Delhi: Director, Publications Division, Ministry of Information and Broadcasting, 1992), [on behalf of Baba Saheb Dr. B.R. Ambedkar Birth Centenary Celebrations Committee, Ministry of Welfare, Government of India].

Heggade, Odeyar D., *Economic Thought of Dr. B.R. Ambedkar*, (New Delhi: Mohit Publications, 1998).

Heggade, O.P., "Ambedkar's Social Theory of Labour Exploitation", in V.T. Patil (ed.), *Studies in Ambedkar*, (Delhi: Devika Publications, 1995).

Henninger, F., *The Bhangis*, (Calcutta: Association Press, n.d.), [Religious Life of India Series].

Henrich, J.C., *The Psychology of a Suppressed People*, (London: George Allen & Unwin, 1937). [Perhaps one of the earliest comparison of the problem of untouchability with that of race].

Henriques, Jude and G.G. Wankhede, "One Step Forward Yet Two Steps Behind: A Study of Wastage and Stagnation in Education of Scheduled Castes and Scheduled Tribes in Maharashtra", (Bombay: Unit for Research in the Sociology of Education, Tata Institute of Social Sciences, 1985), [A research monograph, out of a project financed by the Ministry of Human Resource Development].

Heptulla, Najma, "Life Mission, Contribution and Relevance of Babasaheb", in *Ambedkar and Social Justice*, Vol. II, (New Delhi: Director, Publications Division, Ministry of Information and Broadcasting, 1992), [on behalf of Baba Saheb Dr. B.R. Ambedkar Birth Centenary

Celebrations Committee, Ministry of Welfare, Government of India].

Herbert, Tony, "Naxalite Violence and Varna Ideology: Ganjhus in Turmoil", in Walter Fernandes (ed.), *The Emerging Dalit Identity: The Reassertion of Subalterns,* (New Delhi: Indian Social Institute, 1996).

Hibbert-Ware, G., *Christian Missions in the Telugu Country,* (Westminster: Society for the Propagation of the Gospel in foreign parts, 1912), [Gives an excellent account of the life and surrounds of the Dalits of the Telugu speaking areas, as well as of conditions of mission work among them].

Hiro, Dilip, *The Untouchables of India,* (London: Minority Rights Group, 1982), (Second edition), [Indian edition published by Dalit Sahitya Academy, 1984].

History of the Harijan Sevak Sangh, 1932-1968, (Delhi: Harijan Sevak Sangh, 1971).

Hodgson, Brian Huaghton, *Essay on the Koch, Bodo and Dhimal Tribes,* (Calcutta: Baptist Mission Press, 1847), [This was a three-part (Part I- Vocabulary; Part II- Grammer; Part III- Location, Customs and their moral Characters) book on three communities. *Koch* is a Scheduled Caste community in West Bengal and Tripura].

Horimoto, T., "Politicisation of Scheduled Castes in Independent India", in M. Naito (ed.), *Anti-Untouchability Ideologies and Movements in Modern India,* (Tokyo: Akashi Shoten Publishers, 1994).

Hunt, William S., *India's Outcastes: A New Era,* (London: Church Missionary Society, 1924).

Huq, Afzal, *Pakistan and Untouchability,* (Lahore: Muktaba-I-Urdu, 1941).

Hutton, J.H., 'Exterior Castes', in *Census of India, 1931,* (Delhi, Manager of Publications, 1933).

Hutton, J.H., *Caste in India,* (Bombay: 1951).

Ibbetson, Denzil, *Punjab Castes*, (Lahore: Author, 1916). [This is a reprint of chapters from *The Races, Castes and Tribes in the Census of Punjab, 1881*].

Ilaiah, Kancha, "The Chundur Carnage–The Struggle of Dalits", in Sandeep Pendse (ed.), *Dalit Movement Today*, (Bombay: Vikas Adhyayana Kendra, 1994), [Vikas Adhyayan Kendra, Bombay, *Perspectives* 1].

Ilaiah, Kancha, "Productive Labour, Consciousness and History: The Dalitbahujan Alternative", in Shahid Amin and Dipesh Chakravarthy (eds.), *Subaltern Studies IX*, (Delhi: OUP, 1997).

Ilaiah, Kancha, "Constructing a concept of Dalit-Bahujans and Human Rights", G.S. Bhargava and R.M. Pal (eds.), *Human Rights of Dalits: Societal Violation*, (New Delhi: Gyan Publishing House, 1999).

Ilaiah, Kancha, "Dalitism Vs. Brahminism: The Epistemological Conflict in History", in Ashish Ghosh (ed.), *Dalits and Peasants*, (Delhi: Gyan Sagar, 1999).

Ilaiah, Kancha, "Dalit Bahujans and Human Rights: A New Perspective", in R.M. Pal (ed.), *Protection of Human Rights: A Critique (With Special Reference to SC/STs, the Girl Child/Women belonging to SC/STs, marginalized Section and the Minorities*, (New Delhi: Indian Social Institute, 1999), [Proceedings of the National Seminar held on 13 and 14 November 1998 at the Indian Social Institute].

Ilaiah, Kancha, "Dalitism vs. Brahminism: The Epistemological Conflict in History", in Ghanshyam Shah (ed.), *Dalit Identity and Politics*, (New Delhi: Sage Publications, 2001), [Cultural Subordination and the Dalit Challenge, Vol. 2 of Sage series].

Independent Labour Party: Its Formation and Its Aims, (Reprinted from *Times of India*, August 15, 1936), (Bombay: Independent Labour Party Publications No. I, 1936).

Indian Institute of Psychometry, "Comparison of the Performance of the Scheduled Caste and Scheduled Tribe Candidates in Aptitude and Knowledge Tests with that of General Candidates", (Calcutta: IIP, 1982), [A research monograph].

Indian National Social Action Forum (INSAF), "Commission on Dalits and Other Oppressed Castes", *Appendix II*, in Sandeep Pendse (ed.), *Dalit Movement Today*, (Bombay: Vikas Adhyayana Kendra, 1994), [Vikas Adhyayan Kendra, Bombay, *Perspectives* 1].

Indian (First) Round Table Conference, London, 1930-31, *Indian Round Table Conference, 12 November 1930 – 19 January 1931: Proceedings*, (London: H.M.S.O. Cmd. 3778, 1931). [Dr. B.R. Ambedkar speaks on behalf of the 'Untouchables'].

Indian (Second) Round Table Conference, London, 1931, *Indian Round Table Conference, 7th September, 1931 – 1st December, 1931: Proceedings*, (London: H.M.S.O. Cmd. 3997, 1932). [N. Srinivasan speaks on behalf of 'Untouchables'].

Indian Council of Social Science Research, *Report on a Survey of Scheduled Caste High School and College Students in Fifteen States of India*, (Prepared by Suma Chitnis), (New Delhi: Centre for Social Studies, 1977).

Indian Round Table Conference, London, *Proceedings of the Federal Structure Committee and Minorities Committee*, (London: H.M.S.O., 1932). [The famous controversy/debate between Dr. B.R. Ambedkar and M.K. Gandhi].

Indian School of Social Sciences, *Bonded Labour in India: a Shocking Tale of Slave Labour in Rural India*, (Calcutta: ISSS, 1975).

Indian Statutory Commission (1928), "Chapter X: Education of the Depressed Classes", in *Review of Growth of Education in British India*, (Auxiliary Committee of Indian Statutory Commission, Chairman: Sir Phillip Hartog), (London: H.M.S.O. Cmd. 3407, 1929).

IPHRC, *Gunning Down Dalits: Police Firing at Ramabai Ambedkar Colony, Mumbai on 11th July 1997*, (Bombay: An Indian People's Human Rights Commission Report, 1997).

Irudayaraj, Xavier (ed.), *Emerging Dalit Theology*, (Madras: Jesuit Theological Secretariat, 1990).

Islam, Shamsul, *Untouchables in Manu's India*, (Delhi: Media House, 2002).

Issacs, Harold R., *India's Ex-Untouchables*, (New York: John Day Co., 1965).

Iyar, T. Sadasiva, *Problems of the Depressed Classes*, Presidential Address, (Madras: Cochin Pulaya Conference, May 14, 1923).

Iyengar, G. Aravamuda, *The Temple Entry by Harijans*, (Nellore: Sanatana Dharma Printing Agency, 1935), 2nd edition.

Iyengar, K.V. Sesha, *The Passing away of Untouchability*, (Madras: 1932).

Iyer, L.A.K., *The Cochin Tribes and Castes*, (New Delhi: Cosmos, 1981), (First edition 1909-12), 3 vols.

Iyer, L.A.K. and H.V. Nanjundayya, *The Mysore Tribes and Castes*, 4 vols., (Mysore: Published under the auspices of the Mysore University, 1928-36).

Iyer, L.A.K., *The Travencore Tribes and Castes*, 3 vols., (Trivandrum: Printed by the Superintendent of Government Press, 1937-41).

Iyer, V.R. Krishna, *Ambedkar Memorial Lectures, 1976, (Delivered by Mr. Justice V.R. Krishna Iyer in December 16, 17 and 18, 1976)*, (organized by the Jawaharlal Nehru University under the sponsorship of the Government of India in the Ministry of Education and Social Welfare, the University Grants Commission, and the Ambedkar Institute of Social Research and Training, New Delhi, (New Delhi: 1976).

Iyer, V.R. Krishna, *Social Democracy and Dalit Egalite: Ambedkar Memorial Lectures 1986-87*, (Madras: University of Madras, 1989).

Iyer, V.R. Krishna, *Dr. Ambedkar and the Dalit Future*, (Delhi: B.R. Publishing Corporation, 1990).

Iyer, V.R. Krishna, *Ambedkar Centenary: Social Justice and the Undone Vast*, (New Delhi: B.R. Publishing Corporation, 1991).

Iyer, V.R. Krishna, "Social Justice to Dalits and Sophists", in *Ambedkar and Social Justice*, Vol. I, (New Delhi:

Director, Publications Division, Ministry of Information and Broadcasting, 1992), [on behalf of Baba Saheb Dr. B.R. Ambedkar Birth Centenary Celebrations Committee, Ministry of Welfare, Government of India].

Iyer, V.R. Krishna, "Ambedkar: A Creative Iconoclast", in K.S. Chalam (ed.), *The Relevance of Ambedkarism in India*, (Jaipur: Rawat, 1993).

Jabbi, Mona and C. Rajyalakshmi, "Education of Marginalised Social Groups in Bihar", in A. Vaidyanathan and P.R. Gopinathan Nair (eds.), *Elementary Education Rural India: A Grassroots View*, (New Delhi: Sage, 2001).

Jadhav, A.S., "Dalit Among Dalits: Scheduled Caste and Scheduled Tribe Women", in P.G. Jogdand (ed.), *Dalit Women in India: Issues and Perspectives*, (New Delhi: Gyan Publishing House, in collaboration with University of Poona, Pune, 1995).

Jadhav, Narendra, *Dr. Ambedkar's Economic Thought and Philosophy*, (Bombay: Popular Prakashan, 1993).

Jadhav, Ujwala, "Dalit Women: Issues and Redressal", in P.G. Jogdand (ed.), *Dalit Women in India: Issues and Perspectives*, (New Delhi: Gyan Publishing House, in collaboration with University of Poona, Pune, 1995).

Jaganmohan Rao, R., "Ambedkar: An Architect of Indian Constitution", in K.S. Chalam (ed.), *The Relevance of Ambedkarism in India*, (Jaipur: Rawat, 1993).

Jaganmohan Rao, R., "Ambedkar – Architect of the Indian Constitution", in J.S. Narayana Rao, A. Somasekhar and K. Audiseshaiah (eds.), *B.R. Ambedkar: His Relevance Today*, (New Delhi: Gyan Publishing House, 1994).

Jahan, Qamar, "Prejudice among High and Low Self-Disclosee Scheduled Caste and Scheduled Tribe Females", in N. Hasnain (ed.), *Weaker Sections: The Psycho-Social Perspective*, (New Delhi: Gyan, 1998).

Jain, Akshay Kumar, "Baba Saheb Dr. B.R. Ambedkar: Some Reminiscences", in Rabi Ray (ed.), *Dr. B.R. Ambedkar*, (New Delhi: Lok Sabha Secretariat, 1991), [Eminent Parliamentarians Monograph Series 12].

Jain, P.C., Shashi Jain and Sudha Bhatnagar, *Scheduled Caste Women*, (Jaipur: Rawat, 1997).

Jain, Subhash Kumar, "Ambedkar on the Indian Federalism", in Nazeer H. Khan (ed.), *B.R. Ambedkar on Federalism, Ethnicity and Gender Justice*, (New Delhi: Deep & Deep, 2001).

Jain, Uday and Girishwar Misra, "Deprivation: A Socio-Psychological Analysis", in S.N. Chaudhary (ed.), *Changing Status of Depressed Castes in Contemporary India: Essays in Honour of Professor S.C. Dube*, (Delhi: Daya Publishing House, 1988).

Jairamdas, Jiwanlal, "*Bhangi Kasht Mukti and Bhangi Mukti*, (New Delhi: National Committee for Gandhi Centenary and Udyogshala Press, n.d.).

Jangam, R.T., "A Study and an estimate of Ambedkar's Movement", in V.T. Patil (ed.), *Studies in Ambedkar*, (Delhi: Devika Publications, 1995).

Jans, Rev. Fr. J., *The Depressed Classes: A Chronological Documentation*, (Ranchi: Part I, 1935-37, Parts II-XI, St. Mary's College, Kurseong).

Jashua, Gurram, *Gabbilam (The Bat)*, (Translated from Telugu by M.B. Raja Rao),(Hyderabad: Nava Veda Publications, 1975).

Jashua, Gurram, *Gabbilam (Bat)*, (Translated from Telugu by K.Madhava Rao), (Hyderabad: Joshua Foundation, 1996).

Jaswal, Surinder Singh, *Reservation Policy and the Law: Myth and Reality of Constitutional Safeguards to Scheduled Castes*, (New Delhi: Deep and Deep, 2000).

Jatava, Daya Ram, *Social Philosophy of B.R. Ambedkar*, (Agra: Phoenix Publishing Agency, 1965).

Jatava, Daya Ram, "Ambedkar and Manu", in *Dr. Babasaheb Ambedkar Amrat Mahotsab Visesanka*, (Nagpur: 1966).

Jatava, D.R., *Dr. Ambedkar's Role in National Movement*, (New Delhi: Bauddha Sahitya Sammelan, 1979).

Jatava, D.R., "The Philosopher", in B.K. Ahluwalia and Shashi

Ahluwalia (eds.), *B.R. Ambedkar and Human Rights*, (New Delhi: Vivek Publishing Company, 1981).

Jatava, D.R., "Dr. Ambedkar's Philosophy of Religion", in *Ambedkar and Social Justice*, Vol. II, (New Delhi: Director, Publications Division, Ministry of Information and Broadcasting, 1992), [on behalf of Baba Saheb Dr. B.R. Ambedkar Birth Centenary Celebrations Committee, Ministry of Welfare, Government of India].

Jatava, D.R., "The Philosophy of Dr. Ambedkar", in K.N. Kadam (ed.), *Dr. B.R. Ambedkar: The Emancipator of the Oppressed*, (Bombay: Popular Prakashan, 1993).

Jatava, D.R., *Dr. Ambedkar: Unique and Versatile*, (New Delhi: Blumoon, 1993).

Jatava, D.R., "Ambedkar's Philosophy of Religion", in V.T. Patil (ed.), *Studies in Ambedkar*, (Delhi: Devika Publications, 1995).

Jatava, D.R., *Indian Politics and Democracy*, (Jaipur: Surabhi, 1997).

Jatava, D.R., *The Critics of Dr. Ambedkar*, (Jaipur: Surabhi, 1997), (First published in 1975 by the Bharatiya Shoshit Jan Utthan Parishad, New Delhi).

Jatava, D.R., *Social Justice in India*, (Jaipur: INA Shree Publishers, 1998).

Jatava, D.R., *Ambedkar's Philosophy of Religion*, (Jaipur: INA Shree Publishers, 1998).

Jatava, D.R., *B.R. Ambedkar: Study in Society and Politics*, (Jaipur: National Publishing House, 1998).

Jatava, D.R., *B.R. Ambedkar: A Vision of Man and Morals*, (Jaipur: ABD Publishers, 1999).

Jatava, D.R., *Ambedkar and Humanism*, (Jaipur: ABD Publishers, 1999).

Jatava, D.R., *A Silent Soldier: An Autobiography*, (Jaipur: Samata Sahitya Sadan, 2000).

Javaraiah, M.N., "Dalit Literature in Kannada", in Bojja Tharakam (ed.), *The First All India Dalit Writers Conference:*

A Commemorative Volume and Who's Who, (Hyderabad: Dr. B.R. Ambedkar Memorial Trust, 1994).

Jayal-Chand, Neerja, "Moving the Centre: Black-Canadian and Dalit Literature", in Harish Narang (ed.), *Writing Black Writing Dalit: Essays in Black African and Dalit Indian Writings*, (Shimla: Indian Institute of Advanced Studies, 2002).

Jayakar, Samuel, *Rural sweepers in the City*, (Mysore: Wesley Press and Publishing House, 1952). [This Study was of Christian Sweepers of Jabalpur, Madhya Pradesh].

Jayakumar, Samuel, *Dalit Consciousness and Christian Conversion: Historical Resources for a Contemporary Debate, Mission Theology in an Asian Context*, (Delhi: ISPCK, and Oxford: Regnum International, 1999).

Jayaram, E.D., "The Thinker", in B.K. Ahluwalia and Shashi Ahluwalia (eds.), *B.R. Ambedkar and Human Rights*, (New Delhi: Vivek Publishing Company, 1981).

Jayaram, N., "Protective Discrimination and Education: A Critique of Strategy for Change", in Vimal P. Shah and Binod C. Agrawal (eds.), *Reservation Policy, Programmes and Issues*, (Jaipur: Rawat Publications, 1986).

Jayaraman, Raja, *Caste and Class: Dynamics of Inequality in Indian Society*, (Delhi: Hindustan Publishing Corporation, 1981).

Jeanetta, Robin, *Dr. Ambedkar and His Movement*, (Hyderabad: Dr. Ambedkar Publications Society, 1964).

Jeevan Kumar, D., "Quest for Social Justice", in *Ambedkar and Social Justice*, Vol. I, (New Delhi: Director, Publications Division, Ministry of Information and Broadcasting, 1992), [on behalf of Baba Saheb Dr. B.R. Ambedkar Birth Centenary Celebrations Committee, Ministry of Welfare, Government of India].

Jeevan, Kumar, D., "Ambedkar's Quest for Social Justice Through Constitutional Rights and Safeguards: An Analysis", in V.T. Patil (ed.), *Studies in Ambedkar*, (Delhi: Devika Publications, 1995).

Jena, Jyotsna Rani, "Multi-dimensional Exploitation", in Ambrose Pinto (ed.), *Dalit Assertion for Identity*, (New Delhi: Indian Social Institute, 1999), [Proceedings of the National Seminar of Dalit Postgraduate and Research Students held on 23-25 January 1999 in the Indian Social Institute].

Jha, Chandra Mouli, "Impact of Indira Awas Yojana on the Harijans Chotanagpur: A Case Study of Mandar Block, District Ranchi", in Makhan Jha (ed.), *Scheduled Castes Today*, (New Delhi: M.D. Publications, 1997).

Jha, Dilip Kumar, "Socio-Economic Problems of the Chamars of Madhubani District: A Case Study of Dhanauja Village", in Makhan Jha (ed.), *Scheduled Castes Today*, (New Delhi: M.D. Publications, 1997).

Jha, Ganganath, "Conditions of the Bhangis in the 50th Year of Independence", in Makhan Jha (ed.), *Scheduled Castes Today*, (New Delhi: M.D. Publications, 1997).

Jha, Hetkur, "The Plight of the Scheduled Caste People in Bihar", in Bindeshwar Pathak (ed.), *Social Justice and Development of Weaker Sections*, (New Delhi: Inter India, 1997).

Jha, M.L., *Untouchability and Education: A Socio-psychological Study of Attitudes*, (Meerut: Namita Publications, 1973).

Jha, M.L., *A Study of Change in Attitude Toward Untouchability*, (Allahabad: Allahabad University, 1978).

Jha, Makhan (ed.), *Scheduled Castes Today*, (New Delhi: M.D. Publications, 1997).

Jha, R.K., *Commentary on Reservations for Scheduled Castes, Scheduled Tribes, OBCs and Others*, (Patna: Shail and Neeraj Law House, 2001).

Jha, Shrawan Kumar, "The Khatbe of North Bihar: An Anthropological Perspective", in Makhan Jha (ed.), *Scheduled Castes Today*, (New Delhi: M.D. Publications, 1997).

Jha, Vivekanand, "From Tribe to Untouchable: The Case of Nisadas", in R.S. Sharma and V. Jha (eds.), *Indian Society:*

Historical Probings (In Memory of D.D. Kosambi), (New Delhi: People's Publishing House, 1974).

Jhali, Naresh Kumar, *A Study of the Life and Work of the Great Peaceful Revolutionary of Modern Times and Father of the Indian Constitution Dr. B.R. Ambedkar*, [Submitted as a Dissertation to Satisfy the requirements of the B.A. (Hons), International and Political Studies Degree Coventry University, April 1994).

Jijnasu, Chandrika Prasad, *Adi Hindu Andolan ka Prabartak Sri Swami Acchutanand Harihar*, 2nd ed. (Lucknow: Hindu Samaj Sudhar Karyalay, 1968), [Biography of Swami Achutanand, Founder of Adi Hindu Andolan].

Jogdand, Prahlad Gangaram, *Dalit Movement in Maharashtra*, (New Delhi: Kanak Publications, 1991).

Jogdand, P.G., "The Dalit Protest Movement: An Urge for Social Change", in K.N. Kadam (ed.), *Dr. B.R. Ambedkar: The Emancipator of the Oppressed*, (Bombay: Popular Prakashan, 1993).

Jogdand, P.G., "Dalit Movement: Patterns and Consequences", in Sandeep Pendse (ed.), *Dalit Movement Today*, (Bombay: Vikas Adhyayana Kendra, 1994), [Vikas Adhyayan Kendra, Bombay, *Perspectives* 1].

Jogdand, Prahlad Gangaram (ed.), *Dalit Women: Issues and Perspectives*, (New Delhi: Gyan Publishing House, in Collaboration with University of Poona, Pune, 1995).

Jogdand, P.G., "Consequences of New Economic Policy on Dalits: Some Observations", in P.G. Jogdand (ed.), *New Economic Policy and Dalits*, (Jaipur: Rawat, 2000).

Jogdand, P.G. (ed.), *New Economic Policy and Dalits*, (Jaipur: Rawat, 2000).

Joglekar, S.B., *A Reply to Ambedkar's Pakistan*, (Bombay: 1941).

Joliha, R.C., *The Native Indian: In search of Identity*, (New Delhi: Blumoon Books, 1995).

Jondhale, Surendra, "Theoretical Underpinning of Emancipation of Dalit Women", in P.G. Jogdand (ed.), *Dalit Women in India: Issues and Perspectives*, (New Delhi:

Gyan Publishing House, in collaboration with University of Poona, Pune, 1995).

Joshi, B.R., "Crypto-Capitalistic Constitution of India and Socialist Ambedkar", in *Ambedkar and Social Justice*, Vol. II, (New Delhi: Director, Publications Division, Ministry of Information and Broadcasting, 1992), [on behalf of Baba Saheb Dr. B.R. Ambedkar Birth Centenary Celebrations Committee, Ministry of Welfare, Government of India].

Joshi, Barbara R., *Democracy in Search of Equality: Untouchable Politics and Indian Social Change*, (Delhi: Hindustan Publication Corporation; and Atlantic Highlands, New Jersey: Humanities Press, 1982).

Joshi, Barbara R. (ed.), *Untouchables! Voices of the Dalit Liberation Movement*, (London: Zed Press, 1986), Indian edition published by Selectbook Service Syndicate, New Delhi.

Joshi, Barbara R., "Crypto-Capitalist Constitution of India and Socialist Ambedkar", in V.T. Patil (ed.), *Studies in Ambedkar*, (Delhi: Devika Publications, 1995).

Joshi, Hemant and Sanjay Kumar (eds.), *Asserting Voices: Changing Culture, Identity and Livelihood of the Musahars in the Gangetic Plains*, (Delhi: Deshkal Publications, 2002).

Joshi, Hemant, "Relevance of Folklore in Development Communication", in Hemant Joshi and Sanjay Kumar (eds.), *Asserting Voices: Changing Culture, Identity and Livelihood of the Musahars in the Gangetic Plains*, (Delhi: Deshkal Publications, 2002).

Juergensmeyer, Mark, *Religion as Social Vision: The Movement against Untouchability in 20th Century Punjab*, (Berkeley: University of California Press, 1982).

Juergensmeyer, Mark, *Religious Rebels in Punjab*, (Delhi: Ajanta Books, 1988).

Kabra, Lalita, *Scheduled Caste Girls*, (New Delhi: Mittal, 1991).

Kadam, K.N., *Dr. Ambedkar and the Significance of His Movement: A Chronology*, (Bombay: Popular Prakashan, 1991).

Kadam, K.N. (ed.), *Dr. B.R. Ambedkar: The Emancipator of the Oppressed*, (Bombay: Popular Prakashan, 1993).

Kadam, K.N., "Buddhism, Secularism and Ambedkar", in K.S. Chalam (ed.), *The Relevance of Ambedkarism in India*, (Jaipur: Rawat, 1993).

Kadam, K.N., "Dr. Ambedkar: The Rationalist and Humanist", in K.N. Kadam (ed.), *Dr. B.R. Ambedkar: The Emancipator of the Oppressed*, (Bombay: Popular Prakashan, 1993).

Kadam, K.N., *Dr. Ambedkar: The Rationalist and Humanist*, (Bombay: 1995).

Kadam, K.N., *Currents and Counter-Currents in Ancient India: An Ambedkarite Approach*, (Bombay: 1996).

Kadam, K.N., *The Meaning of the Ambedkarite Conversion to Buddhism and Other Essays*, (Mumbai: Popular Prakashan, 1997).

Kadetotad, N.K., *Religion and Society Among the Harijans*, (Dharwar: Karnataka University, 1977).

Kagazi, M.C. Jain, *Segregation and Untouchability Abolished*, (New Delhi: Metropolitan, 1984).

Kakade, Raghunath Govind, *Depressed Classes of South Kanara (A Socio-Economic Survey)*, (Poona: Servants of India Society, 1949).

Kakade, S.R., "Scheduled Caste Movement in Maharashtra", in K.K. Kavlekar and A.S. Chausalkar (eds.), *Ideas, Movements and Politics in India*, (Kolhapur: Ajab Pustakalaya, 1986).

Kakade, S.R., *Integration of Scheduled Castes in Indian Society*, (Pune: Dastane, 1987).

Kakade, S.R., "Nature of the Leadership of Dr. Ambedkar", in K.K. Kavlekar and A.S. Chausalkar (eds.), *Political Ideas and Leadership of Dr. B.R. Ambedkar*, (Pune: Vishwanil Publications, 1989).

Kakade, S.R., *Scheduled Castes and National Integration: A Case Study of Marathwada*, (New Delhi: Radiant, 1990).

Kakkar, S.P., "The Personality Characteristics and Educational Problems of Scheduled Caste Students", (1990), [A research monograph, out of a project financed the ICSSR].

Kaldate, S., "Survey of the Provision, Administration and Effective Utilization of Facilities such as Textbooks, Libraries, Living Accommodation, Meals, Health Services Available to Students of Scheduled Caste in Aurangabad District", (Pune: Indian Institute of Education, 1985).

Kale, Promod, "The Burden On the Head is Always There", in J. Michael Mahar (ed.), *The Untouchables in Contemporary India*, (Tucson: University of Arizona Press, 1972).

Kalgaonkar, Ramesh Kumar, "The Role of Scheduled Castes in the Structuring and Functioning of Indian Society", in R.G. Singh (ed.), *The Depressed Classes of India: Problems and Prospects*, (New Delhi: B.R. Publishing Corporation, 1986).

Kallur, M.S., "Dr. Ambedkar's Economic Philosophy: A Few Reflections", in J.S. Narayana Rao, A. Somasekhar and K. Audiseshaiah (eds.), *B.R. Ambedkar: His Relevance Today*, (New Delhi: Gyan Publishing House, 1994).

Kalwankar, S.R., *An Appeal to Gandhiji: To desist from Anti-Untouchability Campaign*, (Malegaon: Author, 1934).

Kamal, K.L., *Karmayogi: Bharat Ratna Dr. B.R. Ambedkar (Historical Novel)*, (New Delhi: Intellectual, 1994).

Kamalanathan, T.P., *Mr. K. Veeramani is Refuted and the Historical Facts about Scheduled Castes Struggle for Emancipation in South India*, (Tiruppattur: Ambedkar's Self Respect Movement, 1985).

Kamat, A.R., "Education and Social Change among Weaker Sections: Scheduled Castes and Scheduled Tribes", in his *Education and Social Change in India,* (Bombay: Somaiya, 1985).

Kamble, B.N., "The Determinants of Effectiveness of Developmental Programmes for Dalits", in P.G. Jogdand (ed.), *New Economic Policy and Dalits,* (Jaipur: Rawat, 2000).

Kamble, J.R., *Awakening of Depressed Classes from the Advent of British Rule to the Present Day,* (Indore: 1977).

Kamble, J.R., *Rise and Awakening of Depressed Classes in India,* (New Delhi: National Publishing House, 1979).

Kamble, N.D., *Poverty Within Poverty: A Study of Weaker Sections in a Deccan Village,* (New Delhi: Sterling Publications, 1979).

Kamble, N.D., *The Scheduled Castes,* (New Delhi: Ashish, 1982).

Kamble, N.D., *Atrocities on Scheduled Castes and Scheduled Tribes in Post-Independence India (15th August 1947 to 15th August 1979),* (Delhi: Ashish Publishing, 1982).

Kamble, N.D., *Deprived Castes and their Struggle for Equality,* (New Delhi: Ashish, 1983).

Kamble, N.G., K.M. Kamble and Casare (Compilers), *Essential Dr. Babasaheb Ambedkar,* (Nagpur: Dr. Babasaheb Ambedkar Officers' Social Forum Publications, 1991).

Kamble, Ramdas, "Dalit Theatre: A New Perspective", in Bojja Tharakam (ed.), *The First All India Dalit Writers Conference: A Commemorative Volume and Who's Who,* (Hyderabad: Dr. B.R. Ambedkar Memorial Trust, 1994).

Kamble, Ramesh, "Untouchability in Urban Setting: Everyday Social Experience of Ex- Untouchables in Bombay", in Ghanshyam Shah (ed.), *Dalits and the State,* (New Delhi: Concept Publishing Company, 2002), [Published for Centre for Rural Studies, Lal Bahadur Shastri National Academy of Administration, Mussoorie].

Kanagali, Chandrama S., *B.R. Ambedkar: A Writer Statesman–A Panoramic View,* (New Delhi: CBS Publications, 1995).

Kananaikil, Jose, *Scheduled Castes in the Constituent Assembly: Rebirth in a New Nation*, (New Delhi: Indian Social Institute, 1982).

Kananaikil, Jose, (ed.), *Scheduled Castes and the Struggle Against the Inequality: Strategies to Empower the Marginalized*, (New Delhi: Indian Social Institute, 1983).

Kananaikil, Jose, "Marginalisation of the Scheduled Castes: A Sociological Interpretation", in Jose Kananaikil, (ed.), *Scheduled Castes and the Struggle Against the Inequality*, (New Delhi: Indian Social Institute, 1983).

Kananaikil, Jose, *Christians of Scheduled Caste Origin*, (New Delhi: Indian Social Institute, 1983).

Kananaikil, Jose, *Constitutional Provisions for the Scheduled Castes*, (New Delhi: Indian Social Institute, 1984).

Kananaikil, Jose, "Equal Rights, Unequal Opportunities and the Future of Democracy", in Vimal P. Shah and Binod C. Agrawal (eds.), *Reservation Policy, Programmes and Issues*, (Jaipur: Rawat Publications, 1986).

Kananaikil, Jose, *Scheduled Castes in Search of Justice, Part II: The Verdict of the Supreme Court*, (New Delhi: Indian Social Institute, 1986).

Kananaikil, Jose, "The Scheduled Castes and their Status in India", in W. Fernandes (eds.), *Inequality, its bases and Search for Solutions: Dr. Alfred D'Souza Memorial Essays*, (New Delhi: Indian Social Institute, 1986).

Kananaikil, Jose, "Dalit Women and Social Change: Reflections from a Micro-Experience", in Rekha Pandey and Neelam Upadhyaya (eds.), *Women in India: Past and Present*, (Allahabad: Chugh Publications, 1990).

Kananaikil, Jose, *Scheduled Caste Converts and Social Disabilities: A Survey of Tamil Nadu*, (New Delhi: Indian Social Institute, 1990).

Kananaikil, Jose, *Scheduled Castes in Search of Justice: Constitution (Scheduled Castes Order Amendment) Bill 1990, Part III*, (New Delhi: Indian Social Institute, 1993).

Kanishka, K. and M. Christopher, "Plan of Action for Liberation", in Ambrose Pinto (ed.), *Dalit Assertion for*

Identity, (New Delhi: Indian Social Institute, 1999), [Proceedings of the National Seminar of Dalit Postgraduate and Research Students held on 23-25 January 1999 in the Indian Social Institute].

Kapoor, Archana, "Jatavs of Dehradun City ", in S.K. Sharma, *Reform and Social Transformation*, (New Delhi: Ashish Publishing House, 1982).

Karashima, Noboru, "The Untouchables in Tamil Inscriptions and other Historical Sources in Tamil Nadu", in H. Kotani (ed.), *Caste System, Untouchability and the Depressed*, (New Delhi: Manohar, 1997).

Karlekar, Malavika, *Balmiki Women in Delhi*, (New Delhi: ICSSR, 1979).

Karlekar, Malavika, *Poverty and Women's Work: A Study of Sweeper Women in Delhi*, (Delhi: Vikas, 1982).

Karlekar, Malavika, "Education and Inequality", in Andre Beteille (ed.), *Equality and Education*, (Delhi: OUP, 1983).

Karlekar, Malavika, "A study of Balmiki women in Delhi", in L. Dube (ed.), *Visibility and Power: Essays on Women in Society and Development*, (Delhi: OUP, 1986).

Karnad, Sunanda, "Ambedkar and National Integration", in *Ambedkar and Social Justice*, Vol. I, (New Delhi: Director, Publications Division, Ministry of Information and Broadcasting, 1992), [on behalf of Baba Saheb Dr. B.R. Ambedkar Birth Centenary Celebrations Committee, Ministry of Welfare, Government of India].

Karnataka, Bureau of Economics and Statistics, *Demographic Study of Scheduled Caste Population of Karnataka*, (Bangalore: Government Press, 1977).

Karunyakara, Lella, *Modernization of Buddhism: Contributions of Ambedkar and Dalailama – XIV*, (New Delhi: Gyan, 2002).

Kasare, M.L., *Economic Philosophy of Dr. B.R. Ambedkar*, (New Delhi: B.J. Publications, 1996).

Kasare, M.L., "New Economic Policy and Its Impact on Scheduled Castes and Scheduled Tribes", in Yeshwant

Khillare (ed.), *Present Status of Backward Classes in India*, (Aurangabad: Centre for Studies in SCs/STs, 1997).

Kasbe, Raosaheb, *Dalit Movement in Maharashtra*, (Mumbai: Keshav Gore Memorial Trust, 1999).

Kasbe, Raosaheb, "The Ambedkarian Ideology: A Perspective", in K.C. Yadav, (ed.), *From Periphery to Centre Stage: Ambedkar, Ambedkarism and Dalit Future*, (New Delhi: Manohar, 2000).

Kashi Vidyapitha, *The Scheduled Castes in Eastern Uttar Pradesh: A Sample Survey*, (Lucknow: The Director, Harijan Welfare Department, 1955).

Kassebaum, Gene, "The Relevance of Sociology to Policies on Inequality", in Vimal P. Shah and Binod C. Agrawal (eds.), *Reservation: Policy, Programmes and Issues*, (Jaipur: Rawat Publications, 1986).

Kaur, Bhajan (ed.), *The Philosophy of Dr. B.R. Ambedkar*, (Chandigarh: Dr. Ambedkar Study Circle, 1999).

Kaur, Bhajan, "Dr. Ambedkar's Mission: Justice, Social, Economic and Political", in Bhajan Kaur (ed.), *The Philosophy of Dr. B.R. Ambedkar*, (Chandigarh: Dr. Ambedkar Study Circle, 1999).

Kausalyaayan, Bhandant Aanand, *Baabaa Saaheb*, (Vardhaa: Sugat Prakaashan Griha, n.d.), [in Hindi].

Kavathekar, Balakrishna, *Dalit Sahitya: Ek Akaloan*, (Kolhapur: Ajab Pustakalaya, 1981), [in Marathi].

Kavlekar, K.K. and A.S. Chausalkar (eds.), *Political Ideas and Leadership of Dr. B.R. Ambedkar*, (Pune: Vishwanil Publications, 1989).

Kavlekar, K.K., "Dr. Ambedkar and Social Reform Movement", in K.K. Kavlekar and A.S. Chausalkar (eds.), *Political Ideas and Leadership of Dr. B.R. Ambedkar*, (Pune: Vishwanil Publications, 1989).

Kazimi, M.R., "Case Study of the Harijan Legislators", in *Ambedkar and Social Justice*, Vol. I, (New Delhi: Director,

Publications Division, Ministry of Information and Broadcasting, 1992), [on behalf of Baba Saheb Dr. B.R. Ambedkar Birth Centenary Celebrations Committee, Ministry of Welfare, Government of India].

Keer, Dhananjay, *Dr. Ambedkar: Life and Mission*, (Bombay: Popular Prakashan, 1962, second edition); (Third Edition, New Delhi: D.K. Publishers, 1987), (First Published in 1951), [also available in Marathi and Malayalam].

Keer, Dhananjay, *Mahatma Jotirao Phooley: Father of Our Social Revolution*, (Bombay: Popular Prakashan, 1964).

Keer, Dhananjay, "The Lover of Books", in B.K. Ahluwalia and Shashi Ahluwalia (eds.), *B.R. Ambedkar and Human Rights*, (New Delhi: Vivek Publishing Company, 1981).

Keer, Dhananjay, *Dr. Ambedkar: Memorial Album*, (Bombay: Popular Prakashan, 1982).

Kelkar, N.C., "The Elevation of the Depressed Classes", in his *Pleasures and Privileges of the Pen*, (Poona: Kashinath N. Kelkar, 1929), (Originally published in *Mahratta*, November 7, 1909).

Kenadi, L., *Revival of Buddhism in Modern India: The Role of Ambedkar and the Dalai Lama XIV*, (Delhi: Ashish, 1995).

Keshavsut, "The First Question of the Untouchable Boy", (Tr. by Prabhakar Machwe), *Keshavsut*, (New Delhi: Sahitya Academy, 1966).

Khadbe, Dinkar, *Dr. Ambedkar and Western Thinkers*, (Pune: Sugava Prakashan, 1989).

Khan, Iqbal A., "Ambedkar on Gender Justice: A New Approach", in Nazeer H. Khan (ed.), *B.R. Ambedkar on Federalism, Ethnicity and Gender Justice*, (New Delhi: Deep & Deep, 2001).

Khan, Mumtaz Ali, "Research on Development of Scheduled Castes", in V.K.R.V. Rao, H.K. Mazumdar and Amal Ray (eds.), *Planning for Change*, (Delhi: Vikas, 1975).

Khan, Mumtaz Ali, *Seven Years of Change: A Study of Some Scheduled Castes in Bangalore District*, (Madras: Christian Literature Society, 1979), [published for the Christian Institute for the Study of Religion and Society].

Khan, Mumtaz Ali, *Scheduled Castes and their Status in India*, (New Delhi: Uppal Publishing House, 1980).

Khan, Mumtaz Ali, *Mass Conversion of Meenakshipuram: A Sociological Enquiry*, (Madras: Christian Literary Society, 1983).

Khan, Mumtaz Ali, "Protective Discrimination: Implementation Reservation Policy", in Vimal P. Shah and Binod C. Agrawal (eds.), *Reservation: Policy, Programmes and Issues*, (Jaipur: Rawat Publications, 1986).

Khan, Mumtaz Ali, *Social Legislation and Civil Rights of Scheduled Castes in India*, (New Delhi: Uppal, 1993).

Khan, Mumtaz Ali, "Dr. Ambedkar and Minorities", in J.S. Narayana Rao, A. Somasekhar and K. Audiseshaiah (eds.), *B.R. Ambedkar: His Relevance Today*, (New Delhi: Gyan Publishing House, 1994).

Khan, Mumtaz Ali, *Reservation for Scheduled Castes: Gaps Between Policy and Implementation*, (New Delhi: Uppal, 1994).

Khan, Mumtaz Ali, *Identity Formation and Self Identity among Harijan Elite*, (New Delhi: Uppal, 1994), [published for the Christian Institute of Study of Religion Society].

Khan, M.Z. and Archana Dassi, *Road to Dignity: Socio-Economic Rehabilitation of Valmikis*, (New Delhi: Concept, 1998), [published for Sulab International Social Service Organisations].

Khan, Nazeer H., "Ambedkar on Gender Equality: Myth and Reality", in Nazeer H. Khan (ed.), *B.R. Ambedkar on Federalism, Ethnicity and Gender Justice*, (New Delhi: Deep & Deep, 2001).

Khan, Nazeer H. (ed.), *B.R. Ambedkar on Federalism, Ethnicity and Gender Justice*, (New Delhi: Deep & Deep, 2001).

Khan, Q.U., *Harijan Vegetable Growers (A Caste Study of Mesihgarh, a Settlement of Chamars, Near Okhla Sewage Works, New Delhi)*, (New Delhi: Jamia Institute of Agriculture Economics and Rural Sociology, 1961).

Khan, Zafar Ahmad, "Concept of Confederacy in Ambedkar's Opinion", in Nazeer H. Khan (ed.), *B.R. Ambedkar on Federalism, Ethnicity and Gender Justice*, (New Delhi: Deep & Deep, 2001).

Khanapurkar, D.P., *Chena Dasar*, (Bombay: n.d.), [Pamphlet giving discription of Communities treated as Backward in Old Bombay State].

Khandare, Avinash, "Formation of Dalit Identity", in Ambrose Pinto (ed.), *Dalit Assertion for Identity*, (New Delhi: Indian Social Institute, 1999), [Proceedings of the National Seminar of Dalit Postgraduate and Research Students held on 23-25 January 1999 in the Indian Social Institute].

Khandekar, Tarachandra, "Literature of Revolt and Resurgence", in Bojja Tharakam (ed.), *The First All India Dalit Writers Conference: A Commemorative Volume and Who's Who*, (Hyderabad: Dr. B.R. Ambedkar Memorial Trust, 1994).

Khandewale, Shrinivas, "The New Economic Policy and Its Effects on SC/ST", in Yeshwant Khillare (ed.), *Present Status of Backward Classes in India*, (Aurangabad: Centre for Studies in SCs/STs, 1997).

Khaparde, Saroj, "Dr. Ambedkar's Concern for Dalit Education", in *Ambedkar and Social Justice*, Vol. II, (New Delhi: Director, Publications Division, Ministry of Information and Broadcasting, 1992), [on behalf of Baba Saheb Dr. B.R. Ambedkar Birth Centenary Celebrations Committee, Ministry of Welfare, Government of India].

Kharat, Sankarrao S., *Babasaheb Ambedkar*, (Poona: Thokal Prakashan, 1961).

Khare, P.S., "Scheduled Castes in Transition", in R.S. Tripathi and P.D. Tiwari (eds.), *Dimensions of Scheduled Caste*

Development in India: Problems and Prospects, (New Delhi: Uppal, 1991).

Khare, Ravindra S., *The Untouchable as Himself: Ideology, Identity and Pragmatism among the Lucknow Chamars*, (New York: Cambridge University Press, 1985).

Kharimode, C.B., *B.R. Ambedkar*, Vol. I, (Bombay: Bharat Bhushan Printing Press, 1959).

Kharimode, C.B., *Dr. Ambedkar*, Vol. II, (Bombay: Buddha Jana Panchayat Samiti, 1962).

Kharimode, C.B., *Dr. Ambedkar*, Vol. III, (Bombay: Pratap Prakashan, 1964).

Khobragade, N.T., "A Study of Vocational Aspirations and Interests of SC/ST Students of Class X of Bulsar District of Gujarat State and Providing to Them Vocational Guidance with Reference to Different Variables", (Ahmedabad: Gujarat University, 1990), [A research monograph].

Khobragade, V., "Educational Problems of Postgraduate Scheduled Caste Women Students", (Pune: Indian Institute of Education, 1985), [A research monograph].

Khosla, A.N., *Master Plan for the Education and Socio-Economic Uplift of Scheduled Tribes and Scheduled Castes and Other Backward Sections of Orissa*, (New Delhi: Manager of Publications, 1971).

Khosla, Dinesh, "Untouchability – A Case Study in Law and Life", in A. Podgovecki et al. (eds.), *Legal Systems and Social Systems*, (London: 1985).

Khosla, Dinesh, *Myth and Reality of the Protection of Civil Rights Law: A Case Study of Untouchability in Rural India*, (Delhi: Hindustan Publishing Corporation, 1987).

Kikani, L.T., *Caste in Courts, or Rights and Powers of Castes in Social and Religious matter as recognized by Indian Courts*, (Rajkot: Author, 1912).

Kincaid, C.A., "The Outcastes Story", in *The Anchorite and Other Stories*, (London and Bombay: Humphrey Milford for Oxford University Press, 1922), [A Mahar anchorite from Pandharpur].

Kirpal, Viney, "A Study of Recent Marathi Dalit Poetry", in Harish Narang (ed.), *Writing Black Writing Dalit: Essays in Black African and Dalit Indian Writings*, (Shimla: Indian Institute of Advanced Studies, 2002).

Kishore, Kumkum, "Implementation of Social Justice: A Case Study of Scheduled Caste Girls' Hostels in Uttar Pradesh", in C.P. Barthwal (ed.), *Social Justice in India*, (Lucknow: Bharat Book Centre, 1998).

Kolenda, P., "Widowhood among 'Untouchable' Chuhras", in A. Ostör et al., *Concepts of Person: Kinship, Caste and Marriage in India*, (Cambridge, Mass.: Harvard UP 1982).

Kolenda, Pouline, "Aspects of the Religion of the Untouchables Sweepers of Khalapur", in P. Kolenda, *Caste, Cult and Hierarchy: Essays on the Culture of India*, (Meerut: Folklore Institute, 1983).

Kolenda, Pauline, "The Ideology of Purity and Pollution", in *Caste and Contemporary India: Beyond Organic Solidarity*, (Prospect Heights, Ill.: Waveland Press, 1985).

Kolenda, Pouline, "Untouchable Chuhras through their Humor: 'Equalizing' Marital Kin through Teasing, Pretence, and Farce", in Owen M. Lynch (ed.), *Divine Passions: The Social Construction of Emotion in India*, (Berkeley, CA: University of California Press, 1990).

Knorringa, P., *Economics of Collaboration: Indian Shoe Makers in Between Market and Hierarchy*, (New Delhi: Sage, 1996).

Koshy, Ninan, *Caste in the Kerala Churches*, (Bangalore: Christian Institute for the Study of Religion and Society, 1968).

Kotani, H. (ed.), *Caste System, Untouchability and the Depressed*, (New Delhi: Manohar, 1997), (Japanese Studies on South Asia No. 1).

Kotani, Hiroyuki, "Ati Sudra Castes in the Medieval Deccan", in H.Kotani (ed.), *Caste System, Untouchability and the Depressed*, (New Delhi: Manohar, 1997).

Kotani, Hiroyuki, "Conflict and Controversy over the Mahar Vatan in the Nineteenth-Twentieth Century Bombay Presidency", in H. Kotani (ed.), *Caste System, Untouchability and the Depressed*, (New Delhi: Manohar, 1997).

Kotani, Hiroyuki, "Legal Status of the Depressed Castes under British Colonial Rule", in H. Kotani (ed.), *Caste System, Untouchability and the Depressed*, (New Delhi: Manohar, 1997).

Kothari, Rajni, "Rise of the Dalits and the Renewed Debate on Caste", in Partha Chatterjee (ed.), *State and Politics in India*, (New Delhi: Oxford University Press, 1997).

Kothari, V.N., *A Study of Economic Profiles of the Scheduled Castes in Gujarat*, (Baroda: M.S. University of Baroda, 1976).

Krishna Kanth, T., "The Socio-Political Philosophy of Ambedkar", in K.S. Chalam (ed.), *The Relevance of Ambedkarism in India*, (Jaipur: Rawat, 1993).

Krishna Murty, B., "The Buddhist Dhamma and the Marxist Class Struggle", in *Ambedkar and Social Justice*, Vol. II, (New Delhi: Director, Publications Division, Ministry of Information and Broadcasting, 1992), [on behalf of Baba Saheb Dr. B.R. Ambedkar Birth Centenary Celebrations Committee, Ministry of Welfare, Government of India].

Krishna Murthy, B., "The Buddhist Dhamma, The Marxist Class Struggle and Social Equality: Ambedkar's Viewpoints", in V.T. Patil (ed.), *Studies in Ambedkar*, (Delhi: Devika Publications, 1995).

Krishna Reddy, B., "Anthropological Perspectives on the Vision of Ambedkar for the Upliftment of Dalits", in *Ambedkar and Social Justice*, Vol. I, (New Delhi: Director, Publications Division, Ministry of Information and Broadcasting, 1992), [on behalf of Baba Saheb Dr. B.R. Ambedkar Birth Centenary Celebrations Committee, Ministry of Welfare, Government of India].

Krishna Reddy, B., "Ambedkar and the Dalits: An Anthropological Perspective", in V.T. Patil (ed.), *Studies in Ambedkar*, (Delhi: Devika Publications, 1995).

Krishna Shetty, K.P., *Fundamental Rights and Socio-Economic Justice in the Indian Constitution*, (Allahabad: Chaitanya Publishing House, 1969).

Krishnaiah Chetty, V.B., *Scheduled Castes and Development Programmes in India*, (Allahabad: Vohra, 1991), [This work deals with the impact of IRDP in Nellore and Chittore villages, AP].

Krishnamacharya, U.P., *Temple Worship and Temple Entry*, (Chittoor: 1931).

Krishnan, Asha, *Ambedkar and Gandhi: Emancipants of Untouchables in Modern India*, (New Delhi: Himalaya, 1997).

Krishnan, P.S., "Development of the Scheduled Castes", in Jose Kananaikil (ed.), *Seventh Plan and Development of Weaker Sections: Questions, Challenges and Alternatives*, (New Delhi: 1985).

Krishnan, P.S., "Untouchability and Atrocities", in Walter Fernandes (ed.), *The Emerging Dalit Identity: The Reassertion of Subalterns*, (New Delhi: Indian Social Institute, 1996).

Krishnan, P.S., "Untouchability and Atrocities", in Ghanshyam Shah (ed.), *Dalits and the State*, (New Delhi: Concept Publishing Company, 2002), [Published for Centre for Rural Studies, Lal Bahadur Shastri National Academy of Administration, Mussoorie].

Kshirsagar, R.K., *Untouchability in India: Implementation of the Law and Abolition*, (New Delhi: Deep and Deep, 1986).

Kshirsagar, R.K., *Dalits and Constitutional Safeguards*, (Deenapur: 1986).

Kshirsagar, R.K., "Dr. Ambedkar's Theory of Power", in K.K. Kavlekar and A.S. Chausalkar (eds.), *Political Ideas and Leadership of Dr. B.R. Ambedkar*, (Pune: Vishwanil Publications, 1989).

Kshirsagar, R.K., "Dalit Politics and Leadership", in *National Seminar on Marx, Ambedkar and Polarization of Oppressed and Exploited Classes in India*, (New Delhi: Sanjivayya Institute of Socio-Economic Studies, 1991).

Kshirsagar, R.K., *Political Thought of Dr. B.R. Ambedkar*, (New Delhi: 1992).

Kshirsagar, R.K., *Political Thought of Dr. Babasaheb Ambedkar*, (New Delhi: Intellectual Publishing House, 1992).

Kshirsagar, R.K., "The Political Parties Founded by Dr. Babasaheb Ambedkar", in K.N. Kadam (ed.), *Dr. B.R. Ambedkar: The Emancipator of the Oppressed*, (Bombay: Popular Prakashan, 1993).

Kshirsagar, R.K., *Dalit Movement and Its Leaders 1857-1956*, (New Delhi: M.D. Publishers, 1994).

Kshirsagar, R.K., "Dalit Literature: The Process of Social Change", in Bojja Tharakam (ed.), *The First All India Dalit Writers Conference: A Commemorative Volume and Who's Who*, (Hyderabad: Dr. B.R. Ambedkar Memorial Trust, 1994).

Kuber, W.N., *Dr. Ambedkar: A Critical Study*, (New Delhi: People's Publishing House, 1973).

Kuber, W.N., *Dr. Ambedkar: A Biography*, Builders of Modern India Series, (New Delhi: Government of India, 1978).

Kuber, W.N., "Nature of the Leadership of Dr. Ambedkar", in K.K. Kavlekar and A.S. Chausalkar (eds.), *Political Ideas and Leadership of Dr. B.R. Ambedkar*, (Pune: Vishwanil Publications, 1989).

Kuber, W.N., "A Versatile Personality", in B.K. Ahluwalia and Shashi Ahluwalia (eds.), *B.R. Ambedkar and Human Rights*, (New Delhi: Vivek Publishing Company, 1981).

Kulhalli, R.N., *A Special Study of Scheduled Caste Students in Colleges and High Schools*, (Pune: Gokhale Institute of Politics and Economics, n.d.).

Kulhalli, R.N., *Education and Literacy Among Scheduled Castes of Hubli City*, (Pune: Gokhale Institute of Politics and Economics, n.d.).

Kulkarni, A.R., "Ambedkar and Ranade", in *Ambedkar and Social Justice*, Vol. I, (New Delhi: Director, Publications Division, Ministry of Information and Broadcasting, 1992), [on behalf of Baba Saheb Dr. B.R. Ambedkar Birth Centenary Celebrations Committee, Ministry of Welfare, Government of India].

Kulkarni, A.R., "Ambedkar's Assessment of M.G. Ranade as a Social Reformer", in V.T. Patil (ed.), *Studies in Ambedkar*, (Delhi: Devika Publications, 1995).

Kulkarni, M.G., *Report on the Survey to Assess the Program for the Removal of Untouchability in Maharashtra State*, Part I: Buldana, Part II: Nasik, (Poona: Gokhale Institute of Politics and Economics, 1962), [Manuscript].

Kulkarni, S., "Availability of Facilities such as Text Books, Library, Accommodation, Food, Medical Help etc., to Scheduled Caste Students of Jalana District", (Pune: Indian Institute of Education, 1985), [A research monograph].

Kulkarni, S.G., "Philosophy of Ambedkar: Some Observations", in K.S. Chalam (ed.), *The Relevance of Ambedkarism in India*, (Jaipur: Rawat, 1993).

Kulshreshta, S.B., "Social Engineering and Scheduled Castes and Scheduled Tribes of India", in R.G. Singh (ed.), *The Depressed Classes of India: Problems and Prospects*, (New Delhi: B.R. Publishing Corporation, 1986).

Kulshreshtha 'Noopur', Indira, "Some Reflections on Psycho-Social Development of SC/ST Girls", in her *Education of Women from Socially Backward Communities*, (Delhi: Vikas, 1998).

Kumar "Amar", Ashok, "The Dusadhs of Saharsa District: A Case Study of Four Villages of Sour Bazar Block", in Makhan Jha (ed.), *Scheduled Castes Today*, (New Delhi: M.D. Publications, 1997).

Kumar, Awadesh, "Religious Protest and Status Improvement–A Case Study of Satnamis of Chhattisgarh", in Prakash Pimpley and Satish Sharma (eds.), *Struggle for Status*, (Delhi: B.R. Publishing Corporation, 1985).

Kumar, Dinesh, "The Dusads of the Madhipura District", in Makhan Jha (ed.), *Scheduled Castes Today*, (New Delhi: M.D. Publications, 1997).

Kumar, E.N. Ashok, "Liberalization and Leatherwear Enterprise of Samagars: An Overview", in P.G. Jogdand (ed.), *New Economic Policy and Dalits*, (Jaipur: Rawat, 2000).

Kumar, Guru Das, *The Ethnic Affinities of the Rajbansis of North Bengal*, (Miami Florida: Field Research Project, 1973).

Kumar, Krishna, "Educational Experiences of Scheduled Castes and Tribes", in S.C. Shukla and Krishna Kumar (eds.), *Sociological Perspectives in Education*, (New Delhi: Chanakya, 1985).

Kumar, Narendra, "Dalit Identity and Student Politics in JNU", in Ambrose Pinto (ed.), *Dalit Assertion for Identity*, (New Delhi: Indian Social Institute, 1999), [Proceedings of the National Seminar of Dalit Postgraduate and Research Students held on 23-25 January 1999 in the Indian Social Institute].

Kumar, Rabindra, *Impact of Rural Development on Scheduled Castes*, (New Delhi: Anmol Publications, 2002).

Kumar, Raj, "Globalization and Dalit Culture", in P.G. Jogdand (ed.), *New Economic Policy and Dalits*, (Jaipur: Rawat, 2000).

Kumar, Ravinder, *Gandhi, Ambedkar and the Poona Pact*, (New Delhi: 1985).

Kumar, Ravinder, "Gandhi, Ambedkar and the Poona Pact, 1932", in Jim Masselos (ed.), *Struggling and Ruling*, (New Delhi: Sterling, 1987).

Kumar, Ravinder, "Gandhi, Ambedkar and the Poona Pact, 1932", in his *The Making of a Nation: Essays in Indian History and Politics*, (New Delhi: Manohar, 1989).

Kumar, Sanjay, "What Lies Ahead of 'Kamiot'?", in Hemant Joshi and Sanjay Kumar (eds.), *Asserting Voices: Changing Culture, Identity and Livelihood of the Musahars in the*

Gangetic Plains, (Delhi: Deshkal Publications, 2002).

Kumar, V., "Enrolment and Dropouts among the Harijans of Bihar", (Patna: Harijan Study Cell, A.N. Sinha Institute of Social Sciences, 1983), [A research monograph].

Kumar, Vijay, *Scheduled Caste Panchayat Pradhans in India: A Study of Western Uttar Pradesh*, (Delhi: Ajanta, 1989).

Kumar, Vijendra, *Rise of Dalit Power in India*, (Jaipur: ABD Publishers, 2001).

Kumar, Vivek, "Deconstruction and Reconstruction of Identities in U.P.", in Ambrose Pinto (ed.), *Dalit Assertion for Identity*, (New Delhi: Indian Social Institute, 1999), [Proceedings of the National Seminar of Dalit Postgraduate and Research Students held on 23-25 January 1999 in the Indian Social Institute].

Kumar, Vivek, "Nature and Crisis of Dalit Leadership: A Brief Socio-Historical Profile", in Ashish Ghosh (ed.), *Dalits and Peasants: The Emerging Caste-Class Dynamics*, (Delhi: Gyan Sagar, 1999).

Kumar, Vivek and Uday Sinha, *Dalit Assertion and Bahujan Samaj Party (A Perspective From Below)*, (Lucknow: Bahujan Sahitya Sansthan, 2001).

Kumar, Vivek, *Dalit Leadership in India*, (New Delhi: Kalpaz, 2002).

Kumarappa, B. (ed.), *The Removal of Untouchability*, (Ahmedabad: Navjivan, 1954).

Kunte, B.G. and B.N. Phatak (Compilers), *Source Material on Dr. Babasaheb Ambedkar and the Movement of the Untouchables*, (Bombay: Education Department, Government of Maharashtra, 1982).

Lakshmaiah, T. et al., *Programmes for Scheduled Caste Labourers*, (Jaipur: Printwell, (1995).

Lakshmanan, C., "Activating Social Capital for Dalit Identity", in Ambrose Pinto (ed.), *Dalit Assertion for Identity*, (New Delhi: Indian Social Institute, 1999),

[Proceedings of the National Seminar of Dalit Postgraduate and Research Students held on 23-25 January 1999 in the Indian Social Institute].

Lakshmanna, Chintamani, *Caste Dynamics in Village India*, (Bombay: Nachiketa Publications Ltd., 1973).

Lakshmanna, C., *The Study of Scheduled Castes and Scheduled Tribe High School Students in Andhra Pradesh*, (New Delhi: ICSSR Report, 1974).

Lakshmanna, C., *Harijans and the Social Discrimination (A Study of Some Telangana Villages)*, (Hyderabad: Department of Sociology, Osmania University, 1977).

Lakshmanna, C. and N. Innaiah, *Depressed Group Students: Between Yesterday and Tomarrow*, (Trivandrum: College Book House, 1977).

Lakshmi Narasu, P., *The Essence of Buddhism*, (Preface by B.R. Ambedkar), (Bombay: Thacker, 1912), 2nd edition, (first edition in 1907).

Lal, A.K., "The Educated Harijans as Elite", in Sachchidananda and A.K. Lal (eds.), *Elite and Development*, (New Delhi: Concept, 1980).

Lal, A.K., "Politics of Protection: A Case Study of Bihar", in Vimal P. Shah and Binod C. Agrawal (eds.), *Reservation: Policy, Programmes and Issues*, (Jaipur: Rawat Publications, 1986).

Lal, A.K., "Implications of Fundamentalist Revival for Dalit Identity", in Walter Fernandes (ed.), *The Emerging Dalit Identity: The Reassertion of Subalterns*, (New Delhi: Indian Social Institute, 1996).

Lal, A.K., *Dalit in Action: An Evaluation of Bihar Dalit Vikas Samiti*, (New Delhi: Concept, 1997).

Lal, A.K., "Limited Participation in an Open System: A Study of the Scheduled Castes in Politics", in Bindeshwar Pathak (ed.), *Social Justice and Development of Weaker Sections*, (New Delhi: Inter India, 1997).

Lal, A.K., "Protective Discrimination: Social Necessity or Political Compulsion?", in A.K. Lal (ed.), *Protective Discrimination: Ideology and Praxis*, (New Delhi: Concept, 2002), [Published for B.G. Pant Social Science Institute, Allahabad].

Lal, A.K. (ed.), *Protective Discrimination: Ideology and Praxis*, (New Delhi: Concept, 2002), [Published for B.G. Pant Social Science Institute, Allahabad].

Lal, J.N., "Dr. Ambedkar and Hindu Social System", in R.B. Rao (ed.), *Bharat-Ratna Dr. Ambedkar*, (Allahabad: Chugh Publications, 1993).

Lal, K.S., *Growth of Scheduled Tribes and Castes in Medieval India*, (Delhi: Aditya, 1995).

Lal, Manohar, "Role of Adult Education in the Removal of Civil Disabilities of Harijans: A Case of Study of Harijans' Struggle for Temple Entry", in R.G. Singh (ed.), *The Depressed Classes of India: Problems and Prospects*, (New Delhi: B.R. Publishing Corporation, 1986).

Lal, S.K., "Educational Progress and Problems of Scheduled Caste and Scheduled Tribe College Students in Rajasthan", (Department of Sociology, Jodhpur University, 1974), [A research project financed by the ICSSR].

Lal, S.K. and Umed Raj Nahar, *Higher Education: Scheduled Castes and Scheduled Tribes*, (Jodhpur: Jainsons Publications, 1978).

Lal, S.K. and Umed Raj Nahar, *Extent of Untouchability and Pattern of Discrimination*, (New Delhi: Mittal Publications, 1990).

Lal, Shyam, *Caste and Political Mobilization: The Bhangis*, (Jaipur: Panchsheel Prakashan, 1981).

Lal, Shyam, *The Bhangis in Transition*, (New Delhi: Inter-India Publications, 1984).

Lal, Shyam, *The Bhangi*, (Bombay: Popular Prakashan, 1992).

Lal, Shyam, "Separate Reservation a Must for Sweepers", in Makhan Jha (ed.), *Scheduled Castes Today*, (New Delhi: M.D. Publications, 1997).

Lal, Shyam, *From Higher Caste to Lower Caste: The Process of Asprashyeekaran and the Myth of Sanskritization*, (Jaipur: Rawat, 1997).

Lal, Shyam, "Separate Reservation – A Must for Sweepers", in Bindeshwar Pathak (ed.), *Social Justice and Development of Weaker Sections*, (New Delhi: Inter India, 1997).

Lal, Shyam and K.S. Saxena (eds.), *Ambedkar and Nation-Building*, (Jaipur: Rawat, 1998).

Lal, Shyam, "Ambedkar and Social Justice", in Shyam Lal and K.S. Saxena (eds.), *Ambedkar and Nation-Building*, (Jaipur: Rawat, 1998).

Lal, Shyam, "Asprashyeekaran – Dalitisation", in S.M. Michael (ed.), *Dalits in Modern India: Vision and Values*, (New Delhi: Vistaar Publications, 1999).

Lal, Shyam, *The Changing Bhangis of India: A Study of Caste Association*, (Jaipur: Sublime Publications, 1999).

Lal, Shyam, *Untold Story of a Bhangi Vice-Chancellor*, (Jaipur: University Book House, 2001).

Lal, Shyam, *Untouchables Movement in India*, (Jaipur: Sublime, 2002).

Lalini, V., "Ambedkar on Education", in J.S. Narayana Rao, A. Somasekhar and K. Audiseshaiah (eds.), *B.R. Ambedkar: His Relevance Today*, (New Delhi: Gyan Publishing House, 1994).

Lamb, Frederic, *The Gospel and The Mala: The Story of The Hyderabad Wesleyan Mission*, (Mysore, 1913).

Lanjewar, Jyoti, "Dalit Literature and Dalit Woman", in Prahlad Gangaram Jogdand (ed.), *Dalit Women: Issues and Perspectives*, (New Delhi: Gyan Publications, in collaboration with University of Poona, Pune, 1995).

Lanternari, V., *The Religions of the Oppressed*, (New York: Mentor Books, 1963).

Larbeer, Mohan and V. Alexander (eds.), *The Colours of Liberation*, (Madurai: Dalit Resource Centre, 2002).

Lathwal, P.S., "Dr. Ambedkar's Concept of Democratic System", in Bhajan Kaur (ed.), *The Philosophy of Dr. B.R. Ambedkar*, (Chandigarh: Dr. Ambedkar Study Circle, 1999).

Lazarus, G., *A Brief Life Sketch of Dr. B.R. Ambedkar*, (Deemapur: 1987).

Leitner, G.W., *Appendix to 'Changars' and Linguistic Fragments: Words and Phrases Illustrating the Dialects of the Same and Me as Also of Dancers, Mirasis and Doms*, (Lahore: Punjab Government Civil Secretariat Press, 1882).

Lillingstone, F., "Chamars", in J. Hastings (ed.), *Encyclopedia of Religion and Ethics*, Vol. III, (New York: 1913).

Limaye, Madhu (ed.), *Gandhi and Ambedkar*, (Delhi: Gyan, 1995).

Limaye, Madhu, *Manu, Gandhi and Ambedkar and Other Essays*, (New Delhi: Gyan, 1995).

Limbale, Sharankumar (ed.), *Dalit Panther*, (Pune: Sugawa Prakashan, 1989).

Literary Statistics at a Glance: Scheduled Castes and Scheduled Tribes, (New Delhi: Directorate of Adult Education, 1978).

Lobo, C.H.J. Jacob, *Dr. B.R. Ambedkar: The Champion of Social Democracy in India*, (Bangalore: Hilerina Publishers, 1984).

Lobo, Lancy, "Dalit Religious Movements and Dalit Identity", in Walter Fernandes (ed.), *The Emerging Dalit Identity: The Reassertion of Subalterns*, (New Delhi: Indian Social Institute, 1996).

Lobo, Lancy, "Visions, Illusions and Dilemmas of Dalit Christians in India", in Ghanshyam Shah (ed.), *Dalit Identity and Politics*, (New Delhi: Sage Publications, 2001), [Cultural Subordination and the Dalit Challenge, Vol. 2 of Sage series].

Lockard, Duane, *Toward Equal Opportunity: A Study of State and Local Anti-discrimination Laws*, (New York: Macmillan, 1968).

Lohia, Rammanohar, *The Caste System*, (Hyderabad: Navahind, 1964).

Lokamita, Dhammachari, "Buddhism in the Modern World: An Appreciation of Dr. Ambedkar's Contribution to Buddhism", in K.N. Kadam (ed.), *Dr. B.R. Ambedkar: The Emancipator of the Oppressed*, (Bombay: Popular Prakashan, 1993).

Lokanatha, Salvatore, *Buddhism Will Make You Free!*, (Panadura, Ceylon: Harijan Publishing Society, 1936), [Pamphlet].

Lokhande, Aruna G., "The Contribution of Women Writers to Dalit Sahitya", in Bojja Tharakam (ed.), *The First All India Dalit Writers Conference: A Commemorative Volume and Who's Who*, (Hyderabad: Dr. B.R. Ambedkar Memorial Trust, 1994).

Lokhande, Bhau, "Dr. Ambedkar: A Symbol of Human Rights and Anti-Discrimination Ideology", in Nazeer H. Khan (ed.), *B.R. Ambedkar on Federalism, Ethnicity and Gender Justice*, (New Delhi: Deep & Deep, 2001).

Lokhande, G.S., *Bhimrao Ramji Ambedkar: A Study in Social Democracy*, (New Delhi: Intellectual Publishing House, 2nd Revised edition, 1982), (First Published in 1977 by Sterling Publishers, New Delhi).

Lokhande, G.S., "His Legacy to Modern India", in B.K. Ahluwalia and Shashi Ahluwalia (eds.), *B.R. Ambedkar and Human Rights*, (New Delhi: Vivek Publishing Company, 1981).

Lokhande, G.S., "Dr. Ambedkar's Theory of Social Democracy", in K.K. Kavlekar and A.S. Chausalkar (eds.), *Political Ideas and Leadership of Dr. B.R. Ambedkar*, (Pune: Vishwanil Publications, 1989).

Longer, V., *Forefront Forever: The History of the Mahar Regiment*, (Saugar, M.P.: The Mahar Regimental Centre, 1981).

Louis, Prakash, *Casteism is more Horrendous than Racism: Durban and Dalit Discourse*, (New Delhi: Indian Social Institute, 2001).

Lsyyhr, S.B., *Memoirs of High Highness Shri Shahu Chhatrapati Maharaja of Kolhapur*, 2 vols., (Bombay: Times Press, 1924).

Lucknow University, J.K. Institute of Sociology and Human Relations, *Survey of Living Conditions of Harijans in Uttar Pradesh: A Sample Survey*, (Lucknow: Director, Harijan Welfare Department, U.P., 1955).

Luiz, A.A.D., "Adiyan", *Tribes of Kerala*, (New Delhi: Bhartiya Adimjati Sevak Sangh, 1962).

Luke, P. and J. Carman, *Village Christians and Hindu Culture: Study of a Rural Church in Andhra Pradesh, South India*, (London: Lutterworth, 1968).

Lynch, Owen M., "The Politics of Untouchability: A Case From Agra, India", in M. Singer and B.S. Cohn (eds.), *Structure and Change in Indian Society*, (Chicago: Aldine Publishing Company, 1968).

Lynch, Owen M., *The Politics of Untouchability: Social Change in a City of India*, (New York and London: Columbia University Press, 1969).

Lynch, Owen M., "Dr. B.R. Ambedkar – Myth and Charisma", in J. Michael Mahar (ed.), *The Untouchables in Contemporary India*, (Tucson: University of Arizona, 1972).

Lynch, Owen M., "The Politics of Untouchability: A Case from Agra", in M.S.A. Rao (ed.), *Urban Sociology in India*, (New Delhi: Orient Longman, 1974).

Machwe, Prabhakar (Tr.), *Keshavsut*, (New Delhi: Sahitya Akademi, 1966).

MacMunn, George, *The History of the Sikh Pioneers*, (London: Sampson Low, Marston, 1935).

Madholia, Mata Din, *Supreme Court on Reservations*, (New Delhi: Kamlesh Publications, 1988).

Madras State, Government of, Directorate of Information

and Publicity, *Grants of Concessions to Harijans*, (Madras: 1959).

Madtha, William, "Dalit Theology: Voice of the Oppressed", in James Massey (ed.), *Indigenous People, Dalits: Dalit Issues in Today's Theological Debate*, (Delhi: ISPCK, 1998), (First Published in1994).

Magudkar, M.P. (ed.), *Dr. Ambedkar and Parliamentary Democracy*, (Pune: 1976).

Mahadevaiah, K. (ed.), *Demographic Study of Scheduled Caste Population of Karnataka*, (Bangalore: Bureau of Economics and Statistics, 1972), [This study was prepared by D.B. Kodaganur].

Mahadevan, S., *Mahatma Gandhi's Warning and Flashes in Harijan Tour*, (Madras: Journalists' Publishing House, 1936).

Mahajan, V.S. and B.S. Mann (eds.), *Economic Development of Scheduled Castes*, (New Delhi: Anmol, 1997).

Mahajan, V.S., "Dr. Ambedkar, Scheduled Castes and Punjab's Scenario", in V.S. Mahajan and B.S. Mann (eds.), *Economic Development of Scheduled Castes*, (New Delhi: Anmol, 1997).

Mahapatra, Man Mohan, *Bauri of Bhubaneswar: A Study on the Urbanization Process in a Scheduled Caste*, (Bhubaneswar: Tribal and Harijan Research Training Institute, n.d.).

Mahar, Michael J. (ed.), *The Untouchables in Contemporary India*, (Tucson, Arizona: The University of Arizona Press, 1972).

Mahar-Kolenda, P., "The Mother-Goddess Among North-Indian Sweepers", in G. Gupta (ed.), *Religion in Modern India*, (Delhi: Vikas, 1983).

Mahesh, S., *Hamare Harijan Neta*, (Delhi: Konark, 1981).

Majumdar, A.K. and Bhanwar Singh, *Ambedkar and Social Justice*, (New Delhi: Radha Publications, 1997).

Majumdar, D.N., "The Kinship Terms of the Palias, Babupolias and Rajbanshis in North Bengal", *Proceedings of the Indian Science Congress*, (13th Session, 1926).

Majumdar, D.N., *Bhuiya: The Fortunes of Primitive Tribes*, (Lucknow: The Universal Publishers, 1944), [The Byuiyas or Bhuyans are categorized as Scheduled Castes in Bihar, Uttar Pradesh and West Bengal, but in Orissa they are categorized as Scheduled Tribes].

Majumdar, Nabendu Dutta, "The Backward Classes Commission and Its Work", *Social Welfare in India*, (New Delhi: Government of India, 1955), [Issued on behalf of the Planning Commission].

Mal, Lakkho, *Dr. Ambedkar: Challenger and the Adored (Rejoinder to the Malice 'Worshipping False Gods')*, (Delhi: Pawan Printers, 1998).

Malayadri, P., "Dr. Ambedkar – A Saviour of Indian Women", in J.S. Narayana Rao, A. Somasekhar and K. Audiseshaiah (eds.), *B.R. Ambedkar: His Relevance Today*, (New Delhi: Gyan Publishing House, 1994).

Malhotra, Vinay Kumar, "Adoption of Innovative Measures for Development of Scheduled Castes in Haryana", in V.S. Mahajan and B.S. Mann (eds.), *Economic Development of Scheduled Castes*, (New Delhi: Anmol, 1997).

Malik, Suneila, *Social Integration of Scheduled Castes*, (New Delhi: Abhinav Publications, 1971).

Malik, Suneila, *Society Consequences of Social Mobility Among Scheduled Castes*, (New Delhi: Abhinav, 1979).

Malkani, N.R., *Clean People and an Unclean Country*, (Delhi: Harijan Sevak Sangh, 1965).

Malkani, Naraindas Rattanmal, *A Critical Note on Hindu Temple Entry Bill*, (Delhi: 1934).

Makwana, Yogendra, "Dr. Babasaheb Ambedkar: A Crusade", *Ambedkar and Social Justice*, Vol. I, (New Delhi: Director, Publications Division, Ministry of Information and Broadcasting, 1992), [on behalf of Baba Saheb Dr. B.R. Ambedkar Birth Centenary Celebrations Committee, Ministry of Welfare, Government of India].

Mandal, S.N., "Ambedkar's Work and Mission", in *Ambedkar and Social Justice*, Vol. II, (New Delhi: Director,

Publications Division, Ministry of Information and Broadcasting, 1992), [on behalf of Baba Saheb Dr. B.R. Ambedkar Birth Centenary Celebrations Committee, Ministry of Welfare, Government of India].

Mandal, S.N., "B.R. Ambedkar: His Life, Work and Mission", in V.T. Patil (ed.), *Studies in Ambedkar*, (Delhi: Devika Publications, 1995).

Mander, Harsh, "Status of Dalits and Agenda for State Intervention", in Ghanshyam Shah (ed.), *Dalits and the State*, (New Delhi: Concept Publishing Company, 2002), [Published for Centre for Rural Studies, Lal Bahadur Shastri National Academy of Administration, Mussoorie].

Mane, D.A., "Dalit Movement in Karnataka", in Sandeep Pendse (ed.), *Dalit Movement Today*, (Bombay: Vikas Adhyayana Kendra, 1994), [Vikas Adhyayan Kendra, Bombay, *Perspectives* 1].

Mane, Laxman, *Upara: An Outsider*, (Tr. from the Marathi by A.K.Kamat), (New Delhi: Sahitya Akademi, 1997).

Mane, Suresh, "Glimpses of Constitutional Philosophy of Dr. Ambedkar", in *Ambedkar and Social Justice*, Vol. I, (New Delhi: Director, Publications Division, Ministry of Information and Broadcasting, 1992), [on behalf of Baba Saheb Dr. B.R. Ambedkar Birth Centenary Celebrations Committee, Ministry of Welfare, Government of India].

Mane, Suresh, "Some Reflections on the Constitutional Philosophy of Ambedkar", in V.T. Patil (ed.), *Studies in Ambedkar*, (Delhi: Devika Publications, 1995).

Mane, Suresh, "Ambedkar's Mission and Role of Law", in V.T. Patil (ed.), *Studies in Ambedkar*, (Delhi: Devika Publications, 1995).

Mangalwadi, Vishal, *The Quest for Freedom and Dignity: Caste, Conversion and Cultural Revolution*, (Mumbai: GLS Publishers, 2001).

Mangolpuri, Radhesyam, "Dashrath Manjhi: From Manjhi to Das", in Hemant Joshi and Sanjay Kumar (eds.), *Asserting Voices: Changing Culture, Identity and Livelihood of the Musahars in the Gangetic Plains,* (Delhi: Deshkal Publications, 2002).

Mangudkar, M.P., "Why Dr. Ambedkar was not a Communist", in K.N. Kadam (ed.), *Dr. B.R. Ambedkar: The Emancipator of the Oppressed,* (Bombay: Popular Prakashan, 1993).

Manickam, S., *The Social Setting of Christian Conversion in South India: The Impact of the Wesleyan Methodist Missionaries on the Trichy-Tanjore Diocese to the Harijan Communities of the Mass Movement Area, 1820-1947,* (Wiesbaden: Franz Steiner Verlag, 1977).

Manickam, S., *Nandanar the Dalit Martyr: A Historical Reconstruction of his Time,* (Madras: 1990).

Manickam, S., "Missions' Approaches to Caste", in V. Devasahayam (ed.), *Dalits and Women: Quest for Humanity,* (Madras: The Gurukul Summer Institute, 1992).

Mann, Harold H., "The Untouchable Classes of an India City", in Daniel Thorner (ed.), *The Social Framework of Agriculture,* (Bombay: Vora, 1967), this article was published earlier in *Sociological Review,* (London), Vol. V, (1912).

Mann, Harold H., "The Housing of the Untouchable Classes in an Indian City (Poona)", in Daniel Thorner (ed.), *The Social Framework of Agriculture,* (Bombay: Vora, 1967), this article was originally published in *Social Service Quarterly* (Bombay), Vol. I, (1916).

Manohar, Yashwant, *Dalit Sahitya: Siddhant ani Swaroop,* (Nagpur: Prabodhan Prakashan, 1978).

Manorama, Ruth, "Dalit Women: The Thrice Alienated", in M.E. Prabhakar (ed.), *Towards a Dalit Theology,* (Bangalore: CISRS, 1988).

Manorama, Ruth, "Dalit Women: Downtrodden among the Downtrodden", in James Massey (ed.), *Indigenous People, Dalits: Dalit Issues in Today's Theological Debate,* (Delhi: ISPCK, 1998), (First Published in1994).

Manthara, Fr. Philip, "Communication Through the Dialogue of Life", in Hemant Joshi and Sanjay Kumar (eds.), *Asserting Voices: Changing Culture, Identity and Livelihood of the Musahars in the Gangetic Plains,* (Delhi: Deshkal Publications, 2002).

Martin, Abdul and Mohd. Arshad, "Ambedkar's Perspective on Federalism in India", in Nazeer H. Khan (ed.), *B.R. Ambedkar on Federalism, Ethnicity and Gender Justice,* (New Delhi: Deep & Deep, 2001).

Masihi, E.J. and D.B. Desai, "Dalit Panthers Movement in Gujarat", in Vimal P. Shah (ed.), *Removal of Untouchability,* (Ahmedabad: Gujarat University, 1980).

Massey, James, *Roots: A Concise History of Dalits,* (Delhi: ISPCK, 1991).

Massey, James (ed.), *Indigenous People: Dalits, Dalit Issues in Today's Theological Debate,* (Delhi: ISPCK, 1998), (First Published in1994).

Massey, James, "Historical Roots", in James Massey (ed.), *Indigenous People: Dalits, Dalit Issues in Today's Theological Debate,* (Delhi: ISPCK, 1998), (First Published in1994).

Massey, James, "Ingredients for a Dalit Theology", in James Massey (ed.), *Indigenous People, Dalits: Dalit Issues in Today's Theological Debate,* (Delhi: ISPCK, 1998), (First Published in1994).

Massey, James, *Towards Dalit Hermeneutics: Re-reading the Text, the History and the Literature,* (New Delhi: ISPCK, 1994).

Massey, James, *Dalits in India: Religion as a Source of Bondage or Liberation with Special Reference to Christians,* (New Delhi: Manohar, 1995).

Massey, James, *Roots of Dalit History, Christianity, Theology and Spirituality,* (New Delhi: ISPCK, 1996).

Massey, James, *Down Trodden: The Struggle of Indian Dalits for Identity, Solidarity and Liberation,* (Geneva: WCC Publications, 1997), [Indian edition available from Manohar Publishers, New Delhi, (1997)].

Mathew, Joseph, *Ideology, Protest and Social Mobility: Caste Study of Mahars and Pulayas,* (New Delhi: Inter-India, 1986), [Published for Indian Institute for Regional Development Studies, Kottayam).

Mathew, Thomas, 'The Indigenous People of India and Aryan Colonization' in M. Gopinath and Fr. Lazer (eds.), *The Emergence of Indigenous Peoples,* (Bangalore, Council of Indigenous People – India and Indian Social Institute, 1993).

Mathew, Thomas, *Ambedkar: Reform or Revolution,* (New Delhi: Segment Books, 1991).

Mathew, Thomas, *Caste-Class Dynamics: Radical Ambedkarite Praxis,* (New Delhi: D' Tech, 1992).

Mathur, B.B., *Women and Depressed Caste Population in India,* (Allahabad: Chugh, 1994).

Mathur, S.G., "Vocational Needs and Interests of SC and ST Students of Chiklital and Developing Vocational Guidance Services", (Ahmedabad: F.A. NCERT, 1985), [A research project financed by the NCERT].

Maurya, R.D., "The Challenges of Scheduled Castes' Development and Social Justice in Contemporary India", in Bindeshwar Pathak (ed.), *Social Justice and Development of Weaker Sections,* (New Delhi: Inter India, 1997).

Maurya, R.L., "Changing the Status of the Scheduled Castes", in R.S. Tripathi and P.D. Tiwari (eds.), *Dimensions of Scheduled Caste Development in India: Problems and Prospects,* (New Delhi: Uppal, 1991).

Mavalankar, P.G., "Ambedkar: National Leader, Renowned Parliamentarian, Pre-Eminent Constitution Maker", in Rabi Ray (ed.), *Dr. B.R. Ambedkar,* (New Delhi: Lok Sabha Secretariat, 1991), [Eminent Parliamentarians Monograph Series 12].

McGavran, D.A., *India's Oppressed Classes and Religion*, (Jubbulpore: Mission Press, 1939).

McGaw, A.G., *Out From India's Outcastes*, (New York: Board of Foreign Missions of the Presbyterian Church in the U.S.A., 1914).

Mead, C.S., *The Namasudras and Other Addresses*, (Adelaide: 1911).

Mehta, B.H., *Social and Economic Conditions of the Meghval Untouchables of Bombay City*, Vol. I (no details available).

Mehta, G.S., "Equity Role of Education in Economic Opportunities Between Scheduled Castes/Scheduled Tribes and General Castes Segments", (Lucknow: Giri Institute of Development Studies, 1990), [Working Paper No. 106].

Mehta, Haroobhai and Hasmukh Patel (eds.), *Dynamics of Reservation Policy*, (New Delhi: Patriot Publications, 1985).

Mencher, Joan P., "Continuity and change in an ex-Untouchable community of South India", in Michael J. Mahar (ed.), *The Untouchables in Contemporary India*, (Tucson, Arizona: The University of Arizona Press, 1972).

Mencher, Joan P., "Viewing Hierarchy from the Bottom Up", in A. Beteille and T.N. Madan (eds.), *Encounter and Experience*, (New Delhi: 1975).

Mencher, Joan P., "On Being an Untouchable in India: A Materialist Perspective", in Eric Ross (ed.), *Beyond the Myths of Culture: Essays in Cultural Materialism*, (New York: Academic Press, 1980).

Mendelsohn, Oliver and Marika Vicziany, "The Untouchables Today", in J. Masselos (ed.), *India, Creating a Modern Nation*, (Delhi: Sterling, 1990).

Mendelsohn, Oliver and Marika Vicziany, "The Untouchables", in Oliver Mendelsohn and Upendra Baxi (eds.), *The Rights of the Subordinated People*, (New Delhi: OUP, 1994).

Mendelsohn, Oliver and Marika Vicziany, *The Untouchables: Subordination, Poverty and the State in Modern India*, (Cambridge: Cambridge University Press, 1998).

Menon, D.M., "Intimations of Equality: Shrines and Politics in Malabar, 1900-1924", in P. Robb (ed.), *Dalit Movements and the Meanings of Labour in India*, (Delhi: Oxford University Press, 1993).

Meshram, Tarachand G., "Backward Communities and Conversions", in V.K. Pant and B.S. Bisht (eds.), *Backward Communities: Identity, Development and Transformation*, (New Delhi: Gyan, 1999).

Meshram, Sheshrao, "The Post-Ambedkar Buddhist Missionary Association", in Sanghasen Singh and Priyasen Singh (eds.), *Ambedkar on Buddhist Conversion and Its Impact*, (Delhi: Eastern Book Linkers, 1990).

Meshram, Siddharth G., "The Philosophy of Great Conversion to Buddhism", in Sanghasen Singh and Priyasen Singh (eds.), *Ambedkar on Buddhist Conversion and Its Impact*, (Delhi: Eastern Book Linkers, 1990).

Meshram, Yogendra, "Dalit Literature: Aesthetic Sense and Craftsmanship", in Bojja Tharakam (ed.), *The First All India Dalit Writers Conference: A Commemorative Volume and Who's Who*, (Hyderabad: Dr. B.R. Ambedkar Memorial Trust, 1994).

Michael, S.M. (ed.), *Dalits and Modern India: Vision and Values*, (New Delhi: Vistaar Publications, 1999).

Mimroth, P.L., "An Appraisal of Land Reforms and other Legislative Measures for the uplift of SCs/Sts", in G.S. Bhargava and R.M. Pal (eds.), *Human Rights of Dalits*, (New Delhi: Gyan Publishing House, 1999).

Minority Rights Group, *The Untouchables of India*, (London: MRG, 1982), [Indian edition is available from Bangalore: Dalit Sahitya Academy, 1984).

Minz, Nirmal, "Dalit-Tribal: A Search for Common Ideology", in Arvind P. Nirmal (ed.), *Toward a Common Dalit Ideology*, (Madras: Gurukul Lutheran Theological College and Research Institute, 1990), [Papers presented at the

National Seminar on Dalit Ideology organized by the Department of Dalit Theology, Gugukul Lutheran Theological College and Research Institute].

Minz, Nirmal, "Dalit-Tribal: A Search for a Common Ideology", in James Massey (ed.), *Indigenous People: Dalits, Dalit Issues in Today's Theological Debate,* (Delhi: ISPCK, 1998), (First Published in1994).

Minz, Shashi, "The Dalit Women: The Tribal Perspective", in P.G. Jogdand (ed.), *Dalit Women in India: Issues and Perspectives,* (New Delhi: Gyan Publishing House, in collaboration with University of Poona, Pune, 1995).

Mishra, J.P., "B.R. Ambedkar's Contribution towards the shaping of the Indian Constitution", in V.T. Patil (ed.), *Studies in Ambedkar,* (Delhi: Devika Publications, 1995).

Mishra, Lakshmidhar, *Anguish of the Deprived,* (New Delhi: Har Anand Publications, 1995).

Mishra, Narayan, *Scheduled Education: Issues and Aspects,* (New Delhi: Kalpaz, 2001).

Mishra, P.K., *Harijans in Hidu and Tribal Social Structures,* (New Delhi: Discovery, 1992).

Mishra, Ram Kishore, "Bhim Rao Ambedkar and Education", in R.B. Rao (ed.), *Bharat-Ratna Dr. Ambedkar,* (Allahabad: Chugh Publications, 1993).

Misra, J.P., "Ambedkar and the Constitution-Making", in *Ambedkar and Social Justice,* Vol. I, (New Delhi: Director, Publications Division, Ministry of Information and Broadcasting, 1992), [on behalf of Baba Saheb Dr. B.R. Ambedkar Birth Centenary Celebrations Committee, Ministry of Welfare, Government of India].

Misra, J.P., "Dr. Ambedkar's Contribution to Dalit Upliftment through Political and Constitutional Means", in M.L. Ranga (ed.), *B.R. Ambedkar: His Life, Work and Relevance,* (New Delhi: Manohar, 2000).

Mitra, Asok, *The Tribes and Castes of West Bengal,* (Calcutta: West Bengal Government Press, 1953).

Mitra, Asok, *The Status of Women: Literacy and Employment,* (New Delhi: Allied Publishers, 1979).

Mitra, Joyati, "Education and Attainment: A Study of Women of Dalit Groups", in Joyati Mitra (ed.), *Women and Society: Equality and Empowerment*, (New Delhi: Kanishka Publishers, 1997).

Mizushima, Tsukasa, "The Untouchables and Economic Change in a Dry Village in South India", in H. Kotani (ed.), *Caste System, Untouchability and the Depressed*, (New Delhi: Manohar, 1997).

Modak, Tarabai, *The Meadow School: Experiments in Education*, (New Delhi: Ministry of Education, 1962).

Moffat, Michael, *An Untouchable Community in South India: Structure and Consensus*, (Princeton, NJ: Princeton University Press, 1979).

Mohan, J., *History of Dalit Struggle for Freedom: Dravidian Parties and Dalit Upsurge in Tamil Nadu*, (Pondicherry: Dhamma Institute of Social Sciences, 2001).

Mohan, N. Shantha, *Status of Banjara Women in India: A Study of Karnataka*, (New Delhi: Uppal, 1988), [Banjara is Scheduled Caste in Karnataka, Delhi and Himachal Pradesh; Scheduled Tribe in Bihar, Orissa and West Bengal; Denotified Tribe in Madhya Pradesh, Rajasthan and Uttar Pradesh; and Nomadic Tribe in Gujarat, Karnataka and Rajasthan. They are also referred to as Lamani, Lambadi, Ladhari, Sugali, Vanjara, and Labhan and are identified at the national level].

Mohan, P.E., *Scheduled Castes: History of Elevation: Tamil Nadu, 1900-1955*, (Madras: New Era, 1993).

Mohan, Swadesh, "Some Reflections on Psycho-Social Development of SC/ST Girls", in Indira Kulshreshtha 'Noopur' (ed.), *Education of Women from Socially Backward Communities*, (Delhi: Vikas, 1998).

Molony, J. Chartress, "Minority Communities: The Depressed Classes", in John Cumming (ed.), *Political India, 1832-1932*, (London: Humphrey Milford for Oxford University Press, 1932).

Moneyamma, V.G., "A Study of the Causes and Correlations of Wastage among Scheduled Caste Pupils at the

Primary Stage", (Trivandrum: Department of Education, University of Kerala, 1989), [A research monograph].

Mookerjee, A.K., "Ambedkar and the Ultimate Concern of Religion", in P.K. Mohapatra (ed.), *Religion and Social Change,* (Cuttack: Akash, 1993).

Moon, Vasant, "From Dependence to Protest: The Early Growth of Education and Consciousness among 'Untouchables' of Western India", in Barbara R. Joshi (ed.), *Untouchable! Voices of the Dalit Liberation Movement,* (London: Zed Books Ltd., 1986).

Moon, Vasant, "Compiling Dr. B.R. Ambedkar", in Bojja Tharakam (ed.), *The First All India Dalit Writers Conference: A Commemorative Volume and Who's Who,* (Hyderabad: Dr. B.R. Ambedkar Memorial Trust, 1994).

Moon, Vasant (ed.), *Dr. Baba Saheb Ambedkar Writings and Speeches,* 17 Vols., (Bombay: Government of Maharashtra, (1990–2000).

Moon, Vasant, *Growing Up Untouchable in India: A Dalit Autobiography,* (Tr. From the Marathi by Gail Omvedt, with an Introduction by Eleanor Zelliot, (Lanham, Maryland: Rowman & Littlefield Publishers, 2001.

More, Dado, 'Dalit Writing Achievement and Prospects' in Bojja Tharakam, (Ed), *The First All India Dalit Writers Conference,* (Hyderabad, Dr B R Ambedkar Memorial Trust, 1994).

Moses, D., "Responding to Subordination: Identity and Change among South Indian Untouchable Castes", in J. Campbell and A. Rew (eds.), *Cultural Identity and Affect,* (Harwood: 2001).

Muhlmann, W., "Max Weber and the Concept of Pariah-Communities", in O. Stammer (ed.), *Max Weber and Sociology Today,* (New York: Harper & Row, 1971).

Mujahid, Abdul Malik, *Conversion to Islam: Untouchables' Strategy for Protest in India,* (Chambersburg: 1989).

Mukherjee, A.B., *Study of Scheduled Caste Population in Andhra Pradesh,* (Calcutta: Indian Publications, 1971).

Mukherjee, A.B., *The Chamars of U.P.: A Study of Social Geography*, (New Delhi: Inter-India, 1980).

Mukherjee, Bhabananda, "Caste-Ranking among Rajbanshis in North Bengal", in Bala Ratnam (ed.), Anthropology on the March, (Madras: The Book Centre, 1963). [*Rajbansis* were not considered as a Depressed Classes by the Government until 1931, but later on they were included into Scheduled Castes].

Mukherjee, D., *Caste and Outcaste*, (New York: 1929).

Mukherjee, Hirendranath, *Gandhi, Ambedkar and the Extirpation of Untouchability*, (New Delhi: People's Publishing House, 1982).

Mukherjee, Prabhati, *Beyond the Four Varnas: The Untouchables in India*, (Shimla: Indian Institute of Advanced Study; Delhi: Motilal Banarsidass, 1986).

Mungekar, B.L., "India's Agrarian Problem", in *Ambedkar and Social Justice*, Vol. II, (New Delhi: Director, Publications Division, Ministry of Information and Broadcasting, 1992), [on behalf of Baba Saheb Dr. B.R. Ambedkar Birth Centenary Celebrations Committee, Ministry of Welfare, Government of India].

Mungekar, B.L., "Ambedkar on India's Agrarian Problem", in V.T. Patil (ed.), *Studies in Ambedkar*, (Delhi: Devika Publications, 1995).

Mungekar, B.L., "The Impact of New Economic Policy on the SC/ST Communities: A Macro Perspective", in Yeshwant Khillare (ed.), *Present Status of Backward Classes in India*, (Aurangabad: Centre for Studies in SCs/STs, 1997).

Mungekar, B.L., "State, Market and the Dalits: Analytics of the New Economic Policy", in S.M. Michael (ed.), *Dalits in Modern India: Vision and Values*, (New Delhi: Vistaar Publications, 1999).

Muralidharan, V., *Educational Priorities and Dalit Society*, (New Delhi: Kanishka Publishers, 1997).

Murthi, R.K., "Logic of the Rebel", in B.K. Ahluwalia and Shashi Ahluwalia (eds.), *B.R. Ambedkar and Human Rights*, (New Delhi: Vivek Publishing Company, 1981).

Murthy, C.S., U.N. Murthy and M. Krishna Mohan, "Impact of Development Disparities Between Scheduled Castes/ Scheduled Tribes and 'Others'", in Chandu Subba Rao and D. Francis (eds.), *Development of Weaker Sections (Essays in Honour of Prof. K.S. Chalam)*, (Jaipur: Rawat, 2000).

Murti, S., *On Behalf of the Oppressed: An Inquiry into the Past and Present Condition of the Depressed Classes in Southern India*, (Ambur: Author, 1927), [Pamphlet].

Murty, B.S., *Presidential Address to Depressed Classes League*, (Delhi: Depressed Classes League, 1959).

Murty, B.S., *The Glimmers in Darkness*, (Secunderabad: Lakshmi and Co., 1969).

Murty, B.S., *Depressed and Oppressed: Forever in Agony*, (Delhi: S.Chand and Co., 1972).

Murty, Sri Ram, "Policies of Dr. Ambedkar for Uplift of Weaker Sections", in J.S. Narayana Rao, A. Somasekhar and K. Audiseshaiah (eds.), *B.R. Ambedkar: His Relevance Today*, (New Delhi: Gyan Publishing House, 1994).

Murugkar, Lata, *Dalit Panther Movement in Maharashtra: a Sociological Appraisal*, (Bombay: Popular Prakashan, 1991).

Murugkar, Lata, "Dalit Panthers: A Militant Movement in Maharashtra: An Analysis", in James Massey (ed.), *Indigenous People: Dalits. Dalit Issues in Today's Theological Debate*, (Delhi: ISPCK, 1998), (First Published in1994).

Mustafa, Faizan, "Democracy, Social Disparities and Development: Ambedkar's Vision", in Bhajan Kaur (ed.), *The Philosophy of Dr. B.R. Ambedkar*, (Chandigarh: Dr. Ambedkar Study Circle, 1999).

Mustafa, Faizan, "Democracy, Social Disparities and Development: Ambedkar's Vision", in Nazeer H. Khan (ed.), *B.R. Ambedkar on Federalism, Ethnicity and Gender Justice*, (New Delhi: Deep & Deep, 2001).

Mysore State, Government of, *The Welfare of Scheduled Castes in Mysore State*, (Bangalore: Department of Planning, Housing and Social Welfare, 1961).

Nag, J.P. and Indira Srivastav, "A Comparative Study of Personality Pattern and Adjustment of Harijan and Non-Harijan Girl Students", in R.G. Singh (ed.), *The Depressed Classes of India: Problems and Prospects*, (New Delhi: B.R. Publishing Corporation, 1986).

Nagaich, Sangeeta, "Caste and Work Participation – An Analysis of the Census Data", in V.S. Mahajan and B.S. Mann (eds.), *Economic Development of Scheduled Castes*, (New Delhi: Anmol, 1997).

Nagar, V.D. and K.P. Nagar., *Economic Thought and Policy of Ambedkar*, (New Delhi: Segment, 1992).

Nagraj, D.R., *The Flaming Feet: A Study of the Dalit Movement*, (Bangalore: South Forum Press, 1993).

Naidu, B.N., "Panchama Education", in his *Intellectual History of Colonial India: Mysore, 1831-1920*, (Jaipur: Rawat, 1996).

Naik, J.P., *Education of Scheduled Castes and Scheduled Tribes*, (New Delhi: The Manager of Publications, 1965), [Report of the Seminar on Employment of Scheduled Castes and Scheduled Tribes].

Naik, J.P., *Education of the Scheduled Castes* 1965-66, (New Delhi: ICSSR, 1971), [Occasional Monograph of ICSSR No. 6].

Naik, J.P., *Study of Educational Problems of Scheduled Caste and Scheduled Tribes Secondary Students in Madhya Pradesh*, (1978).

Nair, Adoor K.K.R., *Slavery in Kerala*, (Delhi: Mittal Publishers, 1986).

Nair, V.G. "The Buddhist Revival in India", in *Babasaheb Dr. Ambedkar Jayanti Sandesh*, (Agra: Ambedkar Bhavan, 1966).

Naito, M. (ed.), *Anti-Untouchability Ideologies and Movements in Modern India* ('Caste System and the Depressed' Series, Vol. 3, in Japanese), (Tokyo: Akashi Shoten Publishers, 1994).

Naito, Masao, "Anti-Untouchability Ideologies and Movements in Maharashtra from the Late Nineteenth Century to the 1930s", in H. Kotani (ed.), *Caste System, Untouchability and the Depressed,* (New Delhi: Manohar, 1997).

Naito, Masao, "Circumstances Surrounding and Problems Underlying Liberation Movements of the Depressed Castes", in H. Kotani (ed.), *Caste System, Untouchability and the Depressed,* (New Delhi: Manohar, 1997).

Nalanda Education Society of India, *The Neo-Buddhist Movement in India,* (Bombay: 1964), [Pamphlet].

Nalini, M., "Caste and Patriarchy: Ambedkar's Insight in to the Status of Indian Women", in K.S. Chalam (ed.), *The Relevance of Ambedkarism in India,* (Jaipur: Rawat, 1993).

Nambissan, Geetha, B., "Equity in Education: The Schooling of Dalit Children in India", *Studies in Human Development in India,* [Discussion Paper Series No. 15, Project of UNDP].

Nambissan, Geetha B., "Social Diversity and Regional Disparities in Schooling: A Study of Rural Rajasthan", in A. Vaidyanathan and P.R. Gopinathan Nair (eds.), *Elementary Education Rural India: A Grassroots View,* (New Delhi: Sage, 2001).

Nambissan, Geetha B., "Equity in Education? The Schooling of Dalit Children in India", in Ghanshyam Shah (ed.), *Dalits and the State,* (New Delhi: Concept Publishing Company, 2002), [Published for Centre for Rural Studies, Lal Bahadur Shastri National Academy of Administration, Mussoorie].

Nambissan, Geetha B., "Education for All: The Situation of Dalit Children in India", in R. Govinda (ed.), *India Educational Report,* (New Delhi: OUP, 2003).

Nambissan, Geetha, B., "Human Rights in Education and the Schooling of Dalit Children", in H. Thiagaraj (ed.), *Human Rights From the Dalit Perspective,* (Madras: Dalit Liberation Educational Trust, n.d.).

Namboodiripad, E.M.S., "Multi-Pronged Attach against an Outmoded System", in *Ambedkar and Social Justice,* Vol. I, (New Delhi: Director, Publications Division, Ministry of Information and Broadcasting, 1992), [on behalf of Baba Saheb Dr. B.R. Ambedkar Birth Centenary Celebrations Committee, Ministry of Welfare, Government of India].

Nancharaiah, G., *Land and Caste,* (New Delhi: Himalaya, 1988).

Nancharaiah, G., "Dr. Babasaheb Ambedkar Paradigm of Development", in *Bharat Ratna Dr. Babasaheb B.R. Ambedkar Birth Centenary Commemoration Volume,* (Bombay: Dr. Ambedkar College of Commerce and Economics, 1992).

Nancharaiah, G., "Dr. Ambedkar's Social Economic and Political Thought", in *Ambedkar and Social Justice,* Vol. II, (New Delhi: Director, Publications Division, Ministry of Information and Broadcasting, 1992), [on behalf of Baba Saheb Dr. B.R. Ambedkar Birth Centenary Celebrations Committee, Ministry of Welfare, Government of India].

Nancharaiah, G., "Ambedkar on Economic Development and Social Justice", in K.S. Chalam (ed.), *The Relevance of Ambedkarism in India,* (Jaipur: Rawat, 1993).

Nancharaiah, G., "Dr. B.R. Ambedkar's Strategy of Economic Development and its Relevance", in *Dr. B.R. Ambedkar Memorial Lectures,* (Hyderabad: Dr. B.R. Ambedkar Memorial Trust, 1995), [This Lecture was originally delivered on 6 December 1994].

Nancharaiah, G., "Change in the Structure of Workforce with Special Reference to Scheduled Castes: An Analysis", in Yeshwant Khillare (ed.), *Present Status of Backward Classes in India,* (Aurangabad: Centre for Studies in SCs/STs, 1997).

Nancharaiah, G., "Economic Liberalization and Its Implications for Weaker Sections: A Perspective", in Yeshwant Khillare (ed.), *Present Status of Backward Classes in India*, (Aurangabad: Centre for Studies in SCs/STs, 1997).

Nancharaiah, G., "Development Policy and Social Change with reference to Scheduled Castes", in G.S. Bharava and R.M. Pal (eds.), *Human Rights of Dalits: Societal Violation*, (New Delhi: Gyan Publishing House, 1999).

Nancharaiah, G., "Economic Development of Scheduled Castes", in Chandu Subba Rao and D. Francis (eds.), *Development of Weaker Sections (Essays in Honour of Prof. K.S. Chalam)*, (Jaipur: Rawat, 2000).

Nancharaiah, G., "New Economic Policy and Its Effects on Dalits", in P.G. Jogdand (ed.), *New Economic Policy and Dalits*, (Jaipur: Rawat, 2000).

Nancharaiah, G., "Dalit Education and Economic Inequality", in Sabyasachi Bhattacharya (ed.), *Education and the Disprivileged: Nineteenth and Twentieth Century India*, (New Delhi: Orient Longman, 2002).

Nandi, Purabi, "Impact of Education on Fertility among the Scheduled of Rural Bengal", in Makhan Jha (ed.), *Scheduled Castes Today*, (New Delhi: M.D. Publications, 1997).

Narain, A.K. and D.C. Ahir (eds.), *Dr. Ambedkar, Buddhism and Social Change*, (Delhi: B.R. Publishing Corporation, 1994).

Narain, M.K., "Evaluation of the Centrally Sponsored Girls Hostel Scheme for Scheduled Castes and Scheduled Tribes in Uttar Pradesh and Orissa", (1986), [A research monograph, out of project financed by the Ministry of Human Resource Development financed].

Narang, Harish (ed.), *Writing Black Writing Dalit: Essays in Black African and Dalit Indian Writings*, (Shimla: Indian Institute of Advanced Studies, 2002).

Narasimham, K.V., *Towards Emancipation*, (Madras: Liberation Tigers, 1987).

Narasimham, K.V., *The Alternative*, (Banglore: Dalit Sahitya Academy, 2002).

Narayan, Badri, *Documenting Dissent: Contesting Fables, Contested Memoirs and Dalit Political Discourse,* (Shimla: Indian Institute of Advanced Study, 2001).

Narayana, C.V.L., *Protection of Civil Rights Act 1976,* (Amended Act of Untouchabiliy (Offences) Act of 1955, (Chittoor: Author, 1977).

Narayana, Jitendra, "Protective Discrimination: A Quest for Social Justice", in A.K. Lal (ed.), *Protective Discrimination: Ideology and Praxis,* (New Delhi: Concept, 2002), [Published for B.G. Pant Social Science Institute, Allahabad].

Narayana, T.V., "Dr. Ambedkar's Thoughts and their Relevance in the Present Times", in J.S. Narayana Rao, A. Somasekhar and K. Audiseshaiah (eds.), *B.R. Ambedkar: His Relevance Today,* (New Delhi: Gyan Publishing House, 1994).

Narayana Rao, J.S., A. Somasekhar and K. Audiseshaiah (eds.), *B.R. Ambedkar: His Relevance Today,* (New Delhi: Gyan Publishing House, 1994).

Narayana Rao, J.S. and Y. Pushpalatha, "Socio-Economic Profiles of the Scheduled Castes: A Micro View in Hyderabad", in J.S. Narayana Rao, A. Somasekhar and K. Audiseshaiah (eds.), *B.R. Ambedkar: His Relevance Today,* (New Delhi: Gyan Publishing House, 1994).

Narayana Rao, K.V., *State and the Harijan in Andhra Pradesh,* (New Delhi: Research and Policy Division, Ministry of Home Affairs, 1970).

Narayanan, K.R., "The Rebel", in B.K. Ahluwalia and Shashi Ahluwalia (eds.), *B.R. Ambedkar and Human Rights,* (New Delhi: Vivek Publishing Company, 1981).

Narayanan, Padmini R., "Reservation in Politics and the Scheduled Caste Elite", in Vimal P. Shah and Binod C. Agrawal (eds.), *Reservation Policy, Programmes and Issues,* (Jaipur: Rawat Publications, 1986).

Narotham Reddy, K., "The Hyderabad State Scheduled Caste Federation, 1941–47", *Proceedings of Andhra Pradesh History Congress,* (Srisailam: APHC, 1989).

Narula, Smita, *Broken People: Caste Violence Against India's 'Untouchables'*, (New York: Human Rights Watch, 1999).

Natesan, G.A., "The Depressed Classes", in Rajendra Singh Vatsa (ed.), *The Depressed Classes of India*, (New Delhi: Gitanjali Prakashan, 1977), (This was the text of the Presidential Address delivered by Mr. G.A. Natesan, Editor of the Indian Review, at the Second Session of the Depressed Classes Conference, held at Madras, on the 8th July, 1911).

Nath, Prem, "Ambedkar and Indian Democracy", in Bhajan Kaur (ed.), *The Philosophy of Dr. B.R. Ambedkar*, (Chandigarh: Dr. Ambedkar Study Circle, 1999).

Nath, Ram, *Dalit-Muslim Unity: Why? And How?*, (Bangalore: Dalit Sahitya Akademy, 1995).

Nath, Trilok, *Politics of the Depressed Classes*, (Delhi: Deputy Publications, 1987).

National Campaign on Dalit Human Rights, *Black Paper: Broken Promises and Dalits Betrayed*, (Secunderabad: 1998-99).

National Campaign on Dalit Human Rights, *National Campaign Manifesto: Dalit Human Rights*, (Secunderabad: 1998-99).

National Council of Educational Research and Training, *Stagnation and Dropout at Primary Stage*, (New Delhi: 1981), [This is a report on a sample survey on stagnation and dropout at primary stated conducted by the NCERT in Andhra Pradesh, Bihar, Madhya Pradesh, Orissa, Punjab, Tamil Nadu and Uttar Pradesh].

National Institute of Educational Planning and Administration, *District Profiles of India: Data Base*, (New Delhi: NIEPA, 1980).

National Institute of Educational Planning and Administration, *Selected Statistical, Indicators of Educational Development in India*, (New Delhi: NIEPA, 1980).

National Institute of Educational Planning and Administration, *Educational Administration in States and*

Union Territories: A Survey Report, (New Delhi: NIEPA, 1980).

National Sample Survey Organisation, *Employment Unemployed Situation of SC and ST Population during late eighties*, NSS 43rd Round, (July 1987–June 1988, Department of Statistics), (New Delhi: Government of India, 1990].

National Seminar on Marx, Ambedkar and Polarization of Oppressed and Exploited Classes in India, (New Delhi: Sanjivayya Institute of Socio-Economic Studies, 1991).

Nautiyal, K.C. and Y.D. Sharma, *Equalisation of Educational Opportunities for Scheduled Castes and Scheduled Tribes*, (New Delhi: NCERT, 1979).

Naval, T.R., *Law of Prevention of Atrocities On the Scheduled Castes and the Scheduled Tribes*, (New Delhi: Concept, 2001).

Navare, Savita R., "The Role of Education in Socialization of Scheduled Caste Women: A Case Study of Primary School Teachers in Pune", (Pune: Centre for Education, Indian Institute of Education, 1990), [A research monograph].

Nayak, Radhakant (ed.), *The Fourth World: Appraisal and Aspirations*, (New Delhi: Manohar, 1997).

Nayakar-Mahathera, L. Ariyawansa, "Ambedkar's Embracement of Buddhism", in Sanghasen Singh and Priyasen Singh (eds.), *Ambedkar on Buddhist Conversion and Its Impact*, (Delhi: Eastern Book Linkers, 1990).

Nayar, P.K.B., "The Scheduled Caste and Tribe High School Students in Kerala", (Trivandrum: Department of Sociology, Kerala University, 1975), [A research monograph, out of a project financed by the ICSSR].

Nehru, Rameshwari, *The Harijan Movement*, (Delhi: Harijan Sevak Sangh, 1940), [Pamphlet].

Neihoff, Arthur, *Factory Workers in India*, (Milwaukee, Wisconsin: Milwaukee Public Museum Publications in Anthropology, No. 5, 1959), [There is much material about 'untouchable' industrial workers of Kanpur, Uttar Pradesh].

Nerurkar, P.S., "Rising from the Grass Roots", in Bojja Tharakam (ed.), *The First All India Dalit Writers Conference: A Commemorative Volume and Who's Who*, (Hyderabad: Dr. B.R. Ambedkar Memorial Trust, 1994).

Nicholas, Beverley, "'Below the Bottom Rung': A British Estimate of Dr. Ambedkar, 1944", in K.C. Yadav, (ed.), *From Periphery to Centre Stage: Ambedkar, Ambedkarism and Dalit Future*, (New Delhi: Manohar, 2000).

Nigam, M.N. and Bhawana Mathur, "B.R. Ambedkar – The Militant Champion of the Untouchables", in R.B. Rao (ed.), *Bharat-Ratna Dr. Ambedkar*, (Allahabad: Chugh Publications, 1993).

Nijalingappa, S., "Dr. B.R. Ambedkar", in Rabi Ray (ed.), *Dr. B.R. Ambedkar*, (New Delhi: Lok Sabha Secretariat, 1991), [Eminent Parliamentarians Monograph Series 12].

Nikam, Shriram, *Destiny of Untouchables in India: Divergent Approaches and Strategies of Mahatma Gandhi and Dr. B.R. Ambedkar*, (New Delhi: Deep and Deep, 1998).

Nim, Hoti Lal (Compiler), *Thoughts on Dr. Ambedkar*, (Agra: Siddartha Educational and Cultural Society, 1969).

Nimbalkar, Waman, "Dalit Poetry", in Bojja Tharakam (ed.), *The First All India Dalit Writers Conference: A Commemorative Volume and Who's Who*, (Hyderabad: Dr. B.R. Ambedkar Memorial Trust, 1994).

Nirmal, Arvind P. (ed.), *Toward a Common Dalit Ideology*, (Madras: Gurukul Lutheran Theological College and Research Institute, 1990), (Published for the Department of Dalit Theology), [Papers presented at the National Seminar on Dalit Ideology organized by the Department of Dalit Theology, Gugukul Lutheran Theological College and Research Institute].

Nirmal, Arvind P. and V. Devasahayam (eds.), *Dr. B.R. Ambedkar: A Centenary Tribute*, (Madras: Gurukul, 1991).

Nirmal, Arvind P., "Doing Theology from a Dalit Perspective: in Arvind P. Nirmal (ed.), *A Reader in Dalit Theology*, (Madras: Gurukul, 1992).

Nirmal, Arvind P. (ed.), *A Reader in Dalit Theology*, (Madras: Gurukul, 1992).

Nirmal, Arvind P., "Towards a Christian Dalit Theology", in James Massey (ed.), *Indigenous People: Dalits, Dalit Issues in Today's Theological Debate*, (Delhi: ISPCK, 1998), (First Published in1994).

Nirmata, Bhai, *Harijan Women in Independent India*, (New Delhi: B.R. Publishing Corporation, 1986).

Nisaegandha, S.A., "Dalit Identity", in Ambrose Pinto (ed.), *Dalit Assertion for Identity*, (New Delhi: Indian Social Institute, 1999), [Proceedings of the National Seminar of Dalit Postgraduate and Research Students held on 23-25 January 1999 in the Indian Social Institute].

Nomani, Md. Zafar Mahfooz, "Ambedkar on Indian Federalism: An Appraisal of Water Law and Policy in Contemporary Perspective", in Nazeer H. Khan (ed.), *B.R. Ambedkar on Federalism, Ethnicity and Gender Justice*, (New Delhi: Deep & Deep, 2001).

Nye, Robert, *Conflict among Harijans*, (Springer Publications, 1973).

O'Hanlon, Rosalind, *Caste, Conflict and Ideology: Mahatma Jotirao Phule and Low Caste Protest in Nineteenth Century Western India*, (Hyderabad: Orient Longman, 1986).

Ohlayan, S.K., "Administrative Process and Dr. Ambedkar's Conception of New Socio-Economic Rights under the Constitution of India", in Bhajan Kaur (ed.), *The Philosophy of Dr. B.R. Ambedkar*, (Chandigarh: Dr. Ambedkar Study Circle, 1999).

Ojha, G.P., *Politicisation of Scheduled Castes in Bihar*, (Patna: Jagjivan Ram Institute of Parliamentary Studies and Political Research, 1990).

Olcott, Henry S., *The Poor Paraih*, (Madras: 1902), [Pamphlet].

Om Prakash, S., *Caste and Politics in Indian Education*, (New Delhi: Deep and Deep, 1986).

Omvedt, Gail, 'Who Are The Indigenous People of India' in M Gopinath and Fr Lazer, (eds.), *The Emergence of Indigenous Peoples: Collection of Papers Presented at the First All India Conference of Indigenous Peoples of India* (24-25 Dec.), (Bangalore: Council of Indigenous People-India and Indian Social Institute, 1993).

Omvedt, Gail, *Dalits and the Democratic Revolution: Dr. Ambedkar and the Dalit Movement in Colonial India,* (New Delhi: Sage Publications, 1994).

Omvedt, Gail, "Kanshiram and the Bahujan Saman Party", in K.L. Sharma (ed.), *Caste and Class in India,* (Jaipur: Rawat Publications, 1994).

Omvedt, Gail, "Dalit Women and Communalism", in P.G. Jogdand (ed.), *Dalit Women in India: Issues and Perspectives,* (New Delhi: Gyan Publishing House, in collaboration with University of Poona, Pune, 1995).

Omvedt, Gail, *Dalit Visions: The Anti-Caste Movement and the Construction of an Indian Identity,* (Hyderabad: Orient Longman, 1995).

Omvedt, Gail, "Gandhi and Ambedkar: A Comparative Analysis", in V.T. Patil (ed.), *Studies in Ambedkar,* (Delhi: Devika Publications, 1995).

Omvedt, Gail, "Dalits and Economic Policy: Contributions of Dr. B.R. Ambedkar", in S.M. Michael (ed.), *Dalits in Modern India,* (New Delhi: Vistaar Publications, 1999), (An earlier version of this article was published in the *Fourth World,* Vol. 4, No. 1, (1997).

Omvedt, Gail, "Peasants, Dalits and Women: Democracy and India's New Social Movement", in M. Mohanty, Partha N. Mukerji and Olle Tornquist (eds.), *People's Rights, Social Movements and the State in the Third World,* (New Delhi: Sage Publications, 1998).

Omvedt, Gail, "Undoing the Bondage: Dr. Ambedkar's Theory of Dalit Liberation", in K.C. Yadav, (ed.), *From Periphery to Centre Stage: Ambedkar, Ambedkarism and Dalit Future,* (New Delhi: Manohar, 2000).

Omvedt, Gail, "Economic Policy, Poverty and Dalits", in P.G. Jogdand (ed.), *New Economic Policy and Dalits,* (Jaipur: Rawat, 2000).

Omvedt, Gail, "Gandhi and Ambedkar: Why the Confrontation?", in M.L. Ranga (ed.), *B.R. Ambedkar: His Life, Work and Relevance,* (New Delhi: Manohar, 2000).

Omvedt, Gail, "Ambedkar and After: The Dalit Movement in India", in Ghanshyam Shah (ed.), *Dalit Identity and Politics,* (New Delhi: Sage Publications, 2001), [Cultural Subordination and the Dalit Challenge, Vol. 2 of Sage series].

Oommen, George, *Paths of Dalit Liberation in Kerala: Interaction with Christianity and Communism, 1854-1966,* (Surrey: Curzon Press, 1996).

Oommen, George, "Strength of Tradition and Weakness of Communication: Central Kerala Dalit Conversion", in Geoffrey A. Oddie (ed.), *Religious Conversion Movements in South Asia: Continuities and Change, 1800-1900,* (Surrey: Curzon Press, 1997).

Oommen, T.K., "Scheduled Castes: Then and Now", in B.N. Pande (ed.), *The Spirit of India,* (Bombay: Asia Publishing House, 1975).

Oommen, T.K., *Scheduled Castes and Scheduled Tribes in India since Independence,* (New Delhi: Vikas, 1977), [edited by S.C. Dube].

Oommen, T.K., "Scheduled Castes and Scheduled Tribes", in S.C. Dube (ed.), *India Since Independence,* (New Delhi: Vikas, 1977).

Oommen, T.K., "State Policy and the Socially Deprived in India", in V. Devasahayam (ed.), *Dalits and Women: Quest for Humanity,* (Madras: The Gurukul Summer Institute, 1992).

Opler, M., "North Indian Themes: Caste and Untouchability", in J.M. Mahar (ed.), *The Untouchables in Contemporary India,* (Tucson: University of Arizona Press, 1972).

Orissa, State Government of, Tribal and Rural Welfare Department, *Welfare of Backward Classes in Orissa,* (Bhubaneswar: 1958).

Ouwerkerk, Louise, *The Untouchables of India,* (London: Oxford University Press, 1945).

Padgaonkar, Dilip, "Voice of Protest", in Bojja Tharakam (ed.), *The First All India Dalit Writers Conference: A Commemorative Volume and Who's Who,* (Hyderabad: Dr. B.R. Ambedkar Memorial Trust, 1994).

Padalia, Munni, "On the Reservation of Scheduled Castes and Scheduled Tribes: Problems and Solutions", in M.P. Dube and Neeta Bora (eds.), *Social Justice and Women in India,* (Delhi: Swaraj Prakashan, 1999).

Padma Rao, Katti, *Journey Towards Dalit Dignity,* (Tr. M. Chandrasekhar), (Bombay: The All India Telugu Bahujan Welfare Society, 1999).

Padmanabhan, A., "Ambedkar's Life and Legacy", in *Ambedkar and Social Justice,* Vol. II, (New Delhi: Director, Publications Division, Ministry of Information and Broadcasting, 1992), [on behalf of Baba Saheb Dr. B.R. Ambedkar Birth Centenary Celebrations Committee, Ministry of Welfare, Government of India].

Padmanabhan, A., *Mandal Commission Judgement and the Scheduled Castes and Scheduled Tribes,* (New Delhi: Indian Social Institute, 1993).

Padmanabhan, A., *Dalits at the Cross Roads: Their Struggle – Past and Present,* (Madras: Poompugar Pathippagam, 1996).

Pai Panandiker, V.A. (ed.), *The Politics of Backwardness: Reservation Policy in India,* (New Delhi: Konark Publishers, 1997), [Under the auspices of Centre for Policy Research, New Delhi].

Pai, Sudha, "Politicization of Dalits and Most Backward Castes", in her *State Politics: New Dimensions (Party System, Liberalisation and Politics of Identity),* (Delhi: Shipra Publications, 2000).

Pai, Sudha, "From Harijans to Dalits: Identity Formation, Political Consciousness and Electoral Mobilisation of the Scheduled Castes in Uttar Pradesh", in Ghanshyam Shah (ed.), *Dalit Identity and Politics,* (New Delhi: Sage Publications, 2001), [Cultural Subordination and the Dalit Challenge, Vol. 2 of Sage series].

Pai, Sudha, *Dalit Assertion and the Unfinished Democratic Revolution: The Bahujan Samaj Party in Uttar Pradesh,* (New Delhi: Sage, 2002).

Pai, Sudha, "Theory and Practice of BSP's Concept of Social Justice: Implications for Politics", in A.K. Lal (ed.), *Protective Discrimination: Ideology and Praxis,* (New Delhi: Concept, 2002), [Published for B.G. Pant Social Science Institute, Allahabad].

Pais, Richard, "Scheduled Castes, Employment and Social Mobility", in S.M. Michael (ed.), *Dalits and Modern India,* (New Delhi: Vistaar Publications, 1999).

Pakhiddey, Bapurao, *Dalit Panther: Thoughts and Vision,* (Delhi: 1983).

Pakhiddey, Bapurao, *Emancipation of Bonded Labor in Unorganized Sector,* (Delhi: Bharatiya Bhatta Mazdoor Sangharsh Samiti, 1984).

Pal, Mahendra, "Ambedkar – Life and Conversion Movement", in Sanghasen Singh and Priyásen Singh (eds.), *Ambedkar on Buddhist Conversion and Its Impact,* (Delhi: Eastern Book Linkers, 1990).

Pal, R.M. (ed.), *Protection of Human Rights: A Critique (With Special Reference to SC/STs, the Girl Child/Women belonging to SC/STs, marginalized Section and the Minorities,* (New Delhi: Indian Social Institute, 1999), [Proceedings of the National Seminar held on 13 and 14 November 1998 at the Indian Social Institute].

Palshikar, Vasant, "Gandhi and Ambedkar", in K.K. Kavlekar and A.S. Chausalkar (eds.), *Political Ideas and Leadership of Dr. B.R. Ambedkar,* (Pune: Vishwanil Publications, 1989).

Pandere, Shantaram, "Patterns of Dalit Militancy", in Sandeep Pendse (ed.), *Dalit Movement Today*, (Bombay: Vikas Adhyayana Kendra, 1994), [Vikas Adhyayan Kendra, Bombay, *Perspectives* 1].

Pandey, Gaya, "In Search of an Institution of Exploitation and Oppression among the Scheduled Castes in Palamau", in S.N. Chaudhary (ed.), *Changing Status of Depressed Castes in Contemporary India: Essays in Honour of Professor S.C. Dube*, (Delhi: Daya Publishing House, 1988).

Pandey, N. and Tripathi, R.C., "Scheduled Caste Children in High Caste Schools", in D. Sinha and G. Mishra (eds.), *Deprivation: Its Social Roots and Psychological Consequences*, (New Delhi: Concept Publishing Co., 1982).

Pandey, Prem Narain, *Education and Social Mobility: A Text with Reference Scheduled Castes*, (Delhi: Daya, 1988).

Pandey, R.N., "Dr. B.R. Ambedkar and His Concept of Social Justice", in R.B. Rao (ed.), *Bharat-Ratna Dr. Ambedkar*, (Allahabad: Chugh Publications, 1993).

Pandey, R.S., "Social Profiles of Scheduled Castes in Perspective of Development Programmes: A Case Study of Koraon Block (Allahabad District", in R.S. Tripathi and P.D. Tiwari (eds.), *Dimensions of Scheduled Caste Development: Problems and Prospects*, (New Delhi: Uppal, 1991).

Pandey, Yadunath, "Demographic and Socio-Economic Structure of Chamars and Dusads of Bihar", in Makhan Jha (ed.), *Scheduled Castes Today*, (New Delhi: M.D. Publications, 1997).

Pandhya, K.S. and Jayashree Mahapatra, *Reservation Policy in India*, (New Delhi: Ashish, 1988).

Pandian, M.S.S., "Stepping Outside History? New Dalit Writings from Tamil Nadu", in Partha Chatterjee (ed.), *Wages of Freedom: Fifty Years of the Indian Nation State*, (Delhi: OUP 1998).

Pandian, T.B., *Slaves of the Soil in Southern India*, (Madras: Cosmopolitan Press, 1893; foreign reprint at Amsterdam,

Holland: 1899). [Perhaps the earliest book on Untouchables, from Christian viewpoint].

Pandian, T.B., *Pandian and the Pariahs (A Comprehensive Account of His Visit to England in the interest of the Pariahs)*, (Madras: Britannia Press, 1895).

Pandit, Nalini, "Dalits and Hindu Communalism", in Sandeep Pendse (ed.), *Dalit Movement Today*, (Bombay: Vikas Adhyayana Kendra, 1994), [Vikas Adhyayan Kendra, Bombay, *Perspectives* 1].

Pandit, S.B., "Economic Ideas of Dr. Ambedkar", in K.K. Kavlekar and A.S. Chausalkar (eds.), *Political Ideas and Leadership of Dr. B.R. Ambedkar*, (Pune: Vishwanil Publications, 1989).

Pandya, B.V., *Striving for Economic Equality*, (Bombay: Popular Book Depot, 1959).

Pandyan, K. David, *Dr. B.R. Ambedkar and the Dynamics of Neo-Buddhism*, (New Delhi: Gyan, 1996).

Panikkar, K.N., "Vaikkam Satyagraha: Struggle against Untouchability", in Ravi Dayal (ed.), *We Fought for Freedom Together: Chapters from the Indian National Movement*, (New Delhi: ICHR and OUP, 1995).

Pant, S.K., "Protection Discrimination: How much Relevant, How much Obsolete?", in A.K. Lal (ed.), *Protective Discrimination: Ideology and Praxis*, (New Delhi: Concept, 2002), [Published for B.G. Pant Social Science Institute, Allahabad].

Pantavane, G., *Patrikar Dr. Babasaheb Ambedkar*, (Nagpur: Abhijit, 1987).

Pantawane, Gangadhar, "Evolving a New Identity: The Development of a Dalit Culture", in Barbara R. Joshi (ed.), *Untouchable! Voices of the Dalit Liberation Movement*, (London: The Minority Rights Groups Ltd. and Zed Books Ltd., 1986).

Panwar, Lalit K., "B.R. Ambedkar: Architect", in Shyam Lal and K.S. Saxena (eds.), *Ambedkar and Nation-Building*, (Jaipur: Rawat, 1998).

Paradkar, B., "The Religious Quest of Ambedkar", in T. Wilkinson and M. Thomas (eds.), *Ambedkar and the Neo-Buddhist Movement*, (Madras: The Christian Literature Society, 1972).

Paramjit Judge, S., *Scheduled Caste Women in the Workforce in Rural Punjab*, (Surat: Centre for Social Studies, 1990), [Occasional Paper No. 9].

Pardeshi, Pratima, *Dr. Babasaheb Ambedkar and the Question of Women's Liberation in India*, (Pune: University of Pune, 1998).

Parekh, Bhikhu, *Discourse on Untouchability*, (New Delhi: Sage Publications, 1989).

Parish, Steven, M., "The Indian Untouchables' Critique of Culture", in his *Hierarchy and Its Discontents: Culture and the Politics of Consciousness in Caste Society*, (Delhi: OUP, 1997).

Parmaji, S., *Caste Reservation & Performance*, (Warangal: Mamta Publications, 1985).

Parmar, S.B. Singh, "Women's Age at Marriage Among Scheduled Castes and its Implications: Theoretical and Empirical Explorations", in R.S. Tripathi and P.D. Tiwari (eds.), *Dimensions of Scheduled Caste Development in India: Problems and Prospects*, (New Delhi: Uppal, 1991).

Parmar, Y.A., *The Mahyavanshi: The Success Story of a Scheduled Caste*, (Delhi: Mittal, 1987).

Parthasarathy, Jakka, "Dr. B.R. Ambedkar and Tribal Welfare: An Anthropological Perspective", in *Ambedkar and Social Justice*, Vol. I, (New Delhi: Director, Publications Division, Ministry of Information and Broadcasting, 1992), [on behalf of Baba Saheb Dr. B.R. Ambedkar Birth Centenary Celebrations Committee, Ministry of Welfare, Government of India].

Parvate, T.V., "Bhimrao Ramji Ambedkar", in B.K. Ahluwalia and Shashi Ahluwalia (eds.), *B.R. Ambedkar and Human Rights*, (New Delhi: Vivek Publishing Company, 1981).

Parvathamma, C., "Buddhism: Its Relevance to Buddhist Converts in India", in *Dharma Chakra Pravartan, Buddhist Souvenir*, (Hyderabad: Buddhist Society of India, 1965).

Parvathamma, C., *Politics and Religion*, (New Delhi: Sterling, 1971).

Parvathamma, C., "The Study of Scheduled Caste and Scheduled Tribe College Students in Karnataka', (Mysore: Department of Post-graduate Studies and Research in Sociology, Mysore University, 1974), [A research monograph, out of a project financed by the ICSSR].

Parvathamma, C., "Ambedkar's Analysis of the Hindu Social Order", in A.M. Rajasekharaiah (ed.), *The Socio-Economic Transformation of India—Ambedkar's Vision*, (Dharwad: Karnatak University, 1983).

Parvathamma, C., "Conversion Movements among Untouchables: A Brief Historical Survey", in Jose Kananaikil (ed.), *Scheduled Castes and the Struggle against Inequality*, (New Delhi: Indian Social Institute, 1983).

Parvathamma, C., *Scheduled Castes and Scheduled Tribes: A Socio-Economic Survey*, (New Delhi: Ashish, 1984).

Parvathamma, C. and Satyanarayana, *New Horizons and the Scheduled Castes*, (New Delhi: Ashish, 1984).

Parvathamma, C., *Scheduled Castes at the Cross Roads*, (New Delhi: Ashish Publishing House, 1989).

Paswan, Sanjay and Paramanshi Jaideva, *Encyclopedia of Dalits in India*, 11 Vols., (New Delhi: Kalpaz, 2002).

Paswan, Yogeshwar, *Economic Development of Scheduled Castes in Bihar*, (Batho, Nehra, Darbhanga: Amita Kumari, 1995).

Patankar, Bharat, "Caste System, New Economic Policy and Dalits: Alternatives of the Movement", in P.G. Jogdand (ed.), *New Economic Policy and Dalits*, (Jaipur: Rawat, 2000).

Patauria, Kusum, "National Unity – Problem and its Solution in view of Dr. Ambedkar", in R.B. Rao (ed.), *Bharat-Ratna Dr. Ambedkar*, (Allahabad: Chugh Publications, 1993).

Patel, S.G., "Dr. B.R. Ambedkar", in *Ambedkar and Social Justice*, Vol. II, (New Delhi: Director, Publications

Division, Ministry of Information and Broadcasting, 1992), [on behalf of Baba Saheb Dr. B.R. Ambedkar Birth Centenary Celebrations Committee, Ministry of Welfare, Government of India].

Pathak, Bindeshwar, *Road to Freedom: A Sociological Study on the Abolition of Scavenging in India,* (New Delhi: Motilal Banarsidass and Sulabh Foundation, 1991).

Pathak, Bindeshwar, "Emerging Identity of Untouchables: Gandhi, Ambedkar and Sulabh", in Walter Fernandes (ed.), *The Emerging Dalit Identity: The Reassertion of Subalterns,* (New Delhi: Indian Social Institute, 1996).

Pathak, Bindeshwar, "Liberation of Scavengers from Social and Occupational Bondage", in Bindeshwar Pathak (ed.), *Social Justice and Development of Weaker Sections,* (New Delhi: Inter India, 1997).

Pathak, Bindeshwar, *Social Justice and Development of Weaker Sections,* (New Delhi: Inter India, 1997).

Pathak, Bindeshwar (ed.), *Social Justice and Development of Weaker Sections,* (New Delhi: Inter India, 1997).

Pathak, Bindeshwar, "The Psycho-Social Scenario of Scavengers and the Role of Sulabh International", in N. Hasnain (ed.), *Weaker Sections: The Psycho-Social Perspective,* (New Delhi: Gyan, 1998).

Pathak, Bindeshwar and B.N. Srivastava, *Constitutional Safeguards for Weaker Sections and the Minorities in India,* (New Delhi: Concept, 1999).

Pathak, Indira, "The Chamars of a Tribal City: A Case Study of Kumhartoli of Ranchi", in Makhan Jha (ed.), *Scheduled Castes Today,* (New Delhi: M.D. Publications, 1997).

Pathak, Suman Lata, "Self-Images of Scheduled Castes Girl Students of Chandigarh", in Prakash Pimpley and Satish Sharma (eds.), *Struggle for Status,* (Delhi: B.R. Publishing Corporation, 1985).

Pathak, T., *Occupational Structure of a Scheduled Castes in a Village,* (Dibrugarh University, 1970).

Pati, Jagannath, "Mass Communication, Development and Scheduled Castes", in Makhan Jha (ed.), *Scheduled Castes Today,* (New Delhi: M.D. Publications, 1997).

Patil, R.B., "Employment of the Scheduled Castes in Maharashtra", in R.G. Singh (ed.), *The Depressed Classes of India: Problems and Prospects*, (New Delhi: B.R. Publishing Corporation, 1986).

Patil, R.B. and M.D. Koli, "Atrocities on Scheduled Castes and Scheduled Tribes in India and Social Justice: Some Issues", in Yeshwant Khillare (ed.), *Present Status of Backward Classes in India*, (Aurangabad: Centre for Studies on SCs/STs, Dr. Babasaheb Ambedkar Marathwada University, 1997).

Patil, Rajendra, "Jawahar Rojgar Yojana and Employment of Dalits: Some Observations", in P.G. Jogdand (ed.), *New Economic Policy and Dalits*, (Jaipur: Rawat, 2000).

Patil, Sharad, *Dasa-Sudra Slavery: Studies in the Origins of Indian Slavery and Feudalism and their Philosophies*, (New Delhi: Allied Publishers, 1982).

Patil, Sharad, "Phule-Ambedkar Vada and Indian Social Revolution", in K.K. Kavlekar and A.S. Chausalkar (eds.), *Political Ideas and Leadership of Dr. B.R. Ambedkar*, (Pune: Vishwanil Publications, 1989).

Patil, Sharad, "The Historic Convergence of Marx and Ambedkar", in *National Seminar on Marx, Ambedkar and Polarization of Oppressed and Exploited Classes in India*, (New Delhi: Sanjivayya Institute of Socio-Economic Studies, 1991).

Patil, Sharad, "Ambedkar and Marxism: A Critical Examination of the Case for Synthesis", in K.S. Chalam (ed.), *The Relevance of Ambedkarism in India*, (Jaipur: Rawat, 1993).

Patil, V.T. (ed.), *Studies in Ambedkar*, (Delhi: Devika Publications, 1995).

Patil, V.T. and Narayana, "Nehru, Gandhi, Congress Ideology and Ambedkar's Role in the Making of the Indian Constitution", in V.T. Patil (ed.), *Studies in Ambedkar*, (Delhi: Devika Publications, 1995).

Patil, V.T. and Narayana, "Ambedkar's Perception of Justice under the Constitution – An Overview", in V.T. Patil (ed.), *Studies in Ambedkar*, (Delhi: Devika Publications, 1995).

Patouria, Rajendra, "Ambedkar – A Successful and Powerful Journalist", in R.B. Rao (ed.), *Bharat-Ratna Dr. Ambedkar*, (Allahabad: Chugh Publications, 1993).

Patwardhan, Sunanda, *Change Among India's Harijans: Maharashtra – A Case Study*, (New Delhi: Orient Longman, 1973).

Patwardhan, S., *Dalit Panther*, (New Delhi: Krishnamurthi Foundation of India, 1974-5).

Patwardhan, Sunanda, "Aspects of Social Mobility Among Scheduled Castes in Poona", in M.S.A. Rao (ed.), *Urban Sociology in India*, (New Delhi: Orient Longman, 1974).

Pawade, Kumud, "The Life of a Dalit Women", in P.G. Jogdand (ed.), *Dalit Women in India: Issues and Perspectives*, (New Delhi: Gyan Publishing House, in collaboration with University of Poona, Pune, 1995).

Pawade, Kumud, "The Position of Dalit Women in Indian Society", in Bhagwan Das and James Massey (eds.), *Dalit Solidarity*, (Delhi: ISPCK, 1995), [This article also been reprinted in James Massey (ed.), *Indigenous People, Dalits: Dalit Issues in Today's Theological Debate*, (Delhi: ISPCK, 1998), (First Published in1994).

Pawar, D., *Ma vie d'intouchable*, (Paris: La Decouverte, 1990).

Pawar, Daya, "History of Dalit Literature", in Bojja Tharakam (ed.), *The First All India Dalit Writers Conference: A Commemorative Volume and Who's Who*, (Hyderabad: Dr. B.R. Ambedkar Memorial Trust, 1994).

Pawar, D.V., "Maharshi V.R. Shinde and Dr. Ambedkar", in K.K. Kavlekar and A.S. Chausalkar (eds.), *Political Ideas and Leadership of Dr. B.R. Ambedkar*, (Pune: Vishwanil Publications, 1989).

Pawar, Eswar Das, *Reservation for Scheduled Castes*, (Chandigarh: I.D. Pawar, 1980).

Pawar, Eswar Das, *My struggle in Life*, (Chandigarh: I.D. Pawar, 1993), 3rd edition.

Pawar, J.P., "Dr. B.R. Ambedkar – Man and Mission", in R.B. Rao (ed.), *Bharat-Ratna Dr. Ambedkar*, (Allahabad: Chugh Publications, 1993).

Pawar, P.J., "Dr. Ambedkar and Social Revolution", in R.B. Rao (ed.), *Bharat-Ratna Dr. Ambedkar*, (Allahabad: Chugh Publications, 1993).

Pawar, Urmila, "What Has the Dalit Movement Offered to Women?", in Sandeep Pendse (ed.), *Dalit Movement Today*, (Bombay: Vikas Adhyayana Kendra, 1994), [Vikas Adhyayan Kendra, Bombay, *Perspectives* 1].

Pendse, Sandeep (ed.), *Dalit Movement Today*, (Bombay: Vikas Adhyayana Kendra, 1994), [Vikas Adhyayan Kendra, Bombay, *Perspectives* 1].

Pfaffenberger, B., *Report of the Task Force for Tackling the Problems of Scavengers and Suggesting Measures to Abolish Scavenging with Particular Emphasis on Their Rehabilitation*, (New Delhi: Planning Commission, 1990-91).

Phadke, Balachandra, *Dalita Sahitya: Vedana Va Vidroh*, (Pune: Sri Vidya Prakashan, 1977), (in Marathi).

Phadke, B.D. and Vijay Surwade (eds.), *Selected Writings and Speeches of Dr. B.R. Ambedkar*, (Aurangabad: Anand Prakashan, 1989).

Philip, P.O., *The Depressed Classes and Christianity*, (Calcutta: National Christian Council, 1925).

Philips, Godfrey E., *The Outcastes' Hope or Work Among the Depressed Classes in India*, (Edinburgh: The Foreign Mission Committee of the Church of Scotland and the Mission Study Council of the United Free Church of Scotland, 1913).

Phillips, Godfrey E., *The Untouchables' Quest: The Depressed Classes of India and Christianity*, (Foreword by B.R. Ambedkar), (London: Edinburgh House Press, 1936).

Pickett, J. Waskom, "The Untouchables", in Gertrude C. Warner, et.al. (eds.), *Moving Millions: The Pageant of Modern India*, (Boston: 1938).

Pickett, J. Waskom, *Christ's Way to India's Heart: Present Day Mass Movements to Christianity*, (London: The United

Society for Christian Literature, 1938), (revised and reprint).

Pickett, J. Waskom, *Christian Mass Movements in India: A Study with Recommendations*, (New York, Cincinnati: The Abingdon Press, 1933).

Pilchick, Terry, *Jai Bhim: Dispatches from a Peaceful Revolution*, (Glasgow: Windhorse Publications and Berkeley: Parrallax Press, 1988).

Pillai, N.K., "Adi Dravida", *Census of India, 1931, Vol. XXVIII, Travancore, Part I: Report*, (Trivandrum: 1932).

Pillai, P. Chidambaram, *Right of Temple Entry*, (Nagarcoil: Author, 1933).

Pillai, R.V., "Manual Scavenging: A Challenge to Human Rights", in R.M. Pal (ed.), *Protection of Human Rights: A Critique (With Special Reference to SC/STs, the Girl Child/ Women belonging to SC/STs, marginalized Section and the Minorities*, (New Delhi: Indian Social Institute, 1999), [Proceedings of the National Seminar held on 13 and 14 November 1998 at the Indian Social Institute].

Pillai, Thakazhi S., *Two Measures of Rice*, (Tr. By M.A. Shakoor), (Bombay: Jaico, 1967), [A novel of Praiyan and Pulia life in Travancore].

Pillai-Vetchera, Traude, *The Mahars: A Study of Their Culture, Religion and Socio Economic Life*, (New Delhi: Intercultural Publications, 1994).

Pillai-Vetschera, Traude, "Ambedkar's Daughters: A Study of Mahar Women in Ahmednagar District of Maharashtra", in S.M. Michael (ed.), *Dalits and Modern India*, (New Delhi: Vistaar Publications, 1999).

Pimpley, P.N., "Educational Problems of Scheduled Caste Students in the Punjab: School Students", (Chandigarh: Department of Sociology, Punjab University, 1974), [A research monograph, out of a project financed by the ICSSR].

Pimpley, P.N., "Educational Problems of Scheduled Caste Students in the Punjab: College Students", (Chandigarh:

Department of Sociology, Punjab University, 1974), [A research monograph, out of a project financed by the ICSSR].

Pimpley, P.N., *Profile of Scheduled Castes Students: The Case of Punjab,* (Chandigarh: Department of Sociology, Panjab University, 1980), [Occasional Monograph Series: 2].

Pimpley, P.N., "The Problem of Non-Attendance in Schools of the Children (6-14 years) of Scheduled Castes in Haryana", (Chandigarh: Department of Sociology, Punjab University, 1981), [A research monograph, out of a project financed by the ICSSR].

Pimpley, P.N., "Problem of Non-Attendance of School among Scheduled Castes Children", S.K. Sharma (ed.), *Reform, Protest and Social Transformation,* (New Delhi: Ashish Publishing House, 1982).

Pimpley, Prakash N. and Satish Sharma, "De-Sanskritization of Untouchables: Arya Samaj Movement in Punjab", in Prakash Pimpley and Satish Sharma (eds.), *Struggle for Status,* (Delhi: B.R. Publishing Corporation, 1985).

Pinto, A., *Dalit Christians: A Socio-Economic Survey,* (Bangalore: Aashirvad, Centre for Non-Formal and Continuing Education, 1992).

Pinto, A., "Conversion to Christianity among Indigenous People", in Gopinath, M. and Fr. Lazer, (eds.), *The Emergence of Indigenous Peoples: Collections of Papers Presented at the First All India Conference of Indigenous Peoples of India,* (Bangalore: Council of Indigenous People-India and Indian Social Institute, 1993).

Pinto, A., "Karnataka: Atrocities on Dalits and Dalit Sangarshan Samiti's Response", in Walter Fernandes (ed.), *The Emerging Dalit Identity,* (New Delhi: Indian Social Institute, 1996).

Pinto, A., "Marginalisation of the Marginalised", in *Indian Economy: An Alternative Economic Survey, 1998-99,* (Delhi: Delhi Science Forum, 1999).

Pinto, A. (ed.), *Dalits: Assertion for Identity*, (New Delhi: Indian Social Institute, 1999).

Pinto, A., "Dalits Victims of an Oppressive Caste System", in Stan D'Souza (ed.), *Population and Poverty: Issues at the Dawn of the 21st Century*, (Delhi: 2001).

Poddar, Bhagirath, *The Untouchables in Modern India*, (New Delhi: Sarup and Sons, 2001).

Prabhakar, M.E. (ed.), *Towards a Common Dalit Theology*, (Delhi: Indian Society for Promoting Christian Knowledge, 1989).

Prabhakar, M.E., "Developing a Common Ideology for Dalits of Christian and Other Faiths", in Arvind P. Nirmal (ed.), *Toward a Common Dalit Ideology*, (Madras: Gurukul Lutheran Theological College and Research Institute, 1990), [Papers presented at the National Seminar on Dalit Ideology organized by the Department of Dalit Theology, Gugukul Lutheran Theological College and Research Institute].

Prabhakar, M.E., "Mission in a Dalit Perspective", in V. Devasahayam (ed.), *Dalits and Women: Quest for Humanity*, (Madras: The Gurukul Summer Institute, 1992).

Prabhakar, M.E., "Dalit Concerns in the Context of Religious Fundamentalism in India", in *Religious Fundamentalism: An Asian Perspective*, (New Delhi: 1992).

Prabhakar, M.E., "The Search for a Dalit Theology", in James Massey (ed.), *Indigenous People: Dalits, Dalit Issues in Today's Theological Debate*, (Delhi: ISPCK, 1998), (First Published in1994).

Prabhavathi, M., "Dalit Women in Contemporary Indian Situation", in P.G. Jogdand (ed.), *Dalit Women in India: Issues and Perspectives*, (New Delhi: Gyan Publishing House, in collaboration with University of Poona, Pune, 1995).

Prabhu, P.N., *Report of the Seminar on Casteism and Removal of Untouchability*, (Bombay: Indian Conference of Social Work, 1955).

Pradhan, Atul Chandra, *The Emergence of the Depressed Classes,* (Bhubaneshwar: Bookland International, 1986).

Pradhan, A.C., "Dr. Ambedkar's Quest for Social Justice in Indian Tradition", in P.K. Mohapatra (ed.), *Religion and Social Change,* (Cuttack: Akash, 1993).

Pradhan, G.R., *Untouchable Workers of Bombay City,* (Foreword by B.R. Ambedkar), (Bombay: Karnatak Publishing House, 1938).

Prakash, D.R., *How to Erase Untouchability,* (New Delhi: Bookwala, 1979).

Prakash, Nirupama, *Scheduled Castes: Socio-Economic Changes,* (Allahabad: Chugh, 1989).

Prakash, Om and Arun K. Sen, *Caste Hindu and Scheduled Caste Children in Rural India,* (New Delhi: Ess Ess Publications, 1985).

Prakash, Prem, *Ambedkar, Politics and Scheduled Castes,* (New Delhi: Ashish, 1993).

Prakasham, Gnana, *Social Separatism: Scheduled Castes and the Caste System,* (Jaipur: Rawat, 1998).

Pranjpe, A.C., "The 'Becoming' of Dr. Ambedkar: A Socio-Psychological Study", in M.L. Ranga (ed.), *B.R. Ambedkar: His Life, Work and Relevance,* (New Delhi: Manohar, 2000).

Prasad, Anirudh, *Voluntary Effort in the Development of Musahar Community in Bihar: A Case Study of Samangwaya Ashram, Bodh-Gaya,* (Patna: A.N. Sinha Institute of Social Sciences, 1985).

Prasad, Anirudh, *Samnavaya Ashram in the Service of Harijans,* (New Delhi: Janaki Prakashan, 1986).

Prasad, Anirudh, "People's Perception of the Atrocities committed on Scheduled Castes in Bihar", in S.N. Chaudhary (ed.), *Changing Status of Depressed Castes in Contemporary India: Essays in Honour of Professor S.C. Dube,* (Delhi: Daya Publishing House, 1988).

Prasad, Hari, "The Socio-Economic Problems of the Chamars of Palamau", in Makhan Jha (ed.), *Scheduled Castes Today,* (New Delhi: M.D. Publications, 1997).

Prasad, Ishwari, *Reservation: Action for Social Equality*, (New Delhi: Criterion Books, 1986).

Prasad, Iswari, Jasvir Singh and Sunil, *Caste Merit and Reservations*, (New Delhi: Samata Era Publications, 1987).

Prasad, Manohar Chandra, *Dalit Christian Consciousness*, (New Delhi: Blumoon, 1998), (first published in 1994).

Prasad, R.C., *Preface to Ambedkarism*, (Delhi: Motilal Banarsidass, 1993).

Prasad, R.C., *Ambedkarism*, (New Delhi: Blumoon, 1998).

Prasad, R.R. and G. Rajani Kanth, *Development of Scheduled Caste Leather Artisans: Profile, Problems and Prospects*, (NewDelhi: Discovery, 1991).

Prasad, R.R., *Change and Continuity among SC Leather Workers*, (Rajendranagar, Hyderabad: National Institute for Rural Development, 1986).

Prasad, Shidheswar, "In Quest of Social Justice", in Rabi Ray (ed.), *Dr. B.R. Ambedkar*, (New Delhi: Lok Sabha Secretariat, 1991), [Eminent Parliamentarians Monograph Series 12].

Prasanna Kumar, V., "Ambedkar in Search of Lenin – Dilemmas of Dalit Movement", in J.S. Narayana Rao, A. Somasekhar and K. Audiseshaiah (eds.), *B.R. Ambedkar: His Relevance Today*, (New Delhi: Gyan Publishing House, 1994).

Prashad, Vijay, *Untouchable Freedom: A Social History of a Dalit Community*, (New Delhi: Oxford University Press, 2000).

Premi, Kusum K., *Trends of Enrolment of the Scheduled Caste Students in Higher Education (1964-77)*, (New Delhi: NIEPA, 1983).

Premi, Kusum K., Meena Srivastava, D.R. Pratap, Moshin Nadeem, K.R. Shah, P.C. Sharma and Madhu Singh, *Scheduled Castes and Scheduled Tribes in Industrial Training Institutes: A Study of Five States*, (New Delhi: NIEPA, 1983).

Premi, Kusum K., *Scheduled Castes and Scheduled Tribes in Industrial Training Institutes: A Study of Five States*, (New Delhi: Vikas, 1989).

Premlatha, P.N., "Ambedkar and Communal Award: Its Impact on Tamil Nadu", in *Ambedkar and Social Justice*, Vol. I, (New Delhi: Director, Publications Division, Ministry of Information and Broadcasting, 1992), [on behalf of Baba Saheb Dr. B.R. Ambedkar Birth Centenary Celebrations Committee, Ministry of Welfare, Government of India].

Price, John, "Outcaste Status and Untouchability in Asia", in G. De Vos and H. Wagatsuma (eds.), *Japan's Invisible Race: Caste in Culture and Personality*, (Berkeley, CA: University of California Press, 1967).

Price, John, "A History of the Outcastes: Untouchability in Japan", in G. De Vos and H. Wagatsuma (eds.), *Japan's Invisible Race: Caste in Culture and Personality*, (Berkeley, CA: University of California Press, 1967).

The Problem of Untouchability in Mysore, (Banglore: The Mysore State Anti-Untouchability League, 1933).

Proceedings of the Workshop and Exhibition on Traditional Leather Industry, (Chennai: A.V. PPST Centre, Anna University, 1998).

Progress of Education of Scheduled Caste and Scheduled Tribes in Rajasthan, 1977-78, (Bikaner: Directorate of Primary and Secondary Education, 1979), [Studies in Educational Statistics, 1979].

Pulloppillil, Thomas, *Church, Private Property and the Scheduled Castes*, (New Delhi: Intercultural Publications, 1998).

Punalekar, Devyani, "Atrocities on and Agonies of Gujarat Dalit Women", in P.G. Jogdand (ed.), *Dalit Women in India: Issues and Perspectives*, (New Delhi: Gyan Publishing House, in collaboration with University of Poona, Pune, 1995).

Punalekar, S.P., *School Dropout Among Harijan Children: Causes and Cure*, (New Delhi: Central Institute of Research and Training in Public Cooperation, 1975).

Punalekar, S.P., *Aspects of Class and Caste in Social Tensions: A Study of Marathwada Riots*, (Surat: Centre for Social Studies, 1981).

Punalekar, S.P., "On Dalitism and Gender", in P.G. Jogdand (ed.), *Dalit Women in India: Issues and Perspectives*, (New Delhi: Gyan Publishing House, in collaboration with University of Poona, Pune, 1995).

Punalekar, S.P., *Dalit Literature in Western India: An Annotated Bibliography*, (Surat: Centre for Social Studies, 1996).

Punalekar, S.P., "Development Against Empowerment of the Poor? A Case Study of Rural Dalit Masses", in S.M. Michael (ed.), *Dalits in Modern India*, (New Delhi: Vistaar Publications, 1999).

Punalekar, S.P., "Dalit Literature and Dalit Identity", in Ghanshyam Shah (ed.), *Dalit Identity and Politics*, (New Delhi: Sage Publications, 2001), [Cultural Subordination and the Dalit Challenge, Vol. 2 of Sage series].

Pundir, J.K., "Law and Weaker Sections", in I.N. Tiwary et.al. (eds.), *Challenges and Alternatives*, (U.P. Political Association, 1980).

Pundir, J.K., "Weaker Sections: Scheduled Castes and Beyond in Rural Settling", in A.P. Sarasevat (ed.), *The Poor and the Poverty – Social, Economic and Political Dimensions*, (Meerut: Sawrup, 1989).

Pundir, J.K., "Social Development Through New Institutions and Scheduled Castes in the Rural Setting", in R.S. Tripathi & P.D. Tiwari (eds.), *Dimensions of Scheduled Caste Development: Problems and Prospects*, (New Delhi: Uppal, 1991).

Pundir, J.K., *Changing Patterns of Scheduled Castes*, (Jaipur: Rawat, 1997).

Pundir, J.K., *Banking Bureaucracy and Social Networks: Scheduled Castes in the Process of Development*, (New Delhi: Sarup and Sons, 1998).

Pundir, J.K., "State Measures for Rural Development of Scheduled Castes", in V.K. Pant and B.S. Bisht (ed.),

Backward Communities: Identity, Development and Transformation, (New Delhi: Gyan, 1999).

Pundit, Nalini, *Swatantryottar Kalatil Dalianche Prashna*, (Pune: Sadhana Prakashan, 1982), (in Marathi).

Punekar, S.M., *Harijan Contribution to Medieval Thought*, (Bangalore: Prasaranga, Bangalore University, 1991).

Punjab State, Government of, Public Relations Department, *Harijan Welfare in Punjab*, (Chandigarh: 1961).

Purandare, C.K., "'People of India': Some Prima Facie Inferences with Reference to Scheduled Castes and Scheduled Tribes", in P.G. Jogdand (ed.), *Dalit Women in India: Issues and Perspectives*, (New Delhi: Gyan Publishing House, in collaboration with University of Poona, Pune, 1995).

Purane, K.D., *Untouchability and the Law: "The Ground Reality"*, (New Delhi: Gyan, 2000).

Puri, Harish K., "Dr. B.R. Ambedkar and National Unity", in Bhajan Kaur (ed.), *The Philosophy of Dr. B.R. Ambedkar*, (Chandigarh: Dr. Ambedkar Study Circle, 1999).

Purohit, B.D. and S.D. Purohit, *Handbook of Reservations for Scheduled Castes and Scheduled Tribes (in the Matters of Concerning Employment, Education and Election)*, (New Delhi: Jain Sons Publications, 1990).

Pushpa Kumari, V., *Poverty Alleviation and Rural Harijans*, (New Delhi: Discovery Publishing House, 1991).

Pushparaj, P.K., *As an Untouchable Feels Untouchability*, (Delhi: Servants of Untouchables Society, Tract No. I, 1933), [Pamphlet].

Pushpendra, "Dalit Assertion through Electoral Politics", in Ghanshyam Shah (ed.), *Dalit Identity and Politics*, (New Delhi: Sage Publications, 2001), [Cultural Subordination and the Dalit Challenge, Vol. 2 of Sage series].

Pyarelal (Nair or Nayyar), *The Epic Fast*, (Ahmedabad: Mohanlal Maganlal Bhatt, 1932).

Pye-Smith, Charlie, *Rebels and Outcastes: A Journey through Christian India*, (London: Viking, 1997).

Radhakrishna, P., "Ambedkar on Marx, Buddha and the Oppressed", in *National Seminar on Marx, Ambedkar and Polarization of Oppressed and Exploited Classes in India,* (New Delhi: Sanjivayya Institute of Socio-Economic Studies, 1991).

Radhakrishna, P., "Ambedkar's Legacy to Dalits: Has the Nation Reneged on its Problems", in V.T. Patil (ed.), *Studies in Ambedkar,* (Delhi: Devika Publications, 1995).

Radhakrishnan, S., "Ambedkar: A True Patriot", in B.K. Ahluwalia and Shashi Ahluwalia (eds.), *B.R. Ambedkar and Human Rights,* (New Delhi: Vivek Publishing Company, 1981).

Radhakrishnan, S. and Ranjana Kumari, *Impact of Education on Scheduled Caste Youth in India: A Study of Social Transformation in Bihar and Madhya Pradesh,* (New Delhi: Radiant Publishers, 1989).

Raghavaiah, V., *Nomads,* (Delhi: Bhartiya Adim Jati Sevak Sangh, 1968).

Raghavakumari, A.S., "Social Attitudes and Problems of Scheduled Caste and Scheduled Tribe Girls in Secondary Schools", (Mysore: Department of Education, Mysore University, 1986), [A research monograph, out of project financed by the NCERT].

Raghavendra Rao, J.V., "Dr. Ambedkar and Education", in *Ambedkar and Social Justice,* Vol. II, (New Delhi: Director, Publications Division, Ministry of Information and Broadcasting, 1992), [on behalf of Baba Saheb Dr. B.R. Ambedkar Birth Centenary Celebrations Committee, Ministry of Welfare, Government of India].

Raghavendra Rao, J.V., "Education and Emancipation of Dalits: Dr. B.R. Ambedkar's Perspective", in *Dr. B.R. Ambedkar Memorial Lectures,* (Hyderabad: Dr. B.R. Ambedkar Memorial Trust, 1993), [This Lecture was originally delivered on 6 December 1988].

Raghavendra Rao, J.V., "Dr. Ambedkar on Education", in M.L. Ranga (ed.), *B.R. Ambedkar: His Life, Work and Relevance,* (New Delhi: Manohar, 2000).

Raghavendra Rao, K., "Ambedkar's Concept of Socio-Economic Development", in A.M. Rajasekharaiah (ed.), *The Socio-Economic Transformation of India—Dr. Ambedkar's Vision,* (Dharwad: Karnatak University, 1983).

Raghavendra Rao, K., "Dr. Ambedkar's Political Ideas: The Limits of Liberalism—A Brief Comment", in K.K. Kavlekar and A.S. Chousalkar (eds.), *Political Ideas and Leadership of Dr. B.R. Ambedkar,* (Pune: Vishwanil, 1989).

Raghavendra Rao, K., *Babasaheb Ambedkar,* (New Delhi: Sahitya Academy, 1993), [Makers of Indian Literature Series].

Raghavendra Rao, K., "Babasaheb Ambedkar: History, Society and Polity – An Exploration in Indian Theory", in V.T. Patil (ed.), *Studies in Ambedkar,* (Delhi: Devika Publications, 1995).

Rai, B., "Dr. Ambedkar's Vision of New India", in Bhajan Kaur (ed.), *The Philosophy of Dr. B.R. Ambedkar,* (Chandigarh: Dr. Ambedkar Study Circle, 1999).

Rai, Lala Lajpat, *Presidential Speech at the Depressed Classes Conference,* (Lahore: 1913).

Rai, Lala Lajpat, *On the Upliftment of the Depressed Classes,* (Lahore: 1914).

Raj, Anthony, "Disobedience: A Legitimate Act or Dalit Liberation ", in M.E. Prabhakar (ed.), *Towards a Common Dalit Theology,* (Delhi: Indian Society for Promoting Christian Knowledge, 1989).

Raj, Anthony, "Disobedience: A Legitimate Act or Dalit Liberation", in Arvind P. Nirmal (ed.), *Toward a Common Dalit Ideology,* (Madras: Gurukul Lutheran Theological College and Research Institute, 1990), [Papers presented at the National Seminar on Dalit Ideology organized by the Department of Dalit Theology, Gugukul Lutheran Theological College and Research Institute].

Raj, Anthony, *Children of a Lesser God (Dalit Christians),* (Madurai: DCLM, 1992).

Raj, Anthony, "The Dalit Christian Reality in Tamil Nadu", in A. Kanjamala (ed.), *Integral Mission Dynamics: An*

Interdisciplinary Study of the Catholic Church in India, (New Delhi: Intercultural Publications, 1995).

Raj, E.S., Lourdswamy, J. Daniel, J. Masish and M. Augustine, *Demand for Restoration of Equal Rights for Christian Dalits*, (New Delhi: National Co-ordination Committee for Dalit Christians, 1996).

Raj, Inder, "Dr. Ambedkar Study Circle's Vision", in Bhajan Kaur (ed.), *The Philosophy of Dr. B.R. Ambedkar*, (Chandigarh: Dr. Ambedkar Study Circle, 1999).

Raj, M.C., *From Periphery to Centre: Analysis of the Paradigm of Globalization, Casteism and Dalitism*, (Tumkur: Ambedkar Resource Centre and Rural Education for Development Society, 1998).

Raj, M.C., *From the Year 2000...Ambedkar Era*, (Tumkur, Karnataka: Ambedkar Resource Centre, Rural Education for Development Society, 2000).

Raj, M.C., *Dalitology: The Book of the Dalit People*, (Tumkur, Karnataka: Ambedkar Resource Centre, Rural Education for Development Society, 2002).

Rajagopalachari, C., *Plighted Word: Being an Account of the History and Objects of the Untouchability Abolition and Temple Entry Bills*, (Delhi: Servants of Untouchables Society, 1933).

Rajagopalachari, C., *The Impending Fast of Mahatma Gandhi: The Issues Explained*, (Delhi: Servants of Untouchables Society, 1933).

Rajagopalachari, C., *Ambedkar Refuted*, (Bombay: Hind Kitabs, 1946), 2nd edition.

Rajagopalan, C., "Educational Progress and Problems of Scheduled Caste and Scheduled Tribe Students in Karnataka (High Schools)", (Varanasi: Department of Sociology, Banaras Hindu University, 1974), [A research monograph, out of a project financed by the ICSSR].

Rajah, M.C., *The Oppressed Hindus*, (Madras: The Huxley Press, 1925).

Rajan, Ambeth, *My Bahujan Samaj Party*, (New Delhi: ABCDE Publications, 1994).

Rajasekharaiah, A.M., *B.R. Ambedkar: The Politics of Emancipation*, (Bombay: Sindhu Publications, 1971).

Rajasekharaiah, A.M., "Dr. B.R. Ambedkar on Reservation Policy", in B.A.V. Sharma and K. Madhusudhan Reddy (eds.), *Reservation Policy in India*, (New Delhi: Light and Life Publishers, 1979).

Rajasekharaiah, A.M., "The Constitution Maker", in B.K. Ahluwalia and Shashi Ahluwalia (eds.), *B.R. Ambedkar and Human Rights*, (New Delhi: Vivek Publishing Company, 1981).

Rajasekharaiah, A.M. (ed.), *The Socio-Economic Transformation of India—Dr. Ambedkar's Vision (Papers and Proceedings of the National Level Symposium)*, (Dharwad: Karnatak University, 1983), [Dr. Babasaheb Ambedkar Memorial Publications, III].

Rajasekharaiah, A.M., "Ambedkar and Gandhi—Contrasting Vision of Emancipation", in A.M. Rajasekharaiah (ed.), *The Socio-Economic Transformation of India—Dr. Ambedkar's Vision*, (Dharwad: Karnatak University, 1983).

Rajasekharaiah, A.M., *B.R. Ambedkar: The Quest for Social Justice*, (New Delhi: Uppal, 1989).

Rajasekhariah, A.M., "Dr. Ambedkar and Political Mobilization of the Scheduled Castes", in K.K. Kavlekar and A.S. Chausalkar (eds.), *Political Ideas and Leadership of Dr. B.R. Ambedkar*, (Pune: Vishwanil Publications, 1989).

Rajasekhariah, A.M., "Ambedkar as a Philosopher and a Theoretician: An Evaluation", in K.S. Chalam (ed.), *The Relevance of Ambedkarism in India*, (Jaipur: Rawat, 1993).

Rajendran, G., *The Izhava Community and Kerala Politics*, (Trivandrum: The Kerala Akademy of Political Science, 1974).

Rajpramukh, K.E., "Practicability of Ambedkar's View on Annihilation of Caste", in K.S. Chalam (ed.), *The Relevance of Ambedkarism in India*, (Jaipur: Rawat, 1993).

Rajsekhar Shetty, V., *Dalit Movement in Karnataka*, (Madras: The Christian Literature Society, 1978).

Rajsekhar, V.T., *Apartheid in India*, (Banglore: Dalit Sahitya Academy, 1975).

Rajshekar, V.T., *Hinduism Vs Movement of Untouchables in India*, (Bangalore: Dalit Sahitya Academy, 1983).

Rajsekhar, V.T., *Ambedkar and His Conversion*, (Banglore: Dalit Sahitya Academy, 1983).

Rajshekar, V.T., *'Merit', My Foot: (Reply to Anti-Reservation Racists)*, (Bangalore: Dalit Sahitya Akademy, 1987).

Rajshekar, V.T., *Christians and Dalit Liberation*, (Bangalore: Dalit Sahitya Academy, 1987).

Rajsekhar, V.T., "Ambedkar and the Religious Solution", in Sanghasen Singh and Priyasen Singh (eds.), *Ambedkar on Buddhist Conversion and Its Impact*, (Delhi: Eastern Book Linkers, 1990).

Rajshekar, V.T. and M. Gopinath, *Textbook on Dalit Movement in India: Meaning and Message*, (Bangalore: Dalit Sahitya Akademy, 1994).

Rajsekhar, V.T., *Reservation Policy and Ambedkarism (A most comprehensive Thesis on Dalit Human Rights Stolen by the Brahminical Ruling Class of India)*, (Banglore: Dalit Sahitya Academy, 1997), [Pamphlet].

Rajsekhar, V.T., *Aggression on Indian Culture*, (Banglore: Dalit Sahitya Academy, 2001).

Rajsekhar, V.T., *Caste: A Nation within the Nation – Recipe for a Bloodless Revolution*, (Banglore: Books for Change, 2002).

Raju, G.G., *The Life of B.R. Ambedkar*, (Hyderabad: Babasaheb Dr. Ambedkar Memorial Society, 1979).

Raju, K.S., "Bharat Ratna Dr. Ambedkar", in *Ambedkar and Social Justice*, Vol. II, (New Delhi: Director, Publications Division, Ministry of Information and Broadcasting, 1992), [on behalf of Baba Saheb Dr. B.R. Ambedkar Birth Centenary Celebrations Committee, Ministry of Welfare, Government of India].

Raju, K.S., "Basic Programmes for Economic Development of Scheduled Castes in Punjab and their Functioning", in V.S. Mahajan and B.S. Mann (eds.), *Economic Development of Scheduled Castes*, (New Delhi: Anmol, 1997).

Ralhan, O.P. (ed.), *The Depressed Classes in India*, (Delhi: n.d.).

Ram, Chandrika, *Plan for Harijans and Other Backward Classes*, (Foreword by N.V. Gadgil), (New Delhi: Bharatiya Depressed Classes League, 1951).

Ram, Daulat, "Marx, Ambedkar and Polarization of Oppressed and Exploited Classes in India", in *National Seminar on Marx, Ambedkar and Polarization of Oppressed and Exploited Classes in India*, (New Delhi: Sanjivayya Institute of Socio-Economic Studies, 1991).

Ram, Jagjivan, *Caste Challenge in India*, (New Delhi: Vision Books, 1980).

Ram, Nandu, "Social Stratification and Mobility Among the Scheduled Castes in Urban India", in K. Seshadri and Eshanul Haq (eds.), *Studies in the Problems of the Third World*, (New Delhi: Uppal, 1985).

Ram, Nandu, "Law and the Atrocities on the Weaker Sections in India", in R.G. Singh (ed.), *The Depressed Classes of India*, (New Delhi: B.R. Publishing Corporation, 1986).

Ram, Nandu, "Scheduled Castes: Social Stratification and Sources of Mobility in Urban India", in K.L. Sharma (ed.), *Social Stratification in India*, (New Delhi: Manohar, 1986).

Ram, Nandu, "From Atrocities to Protest Movement: An Urge for Social Development", in S.K. Srivastava and A.L. Srivastava (eds.), *Social Movements for Development*, (Allahabad: 1988).

Ram, Nandu, *The Mobile Scheduled Castes: Rise of a New Middle Class*, (Delhi: Hindustan Publishing Corporation, 1988).

Ram, Nandu, "Atrocities and Segregation in an Urban Social Structure: View from the Bottom", in Yogesh Atal (ed.), *Understanding Indian Society*, (New Delhi: Har Anand, 1992).

Ram, Nandu, "Atrocities on the Weaker Sections: Some Developmental Constructs", in S.N. Pawar and R.B. Patil (eds.), *Problems and Prospects of Development in Rural India*, (New Delhi: Mittal Publications, 1994).

Ram, Nandu, *Beyond Ambedkar: Essays on Dalits in India*, (New Delhi: Har-Anand Publications, 1995).

Ram, Nandu, "Dalit Movements in India: A Perspective from the Below", in Murti Desai et. al. (eds.), *Towards People-Centre Development*, (Bombay: Tata Institute of Social Sciences, 1998).

Ram, Nandu, "Forms and Styles of Dalit Movements in India: A Macro Sociological Perspective", in Anand Kumar (ed.), *Nation Building in India*, (New Delhi: Radiant Publications, 1999).

Ram, Nandu, *Encyclopedia of Scheduled Castes in India*, 5 vols., (New Delhi: Gyan Publications, forthcoming).

Ram, Nandu, "Equality Through Legislation: Social Consequences of Gradual Change", in Ghanshyam Shah (ed.), *Dalits and the State*, (New Delhi: Concept Publishing Company, 2002), [Published for Centre for Rural Studies, Lal Bahadur Shastri National Academy of Administration, Mussoorie].

Ram, Pars, *A UNESCO Study of Social Tensions in Aligarh, 1950-51*, (Ahmedabad: New Order Book Co., 1955), [Chapter X is on 'Attitudes of Harijans'].

Rama Naidu, M.B., *The Adi Dravida: His Cult, Past and Present*, (Chidabaram: 1921). [Presidential Address Delivered at the Adi Dravida Conference held at Chidambaram, on 21 April 1921].

Rama Rao, T.S., "Protective Discrimination and Educational Planning", in G.S. Sharma (ed.), *Educational Planning: Its Legal and Constitutional Implications in India*, (Bombay: N.M. Tripathi, 1967).

Ramaiah, A., "The Dalit Issue: A Hindu Perspective", in James Massey (ed.), *Indigenous People: Dalits. Dalit Issues in Today's Theological Debate*, (Delhi: ISPCK, 1998), (First Published in1994).

Ramaiah, Kinjarama, *Educational Performance of Scheduled Castes*, (New Delhi: APH Publishing Co., 1998).

Ramaiah, P. and K. Sateesh Reddy, *Dr. B.R. Ambedkar's Economic Philosophy*, (New Delhi: Delta Publishing House, 1994).

Ramakrishna, H.A., "Hinduism and Dr. B.R. Ambedkar: A Study in Paradox", in *Ambedkar and Social Justice*, Vol. II, (New Delhi: Director, Publications Division, Ministry of Information and Broadcasting, 1992), [on behalf of Baba Saheb Dr. B.R. Ambedkar Birth Centenary Celebrations Committee, Ministry of Welfare, Government of India].

Ramanujachari, K., "The Present Condition of the Low Castes", in C.Y. Chintamani (ed.), *Indian Social Reform*, (Madras: Thompson Press, 1901).

Ramaswami, K., "Ambedkar: The Cornerstone of the Constitution", in *Ambedkar and Social Justice*, Vol. I, (New Delhi: Director, Publications Division, Ministry of Information and Broadcasting, 1992), [on behalf of Baba Saheb Dr. B.R. Ambedkar Birth Centenary Celebrations Committee, Ministry of Welfare, Government of India].

Ramaswami, Periyar E.V., *Why Brahmins Hate Reservation?* (Madras: Periyar Self Respect Propaganda Institute, 1983).

Ramaswami Naicker, E.V., *Untouchablility, History of Vaikom Agitation*, (Madras: Periyar Self Respect Propaganda Institute, 1980).

Ramaswamy, K., "B.R. Ambedkar: A Multi-Dimensional Personality", in Shyam Lal and K.S. Saxena (eds.), *Ambedkar and Nation-Building*, (Jaipur: Rawat, 1998).

Ramaswamy, K., "Ambedkar: A True Democrat and Nationalist", in Shyam Lal and K.S. Saxena (eds.), *Ambedkar and Nation-Building*, (Jaipur: Rawat, 1998).

Ramaswamy, K.V., *India's Untouchable Saints*, (Madras: G.A. Natesan & Co., 1934).

Ramotra, Krishan Chand, "Sex Disparity in Scheduled Caste Literacy in Maharashtra: A Case of Selected Villages", in R.S. Tripathi and P.D. Tiwari (eds.), *Dimensions of Scheduled Caste Development in India: Problems and Prospects*, (New Delhi: Uppal, 1991).

Ramteke, Amar, "Dalit Theatre", in Bojja Tharakam (ed.), *The First All India Dalit Writers Conference: A*

Commemorative Volume and Who's Who, (Hyderabad: Dr. B.R. Ambedkar Memorial Trust, 1994).

Rana, Mahendra Pratap, "Protection of Human Rights or Protection of Rights of Caste in India", in R.M. Pal (ed.), *Protection of Human Rights: A Critique (With Special Reference to SC/STs, the Girl Child/Women belonging to SC/STs, marginalized Section and the Minorities,* (New Delhi: Indian Social Institute, 1999), [Proceedings of the National Seminar held on 13 and 14 November 1998 at the Indian Social Institute].

Rana, Mahendra Pratap, "Dalit Economy and Identity", in Ambrose Pinto (ed.), *Dalit Assertion for Identity,* (New Delhi: Indian Social Institute, 1999), [Proceedings of the National Seminar of Dalit Postgraduate and Research Students held on 23-25 January 1999 in the Indian Social Institute].

Randeria, Shalini, "Death and Defilement: Divergent Accounts of Untouchability in Gujarat", in Gabriella Eichinger Ferro-Luzzi (ed.), *Rites and Beliefs in Modern India,* (New Delhi: Manohar, 1990).

Randhawa, M.S., "Dagis, Kolis", in *Farmers of India,* Vol. I, (New Delhi: 1959).

Ranga, M.L. (ed.), *B.R. Ambedkar: His Life, Work and Relevance,* (New Delhi: Manohar, 2000).

Ranga, N.G., "Dr. B.R. Ambedkar: As I saw him", in Rabi Ray (ed.), *Dr. B.R. Ambedkar,* (New Delhi: Lok Sabha Secretariat, 1991), [Eminent Parliamentarians Monograph Series 12].

Ranga Rao, A.V.P., *Urbanization, Occupational Mobility and Social Integration: A Study of Scheduled Castes,* (New Delhi: Deep and Deep, 1989).

Rangari, Ashok D., *Indian Caste System and Education,* (New Delhi: Deep and Deep, 1984).

Rangnekar, S.B., *The Scheduled Caste Economy of Punjab: A 1961 Census Based Study on Deprivation and Inequality,* (Chandigarh: Department of Economics, Punjab University, 1977-78).

Ranjan, P. Swarnalata, "Christian Dalit Aspirations as expressed by Jashuva Kavi in Gabbilam (The Bat)", in James Massey (ed.), *Indigenous People, Dalits: Dalit Issues in Today's Theological Debate,* (Delhi: ISPCK, 1998), (First Published in1994).

Ranjan, Vinay, "Musahars: Beyond the Stereotype", in Hemant Joshi and Sanjay Kumar (eds.), *Asserting Voices: Changing Culture, Identity and Livelihood of the Musahars in the Gangetic Plains,* (Delhi: Deshkal Publications, 2002).

Ransubhe, Suryanarayana, "Frontiers of Dalit Literature", in Bojja Tharakam (ed.), *The First All India Dalit Writers Conference: A Commemorative Volume and Who's Who,* (Hyderabad: Dr. B.R. Ambedkar Memorial Trust, 1994).

Ranveer, Kashinath, "Dalit Literature and African American Literature: Roots against Dominant Ideology and Cultural Hegemony", in Harish Narang (ed.), *Writing Black Writing Dalit: Essays in Black African and Dalit Indian Writings,* (Shimla: Indian Institute of Advanced Studies, 2002).

Rao, Hemalatha, and M.Devendra Babu, *Scheduled Castes and Tribes: Socio-Economic Upliftment Programmes,* (New Delhi: Ashish, 1994).

Rao, M.J.A., "Sanskritization among the Tiyas of North Malabar", in Bala Ratnam (ed.), *Anthropology on the March,* (Madras: The Book Centre, 1963).

Rao, M.S.A., "Education, Social Stratification and Mobility", in M.S. Gore, I.P. Desai and Suma Chitnis (eds.), *Papers in the Sociology of Education in India,* (New Delhi: NCERT, 1967).

Rao, P. Kodanda and Mary Campbell Rao, "Critique of Group Prejudice with Special Reference to Harijans", in Manilal Balabhai Nanavati and C.N. Vakil (eds.), *Group Prejudices in India: A Symposium,* (Bombay: Vora, 1951).

Rao, Ram Bachan, "Dr. Bhim Rao Ambedkar: A Charismatic Personality", in R.B. Rao (ed.), *Bharat-Ratna Dr. Ambedkar,* (Allahabad: Chugh Publications, 1993).

Rao, R.B. (ed.), *Bharat-Ratna Dr. Ambedkar*, (Allahabad: Chugh Publications, 1993).

Rastogi, S.P., *The Impact of Constitutional Provisions Upon he Uplift of Harijans*, (Lucknow: Account Organisation, Lucknow University, 1977).

Rastogi, Sita Ram, *Economic Status and Fertility: A Study of the Harijans in Mirzapur*, (Lucknow: Lucknow University, 1979).

Ratan, Ram, "The Changing Religion of the Bhangis of Delhi: A Case of Sanskritization", in L.P. Vidyarthi (ed.), *Aspects of Religion in India*, (Meerut: Kedar Rath Nam Rath, 1960).

Rath, R. and S.K. Misra, "The Study of Scheduled Caste and Scheduled Tribe College Students in Orissa", (Department of Psychology, Utkal University, 1974), [A research Monograph, out of project financed by the ICSSR].

Rath, R., A.S. Daste and V.N. Dash, *Cognitive Abilities and School Achievements of the Socially Disadvantaged Children in Primary Schools*, (New Delhi: Allied, 1979).

Rath, Rajalaxmi, "Social Transformation among Scheduled Castes in Bihar due to Job Reservation – Case Study of Three Generations in Bihar", in A.K. Lal (ed.), *Protective Discrimination: Ideology and Praxis*, (New Delhi: Concept, 2002), [Published for B.G. Pant Social Science Institute, Allahabad].

Rath, S.N., "Dr. Ambedkar and His Legacy to Modern India", in P.K. Mohapatra (ed.), *Religion and Social Change*, (Cuttack: Akash, 1993).

Rathnaswamy, A.M. Wamit, *Harijans in a Changing India*, (Madras: Author, 1947).

Rathod, P.V. and Vijay Kumar, "The Working of the Scheduled Castes and Scheduled Tribes (Prevention of Atrocities) Act 1989 in Gujarat", in Ghanshyam Shah (ed.), *Dalits and the State*, (New Delhi: Concept Publishing Company, 2002), [Published for Centre for Rural Studies, Lal Bahadur Shastri National Academy of Administration, Mussoorie].

Ratnaiah, K., *Social Change Among Malas (An Ex-Untouchable Caste in South India)*, (New Delhi: Discovery Publishing House, 1991).

Rattu, Nanak Chand, *Bharatha Rathna Babasaheb Dr. Ambedkar: His Last Days and His Last Message*, (Nellore: Dr. Ambedkar Publications Society, 1991).

Rattu, Nanak Chand, "With Babasaheb till the End", in K.N. Kadam (ed.), *Dr. B.R. Ambedkar: The Emancipator of the Oppressed*, (Bombay: Popular Prakashan, 1993).

Rattu, Nanak Chand, *Reminiscences and Remembrances of Dr. B.R. Ambedkar*, (New Delhi: Falcon Books, 1995).

Rattu, Nanak Chand, *Last Few Years of Dr. Ambedkar*, (New Delhi: Amrit, 1997), [Published for Dr. Ambedkar Memorial Committee of Great Britain, UK].

Rauschenbusch-Clough, Emma, *While Sewing Sandals: Tales of a Telugu Pariah Tribe*, (London: Hodder and Stoughton, 1899), [Experiences and folklore tales of Telugu speaking Dalits. Written by the wife of an American Missionary who baptized thousands of Andhra Dalits in the years 1878 and following. Reprinted after nearly one hundred years of its first publication by Asia Educational Services, New Delhi].

Ravankar, Ratna G., *The Indian Constitution: A Case Study of Backward Classes*, (Gramburry: Fairleigh Dickinson University Press, 1971).

Ravi Prasad, D.M., *Dalit Youth: A Sociological Study*, (New Delhi: A.P.H., 1997).

Ravindran, T.K., *Vaikkam Satyagraha and Gandhi*, (Trichur: Narayana Institute of Social and Cultural Development, 1975).

Ray, Baren, (edited with an Introductory Essay), *Gandhi's Campaign Against Untouchability, 1933-34: An Account from the Raj's Secret Official Reports*, (New Delhi: Gandhi Peace Foundation, 1996).

Ray, Rabi (ed.), *Dr. B.R. Ambedkar*, (New Delhi: Lok Sabha Secretariat, 1991), [Eminent Parliamentarians Monograph Series 12].

Ray, Renuka, "Dr. Ambedkar: A Social Revolutionary", in Rabi Ray (ed.), *Dr. B.R. Ambedkar*, (New Delhi: Lok Sabha Secretariat, 1991), [Eminent Parliamentarians Monograph Series 12].

Ray, S.N. and S. Chakravarti, *Brahmo Samaj: The Depressed Classes and Untouchables*, (Calcutta: 1933).

Rayan, Samuel, "The Challenge of the Dalit Issue: Some Theological Perspectives", in V. Devasahayam (ed.), *Dalits and Women: Quest for Humanity*, (Madras: The Gurukul Summer Institute, 1992).

Rayappa, P. Hanumantha and Deepak Grover, *Employment Planning for the Rural Poor: The Case of Scheduled Castes and Scheduled Tribes*, (New Delhi: Sterling Publishers, 1980).

Rayappa, P. Hanumantha and P. Mutharayappa, *Backwardness and Welfare of Scheduled Castes and Scheduled Tribes in India*, (New Delhi: Ashish, 1986).

Raza, Moonis and Kusum K. Premi, *Reservation in Higher Education for Scheduled Castes and Scheduled Tribes: A Policy Framework*, (New Delhi: NIEPA, 1982).

Raza, Moonis and S.M. Dubey, *Monitoring of the Functioning of the Post-Matric Scholarship Scheme: Findings and Remedial Measures – National Profile*, (New Delhi: NIEPA, 1983).

Raza, Moonis and S.M. Dubey, *Post-Matric Scholarship Scheme for Scheduled Castes and Scheduled Tribes: A Pilot Study*, (New Delhi: NIEPA, 1983).

Raza, Moonis and S.M. Dubey, *Retention, Failure, Repetition and Dropout in Higher Education: A Cohort Analysis of SC and ST Students, National Profile–3*, (New Delhi: NIEPA, 1984).

Raza, Moonis and S.M. Dubey, *Social Background, Living Conditions and Academic Performance of Post-Matric Scholarship Holders: A National Study of SC and ST Students, National Profile – 4*, (New Delhi: NIEPA, 1984).

Raza, Moonis, Aijazuddin Ahmed and Sheel Chand Nuna, *Educational Development in India: Some Aspects of Equity*, (New Delhi: Indian Association of Educational Planning and Administration, 1985), [Second National Conference, 5-6 January 1985].

Reddy, M. Gopalakrishna, "The Relevance of Ambedkarism in India Today", in K.S. Chalam (ed.), *The Relevance of Ambedkarism in India*, (Jaipur: Rawat, 1993).

Rege, Sharmila, "Caste and Gender: The Violence Against Women in India", in P.G. Jogdand (ed.), *Dalit Women in India: Issues and Perspectives*, (New Delhi: Gyan Publishing House, in collaboration with University of Poona, Pune, 1995).

Renukarya, C.K., "Land Reforms and Industrialisation", in *Ambedkar and Social Justice*, Vol. II, (New Delhi: Director, Publications Division, Ministry of Information and Broadcasting, 1992), [on behalf of Baba Saheb Dr. B.R. Ambedkar Birth Centenary Celebrations Committee, Ministry of Welfare, Government of India].

Renukarya, C.K., "Ambedkar's Views on Land Reforms and Industrialization: An Evaluation", in V.T. Patil (ed.), *Studies in Ambedkar*, (Delhi: Devika Publications, 1995).

Report of Activities of Bombay Board of Harijan Sevak Sangh, (Bombay: H.N. Trivedi, 1969).

Republican Party [of India], *Charter of Demands: Submitted to Shri Lal Bahadur Shastri, the Honorable Prime Miister of India*, (Delhi: Dada Sahib B.K. Gaikwad, B.P. Maurya and B.D. Khobaragade, 1964).

Republican Party [of India], *Election Manifesto of 1957*, (Delhi: B.D. Khobaragade, 1957).

Republican Party [of India], *Presidential Address by R.D. Bhandare*, (Bombay: R.D. Bhandare, (1965).

Research Team (S.P. Punalekar, Project Officer), *School Dropout Among Harijan Children: Causes and Cure*, (New Delhi: Central Institute of Research and Training in Public Cooperation, 1975).

Risley, Herbert Hope, *The Tribes and Castes of Bengal*, 4 vols., (Calcutta: Bengal Secretariat Press, 1891).

Robb, Peter (ed.), *Dalit Movements and the Meanings of Labour in India*, (Delhi: Oxford University Press, 1993).

Robertson, Alexander, *The Mahar Folk: A Study of Untouchables in Maharashtra*, (Calcutta: Y.M.C.A. Publishing House and Oxford University Press, 1938).

Robertson, B., *A Study of Untouchables in Maharashtra*, (Bombay: Y.M.C.A., n.d.).

Rodrigues, Valerian, "Making a Tradition Critical: Ambedkar's Reading of Buddhism", in P. Robb (ed.), *Dalit Movements and the Meanings of Labour in India*, (Delhi: Oxford University Press, 1993).

Rodrigues, Valerian, "Between Tradition and Modernity: The Gandhi – Ambedkar Debate", in A.K. Narain and D.C. Ahir (eds.), *Dr. Ambedkar, Buddhism and Social Change*, (Delhi: B.R. Publishing Corporation, 1994).

Rodrigues, Valerian, "Viewing Dalit Movement: Contending Perspectives", in Sandeep Pendse (ed.), *Dalit Movement Today*, (Bombay: Vikas Adhyayana Kendra, 1994), [Vikas Adhyayan Kendra, Bombay, *Perspectives* 1].

Rose, Horace Arther, *A Glossary of the Tribes and Castes of the Punjab and North-West Frontier Provinces*, based on the census report for the Punjab, 1893, by the late Sir Denzil Ibbetson and the census report for the Punjab, 1892, by Sir Edmond Maclagan and compiled by H.A. Rose, 3 vols., (Lahore: Printed by the Superintendent of Government Printing, 1916).

Roy Burman, B.K., *Report on the Practice of Untouchability and Other Social Disability in West Bengal*, (Calcutta: Cultural Research Institute, 1957), [Booklet].

Roy Burman, B.K. (ed.), *Bibliography on Scheduled Castes, Scheduled Tribes and Selected Marginal Communities of India*, 2 Vols., (New Delhi: Office of Registrar General of India, 1968). [This was a part of series in Census of India, 1961].

Roy Burman, B.K., *Social Mobility Movements among the Scheduled Castes and Scheduled Tribes of India*, (New Delhi: Registrar General of India, Ministry of Home Affairs, 1970).

Roy Burman, B.K. (ed.), *Social Mobility among the Sweepers of India*, (New Delhi: Registrar General of India, Ministry of Home Affairs, n.d.), [Mimeo].

Roy Burman, B.K., "The Problems of Untouchables", in Romesh Thaper (ed.), *Tribe, Caste and Religion in India*, (Meerut: The Macmillan Company India Limited, 1974).

Roy, A.K., *New Dalit Revolution*, (Patna: 1980).

Roy, Ajit, "The Nature of the Dalit Question Today", in Sandeep Pendse (ed.), *Dalit Movement Today*, (Bombay: Vikas Adhyayana Kendra, 1994), [Vikas Adhyayan Kendra, Bombay, *Perspectives* 1].

Roy, Nirode Bihar, *On the Origin of the Namasudras*, (Calcutta: Kirti Publishing Concern, 1967).

Roy, Ramashray and V.B. Singh, *Between Two Worlds: A Study of Harijan Elites*, (Delhi: Discovery Publishing House, 1987).

Roy, Ramshray, "The Political Dilemma of the Scheduled Castes", in Ramashray Roy and Richard Sisson (eds.), *Diversity and Dominance in India Politics*, Vol. 2: *Division, Deprivation and the Congress*, (New Delhi: 1990).

Roy, Ramashray and Vijay Bahadur Singh, "The Harijan Elite at the Cross Roads: Results from a Survey", in Subrata Kumar Mitra (ed.), *Politics of Positive Discrimination: A Cross National Perspective*, (Bombay: Popular Prakashan, 1990).

Roy, Ramshray, *Dalits, Development and Democracy*, (Delhi: Shipra Publications, 1999).

Rozario, Mary Rita, *Broken Lives: Dalit Women and Girls in Prostitution*, (Tumkur: Ambedkar Resource Centre, 2000).

Rudolph, Lloyd I. and Susanne Hoeber Rudolph, "Untouchability: The Test of Fellow Feeling", in their *The Modernity of Tradition: Political Development in India*, (Chicago: University of Chicago, 1967).

Russell, R.V. and Hira Lal, *The Tribes and Castes of the Central Provinces*, (Assisted by Hira Lal, 4 Vols., (London: Macmillan, 1916).

Saberwal, Satish, *Mobile Men: Limits to Social Change in Urban Punjab*, (New Delhi: Vikas, 1989).

Sachchidananda, "Research on Scheduled Caste: With Special reference to Change", in M.N. Srinivas et. al. (eds.), *A Survey of Research in Sociology and Social Anthropology*, I.C.S.S.R., Vol. I, (Bombay: Popular Prakashan, 1974).

Sachchidananda, *Education of Scheduled Castes and Scheduled Tribes in Bihar, Vol. I: School Students*, (Patna: A.N. Sinha Institute of Social Sciences, 1974), and Volume II: *College Students*, [financed by the ICSSR].

Sachchidananda, *The Harijan Elite: A Study of the Status, Networks, Mobility and Role in Social Transformation*, (Faridabad: Thomson Press, 1976).

Sachchidananda, K.D. Verma, Manohar Lal and Mishra, *Voluntary Effort in Adult Education*, (Calcutta: Naya Prakashan, 1981).

Sachchidananda, *Congress and the Harijans*, (New Delhi: Congress Centenary Celebrations Committee, 1985).

Sachidanand and Ramesh P. Sinha,. *Education and the Disadvantaged: A Study of Scheduled Castes and Tribes*, (New Delhi: Uppal, 1989).

Sachchidananda, *People at the Bottom: A Portrait of the Scavengers*, (New Delhi: Concept, 2001).

Sachchidananda, "Rethinking Scheduled Caste Reservation" in A.K. Lal (ed.), *Protective Discrimination: Ideology and Praxis*, (New Delhi: Concept, 2002), [Published for B.G. Pant Social Science Institute, Allahabad].

Sada, Asha, "Striding on the Difficult Paths of Life", in Hemant Joshi and Sanjay Kumar (eds.), *Asserting Voices: Changing Culture, Identity and Livelihood of the Musahars in the Gangetic Plains*, (Delhi: Deshkal Publications, 2002).

Saibaba, G., "Ambedkar as a Theoretician and Policy Maker", in K.S. Chalam (ed.), *The Relevance of Ambedkarism in India*, (Jaipur: Rawat, 1993).

Saksena, H.S., *Safeguards for Scheduled Castes and Scheduled Tribes: Founding Fathers' Views (An Exploration of the Constituent Assembly Debates)*, (New Delhi: Uppal Publishing House, 1981).

Salim, M., "Dr. B.R. Ambedkar: A Great Warrior against Untouchability", in R.B. Rao (ed.), *Bharat-Ratna Dr. Ambedkar*, (Allahabad: Chugh Publications, 1993).

Salve, R.N., "Impact of Government Welfare Measures on Scheduled Castes in India: A Sociological Study", in Yeshwant Khillare (ed.), *Present Status of Backward Classes in India*, (Aurangabad: Director, Centre for Studies on SCs/STs, 1997).

Samant, Anuradha, *A Study in the Motivational Background of the Scheduled Caste Teachers and Their Role in Social Transformation*, (Kolhapur: Department of Sociology, Shivaji University, 1992).

Samanta, D.K., *The Dominant Weak: A Case Study of the Nava Bouddha of Maharashtra*, (Calcutta: Anthropological Survey of India, 1991).

Samdani, Shakeel A., "Dr. Ambedkar: A Man of Principles and Saviour of Untouchables", in Nazeer H. Khan (ed.), *B.R. Ambedkar on Federalism, Ethnicity and Gender Justice*, (New Delhi: Deep & Deep, 2001).

Sanajaoba, Naorem, "De-stabilising Indian Apartheid: Ambedkarian Approach", in *Ambedkar and Social Justice*, Vol. I, (New Delhi: Director, Publications Division, Ministry of Information and Broadcasting, 1992), [on behalf of Baba Saheb Dr. B.R. Ambedkar Birth Centenary Celebrations Committee, Ministry of Welfare, Government of India].

Sanal Mohan, P., *Dalit Discourse and the Evolving New Self: Contest and Strategies*, (Kottayam: Mahatma Gandhi University, n.d.), [Lateral Study Series, School of Social Sciences, No. 13].

Sandanshiv, D.N., *Reservations for Social Justice: A Socio-Constitutional Approach*, (Bombay: Current Law Publishers, 1986).

Sandanshiv, D.N., "Ambedkar's Expounding of Social Justice", in Radhakant Nayak (ed.), *The Fourth World: Appraisal and Aspirations*, (New Delhi: Manohar, 1997).

Sangal, P.S., "Ambedkar: The Father of Indian Constitution", in *Ambedkar and Social Justice*, Vol. I, (New Delhi: Director, Publications Division, Ministry of Information and Broadcasting, 1992), [on behalf of Baba Saheb Dr. B.R. Ambedkar Birth Centenary Celebrations Committee, Ministry of Welfare, Government of India].

Sangavakshita, Mahasthavira, *Ambedkar and Buddhism*, (Glasgow: Windhorse Publications, 1986).

Sangeetha Rao, R., *Giants of the East: Ambedkar and Mao*, (New Delhi: Blumoon Books, 1997).

Sangeetha Rao, R., *Marx and Ambedkar*, (New Delhi: Blumoon Books, 1997).

Sangeetha Rao, R., *Dr. Ambedkar on Democracy and Social Justice*, (New Delhi: Blumoon Books, 1998).

Sangeetha Rao, R., *Ambedkar and Mao Tsetung*, (New Delhi: Sanjeevayya Institute of Socio-Economic Studies, n.d.).

Sangwan, O.P. (ed.), *Social System and the Dalit Identity*, (New Delhi: Commonwealth, 1996).

Sangwan, O.P. (ed.), *Dalit Society and the Challenge of Development*, (New Delhi: Commonwealth Publishers, 1996).

Sanjana, J.E., *Caste and Outcaste*, (Bombay: Thacker and Co., 1946).

Sankaran, S.R., "Administration and the Poor", in Ghanshyam Shah (ed.), *Dalits and the State*, (New Delhi: Concept Publishing Company, 2002), [Published for Centre for Rural Studies, Lal Bahadur Shastri National Academy of Administration, Mussoorie].

Santakumari, R., *Scheduled Castes and Welfare Measures*, (New Delhi: Classical Publishing Company, 1982).

Santanam, K., *Ambedkar's Attack*, (New Delhi: The Hindustan Times, 1946).

Santanam, K., *The Fight Against Untouchability: A Brief Review of the Phenomenal Progress Made During the Last Three Decades in the Eradication of an Ancient Evil,* (New Delhi: The Hindustan Times, 1949).

Sanyal, Annapurna, *Scheduled Castes and Scheduled Tribes in Indian Politics,* (Calcutta: Minerva, 1992).

Sanyal, Charu Chandra, *The Rajbanshis of North Bengal,* (Calcutta: The Asiatic Society, 1965).

Sanyal, S. and B.K. Roy Burman, *Social Mobility Movements among Scheduled Castes and Scheduled Tribes of India,* (New Delhi: Government of India, 1970).

Saradamani, K., *Emergence of a Slave Caste: Pulayas of Kerala,* (Delhi: People's Publishing House, 1980).

Saradamani, K., *Divided Poor: Study of a Kerala Village,* (Delhi: Ajanta Publications, 1981).

Sardar, G.B., *Gandhi and Ambedkar,* (Pune: Sugawa, 1987).

Sarkar, K.T., *Theory and Practice of Leather Manufacture,* (Chennai CCS Press, 1997).

Sarkar, S.K., "Socio-Economic Ideas of Ambedkar and their Relevance", in K.S. Chalam (ed.), *The Relevance of Ambedkarism in India,* (Jaipur: Rawat, 1993).

Sastry, E.S., *Socio-Economic Survey of Harijan Families in Andhra Pradesh,* (Hyderabad: Institute of Public Enterprise, 1976).

Sath Brahmana Ashram, Bezwada, *A Memorandum of the Real Indian Nationalist Congress Party, Bezwada, Submitted to the Government of India Regarding the Temple-entry Bill,* (Bezwada: 1934).

Sathe, S.P., "Reservation of Seats in Legislatures for Scheduled Castes", in Mohammed Imam (ed.), *Minorities and the Law,* (Bombay: N.M. Trip Ltd., 1972).

Sato, Masanori, "The Chamars of South-Eastern Rajasthan: A.D 1650-1800", in H. Kotani (ed.), *Caste System, Untouchability and the Depressed,* (New Delhi: Manohar, 1997).

Sattar, S. Abdul, "Dr. Ambedkar's Contribution to Buddhism", in *Ambedkar and Social Justice*, Vol. II, (New Delhi: Director, Publications Division, Ministry of Information and Broadcasting, 1992), [on behalf of Baba Saheb Dr. B.R. Ambedkar Birth Centenary Celebrations Committee, Ministry of Welfare, Government of India].

Satyanarayana, A., "Upper Caste Violence Against Dalits in Andhra Pradesh, 1947-1985", in Chandu Subba Rao and D. Francis (eds.), *Development of Weaker Sections (Essays in Honour of Prof. K.S. Chalam)*, (Jaipur: Rawat, 2000).

Satyanarayana, A., "Growth of Education Among the Dalit-Bahujan Communities in Modern Andhra, 1893 – 1947", in S Bhattacharya (ed), *Education and the Disprivileged: Nineteenth and Twentieth Century India*, (New Delhi, Orient Longman, 2002).

Satyanarayana Moorthy, A. and M.P. Narasimha Raju, "Harijans: Their Conversion and Problems", in R.S. Tripathi and P.D. Tiwari (eds.), *Dimensions of Scheduled Caste Development in India: Problems and Prospects*, (New Delhi: Uppal, 1991).

Sauter, Johannes A., *Unter Brahminen und Parias*, (Leipzig: K.E. Koehler, 1932).

Sawai, Pradnyashailee Bhagwan, "Dalit Women's Quest for Identity", in Ambrose Pinto (ed.), *Dalit Assertion for Identity*, (New Delhi: Indian Social Institute, 1999), [Proceedings of the National Seminar of Dalit Postgraduate and Research Students held on 23-25 January 1999 in the Indian Social Institute].

Saxena, P.K., *The Scheduled Caste Voter*, (New Delhi: Radha Publications, 1990).

Sayaji Rao III, Maharaja, *Speeches and Addresses of His Highness Sayaji Rao III Maharaja of Baroda*, (London: Macmillan, 1928), [This work contains addresses to Depressed Classes Mission Conferences in 1909 and 1918 speech on untouchability].

SCERT, *Career and Placement Study of Scheduled Caste and Scheduled Tribe Students in Select Districts of Tamil Nadu (1974-76)*, (Madras: State Council of Educational Research and Training, Tamil Nadu, 1979), [A research monograph, out of a project financed by the ICSSR].

Scheduled Caste Federation, *Resolutions Passed by the Working Committee of the All-India Scheduled Castes Federation on 21st August, 1955, Bombay*, (Chanda: All India Scheduled Castes Federation, 1955).

Scheduled Castes Students' Federation, *Report of the Second Session of the All India Scheduled Castes Students' Federation*, (held at Nagpur December 25-26 and 27, 1946), (Nagpur: 1947).

Scheduled Castes' Federation, *Election Manifesto of the All India Scheduled Castes Federation*, (New Delhi: P.N. Rajbhoj, General Secretary, 1951), [Pamphlet].

Schwartz, Michael B., "Indian Untouchable Texts of Resistance: Symbolic Domination and Historical Knowledge", in H.L. Seneviratne (ed.), *Identity, Consciousness and the Past: Forging of Caste and Community in India and Srilanka*, (Delhi: OUP, 1997).

Searle-Chatterjee, Mary, "The Polluted Identity of Work: A Study of Benares Sweepers", in Sandra Wallman (ed.), *Social Anthropology of Work*, (London: Academic Books, 1979).

Searle-Chatterjee, Mary, *Reversible Sex Roles: The Special Case of the Benares Sweepers*, (Oxford: Pergamon Press, 1981).

Searle-Chatterjee, "At the Threshold of Untouchability: Pallars and Valaiyars in a Tamil Village", in C. Fuller (ed.), *Caste Today*, (Oxford: Oxford University Press, 1996).

Sebastian, M., *Liberating the Caged Dalit Panther*, (Madras: Emerald Publishers, 1994).

Sekine, Y., *Theories of Pollution: Theoretical Perspective and Practice in a South Indian Tamil Village*, (Tokyo: Institute for the Study of Language and Culture of Asian and Africa, 1989).

Selected Statistics on Scheduled Caste, (New Delhi: Ministry of Home Affairs, 1984), [Occasional Papers on Development of Scheduled Castes].

Selvanathan, S., *Status of Scheduled Castes.* (New Delhi: Ashish Publishing House, 1989).

Sengupta, Nirmal, *Destitutes and Development: A Study of the Bauri Community in the Bokaro Region,* (New Delhi: Concept, 1979).

Sequeira, Fr. Leo, "Human Response to Dalit Women Today", in P.G. Jogdand (ed.), *Dalit Women in India: Issues and Perspectives,* (New Delhi: Gyan Publishing House, in collaboration with University of Poona, Pune, 1995).

Seth, Baij Nath, "The Social, Religious and Economic Conditions of the Chamars of Panchapargana in Chotanagpur", in Makhan Jha (ed.), *Scheduled Castes Today,* (New Delhi: M.D. Publications, 1997).

Seth, V.N., "Caste System and Status Change: A Study of Harijan Protest in Banda", in Satish K. Sharma (ed.), *Reforms Protest and Social Transformation,* (New Delhi: Ashish Publishing House, 1987).

Seviaray, B.R., "Marx, Ambedkar and Polarization of Oppressed and Exploited Classes in India", in *National Seminar on Marx, Ambedkar and Polarization of Oppressed and Exploited Classes in India,* (New Delhi: Sanjivayya Institute of Socio-Economic Studies, 1991).

Shabbir, M., *B.R. Ambedkar: Study in Law and Society,* (Jaipur: Rawat, 1997).

Shah, A.M., "Untouchability, the Untouchables and Social Change in Gujarat", in P. Hockings (ed.), *Dimensions of Social Life,* (Berlin: Mouton, 1987).

Shah, B.V. and J.D. Thaker, *Educational Problems of Scheduled Caste and Scheduled Tribe College Students in Gujarat,* (Vidyanagar: Department of Sociology, Sardar Ballabh Patel University, 1974), [A research monograph, out of a project financed by the ICSSR].

Shah, B.V. and J.D. Thaker, "Occupational Status of the Scheduled Castes in Gujarat", in Vimal P. Shah (ed.),

Removal of Untouchability, (Ahmedabad: Gujarat University, 1980).

Shah, Ghanshyam, *Politics of Scheduled Castes and Tribes (Adivasi and Harijan Leaders of Gujarat)*, (Bombay: Vora & Co., 1975).

Shah, Ghanshyam, "Anti-Untouchability Movements", in Vimal P. Shah (ed.), *Removal of Untouchability*, (Ahmedabad: Gujarat University, 1980).

Shah, Ghanshyam, "Anti-Untouchability Movements", in Centre For Social Studies, *Caste, Caste-Conflict and Reservation*, (Surat and Delhi: Ajanta Publications, 1985).

Shah, Ghanshyam, "Caste, Class and Reservation", in Haroobhai Mehta and Hasmukh Patel (eds.), *Dynamics of Reservation Policy*, (NewDelhi: 1985).

Shah, Ghanshyam, "Protective Discrimination, Equality and Political Will", in Vimal P. Shah and Binod C. Agrawal (eds.), *Reservation Policy, Programmes and Issues*, (Jaipur: Rawat Publications, 1986).

Shah, Ghanshyam, "Congress and the Deprived Communities", in Ram Joshi and R.K. Hebsur (eds.), *Congress in Indian Politics: A Centenary Perspectives*, Bombay: Popular Prakashan, 1988).

Shah, Ghanshyam, *Social Movements in India: A Review of the Literature*, (Delhi: Sage, 1990), [There is a good chapter on the review of Dalit Movements].

Shah, Ghanshyam, "Politics of Dalit Movement: From Direct Action to Pressure Group?", in Sandeep Pendse (ed.), *Dalit Movement Today*, (Bombay: Vikas Adhyayana Kendra, 1994), [Vikas Adhyayan Kendra, Bombay, *Perspectives* 1].

Shah, Ghanshyam, "Dalit Movements and Search for Identity", in Manorama Savur and Indra Munshi (eds.), *Contradictions in Indian Society*, (Jaipur: Rawat Publications, 1995).

Shah, Ghanshyam (ed.), *Dalit Identity and Politics*, (New Delhi: Sage Publications, 2001), [Cultural Subordination and the Dalit Challenge, Vol. 2 of Sage series].

Shah, Ghanshyam, "Introduction: Dalit Politics", in Ghanshyam Shah (ed.), *Dalit Identity and Politics*, (New Delhi: Sage Publications, 2001), [Cultural Subordination and the Dalit Challenge, Vol. 2 of Sage series].

Shah, Ghanshyam, "Dalits and the State: An Overview", in Ghanshyam Shah (ed.), *Dalits and the State*, (New Delhi: Concept Publishing Company, 2002), [Published for Centre for Rural Studies, Lal Bahadur Shastri National Academy of Administration, Mussoorie].

Shah, Ghanshyam (ed.), *Dalits and the State*, (New Delhi: Concept Publishing Company, for Centre for Rural Studies, Lal Bahadur Shastri National Academy of Administration, Mussoorie, 2002).

Shah, Ghanshyam, "Untouchability in Rural Gujarat: Revisited", in Ghanshyam Shah (ed.), *Dalits and the State*, (New Delhi: Concept Publishing Company, 2002), [Published for Centre for Rural Studies, Lal Bahadur Shastri National Academy of Administration, Mussoorie].

Shah, P., *The Dublas of Gujarat*, (Delhi: Bharatiya Adimjati Sevak Sangh, 1958).

Shah, Vimal P., *Educational Achievements of the Scheduled Castes in Gujarat: Removal of Untouchability in Gujarat*, (Ahmedabad: Gujarat University, 1973).

Shah, Vimal P. and Tara Patel, *Who goes to College: Scheduled Caste/Tribe Post-Matric Scholars in Gujarat*, (Ahmedabad: Rachana Prakashan, 1977).

Shah, Vimal P. (ed.), *Removal of Untouchability*, (Ahmedabad: Gujarat University, 1980).

Shah, Vimal P., *The Educational Problems of Scheduled Caste and Scheduled Tribe College Students: A Statistical Profile*, (Delhi: Allied Publishers, 1982), [for Indian Council of Social Science Research].

Shah, Vimal P. and Binod C. Agarwal (eds.), *Reservation: Policy Programmes, Issues*, (Jaipur: Rawat, 1986).

Shahare, M.L., *Dr. Bhimrao Ambedkar: His Life and Work*, (New Delhi: NCERT, 1988).

Shakir, Moin, "The Social Reformer", in B.K. Ahluwalia and Shashi Ahluwalia (eds.), *B.R. Ambedkar and Human Rights*, (New Delhi: Vivek Publishing Company, 1981).

Shakir, Moin, "Ambedkar's Theory of Social Reforms", in A.M. Rajasekharaiah (ed.), *The Socio-Economic Transformation of India—Dr. Ambedkar's Vision*, (Dharwad: Karnatak University, 1983).

Shamkanwar, M.R., *Scheduled Castes: A Socio-Economic Survey*, (Allahabad: Kitab Mahal, 1985).

Shankar, Jogan, *Devadasi Cult: A Sociological Analysis*, (New Delhi: Ashish Publishing House, 1990).

Shankdher, S.L., "Dr. B.R. Ambedkar and His Contribution in the Constituent Assembly and Parliament", in Rabi Ray (ed.), *Dr. B.R. Ambedkar*, (New Delhi: Lok Sabha Secretariat, 1991), [Eminent Parliamentarians Monograph Series 12].

Sharan, D.K., *Scheduled Castes in the Freedom Struggle in India*, (New Delhi: Classical, 1999).

Sharda, Bam Dev (ed.), *Tribes, Castes and Harijans: Structured Inequalities and Social Mobility*, (Delhi: Ajanta, 1991).

Sharma, B.A.V. and K. Madhusudhan Reddy, *Reservation Policy in India*, (New Delhi: Light and Life, 1982).

Sharma, B.D., *Dalits Betrayed*, (New Delhi: Har-Anand, 1994), (second edition was published by Sahyog Pustak Kuteer Trust, New Delhi 2000).

Sharma, B.K., "Dr. Ambedkar and His Educational Thoughts", in R.B. Rao (ed.), *Bharat-Ratna Dr. Ambedkar*, (Allahabad: Chugh Publications, 1993).

Sharma, B.L., "Teachings of Ambedkar", in Shyam Lal and K.S. Saxena (eds.), *Ambedkar and Nation-Building*, (Jaipur: Rawat, 1998).

Sharma, C.L., "The Problem of Scheduled Castes in Urban Rajasthan", in R.G. Singh (ed.), *The Depressed Classes of India: Problems and Prospects*, (New Delhi: B.R. Publishing Corporation, 1986).

Sharma, C.L., "Constitutional Provisions and Welfare Measures for SCs/STs", in V.K. Pant and B.S. Bisht (eds.), *Backward Communities: Identity, Development and Transformation*, (New Delhi: Gyan, 1999).

Sharma, C.L., *Social Mobility Among Scheduled Castes: An Empirical Study in an Indian State*, (New Delhi: M.D. Publications, 1996).

Sharma, G.S., *Legislation and Cases on Untouchability and Scheduled Castes in India*, (Delhi: Indian Council of Social Sciences Research, 1975).

Sharma, H.D., *B.R. Ambedkar: A Crusader for Equality*, (New Delhi: Rupa and Co., 2002).

Sharma, Krishna Dutt, "Dr. Bhim Rao Ambedkar and the Upliftment of the Depressed Classes", in R.B. Rao (ed.), *Bharat-Ratna Dr. Ambedkar*, (Allahabad: Chugh Publications, 1993).

Sharma, K.S., "Dr. Ambedkar's Contribution to Class Polarisation in India", in A.M. Rajasekharaiah (ed.) *The Socio-Economic Transformation of India—Dr. Ambedkar's Vision*, (Dharwad: Karnatak University, 1983).

Sharma, Kusum, *Ambedkar and Indian Constitution*, (New Delhi: Ashish, 1997).

Sharma, Mukul, "The Untouchable Present: Everyday Life of the Masahar in North Bihar", in Hemant Joshi and Sanjay Kumar (eds.), *Asserting Voices: Changing Culture, Identity and Livelihood of the Musahars in the Gangetic Plains*, (Delhi: Deshkal Publications, 2002).

Sharma, Nalin Vilochan, "A Biography of Jagjivan Ram", in *The Working Man*, (Patna: Jagjivan Ram Abhinandan Granth Committee, 1957).

Sharma, Neena, *Politicization and its Impact on Attitudinal Change Towards Social and Political System: A Case Study of Harijan Women of Delhi*, (New Delhi: Inter-India Publications, 1985).

Sharma, O.P., *Scheduled Castes: Population and Literates*, (New Delhi: KarKripa Publishers, 1990).

Sharma, O.P., *Reservation: A Gimmick*, (New Delhi: Karkripa Publishers, 1994).

Sharma, Premlata, *The Problems of Dalits and OBCs*, (Jaipur: Book Enclave, 2002).

Sharma, R.S., *Shudras in Ancient India: A Survey of the Position of the Lower Orders Down to Circa AD 500*, (Delhi: Motilal Banarasidas, 1958).

Sharma, Rama, *Bhangi: Scavenger in Indian Society – Marginality, Identity and Politicization of the Community*, (New Delhi: M.D. Publications, 1995).

Sharma, S.K., *The Chamar Artisans (Industrialization, Skills and Social Mobility)*, (Delhi: B.R. Publications, 1986).

Sharma, Satish Kumar, *Social Movements and Social Changes: A Study of Arya Samaj and Untouchables in Punjab*, (Delhi: B.R. Publishing Corporation, 1985).

Sharma, Ursula, "The Debate about Untouchables: Consensus or Resistance?", in her *Caste: Concepts in the Social Sciences series*, (Buckingham: Open University Press, 1999).

Shashi, S.S. (ed.), *Ambedkar and Social Justice*, (New Delhi: Government of India, 1992).

Shasmal, K.C., *The Bauris of West Bengal: A Socio-Economic Study*, (Calcutta: Indian Publications, 1972).

Shastree, *Religious Converts in India: Socio-Political Study of Neo Buddhists*, (New Delhi: Mittal, 1996).

Shastri, Sandeep, "Issues in Indian Federation: The Ambedkar Approach in Perspective", in *Ambedkar and Social Justice*, Vol. I, (New Delhi: Director, Publications Division, Ministry of Information and Broadcasting, 1992), [on behalf of Baba Saheb Dr. B.R. Ambedkar Birth Centenary Celebrations Committee, Ministry of Welfare, Government of India].

Shastri, Sandeep, "Issues in Indian Federalism: An Analytical Discussion of the Ambedkar Approach", in V.T. Patil (ed.), *Studies in Ambedkar*, (Delhi: Devika Publications, 1995).

Shastri, Shankaranand, *My Memoirs and Experiences of Babasaheb Dr. B.R. Ambedkar*, (Gaziabad: Author, 1989).

Shastri, Shankaranand, "Conversion Movement and its Impact on Indian Society", in Sanghasen Singh and Priyasen Singh (eds.), *Ambedkar on Buddhist Conversion and Its Impact*, (Delhi: Eastern Book Linkers, 1990).

Shastri, Shankaranand, "Our Saviour Babasaheb Ambedkar", in K.N. Kadam (ed.), *Dr. B.R. Ambedkar: The Emancipator of the Oppressed*, (Bombay: Popular Prakashan, 1993).

Sheean, Vincent, "The Critique", in B.K. Ahluwalia and Shashi Ahluwalia (eds.), *B.R. Ambedkar and Human Rights*, (New Delhi: Vivek Publishing Company, 1981).

Shekhavat, Bhairon Singh, "Ambedkar: A Profile in Courage", in *Ambedkar and Social Justice*, Vol. II, (New Delhi: Director, Publications Division, Ministry of Information and Broadcasting, 1992), [on behalf of Baba Saheb Dr. B.R. Ambedkar Birth Centenary Celebrations Committee, Ministry of Welfare, Government of India].

Sherring, Matthew Atmore, *Hindu Tribes and Castes as Represented in Benares*, 3 vols., (Calcutta: Thacker, 1872-1881, London: Trubner, 1872).

Shetty, V.T. Rajsekhar, *Dalit Movement in Karnataka*, (Madras: The Christian Literature Society, 1978).

Shetty, V.T.Rajsekhar, *Ambedkar and his Conversion: A Critique*, (Bangalore: Dalit Action Committee, 1980).

Shikhare, D.N., *Dr. Ambedkar*, (Poona: Jayant and Co., 1963).

Shinde, J.R., "From Reform to Revolt: An Analysis of Dr. Ambedkar's Revolutionary Thinking", in K.K. Kavlekar and A.S. Chausalkar (eds.), *Political Ideas and Leadership of Dr. B.R. Ambedkar*, (Pune: Vishwanil Publications, 1989).

Shinde, Pradeep, "Our Crippled Identity: United We Need to Stand", in Ambrose Pinto (ed.), *Dalit Assertion for Identity*, (New Delhi: Indian Social Institute, 1999), [Proceedings of the National Seminar of Dalit Postgraduate and Research Students held on 23-25 January 1999 in the Indian Social Institute].

Shinde, V.R., "The Depressed Class Mission", in *The Theistic Directory*, (Bombay: Depressed Class Mission, 1912).

Shindoba, Takashi, "Socio-Economic Conditions of Sweepers Employed by Local Bodies in Ahmedabad District", in S. Taniuguchi, H. Yanagisawa, T. Shindoba and F. Oshikawa (eds.), *Economic Changes and Social Transformation in Modern and Contemporary South Asia*, (Tokyo: Hitotsubashi University, 1994).

Shinoda, Takashi, "The Structure of Stagnancy: Sweepers in Ahmedabad District", in Ghanshyam Shah (ed.), *Dalits and the State*, (New Delhi: Concept Publishing Company, 2002), [Published for Centre for Rural Studies, Lal Bahadur Shastri National Academy of Administration, Mussoorie].

Shiri, Godwin, "Plight of Christian Dalits in Karnataka", in V. Devasahayam (ed.), *Dalits and Women: Quest for Humanity*, (Madras: The Gurukul Summer Institute, 1992).

Shirke, Suvarna T., "Prejudices Against Dalits", in Ambrose Pinto (ed.), *Dalit Assertion for Identity*, (New Delhi: Indian Social Institute, 1999), [Proceedings of the National Seminar of Dalit Postgraduate and Research Students held on 23-25 January 1999 in the Indian Social Institute].

Shivam, K.S., "Scheduled Caste in India", in Durgabai Deshmukh (ed.), *Social Welfare in India*, (New Delhi: Director, Publication Division, 1960).

Shourie, Arun, *Worshipping False Gods: Ambedkar and the facts which have been erased*, (New Delhi: ASA Publications, 1997).

Showeb, M., *Education and Mobility Among Harijans: A Study based on Students, Government Employees and Traditionally Employed Chamars of Varanasi*, (Varanasi: Institute of Gandhian Studies; Allahabad: Vohra Publishers, 1986).

Shrikant, L.M., "Scheduled Castes and Their Welfare", in M.S. Gore (ed.), *Encyclopaedia of Social Work in India*, Vo. 2, (Delhi: Manager of Publications, 1968).

Shrirama, "Untouchability and Stratification in Indian Civilisation", in S.M. Michael (ed.), *Dalits in Modern*

India: Vision and Values, (New Delhi: Vistaar Publications, 1999).

Shukla, Girish Chandra, "Dr. Ambedkar – As a Human Right Fighter", in R.B. Rao (ed.), *Bharat-Ratna Dr. Ambedkar*, (Allahabad: Chugh Publications, 1993).

Shukla, J.J., *Dr. B.R. Ambedkar on Hinduism*, (Ahmedabad: Globe Books and Periodicals, 1993).

Shukla, J.J., *B.R. Ambedkar, Gandhi and Tagore: A Comparative Study on Education*, (Ahmedabad: Karnavati Publishers, 1998).

Shukla, K.S. and B.M. Verma, *Development of Scheduled Castes and Administration*, (New Delhi: Uppal, 1993).

Shukla, R.K. and Chunna Singh, "Literacy of Scheduled Castes in Bundelkhand Region, Uttar Pradesh: A Spatial Analysis", in R.S. Tripathi and P.D. Tiwari (eds.), *Dimensions of Scheduled Caste Development in India: Problems and Prospects*, (New Delhi: Uppal, 1991).

Shukla, V.N., "Educational Protection Clause, Selective Techniques and Educational Planning", in G.S. Sharma (ed.), *Educational Planning: Its Legal and Constitutional Implications in India*, (N.M. Tripathi, 1967).

Sigrist, Christian, "The Problem of 'Pariahs'", in Otto Stammer (ed.), *Max Weber and Sociology Today*, (New York: Harper & Row, [Harper Torchbooks] 1971).

Sikhamani, (Pen name of Sanjeeva Rao), *The Black Rainbow – Dalit Poems in Telugu*, (Hyderabad: Milinda Publications, 2000), (Tr. by Kiranmayi, D. Kesava Rao, M. Sridhar and Alladi Uma).

Sikligar, P.C., *Atrocities on Scheduled Castes and Scheduled Tribes: Prevention and Implementation*, (Jaipur: Mangal Deep Publications, 2002).

Silvertsen, Dagfinn, *When Caste Barriers Fall*, (Oslo: Universietetsforlaget, 1963).

Singh, Amar, "Ambedkar's Critique of the Four Noble Truths", in Sanghasen Singh and Priyasen Singh (eds.), *Ambedkar on Buddhist Conversion and Its Impact*, (Delhi: Eastern Book Linkers, 1990).

Singh, Ashok Kumar, "Socio-Cultural Characteristics of 'Dusadh': A Case Study of North Bihar Villages", in S.N. Chaudhary (ed.), *Changing Status of Depressed Castes in Contemporary India: Essays in Honour of Professor S.C. Dube*, (Delhi: Daya Publishing House, 1988).

Singh, B.P., "Current Government Policies and Socio-Economic Harmony among Scheduled Castes in Punjab", in V.S. Mahajan and B.S. Mann (eds.), *Economic Development of Scheduled Castes*, (New Delhi: Anmol, 1997).

Singh, B.P., "Wisdom, Skill and Land", in Hemant Joshi and Sanjay Kumar (eds.), *Asserting Voices: Changing Culture, Identity and Livelihood of the Musahars in the Gangetic Plains*, (Delhi: Deshkal Publications, 2002).

Singh, Dharam Raj, *Rural Leadership among Scheduled Castes*, (Allahabad: Chugh Publications, 1985).

Singh, Gulab, "Teacher's Perception of Scheduled Caste Students and their Scholastic Achievement", (Varanasi: Department of Education, Banaras Hindu University, 1988).

Singh, Hoshiar, "Administration of Socio-Economic Change among Scheduled Caste Communities in Haryana", in V.S. Mahajan and B.S. Mann (eds.), *Economic Development of Scheduled Castes*, (New Delhi: Anmol, 1997).

Singh, Hoshiar and Ajmir Singh Malik, "The Scheduled Castes and the Scheduled Tribes (Prevention of Atrocities) Act, 1989: An Analysis", in C.P. Barthwal (ed.), *Social Justice in India*, (Lucknow: Bharat Book Centre, 1998).

Singh, Hoshiar and A.S. Malik, *Socio-Economic Development of Scheduled Castes in India (A Study of Haryana)*, (Jaipur: Aalekh Publishers, 2001).

Singh, K.K., *Patterns of Caste Tension*, (London: Asia Publishing House, 1967). [Detailed explanation about the inter-caste tensions in the village of Senapur and Borsar].

Singh, K.P., "Liberation Movements in Comparative Perspective: Dalit Indian and Black Americans", in S.M.

Michael (ed.), *Dalits in Modern India: Vision and Values*, (New Delhi: Vistaar Publications, 1999).

Singh, K.S., *The Scheduled Castes*, Vol. II of *The Peoples of India*, (Delhi: Oxford University Press in association with Anthropological Survey of India, 1993).

Singh, K.S., "Musahar: Community Context and Equality", in Hemant Joshi and Sanjay Kumar (eds.), *Asserting Voices: Changing Culture, Identity and Livelihood of the Musahars in the Gangetic Plains*, (Delhi: Deshkal Publications, 2002).

Singh, Krishna, "Gender Perceptions of Scheduled Castes and OBCs or Distributive Justice", in D.M. Diwakar (ed.), *Distributive Justice Through Social Mobilization*, (New Delhi: Manak, 1998).

Singh, L.R. (Project Director), *A Diagnostic Survey of Socio-Economic Conditions of the Scheduled Castes in Banda District of Uttar Pradesh*, (Allahabad: Gobind Ballabh Pant Social Science Institute, 1983), [Sponsored by the Ministry of Home Affairs, Government of India].

Singh, M., "End of Untouchability – A Legal Way?", in P.N. Pimply and S.K. Sharma (eds.), *Struggle for Status*, (New Delhi: B.R. Publishing Corporation, 1985).

Singh, Malook, "Study of Welfare Schemes for Scheduled Castes in Tarn Taran Tehsil of Amritsar District", in V.S. Mahajan and B.S. Mann (eds.), *Economic Development of Scheduled Castes*, (New Delhi: Anmol, 1997).

Singh, Mohinder, *The Depressed Classes of India: Their Social and Economic Condition*, (Bombay: Hind Kitabs, 1947), [Introduction by Radhakamal Mukerjee].

Singh, M.N., "Dr. Bhim Rao Ambedkar and the Depressed Classes", in R.B. Rao (ed.), *Bharat-Ratna Dr. Ambedkar*, (Allahabad: Chugh Publications, 1993).

Singh, Nagendra Kumar, *Ambedkar on Religion*, (New Delhi: Anmol, 2000).

Singh, N.K., *Educational Problems of Scheduled Castes and Scheduled Tribes School Students in Rajasthan*, (Jaipur: Jaipur University of Rajasthan, 1975).

Singh, N.K., *Education and Social Change*, (Jaipur: Rawat Publications, 1979).

Singh, N.K., *Dalit Movement in Indian Literature*, (New Delhi: Gyan, 1999).

Singh, Paramanand, *Equality, Reservation and Discrimination in India: A Constitutional Study of Scheduled Castes, Scheduled Tribes, and Other Backward Classes*, (New Delhi: Deep and Deep Publications, 1982).

Singh, Priya Sen, "The After-Effects of the Ambedkar Conversion", in Sanghasen Singh and Priyasen Singh (eds.), *Ambedkar on Buddhist Conversion and Its Impact*, (Delhi: Eastern Book Linkers, 1990).

Singh, Puran, *Problem of Education Among Scheduled Castes: A Comparative Study of Achievement, Adjustment, Attitudes and Problems of First and Subsequent Generation Learners Belonging to Scheduled Caste at Higher Education*, (New Delhi: Mittal, 1989).

Singh, Rekha, "Bhim Rao Ambedkar and Social Reform", in R.B. Rao (ed.), *Bharat-Ratna Dr. Ambedkar*, (Allahabad: Chugh Publications, 1993).

Singh, R.B., *Scheduled Caste Welfare: Myth or Reality*, (New Delhi: A.P.H. Publishing and Co., 2003).

Singh, R.G. (ed.), *The Depressed Classes of India: Problems and Prospects*, (New Delhi: B.R. Publishing Corporation, 1986).

Singh, R.G., "Neo-Buddhist Movement among then Harijans of Ahamadpur: Search for a New Status and Identity", in R.G. Singh (ed.), *The Depressed Classes of India: Problems and Prospects*, (New Delhi: B.R. Publishing Corporation, 1986).

Singh, R.K. Birender, "Special Tables for Scheduled Castes and Scheduled Tribes, Manipur", in *Census of India, 1981*, Series 13, Part 9, (Delhi: Controller of Publications, 1988).

Singh, R.P., "Educational Backwardness of Scheduled Caste Students and a Neer-Oriented Plan for Their

Development", (Patna: Department of Education, Patna University, 1982), [A research monograph, out of project financed by the NCERT].

Singh, R.R., "Adjustment Problems of the Scheduled Caste and the Scheduled Tribe Students in Residential Schools of Rajasthan", (Udaipur: Vidya Bhavan G.S. Teacher's College, 1981), [A research monograph, out of a project financed by the NCERT].

Singh, Rongmuthu D., *The Folk Tales of the Garos,* (Gauhati: Department of Tribal Culture and Folksore Research, University of Gauhati, 1960).

Singh, Sanghasen and Priya Sen Singh (eds.), *Ambedkar on Buddhist Conversion and Its Impact,* (Delhi: Eastern Book Linkers, 1990).

Singh, S.D.N., "Scheduled Castes and Scheduled Tribes in Urban Bihar", in S.N. Chaudhary (ed.), *Changing Status of Depressed Castes in Contemporary India: Essays in Honour of Professor S.C. Dube,* (Delhi: Daya Publishing House, 1988).

Singh, S.K., "The Scheduled Castes and the Scheduled Tribes (Prevention of Atrocities) Act, 1983: Some Contradictions", in C.P. Barthwal (ed.), *Social Justice in India,* (Lucknow: Bharat Book Centre, 1998).

Singh, Soran, *Scheduled Casts of India: Dimensions of Social Change,* (New Delhi: Gian Publishing House, 1987).

Singh, S.N., "A Study of the Pattern of Education and Occupation of Persons Living in Varanasi (Rural) with Special Reference to Scheduled Castes", (Varanasi: Demographic Research Centre, Banaras Hindu University, 1972), [A research monograph, out of a project financed by the ICSSR].

Singh, Sriram, "Bharat Ratna Babasaheb Dr. B.R. Ambedkar: As a Social Reformer and Pilot of the Indian Constitution", in R.B. Rao (ed.), *Bharat-Ratna Dr. Ambedkar,* (Allahabad: Chugh Publications, 1993).

Singh, Sukhdev, "73rd Amendment and Panchayati Raj: A Case Study of Punjab", in V.S. Mahajan and B.S. Mann (eds.), *Economic Development of Scheduled Castes,* (New Delhi: Anmol, 1997).

Singh, Surendra, "Areal Profiles of Scheduled Caste Concentration in the Economic Sectors of Uttar Pradesh", in R.S. Tripathi and P.D. Tiwari (eds.), *Dimensions of Scheduled Caste Development in India: Problems and Prospects,* (New Delhi: Uppal, 1991).

Singh, Surendra, "Ambedkar's Contribution to Social Justice", in Bindeshwar Pathak (ed.), *Social Justice and Development of Weaker Sections,* (New Delhi: Inter India, 1997).

Singh, Surendra Pratap, "Education in view of Dr. Ambedkar", in R.B. Rao (ed.), *Bharat-Ratna Dr. Ambedkar,* (Allahabad: Chugh Publications, 1993).

Singh, S.S. and S. Sundaram, *Emerging Harijan Elite: A Study of Their Identity,* (New Delhi: Uppal Publishing House, 1987).

Singh, Shoran, *The Socio-Economic Condition of the Scheduled Castes in India,* (Allahabad: Programme Book Depot, 1980).

Singh, Shoran, *The Scheduled Castes of India: Dimensions of Social Change,* (Delhi: Gyan Publishing House, 1987).

Singh, Surya Bhan, "Dr. Bhim Rao Ambedkar: A Great Man", in R.B. Rao (ed.), *Bharat-Ratna Dr. Ambedkar,* (Allahabad: Chugh Publications, 1993).

Singh, T.P., B.P. Pandey, G.S. Dubey and D.R. Yadav, "The Study of Scheduled Castes and Scheduled Tribes Students of Secondary Schools in Uttar Pradesh East", [A research monograph, out of a project financed by the ICSSR].

Singh, T.R., *The Madigas: A Study of Social Structure and Changes,* (Lucknow: Ethnographic and Folk Culture Society, 1969).

Singh, V.B., "Deprivation and Political Consciousness: A Case of Scheduled Caste Communities in India", in B.K. Nagla (ed.), *Political Sociology,* (Jaipur: Rawat, 1999).

Singh, Virendra Prakash (ed.), *Caste System and Social Change,* (New Delhi: Commonwealth, 1992), [Caste Culture and Society Series – I].

Sinha, D.N., "Educational Planning: Discrimination and the Equal Protection of the Laws", in G.S. Sharma (ed.), *Educational Planning: Its Legal and Constitutional Implications in India*, (Bombay: N.M. Tripathi, 1967).

Sinha, Jogendra, *Dr. Ambedkar: A Critical Study*, (Patna: Vijay Publications, 1993).

Sinha, Raj Kishore, *Alienation among Scheduled Castes*, (New Delhi: Manas Publications, 1986).

Sinha, Saurabh and Sanjay Sinha, *Indian Leather Industry: The Challenge of Modernization*, (New Delhi: OUP, 1992).

Sinha, Tara, *A Brief Description of the Dalit Women's Movement in the Bhal*, (Ahmedabad: Behavioural Science Centre, 1994).

Singh, Virendra Prakash (ed.), *Caste System and Social Change (Essay on Social Integration of Scheduled Castes and Dr. Ambedkar)*, (New Delhi: Commonwealth Publishers, 1992), [Caste Culture and Society Series, I].

Singhla, Jogendranath, *Dr. B.R. Ambedkar: A Critical Study*, (Patna: Vijay Publication, 1993).

Sivanandan, P., "Economic Emancipation through Institutional Reform and Development Programmes: Experience of the Dalit Community in Kerala", in A.M. Abraham Ayrookuzhiel (ed.), *The Dalit Desiyata: The Kerala Experience in Development and Class Struggle*, (Delhi: 1990).

Sivarama Krishna Rao, C., "Ambedkar's Views on Small Holdings in India", in K.S. Chalam (ed.), *The Relevance of Ambedkarism in India*, (Jaipur: Rawat, 1993).

Siwach, J.R., *Dr. Ambedkar on Presidential and Judicial Impeachment*, (Delhi: Indian Publishers, 1999).

Somanathan, N., "Leather Tanning Techniques of the Tamils of Sangam Society", in *the Proceedings of the Workshop and Exhibition on Traditional Leather Industry*, (Chennai: AU-PPST Centre, Anna University, 1998).

Somasekhar, A., "Perspectives of Research on Ambedkar's Socio-Economic Philosophy", in K.S. Chalam (ed.), *The Relevance of Ambedkarism in India*, (Jaipur: Rawat, 1993).

Somasekhar, A., "Quality of Life of Scheduled Castes – Facts and Issues", in J.S. Narayana Rao, A. Somasekhar and K. Audiseshaiah (eds.), *B.R. Ambedkar: His Relevance Today*, (New Delhi: Gyan Publishing House, 1994).

Sommer, John G., *Empowering the Oppressed: Grassroots Advocacy Movements in India*, (New Delhi: Sage, 2001).

Sonawane, Vijay Cintaman, "Dr. B.R. Ambedkar: A Humanist", in Bhajan Kaur (ed.), *The Philosophy of Dr. B.R. Ambedkar*, (Chandigarh: Dr. Ambedkar Study Circle, 1999).

Soni, B.D., "Educational Problems of Scheduled Caste College Students in Uttar Pradesh (West)", (Agra: Department of Sociology, Agra University, 1975), [A research monograph, out of a project financed by the ICSSR].

Sonkamble, P.I., "Dalit Literature at a Glance", in Bojja Tharakam (ed.), *The First All India Dalit Writers Conference: A Commemorative Volume and Who's Who*, (Hyderabad: Dr. B.R. Ambedkar Memorial Trust, 1994).

Source Materials on Dr. Babasaheb Ambedkar and the Movement of Untouchables, (Bombay: Government of Maharashtra, 1982).

Sreenath, J. and S.H. Ahmad, *All India Anthropometric Survey, South Zone: Andhra Pradesh (Analysis of Data)*, (Calcutta: Anthropological Survey of India, 1989).

Srinivas, M.N. (ed.), *Seminar on Casteism and Untouchability*, (Indian Conference of Social Work,), [no more details available].

Srivastava, Alka, "Dalit Identity in Bihar", in Fernando Franco (ed.), *Pain and Awakening: The Dynamics of Dalit Identity in Bihar, Gujarat and Uttar Pradesh*, (New Delhi: Indian Social Institute, 2002).

Srivastava, A.K., "Development of Scheduled Castes and Scheduled Tribes: An Assessment of U.P.", in V.K. Pant and B.S. Bisht (eds.), *Backward Communities: Identity, Development and Transformation*, (New Delhi: Gyan, 1999).

Srivastava, B., *Manual Scavenging in India: A Disgrace to the Country*, (New Delhi: Concept, 1997), (published for Sulabh International Social Service Organisation, New Delhi).

Srivastava, L.R.N., *Hostel Facilities for Scheduled Castes: Third All India Educational Survey*, (New Delhi: NCERT, 1979).

Srivastava, L.R.N., *An Evaluative Study of Pre-Matric Scholarship Scheme for Scheduled Caste and Scheduled Tribe Students*, (New Delhi: NCERT, 1988).

Srivastava, N.K. and Ram Shanker, *Impact of Adult on Scheduled Caste Women*, (1990).

Srivastava, S.C., "Ambedkar's Approach to Imposition of President's Rule on Failure of Constitutional Machinery in State", in Nazeer H. Khan (ed.), *B.R. Ambedkar on Federalism, Ethnicity and Gender Justice*, (New Delhi: Deep & Deep, 2001).

Srivastava, S.N., *Harijans in Indian Society: A Cultural Study of the Status of Harijans and Other Backward Classes from the Earliest Times to the Present Day*, (New Delhi: S. Chand and Co., 1980), [Foreworded by Jagjivan Ram].

Srivastava, S.P., *Educational Growth in India: Data Base*, (New Delhi: NIEPA, 1982).

Srivastava, S.P., "The Theatre of Injustice: Atrocities on Scheduled Castes and Scheduled Tribes", in Bindeshwar Pathak (ed.), *Social Justice and Development of Weaker Sections*, (New Delhi: Inter India, 1997).

Srivastava Varma, G. and N. Ramaswamy, *Harijan Dialect in Tamil*, (Annamalai Nagar: Annamalai University, 1971).

Stanislans, L., *The Liberating Mission of the Church among Dalit Christians*, (Delhi: ISPCK, 1999).

State-wise Information on Education of Scheduled Castes and Scheduled Tribes, (New Delhi: SC & ST Cell, Ministry of Education, 1985).

Steefland, Pieter H., *The Christian Punjabi Sweepers: Their History and Their Position in Present-Day Pakistan*, (Amsterdam: University of Amsterdam, 1973), [Publication No. 6 of the South and South East Asia Department of Anthropological and Sociological Centre; this was reprinted by the Christian Study Centre Rawalpindi, Pakistan].

Steefland, Pieter H., *The Sweepers of Slaughterhouse: Conflict and Survival in a Karachi Neighbourhood*, (Assen, The Netherlands: Van Gorcum, 1979).

Stevenson, Margaret Sinclair, *Without the Pale: The Life Story of an Outcaste*, (Calcutta: Association Press and Humphrey Milford for Oxford University Press, 1930).

Subba Rao, Chandu and D. Francis (eds.), *Development of Weaker Sections (Essays in Honour of Prof. K.S. Chalam)*, (Jaipur: Rawat, 2000).

Subba Rao, K., "The Visionary", in B.K. Ahluwalia and Shashi Ahluwalia (eds.), *B.R. Ambedkar and Human Rights*, (New Delhi: Vivek Publishing Company, 1981).

Subba Rao, K.P., "Educational Philosophy of Ambedkar", in K.S. Chalam (ed.), *The Relevance of Ambedkarism in India*, (Jaipur: Rawat, 1993).

Subhan, J. and Mohini Dass, *The Good News of Christ for The Depressed Classes*, (Hazratganj, Lucknow: The Lucknow Publishing House, n.d.)

Subramanya Menon, K.P., *The Shame of Free India: A Study of the Social and Economic Disabilities of Scheduled Castes and Scheduled Tribes*, (New Delhi: 1961), [Pamphlet].

Subrahmanian, K.S., *Violence Against the Scheduled Castes in India: Overview, Problems, Prospects*, (New Delhi: NMML, 1986), [Occasional Papers on History and Society, No. XXIX].

Sudhakar Rao, N., "The Structure of South Indian Untouchable Castes: A View", in Ghanshyam Shah (ed.), *Dalit Identity and Politics*, (New Delhi: Sage Publications, 2001), [Cultural Subordination and the Dalit Challenge, Vol. 2 of Sage series].

Sugirtharaj, Felix N., "Developing a Common Dalit Ideology: Is it a Myth or Reality?", in Arvind P. Nirmal (ed.), *Toward a Common Dalit Ideology*, (Madras: Gurukul Lutheran Theological College and Research Institute, 1990), [Papers presented at the National Seminar on Dalit Ideology organized by the Department of Dalit Theology, Gugukul Lutheran Theological College and Research Institute].

Sujata, B.N. and K. Yeshodhara, "A Comparative Study Some Educational Variables of SC/ST Students", (Mysore: Department of Education, Mysore University, 1986), [A research monograph, out of a project financed by the NCERT].

Suman, R.D. (ed.), Dr. *Ambedkar: Pioneer of Human Rights*, (New Delhi: Bodhisattva Publications, Ambedkar Institute of Buddhist Studies, 1977).

Sunda, K.R., "Marx, Ambedkar and Polarization of Oppressed and Exploited Classes in India", in *National Seminar on Marx, Ambedkar and Polarization of Oppressed and Exploited Classes in India*, (New Delhi: Sanjivayya Institute of Socio-Economic Studies, 1991).

Sundar Raj, Victor, *Scheduled Castes of Rural India: Problems and Prospects*, (New Delhi: A.P.H. Publishing and Co., 2000).

Sundarananda, Swami, *Hinduism and Untouchability*, (Foreword by Shyma Prasad Mukherjee), (Calcutta: Udbodhan Office, 1946), (First Published in 1922), [Also reprinted in Delhi: Harijan Sevak Sangh, ca., 1945].

Sundarani, Dwarko, "Education is the Foundation of Culture", in Hemant Joshi and Sanjay Kumar (eds.), *Asserting Voices: Changing Culture, Identity and Livelihood of the Musahars in the Gangetic Plains,* (Delhi: Deshkal Publications, 2002).

Suresh, V., "The Dalit Movement in India", in T.V. Satyamurthy (ed.), Region, *Religion, Caste, Gender and Culture in Contemporary India,* (Delhi: OUP, 1996).

Survade, V.G., *Dr. B.R. Ambedkar Through Correspondence,* Vol. I. (Kalyan (East), Dist. Thane: 1986).

Swart, W.Q., *The Mahar Folk,* (manuscript), (Ahmednagar: Ahmednagar College, 1947).

Tagore, Rabindranath, "Chandalika", in *Three Plays,* (Translated from the Bengali by Marjorie Sykes), (Bombay: Oxford University Press, 1950), [A play based on the Buddhist legend of an outcaste girl becoming a Bhikkuni, written in 1933].

Tagore, Rabindranath, *Mahatmaji and the Depressed Humanity,* (Calcutta: Visvabharati, 1932).

Tambiah, S.J., "From Varna to Caste Through Mixed Unitions", in Jack Goody (ed.), *The Character of Kinship,* (Cambridge: CUP, 1973).

Tandon, Lataprasad, *Rationale of Untouchability,* (Cawnpore: S.G. Rastoji, 1934).

Tanwani, Dhruv, "Raidas Chamar Basti of Ranchi: A Sociological Case Study", in Makhan Jha (ed.), *Scheduled Castes Today,* (New Delhi: M.D. Publications, 1997).

Tarachand, K.C., *Devadasi Custom: Rural Social Structure and Flesh Market,* (New Delhi: Reliance Publishing House, 1992).

Taylor, H.F.L., *In the Land of the Five Rivers,* (Edinburgh: Black, 1906), [Chapters XII-XV deals with mass-movements among Outcastes in Punjab].

Taylor, R., "The Ambedkarite Buddhists", in T. Wilkinson and M. Thomas (eds.), *Ambedkar and the Neo-Buddhist Movement,* (Madras: The Christian Literature Society, 1972).

Tehrani, M.Z. Shamsi, "Dr. Ambedkar's Perspective on Upliftment of Women", in Nazeer H. Khan (ed.), *B.R.*

Ambedkar on Federalism, Ethnicity and Gender Justice, (New Delhi: Deep & Deep, 2001).

Teltumbde, Anand, *'Ambedkar' in and for the Post-Ambedkar Dalit Movement*, (Pune: Sugawa, 1997).

Teltumbde, Anand, "Impact of New Economic Reforms on Dalits", in P.G. Jogdand (ed.), *New Economic Policy and Dalits*, (Jaipur: Rawat, 2000).

Teltumbde, Anand, "Beyond the Torturing Times: Dr. Ambedkar and the Dalit Future", in K.C. Yadav, (ed.), *From Periphery to Centre Stage: Ambedkar, Ambedkarism and Dalit Future*, (New Delhi: Manohar, 2000).

Teltumbde, Anand, *Globalization and the Dalits*, (Nagpur: Sanket Prakashan, 2001).

Tewary, S.N., "Scheduled Caste Women in Rural Bihar – A Study in Sociology of Poverty", in S.N.Chaudhary, and P. Chaudhary, (eds.), *National Development and Women*, (New Delhi: Har-Anand & Vikas, 1992).

Thakkar, A.V., *Aboriginals Cry in the Wilderness: Their Education and Representation in Legislature*, (Bombay: A.W. Thakkar, Servants of India Society, 1945), [Controversy between Dr. Ambedkar and A.W. Thakkar with facts and figures regarding aboriginals and hill tribes].

Thakkar, A.V., *Thakkar Baba Eightieth Birthday Commemoration Volume*, (A.V. Thakker), (Compiled and Edited by T.N. Jagadisan and Shyam Lal), (Madras: 1949), [This volume contains around fifty pages of material on the Harijan Sevak Sangh].

Thakur, Devendra, *Self-Employment Patterns of Scheduled Castes: The Basic Leather Workers (Harijans)*, (New Delhi: Deep and Deep, 1992).

Thangaraj, M., "Access to Land by Scheduled Castes and Scheduled Tribes in India", in Ghanshyam Shah (ed.), *Dalits and the State*, (New Delhi: Concept Publishing Company, 2002), [Published for Centre for Rural Studies, Lal Bahadur Shastri National Academy of Administration, Mussoorie].

Tharakam, Bojja, "Dalit Literature in Telugu", in Bojja Tharakam (ed.), *The First All India Dalit Writers Conference: A Commemorative Volume and Who's Who*, (Hyderabad: Dr. B.R. Ambedkar Memorial Trust, 1994).

Tharakam, Bojja, *The First All India Dalit Writers Conference: A Commemorative Volume and Who's Who*, (Hyderabad: Dr. B.R. Ambedkar Memorial Trust, 1994).

Thaware, G.M., *Gandhiji's Letters Re: Untouchables*, (Nagpur: L.P. Meshram and M.G. Dongre, 1941).

The Bhopal Document: Charting a New Course or Dalits for the 21st Century, (Bhapal: Government of Madhya Pradesh, 2002).

The Depressed Classes: A Chronological Documentation, Part I, (Ranchi: Rev. Fr. J. Jans S.J., Catholic Press, 1935); Part II – Part VII, (Kurseong: St. Mary's College, 1935 – 1937), (Published in one volume).

Theertha, Swami Dharma, *History of Hindu Imperialism*, (Madras: Dalit Educational Literature Centre 1992), [Reprint of *The Menace of Hindu Imperialism* (1941)].

Thiagaraj, Henry, *Asian Dalit Solidarity*, (Delhi: ISPCK, 1999), (published for Dalit Liberation Education Trust, Chennai).

Thiagaraj, Henry, *Dalit Human Rights*, (Madras: Dalit Liberation Education Trust, 1998).

Thimmaiah, G., "Karnataka Government Reservation Policies for Scheduled Castes/Scheduled Tribes and Other Backward Castes", in V.A. Pai Panandiker (ed.), *The Politics of Backwardness: Reservation Policy in India*, (New Delhi: Konark Publishers, 1997), [Under the auspices of Centre for Policy Research, New Delhi].

Thirupathi Kumar, G., "Indian Nation-state and Question: A Study of Vivekananda", in Chandu Subba Rao and D. Francis (eds.), *Development of Weaker Sections (Essays in Honour of Prof. K.S. Chalam)*, (Jaipur: Rawat, 2000).

Thomas, M.M., *Religion and Revolt of the Oppressed*, (Delhi: ISPCK, 1981).

Thomas, P., *The Death of a Harijan: A Novel based on Village Life in Kerala in the third-fourth Decade of the 20th Century*, (Trithur: Horizon Publications, 1984).

Thorat, S.K., "Passage to Adulthood: Perceptions from Below", in Sudhir Kakar (ed.), *Identity and Adulthood*, (Delhi: OUP, 1982).

Thorat, S.K., "Dalit Reality: From an Economic Perspective", in V. Devasahayam (ed.), *Dalits and Women: Quest for Humanity*, (Madras: The Gurukul Summer Institute, 1992).

Thorat, S.K., *Ambedkar's Contribution to Water Resource Development*, (New Delhi: Central Water Commission, Government of India, 1993).

Thorat, S.K., "Ambedkar and the Economics of the Hindu Social Order: Understanding its Orthodoxy and Legacy", in Walter Fernandes (ed.), *The Emerging Dalit Identity: The Reassertion of the Subalterns*, (New Delhi: Indian Social Institute, 1996).

Thorat, S.K., "Ambedkar's Thoughts on Economic Development and Planning", in Radhakant Nayak (ed.), *The Fourth World: Appraisal and Aspirations*, (New Delhi: Manohar, 1997).

Thorat, S.K., "Public Policies and Economic Change: The Case of the Scheduled Castes", in Radhakant Nayak (ed.), *The Fourth World: Appraisal and Aspirations*, (New Delhi: Manohar, 1997).

Thorat, S.K., *Ambedkar's Role in Economic Planning and Water Policy*, (Delhi: Shipra, 1998).

Thorat, S.K., "Hindu Social System and Human Right of Untouchables: Theoretical Perspective and Empirical Evidence", in Wagmore (ed.), *Human Rights of Dalits*, (Pune: Popular Publications, 1998).

Thorat, S.K., "Ambedkar and Nation Building: Reflection on Selected Themes", in Anand Kumar (ed.), *Nation Building in India*, (Delhi: Radiant, 1999).

Thorat, S.K., "Dalits and Human Rights: A part of the Whole, but a part apart", in G.S. Bhargava and R.M. Pal (eds.), *Human Rights of Dalits: Societal Violation*, (New Delhi: Gyan Publishing House, 1999).

Thorat, S.K., "Poverty, Caste and Child Labour: Plight of Scheduled Caste and Tribal Children", in Voll Klues (ed.), *Child Labour in India*, (Delhi: F.E.S. Foundation, 1999).

Thorat, S.K., "New Economic Policy and its Impact on Employment and Poverty of the Scheduled Castes", in P.G. Jogdand (ed.), *New Economic Policy and Dalits*, (Jaipur: Rawat, 2000).

Thorat, S.K. and R.S. Deshpande, "Caste System and Economic Inequality: Economic Theory and Evidence", in Ghanshyam Shah (ed.), *Dalit Identity and Politics*, (New Delhi: Sage Publications, 2001), [Cultural Subordination and the Dalit Challenge, Vol. 2 of Sage series].

Thorat, S.K. (ed.), *Ambedkar in Retrospect: Reflection on Contributions*, (Delhi: Manohar, forthcoming).

Thorat, S.K. (ed.), *Caste System and Economic Inequality: Continuing Deprivation Untouchables in India*, (Delhi: Manohar, forthcoming).

Thorat, S.S.P., *The Regimental History of the Mahar MG (Machine Gun) Regiment*, (Dehra Dun: The Army Press, 1954).

Thorat, Vimal, "Dalit Women and Human Rights: Some Neglected Issues", in G.S. Bhargava and R.M. Pal (eds.), *Human Rights of Dalits*, (New Delhi: Gyan Publishing, 1999).

Thurston, Edgar and Rangachari, *Castes and Tribes of Southern India*, 7 vols., (Madras: Government Press, 1909), (with an assistance of Rangachari).

Tirumala Rao, Jayadheer, 'Hidden Culture of Depressed Castes: A Case Study of Dakkali – A Dalit Community', in R. Soma Reddy, M. Radhakrishna Sharma and A. Satyanarayana (eds.), *Castes, Community and Culture in Andhra Desa: 17th and 18th Century*, (Hyderabad: Osmania University, 1995).

Tiwari, Chitra, *Sudras in Manu*, (Foreword by Jagjiwan Ram), (Delhi: Motilal Banarsidass, 1963).

Tiwari, R.S., R.S. Tripathi and P.D. Tiwari, "Nutrition Problems and Diseases Caused by Malnutrition among Scheduled Castes", in R.S. Tripathi and P.D. Tiwari (eds.), *Dimensions of Scheduled Caste Development in India: Problems and Prospects*, (New Delhi: Uppal, 1991).

Tiwari, Ravi, "The Role of Theological Colleges in the Emergence of Dalit Theology", in James Massey (ed.), *Indigenous People, Dalits: Dalit Issues in Today's Theological Debate*, (Delhi: ISPCK, 1998), (First Published in1994).

Tiwary, Shailendra Kumar, "Protective Discrimination and the Scheduled Castes: Views of Dr. B.R. Ambedkar", in A.K. Lal (ed.), *Protective Discrimination: Ideology and Praxis*, (New Delhi: Concept, 2002), [Published for B.G. Pant Social Science Institute, Allahabad].

Togawa, Masahiko, "Untouchable or Scheduled Castes?: A Gram Panchayat Election in West Bengal in 1993", in H. Kotani (ed.), *Caste System, Untouchability and the Depressed*, (New Delhi: Manohar, 1997).

Tope, T.K., "Protective Discrimination and Educational Planning", in G.S. Sharma (ed.), *Educational Planning: Its Legal and Constitutional Implications in India*, (Bomby: N.M. Tripathi, 1967).

Tope, T.K., Dr. *B.R. Ambedkar: A Symbol of Social Revolt*, (New Delhi: Maharashtra Information Centre, 1964), [Pamphlet].

Tope, T.K., "The Socialist", in B.K. Ahluwalia and Shashi Ahluwalia (eds.), *B.R. Ambedkar and Human Rights*, (New Delhi: Vivek Publishing Company, 1981).

Toppo, S.R., *Caste: A Social Evil*, (New Delhi: Rajat Publications, 2000).

Trawick, M., "Untouchability and the Fear of Death in a Tamil Song", in Lutz A. Catherine and Lila Abu-Lughod (eds.), *Language and Politics of Emotions*, (Cambridge: University of Cambridge Press, 1990).

Trawick, Margaret E., "Internal Iconocity in Paraiyar Crying

Songs", in Stuart Blackburn and A.K. Ramanujan (eds.), *Another Harmony: New Essays on the Foklore of India*, (Berkeley: University of California Press, 1986).

Tripathi, C.B., *Educational Development of the Scheduled Castes and Scheduled Tribes of Madhya Pradesh Since Independence to 1973*, (Bhopal: Ministry of Home Affairs, 1981), [On behalf of the Office of the Zonal Director, Backward Classes Welfare (Central Zone)].

Tripathi, Gyandev Mani, "The Desire for Education", in Hemant Joshi and Sanjay Kumar (eds.), *Asserting Voices: Changing Culture, Identity and Livelihood of the Musahars in the Gangetic Plains*, (Delhi: Deshkal Publications, 2002).

Tripathi, Raj Mani, "Protective Discrimination and Socio-Economic Profile of Scheduled Caste Population in India", in A.K. Lal (ed.), *Protective Discrimination: Ideology and Praxis*, (New Delhi: Concept, 2002), [Published for B.G. Pant Social Science Institute, Allahabad].

Tripathi, R.S. and P.D. Tiwari (eds.), *Dimensions of Scheduled Caste Development in India: Problems and Prospects*, (New Delhi: Uppal, 1991).

Tripathy, A.K., "Religion and Social Change in India: Appreciation of the Role of Dr. Ambedkar", in P.K. Mohapatra (ed.), *Religion and Social Change*, (Cuttack: Akash, 1993).

Tripathy, R.B., *Dalits: A Sub-Human Society*, (New Delhi: Ashish Publishing House, 1994).

Trivedi, H.R., *Scheduled Caste Women: Studies in Exploitation with reference to Superstition, Ignorance and Poverty*, (New Delhi: Concept, 1977).

Trivedi, H.R., *Scheduled Castes' Quest for Land and Social Equality*, (New Delhi: Concept, 1996).

U.S. Office of Strategic Services, Research and Analysis Branch, *The Depressed Classes of India*, (Washington, D.C., Ann Arbor: University of Michigan Microfilms, 1943).

Uke, N.G., "Dr. B.R. Ambedkar and National Unity", in Bhajan Kaur (ed.), *The Philosophy of Dr. B.R. Ambedkar*, (Chandigarh: Dr. Ambedkar Study Circle, 1999).

Underwood, A.S., "The Depressed Classes", in *Contemporary Thought of India,* (New York: Alfred A. Knopf, 1931).

University Grants Commission, *Facilities to Scheduled Castes and Scheduled Tribes in Universities and Colleges,* (New Delhi: UGC, 1982).

'Untouchability' – A Challenge: The Right Approach, (Banglore: Jagarana Prakashana, n.d.).

Upadhyay, H.C., *Harijans of Himalaya: With Special Reference to the Harijans of Kumaun Hills,* (Nainital: Gnanodaya Prakashan, 1990).

Upadhyay, H.C., *Reservations for Scheduled Castes and Scheduled Tribes in India: A Socio-Economic Profile,* (New Delhi: Anmol, 1991).

Uplaonkar, Ambarao R., "Social Background and Occupations Aspirations of College Students: A Case of Scheduled Castes Vis-à-vis non-Scheduled Caste Students in Higher Education", in Vimal P. Shah and Binod C. Agrawal (eds.), *Reservation: Policy, Programmes and Issues,* (Jaipur: Rawat Publications, 1986).

Urade, S.K., *Justice Versus Injustice: Dr. Ambedkar, Mr. Arun Shourie's Invectives and Realities Unveiled,* (Nagpur: Sanket Prakashan, 1997).

Usha Rao, N.J., *Deprived Castes in India,* (Allahabad: Chugh Publications, 1981).

Usha Rao, N.J., "Inter-State Disparities in Literacy Rates in Karnataka with Special Reference to Scheduled Castes", in L.S. Bhat, A. Mathur, K.R.G. Nair and M.S.A. Rao (eds.), *Regional Inequalities in India: An Inter-State and Intra-State Analysis,* (New Delhi: Society for the Study of Regional Disparities, 1982).

Usuda, Masayuki, "Pushed Towards the Partition: Jogendranath Mandal and the Constrained Namasudra Movement", in H. Kotani (ed.), *Caste System, Untouchability and the Depressed,* (New Delhi: Manohar, 1997).

Vadasery, Jose and K.K. Verma, "Dalit Christians of Bihar and the Demand for Reservations", in Makhan Jha (ed.),

Scheduled Castes Today, (New Delhi: M.D. Publications, 1997).

Vadasery, Jose, "Dalit Literacy and Education in Bihar", in A.K. Lal (ed.), *Protective Discrimination: Ideology and Praxis*, (New Delhi: Concept, 2002), [Published for B.G. Pant Social Science Institute, Allahabad].

Vagiswari, A., *Income-Earning Trends and Social Status of the Harijan Community in Tamil Nadu*, (Madras: Sangam Publishers, 1972).

Vaikom Satyagraha Commemoration Volume, (Vaikkam: 1977).

Vairal, Sanjay, "Religious Conversions and Dalit Identity", in Ambrose Pinto (ed.), *Dalit Assertion for Identity*, (New Delhi: Indian Social Institute, 1999), [Proceedings of the National Seminar of Dalit Postgraduate and Research Students held on 23-25 January 1999 in the Indian Social Institute].

Vaishnav, T.K., "Identity and Development of the Scheduled Tribes, Scheduled Castes and Other Backward Classes in Madhya Pradesh", in V.K. Pant and B.S. Bisht (eds.), *Backward Communities: Identity, Development and Transformation*, (New Delhi: Gyan, 1999).

Vakil, A.K., *Reservation Policy and Scheduled Castes in India*, (New Delhi: Ashish, 1985).

Vakil, A.K., *Gandhi-Ambedkar Dispute*, (New Delhi: Ashish, 1991).

Varadarajan, A., *Dr. B.R. Ambedkar and Popular Sovereignty*, (Dharwad: Department of Political Science, Karnatak University, 1982), [Dr. Babasaheb Ambedkar Memorial Publication—I.].

Vatsa, Rajendra Singh (edited with an Introduction), *The Depressed Classes of India: An Enquiry into their Conditions and Suggestions for their Uplift*, (New Delhi: Gitanjali Prakashan, 1977), (First published in 1912).

Veeramani, K., *For Scheduled Castes', Scheduled Tribes' and OBCs: Why Reservation?*, (Madras: The Dravidar Kazhagam Publication, 1983).

Veeramani, K., *The History of the Struggle for Social Justice in Tamil Nadu.* (Madras: Dravidar Kazhagam Publications, 1992).

Venkata Reddy, K., "B.R. Ambedkar and Beyond", in *Ambedkar and Social Justice,* Vol. II, (New Delhi: Director, Publications Division, Ministry of Information and Broadcasting, 1992), [on behalf of Baba Saheb Dr. B.R. Ambedkar Birth Centenary Celebrations Committee, Ministry of Welfare, Government of India].

Venkata Siva Reddy, G., "Competition and Conflict among the Dalits: Madiga Dandora Movement in Andhra Pradesh", in Ghanshyam Shah (ed.), *Dalits and the State,* (New Delhi: Concept Publishing Company, 2002), [Published for Centre for Rural Studies, Lal Bahadur Shastri National Academy of Administration, Mussoorie].

Venkataraman, S.R., *Harijans Through the Ages,* (Madras: Bharati Devi Publications, 1946).

Venkataratnam, R., "Self-fulfilling Prophecy: An insight into Prejudice vs. Reality", in Tripathi R.S. and P.D. Tiwari (eds.), *Dimensions of Scheduled caste Development in India,* (New Delhi: Uppal, 1991).

Venkataswamy, P.R., *Our Struggle for Emancipation,* 2 vols.,(Secunderabad: Universal Art Printers, 1955), [This provides a systematic documented history of Dalit movement in Hyderabad region].

Venkateswarlu, D., *Harijan–Upper Caste Conflict,* (New Delhi: Discovery Publishing House, 1990).

Venkatraman, S.R., *Temple Entry Legislation: Reviewed with Acts and Bills,* (Madras: Bharat Devi Publications, 1946).

Venkatraman, S.R., *Untouchables Liberation Movement,* (Madras: 1952).

Verba, Sidney, Bashiruddin Ahmed and Anil Bhatt, *Race, Caste and Politics: A Comparative Study of India and the U.S.,* (Bevery Hills, New York: Sage, 1972).

Verghese, Sudha, "Dignity and Daily Life", in Hemant Joshi and Sanjay Kumar (eds.), *Asserting Voices: Changing*

Culture, Identity and Livelihood of the Musahars in the Gangetic Plains, (Delhi: Deshkal Publications, 2002).

Verma, B.M., *Welfare Measures for Weaker Sections (A Policy Analysis)*, (New Delhi: Devika Publications, 1996).

Verma, G.P., *Caste Reservation in Indian Law and the Constitution*, (Allahabad: Chugh Publications, 1980).

Verma, Mukut Behari, *History of the Harijan Sevak Sangh, 1932–1968*, (Delhi: Harijan Sevak Sangh, 1971).

Verma, R.B., "Dr. Ambedkar – Buddhism and Marxism", in R.B. Rao (ed.), *Bharat-Ratna Dr. Ambedkar*, (Allahabad: Chugh Publications, 1993).

Verma, R.C., "Welfare Programmes for Scheduled Castes in Punjab: Some observations or Critical Deficiencies in them", in V.S. Mahajan and B.S. Mann (eds.), *Economic Development of Scheduled Castes*, (New Delhi: Anmol, 1997).

Vibhute, Bhalba, "Dr. Ambedkar on Education", in K.K. Kavlekar and A.S. Chausalkar (eds.), *Political Ideas and Leadership of Dr. B.R. Ambedkar*, (Pune: Vishwanil Publications, 1989).

Vidhyarthi, L.P. and N. Mishra, *Harijan Today: Sociological, Economic, Political, Religious and Cultural Analysis*, (Delhi: Classical Publications, 1977).

Vidrohi, M.R., *Dalit Dastavaij*, (New Delhi: Dalit Sahitya Prakashan Sanstha, 1989).

Vijaya Lakshmi, K., Y. Srilatha and T. Rajani, "Dalit Mobilisation through Education", in Ambrose Pinto (ed.), *Dalit Assertion for Identity*, (New Delhi: Indian Social Institute, 1999), [Proceedings of the National Seminar of Dalit Postgraduate and Research Students held on 23-25 January 1999 in the Indian Social Institute].

Vinod, M.J., "The Partition of India: The Ambedkar Viewpoint", in V.T. Patil (ed.), *Studies in Ambedkar*, (Delhi: Devika Publications, 1995).

Vinod Rao, B.N., "Dr. B.R. Ambedkar – A Boon for the Industrial Labour", in J.S. Narayana Rao, A. Somasekhar and K. Audiseshaiah (eds.), *B.R. Ambedkar: His Relevance Today*, (New Delhi: Gyan Publishing House, 1994).

Viramma, Josiane and Jean-Luc Racine, *Viramma: Life of an Untouchable*, (Tr. from the French by Will Hobson), (London: Verso, 1997), (UNESCO Collection of Representative Works).

Viswanadham, G. and K. Narasimha Reddy, *Scheduled Castes: A Study in Educational Achievement*, (Hyderabad: Scientific Services, 1985).

Viswanath, Leela, *Social Mobility Among Scheduled Caste Women in India*, (New Delhi: Uppal, 1993).

Vivek, P.S., *The Scavengers: Exploited Class of City Professionals*, (New Delhi: Himalaya Publishing House, 1998).

Vyas, S.K., *Educational Schemes for Scheduled Castes*, (New Delhi: Shree Publishing House, 1986).

Wadhwa, Kamlesh Kumar, *Minority Safeguards in India (Constitutional Provisions and Their Implementation)*, (Delhi: Thompson Press, 1975).

Wadia, Sophia, *Theosophy and Untouchability*, (Bombay: Servants of Untouchables Society, 1932).

Waghmare, J.M., *A Study of Relationship Between Education and Social Status among Scheduled Caste Students*, (Pune: Indian Institute of Education, 1985).

Wagmore, B.S., "Impact of Protective Discrimination Policy on Marginal Scheduled Caste Groups in Maharashtra", in C.P. Barthwal (ed.), *Social Justice in India*, (Lucknow: Bharat Book Centre, 1998).

Wanger, E.G. and J.N. Lanoix, *Excreta Disposal for Rural Areas and Small Communities*, (Geneva: World Health Organisation, 1958).

Wani, M. Afzal, "Threat of Ethnicity to Indian Union: Ambedkar's Views", in Nazeer H. Khan (ed.), *B.R. Ambedkar on Federalism, Ethnicity and Gender Justice*, (New Delhi: Deep & Deep, 2001).

Wankhade, G.G., *Social Mobility and Scheduled Castes: Recent Horizons*, (New Delhi: Rawat, 1999).

Wankhade, Vaishali, "Experiences of Harassment", in Ambrose Pinto (ed.), *Dalit Assertion for Identity*, (New Delhi: Indian Social Institute, 1999), [Proceedings of the National Seminar of Dalit Postgraduate and Research Students held on 23-25 January 1999 in the Indian Social Institute].

Web, W.C., *Crime Against Humanity*, (New Delhi: Uppal, 1993).

Webster, John C.B., "Who is a Dalit", in S.M. Michael (ed.), *Dalits in Modern India*, (New Delhi: Vistaar Publications, 1999).

Webster, John C.B., *A History of the Dalit Christians of India*, (Lewiston, New York: Edwin Mellen, 1992). There is also an Indian edition: *The Dalit Christians: A History*, (Delhi: ISPCK, 1992).

Webster, John C.B., *The Pastor to Dalits*, (Delhi: ISPCK, 1995), [ISPCK Contextual Theological Education Series No. 8].

Webster, John C.B., Deborah Premraj, Ida Swamidoss, Rashilda Udayakumar and Chandra Yesuratnam, *From Role to Identity: Dalit Christian Women in Transition*, (Delhi: ISPCK, 1997).

Webster, John C.B., *Religion and Dalit Liberation: An Examination of Perspectives*, (New Delhi: Manohar, 1999).

Weibe, P. and S.J. Peter, "The Catholic Church and Caste in Rural Tamil Nadu", in H. Singh (ed.), *Caste Among Non-Hindus in India*, (New Delhi: National, 1977).

Welbon, Guy R., "The Candala's Song", in Guy R. Welbon and Glen E. Yocum (Eds.), *Religious Fest9ivals in South India and Sri Lanka*, (New Delhi: Manohar, 1982).

Whitehead, Henry, *Work Among the India's Outcastes*, (London: CMS, 1912).

Whitehead, Henry, *The Village Gods of South India*, (Delhi: Summit Publications, 1976), (First published in 1921).

Wilkinson, T.S. and M.M. Thomas (eds.), *Ambedkar and the Neo-Buddhist Movement*, (Madras: Christian Literature Society; Bangalore: Christian Institute for the Study of Religion and Society, 1972).

Wilkinson, T.S., "Buddhism and Social Change among Mahars", in T.S. Wilkinson and M.M. Thomas (eds.), *Ambedkar and the Neo-Buddhist Movement*, (Madras: Christian Literature Society; Bangalore: Christian Institute for the Study of Religion and Society, 1972).

Wilson, K., *The Twice Alienated: Culture of Dalit Christians*, (Hyderabad: Booklinks Corporation, 1982).

Wilson, K., "The post-Ambedkar Indian Experience", in K.S. Chalam (ed.), *The Relevance of Ambedkarism in India*, (Jaipur: Rawat, 1993).

Wilson, Kothapalli, "A Dalit Theology of Human Self-Development", in James Massey (ed.), *Indigenous People, Dalits: Dalit Issues in Today's Theological Debate*, (Delhi: ISPCK, 1998), (First Published in1994).

Yadav, C.P. (ed.), *Encyclopedia of Scheduled Castes and Scheduled Tribes*, 4 vols., (Lucknow: Institute for Sustainable Development and New Delhi: Anmol, 2000).

Yadav, K.C. (ed.), *From Periphery to Centre Stage: Ambedkar, Ambedkarism and Dalit Future*, (New Delhi: Manohar, 2000).

Yadav, K.C., "Empowering the Powerless: Dr. Ambedkar's contribution to the Ideology of Dalit Protest", in K.C. Yadav, (ed.), *From Periphery to Centre Stage: Ambedkar, Ambedkarism and Dalit Future*, (New Delhi: Manohar, 2000).

Yadav, K.C. and S.K. Chahal, "Ambedkarian Framework of Nation-Building: A Critical Enquiry", in M.L. Ranga (ed.), *B.R. Ambedkar: His Life, Work and Relevance*, (New Delhi: Manohar, 2000).

Yadav, Karan Deo, "Dr. Bhim Rao Ambedkar – Great Honourable Man of the Nation", in R.B. Rao (ed.), *Bharat-Ratna Dr. Ambedkar*, (Allahabad: Chugh Publications, 1993).

Yadav, R.R., "Ambedkar: A Judicious Evaluation", in Shyam Lal and K.S. Saxena (eds.), *Ambedkar and Nation-Building*, (Jaipur: Rawat, 1998).

Yadav, Subash Singh, "Dr. Bhim Rao Ambedkar – A Creator of Social Justice", in R.B. Rao (ed.), *Bharat-Ratna Dr. Ambedkar*, (Allahabad: Chugh Publications, 1993).

Yadava, S.K., *Harijan Awareness of Educational Schemes*, (Haryana: The Academic Press, 1983).

Yadava, S.K. and N.K. Jangira, *Dynamics of Social Stagnation: An Excursion into Scheduled Caste Families*, (Delhi: Shree Publishing House, 1985).

Yadava, S.K., *Educational Schemes for Scheduled Castes*, (Delhi: Shree Publishing House, 1985).

Yadava, S.K., *Education of Scheduled Castes*, (New Delhi: Common Wealth Publishers, 1991).

Yamazaki, Gen'ichi, "Introduction: Social Discrimination in Ancient India and its Transition to the Medieval Period", in H. Kotani (ed.), *Caste System, Untouchability and the Depressed*, (New Delhi: Manohar, 1997).

Yamazaki, Gen'ichi, *Society in Ancient India: The Social Structure and Middle/Low Classes*, (Tokyo: 1986).

Yasudasan, T.M., "Caste, Gender and Knowledge: Towards a Dalit Feminist Perspective", in Ashish Ghosh (ed.), Dalits and Peasants, (Delhi: Gyan Sagar, 1999).

Yogi, Praveen, *Social Justice and Empowerment*, (Delhi: Kalpaz, 2000).

Youngson, John W., "Chuhras", in James Hastings (ed.), *Encyclopedia of Religion and Ethics*, Vol. III, (New York: 1913),

Yurlova, Eugenia S., *Scheduled Castes in India*, (New Delhi: Patriot, 1990).

Zelliot, Eleanor, "Background of the Mahar Buddhist Conversion", in Robert Sakai (ed.), *Studies on Asia*, (Lincoln: University of Nebraska, 1966).

Zelliot, Eleanor, "Buddhism and Politics in Maharashtra", in Donald Eugene Smith (ed.), *Religion and Politics in South Asia*, (Princeton: Princeton University Press, 1966).

Zelliot, Eleanor, "Learning the Use of Political Means—The Mahars of Maharashtra", in Rajni Kothari (ed.), *Caste in Indian Politics*, (New Delhi: Orient Longmans, 1970), [Reprinted in 1973, 1985 and 1991].

Zelliot, Eleanor, "Gandhi and Ambedkar: A Study in Leadership", in J. Michael Mahar (ed.), *The Untouchables in Contemporary India*, (Tucson: University of Arizona Press, 1972), [This article was reprinted as a pamphlet by Triratna Grantha Mala, Pune, 1983].

Zelliot, Eleanor, "The Medieval Bhakti Movement in History – An Essay on the Literature in English", in Bardwell L. Smith (ed.), *Hinduism: New Essays in the History of Religions*, (Leiden: E.J. Brill, 1976), [Numen Series].

Zelliot, Eleanor, "The American Experience of Dr. B.R. Ambedkar", in R.D. Suman (ed.), *Dr. Ambedkar: Pioneer of Human Rights*, (New Delhi: Bodhisattva Publications, Ambedkar Institute of Buddhist Studies, 1977).

Zelliot, Eleanor, "The Leadership of Babasaheb Ambedkar", in B.N. Pandey (ed.), *Leadership in South Asia*, (New Delhi: Vikas, 1977).

Zelliot, Eleanor, "The Psychological Dimension of the Buddhist Movement in India", in G.A. Oddie (ed.), *Religion in South Asia: Religious Conversion and Revival Movements in Medieval and Modern Times*, (New Delhi: Manohar, 1977).

Zelliot, Eleanor, "Religion and Legitimization in the Mahar Movement", in Bardwell L. Smith (ed.), *Religion and Legitimization in South Asia*, (Leiden: E.J. Brill, 1978).

Zelliot, Eleanor, "Dalit – New Cultural Context of an Old Marathi Word", in Clarence Maloney (ed.), *Language and Civilization Change in South Asia*, (Leiden: E.J. Brill, 1978).

Zelliot, Eleanor, "The Indian Rediscovery of Buddhism, 1855-1956", in A.K. Narain (ed.), *Studies in Pali and Buddhism: A Memorial Volume in Honour of Bhikku Jagdish Kashyap*, (New Delhi: D.K. Publishers, 1978).

Zelliot, Eleanor and Joanna Rogers Macy, "Tradition and Innovation in Contemporary Indian Buddhism", in A.K.

Narain (ed.), *Studies in History of Buddhism,* (Delhi: B.R. Publishing Corporation, 1980).

Zelliot, Eleanor, "An Historical View of the Maharashtrian Intellectual and Social Change", in Yogendra K. Malik (ed.), *South Asian Intellectuals and Social Change: A Study of the Role of Vernacular Speaking Intellectuals,* (Columbia, Mo: South Asia Books and New Delhi: Heritage Publishers, 1982).

Zelliot, Eleanor, "A Medieval Encounter between Hindu and Muslim: Eknath's Drama-poem *Hindu-turk samvad*", in Fred Clothey (ed.), *Images of Man: Religion and Historical Process in South Asia,* (Madras: New Era, 1982).

Zelliot, Eleanor, "Dr. B.R. Ambedkar", in *Encyclopaedia of Religion,* Chief Editor, Mircea Eliade, (New York: Macmillan, 1986).

Zelliot, Eleanor, "The Folklore of Pride: Three Components of Contemporary Dalit Belief", in Gunther D. Sontheimer (ed.), *Folk Culture, Folk Religion and Oral traditions as a Component in Maharashtrian Culture,* (Forthcoming Proceedings of the Third Maharashtrian Conference held in Heidelberg in 1986).

Zelliot, Eleanor, "The Political Thought of Dr. B.R. Ambedkar", in Thomas Pantham and Kenneth L. Deutsch (eds.), *Contemporary Indian Political Thought,* (Delhi: Sage Publications, 1986).

Zelliot, Eleanor, "Four Radical Saints of Maharashtra", in Milton Israel and N.K. Wagle (eds.), *Religion and Society in Maharashtra,* (Toronto: Centre for South Asian Studies, University of Toronto, 1987).

Zelliot, Eleanor, "Untouchability", "Dr. B.R. Ambedkar", in *Encyclopaedia of Asian History,* Ainslee Embree, Chief Editor, (New York: Charles Scribners Sons, 1988).

Zelliot, Eleanor, "Dr. B.R. Ambedkar: Selections from his Writings and Speeches", in Stephen Hay (ed.), *Sources of Indian Civilization,* (New York: Columbia University Press, 1988), [Revised Edition].

Zelliot, Eleanor, "Congress and the Untouchables", in Stanley Wolpert and Richard Sission (eds.), *Congress and Indian Nationalism*, (Berkeley: University of California Press, 1988).

Zelliot, Eleanor, "Dalit—New Perspectives on India's Ex-Untouchables", in Philip Oldenburg (ed.), *India Briefing 1991*, (The Asia Society, 1991).

Zelliot, Eleanor, "Buddhist Women of the Contemporary Maharashtrian Conversion Movement", in Jose Cabezon (ed.), *Buddhism, Sexuality and Gender*, (Albany: State University of New York Press, 1992).

Zelliot, Eleanor and Mulk Raj Anand (eds.), *An Anthology of Dalit Literature*, (New Delhi: Gyan, 1992), [in her own words, "a wretchedly printed thing that I am hiding from almost everyone].

Zelliot, Eleanor, *From Untouchable To Dalit: Essays on the Ambedkar Movement*, (New Delhi: Manohar, 2001), Third Edition, (First Published in 1992).

Zelliot, Eleanor, "Mahar", in Paul Hockings (ed.), *Encyclopaedia of World Cultures*, Vol. II, (Boston: G.K. Hall, 1992).

Zelliot, Eleanor, "Dr. Ambedkar through Western Eyes", in K.N. Kadam (ed.), *Dr. Ambedkar: The Emancipator of the Oppressed*, (Bombay: Popular Prakashan, 1993).

Zelliot, Eleanor, "New Voices of the Buddhists of India", in A.K. Narain and D.C. Ahir (eds.), *Dr. Ambedkar, Buddhism and Social Change*, (Delhi: B.R. Publishing Corporation, 1994).

Zelliot, Eleanor, "Should We Study Caste in Order To Abolish It?", in Sandeep Pendse (ed.), *Dalit Movement Today*, (Bombay: Vikas Adhyayana Kendra, 1994), [Vikas Adhyayan Kendra, Bombay, *Perspectives* 1].

Zelliot, Eleanor, "The New Buddhist Poetry", in A.K. Narain and D.C. Ahir (eds.), *Dr. Ambedkar, Buddhism and Social Change*, (Delhi: B.R. Publishing Corporation, 1994).

Zelliot, Eleanor (tr.), "Daya Pawar's The Buddha", in *Oxford Anthology of Modern Indian Poetry*, (New Delhi: 1994).

Zelliot, Eleanor, "Cokhamela: Piety and Protest" in David Lorenzen (ed.), *Bhakti Religion in North India: Community, Identity and Political Action*, (Albany: State University of New York Press, 1995).

Zelliot, Eleanor, "The Poetry of Dalit Women", in Saral K.Chatterjee and Hunter P. Mabry (eds.), *Culture, Religion and Society: Essays in Honour of Richard W. Tylor*, (Delhi: ISPCK, 1996), (Published for the Christian Institute for he Study of Religion and Society, Bangalore).

Zelliot, Eleanor, "The Folklore of Pride: Three Components of Contemporary Dalit Belief", in Gunther D. Sontheimer (ed.), *Folk Culture, Folk Religion and Oral Traditions as a Component in Maharashtrian Culture*, (University of Heidelberg, 1996).

Zelliot, Eleanor, "Stri Dalit Sahitya: The New Voice of Women Poets", in Anne Feldhaus (ed.), *Images of Women in Maharastrian Literature and Religion*, (Albany: State University of New York Press, 1996).

Zelliot, Eleanor, "Bhimrao Ramji Ambedkar", in Henry Scholberg (ed.), *The Biographical Dictionary of Greater India*, (Delhi: Promilla and Co., 1998).

Zelliot, Eleanor, "Fifty Years of Dalit Politics", in Yogendra K. Malik and Ashok Kapur (eds.), *India, Fifty Years of Independence: Assessment and Prospects*, (New Delhi: APH Publishing Corporation, 1998).

Zelliot, Eleanor, "Dr. Ambedkar Speaks to Government", in Virender Grover (ed.), *Bhimrao Ramji Ambedkar: A Biography of His Vision and Ideas*, (New Delhi: Deep and Deep, 1998).

Zelliot, Eleanor, "The American Experience of Dr. B.R. Ambedkar", in Virender Grover (ed.), *Bhimrao Ramji Ambedkar: A Biography of His Vision and Ideas*, (New Delhi: Deep and Deep, 1998).

Zelliot, Eleanor, "The Process of Securing places of Power for Dalits: A Note on Ambedkar's Contribution", in K.C. Yadav, (ed.), *From Periphery to Centre Stage: Ambedkar, Ambedkarism and Dalit Future*, (New Delhi: Manohar, 2000).

Zelliot, Eleanor, "The Meaning of Ambedkar", in Ghanshyam Shah (ed.), *Dalit Identity and Politics*, (New Delhi: Sage Publications, 2001), [Cultural Subordination and the Dalit Challenge, Vol. 2 of Sage series].

Zelliot, Eleanor, "Dalit Tradition and Socio-Economic Change", in Sudha Pai (ed.), *Democratic Government in India: Challenges of Poverty, Development and Identity*, (New Delhi: Sage, 2001).

Zelliot, Eleanor, "Experiments in Dalit Education: Maharashtra, 1850–1947", in Sabyasachi Bhattacharya (ed.), *Education and the Disprivileged: Nineteenth and Twentieth Century India*, (New Delhi: Orient Longman, 2002).

Zelliot, Eleanor, "Bombay/Mumbai and the Ambedkar Movement: Past and Present", in Sujata Patel, Jasodhara Bagchi and Krishna Raj (eds.), *Thinking Social Science in India: Essays in Honour of Alice Thorner*, (New Delhi: Sage, 2002).

Zelliot, Eleanor, "Dr. B.R. Ambedkar", in *New Dictionary of National Biography*, (Oxford, England: forthcoming).

2

Articles (Published in Periodicals/Journals)

Abbasayulu, Y.B., "The Emergence of Scheduled Caste Elite: Factors and Process", *Indian Journal of Social Research,* Vol.19, (1978).

Abel, Elie, "India's Untouchables—Still the 'Black Sin'", *New York Times Magazine,* (March 1, 1959).

Abraham, A., "Importance of Renaming Marathwada University", *Economic and Political Weekly,* Vol. 14, No. 29, (1979).

Abraham, A.N., "The Fate of an Untouchable God", *Dalit Voice,* Vol. I, No. 14, (1988).

Abraham, A.S., "Caste War in the Villages: The Challenge of Modernisation", *Times of India,* (August 14, 1978).

Abraham, A.S., "Promoting Equal Opportunity: Positive Discrimination Becomes a Force", *Times of India,* (March 21, 1978).

Abraham, Abu, "Ambedkar the Great", *The Hindu,* (31 August 1997).

Abraham, Amrita, "A Report From Marathwada", *Economic and Political Weekly,* Vol. 14, No. 19, (May 12, 1979).

Abraham, Merey and A. Sudharjma, "Role of Financial and Lumpsum Grant in Reducing Wastage and Stagnation

Among the Scheduled Caste/Scheduled Tribe Students in the Secondary Schools of Kerala", *Journal of Education and Psychology*, Vol. 46, Nos. 1-2, (1988).

Achutan, R., "Untouchability – A Myth", *Yojana*, Vol. 3, No. 15, (March 9, 1969).

Adiseshiah, Malcolm, "Scheduled Castes and Tribes in Higher Education in Tamil Nadu", *Journal of Higher Education*, Vol. 1, No. 2, (1975).

Agarwal, D.D., "Ethnographical Notes on the Cheros (Mirzapur, United Provinces)", *Man in India*, Vol. 9, No. 4, (1929).

Aggarwal, H.N., "Blood Group of the Pasis with special Reference to their Genetic Relationship with Other Castes of U.P.", *Eastern Anthropologist*, Vol. 10, No. 2, (1962).

Aggarwal, Yash, "Some Aspects of Educational Development among the Scheduled Caste Population in India", *Journal of Educational Planning and Administration*, Vol. 1, No. 2, (1987).

Aggarwal, Yash, "Some Aspects of Social and Economic Inequities among Scheduled Castes in India", *Journal of Higher Education*, Vol. 21, No. 3, (1998).

Agrawal, Binod C., "Harijan, Chamar No More: A Case Study", *Journal of Social and Economic Studies*, Vol. 2, No. 2, (1974).

Ahir, D.C., "Seven Years of Ambedkar Era", *Maha Bodhi*, No. 72, (1964).

Ahmad, Imtiaz, "Muslims and Scheduled Castes", *New Quest*, Vol. 19, No. 1, (1980).

Ahmad, Imtiaz, "Threats and Responses: Conversions in Tamil Nadu", *Economic and Political Weekly*, Vol. 17, No. 43, (1980).

Ahmad, Karuna, "Towards Equality: The Consequences of Protective Discrimination", *Economic and Political Weekly*, Vol. 13, No. 2, (1978).

Ahmad, Karuna, "Towards Equality: Consequences of

Protective Discrimination", *Economic and Political Weekly,* (Annual Number), (February 1979).

Ahuja, S.P. and K.M.L. Chhabra, "Special Schemes for Scheduled Castes Rural Households: Case for Greater Impetus", *IASSI Quarterly,* Vol. 9, Nos. 1-2, (July-December, 1990).

Aijaz, R. and S. Monga, "Educational Development of Scheduled and Scheduled Tribes in Maharashtra, Tamil Nadu and Orissa", *Social Change,* Vol. 18, No. 1, (1988).

Aikara, Jacob, "Scheduled Castes and Higher Education: A Study of College Students in Bombay", *Education Quarterly,* Vol. 33, No. 3, (1981).

Aikara, Jacob, "Inequality of Educational Opportunities: The Case of Scheduled Castes in India", *Journal Educational Planning and Administration,* Vol. 10, No. 1, (January, 1996).

Aiyappan, A., "Social and Physical Anthropology of the Nayadis of Malabar", *Bulletin of the Madras Government Museum,* (New Series), Vol. 2, No. 4, (1937).

Aiyappan, A., "Blood Groups of the Nayadis of Malabar", *Man,* Vol. 39, (Article No. 199), (1939).

Aiyappan, A., "Iravas and Culture Change", *Bulletin of the Madras Government Museum,* (1945).

Aiyar, T.V. Seshagiri, "The Depressed Classes, *The Indian Review,* (June, 1910).

Aiyer, P.R., "The Depressed Classes", *The Indian Review,* (December, 1910).

Alam, Khurshid, "Educational Aspirations and Dropout Factors among Scheduled Castes", *Indian Journal of Community Guidance Service,* Vol. 4, No. 1, (1987).

Aleaz, K.P., "The Convergence of Dalit-Advaitic Theologies", *Indian Journal of Theology,* Vol. 36, No. 1, (1994).

Alexander, Horace G., "Mr. Gandhi and Untouchability", *Contemporary Review,* No. 147, (1935).

Alexander, K.C., "The Problem of the Neo-Christians of Kerala", *Man in India,* Vol. 47, No. 4, (1960).

Alexander, K.C., "Changing Status of Pulaya Harijans of Kerala", *Economic and Political Weekly*, Vol. 3, Nos. 26-28, (Special Number), (1968).

Alexander, K.C., G.L. Verma and E.C. Jayakumar, "Social Development of Weaker Sections: A Study in Krishna District, Andhra Pradesh", *Behavioural Success and Rural Development*, Vol. 4, No. 2, (1981).

Alone, Y.S., "Dalit Imagery", *Pioneer*, (28 January 2000).

Ambarao, U., "Higher Education and Occupational Mobility Among the Scheduled Castes", *Journal of Higher Education*, Vol. 1, No. 3, (1976).

Ambedkar, B.R., "Castes in India – Their Mechanism, Genesis and Development", *The Indian Antiquary*, XLVI, (1916/7).

Ambedkar, Dr. B.R., "Presidential Address", All India Depressed Classes Conference, *Indian Annual Register*, Vol. II, (1930), [Extracts].

Ambedkar, Dr. B.R., "What Ails the World Today", *The Indian Reader's Digest*, (July 1943).

Ambedkar, Dr. B.R., "Rise and Fall of Hindu Women: Who is Responsible for it?", *Journal of Mahabodhi Society of India*, Nos. 5-6, (May-June, 1951].

Ambedkar, Dr. B.R., "The Original Home of the Hindus", *The Organiser*, (23 July 1952).

Ambedkar, Dr. B.R., "Prospects of Parliamentary Democracy in India", [Talk for the B.B.C., London, 20 May 1956].

Ambirajan, S., "Ambedkar's Contributions to Indian Economics", *Economic and Political Weekly*, Vol. 34, No. 46 and 47, (1999).

Ameerjan, M.S., "A Comparative Study of Academic Achievement of the Scheduled Caste and Tribe Students of Agriculture", *Journal of Education and Psychology*, Vol. 37, No. 2, (1979).

Ameerjan, M.S., "Background Variables of the Scheduled Caste and Tribe Colleges", *Indian Educational Review*, Vol. 19, No. 2, (1984).

Amicus, "The Madras Government and the Pariahs", *Harvest Field*, Vol. 4, Nos. 3 and 4, (1893).

Amicus, "The Madras Government and the Pariahs", *Harvest Field*, Vol. 5, Nos. 3–5, (1894).

Anand, Mulk Raj, "The Story of My Experiment with a White Lie", *Indian Literature*, Vol. X, (1967), [The Story of writing *Untouchable*].

Anand, S., "Sanskrit, English and Dalits", *Economic and Political Weekly*, Vol. 34, No. 30, (1999).

Anandan, P.M., "The Coronation and the Depressed Classes", *Hindustan Review*, Vol. XXIV, No. 138, (December, 1911).

Anandan, Sujata, "Has Neo-Buddhism Lost Relevance?", *Illustrated Weekly of India*, (26 August 1982).

Anant, Santokh Singh, "Caste Hindu Attitudes: The Harijans' Perception", *Asian Survey*, Vol. 11, No. 3, (1971).

Anant, Santosh S., "Caste Prejudice and Its Perceptions by Harijans", *Journal of Social Psychology*, (December, 1970).

Andrews, C.F., "The Untouchable Problem", *Contemporary Review*, (New York), No. 144, (August, 1933).

Annamalai, V., "Wanted Not Jati Identity but Dalit Identity", *Dalit Voice*, Vol. 15, No. 18, (August 15, 1996).

Anonymous, "The Gonds and Bygas of the Eastern Satpuras", *Cornhill Magazine*, Vol. 26, (1872).

Anonymous, "Nayadis of Malabar", *Bulletin of Madras Government Museum*, Vol. 4, No. 1, (1901).

Anonymous, "Origin of the Pods and Chandals", *Journal of Asiatic Society Bengal*, Vol. 72, No. 3, (1903).

Anonymous, "Ad Dharm: Revolt of the Untouchables", *Punjab Census Report, 1931*, Vol. 20, [Chapter: 11].

Anonymous, "The Harijan Movement in India in Relation to Christianity", *International Review of Mission*, Vol. 24, (1935).

Anonymous, "New Awakening among the Scheduled Castes and the Scheduled Caste Federation", *Party Letter*, (N.S), No. 5, (20 May 1946), [This was an interim inner party statement, circulated among the (Communist) party members only].

Anonymous, "Dom and Mushhar", *Vanyajati*, Vol. 4, No. 4, (1956).

Anonymous, "Harijans of Uttar Pradesh", *Eastern Economist*, Vol. 29, No. 1, (1957).

Anonymous, "Harijans of Utter Pradesh", *Easter Economist*, Vol. 29, (1957).

Anonymous, "Dom of Kumaon", *Indian Folklore*, Vol. 2, No. 4, (1959).

Anonymous, "Progress of the Backward", *Economic Weekly*, Vol. XV, (1963).

Anonymous, "Baiga", *Adibasi*, (1963-64).

Anonymous, "Koli (Including Malhar)", *Adibasi*, (1963-64).

Anonymous, "The Plight of Harijans", *Link*, Vol. 10, No. 43, (1968).

Anonymous, "Scheduled Castes: Economic Roots of Oppression", *Economic and Political Weekly*, Vol. 9, No. 36, (1974).

Anonymous, "Eight-Fold Increase in Scheduled Castes Literacy", *Assam Information*, No. 27, (October-November 1975).

Anonymous, "Scheduled Castes: Education and Employment", *Economic and Political Weekly*, Vol. 9, No. 51, (1976).

Anonymous, "Harijans: Thirty Years Later", *Monthly Public Opinion Surveys*, Vol. XXII, No. 9, (1985).

Anonymous, "New Policy to Aim at SC, ST Education: National Core Curriculum Proposed", *Indian Express*, (22 April 1986).

Anonymous, "Implementation of Post-Matric Scholarship Scheme for Scheduled Castes and Scheduled Tribes: A Study of the Procedure", *Management in Government*, Vol. 22, Nos. 2-3, (July-December, 1990).

Anonymous, "Draft Manifesto of the Mahasabha of Joint

Dalit-Adivasi – Rural Literatures", *Olympus*, Vol. 12, No. 4, (1991).

Anonymous, "Ambedkar and Democratic Struggle", *Frontier*, Vol. 23, No. 22, (1991), (A Document circulated by CRC, CPI-ML).

Anonymous, "Condition of Scheduled Castes in Present Day India", *Link*, Vol. 35, No. 15, (November 22, 1992).

Anonymous, "Condition of Scheduled Castes in Present Day India", *Link*, Vol. 35, No. 22, (January 10, 1993).

Anonymous, "Dalit Literature in Tamil: An Interview with P. Sivakami", *Dalit International Newsletter*, (February 1997).

Anveshi Committee, "Caste and the Metropolitan University", *Economic and Political Weekly*, Vol. 37, No. 12, (2002).

Apte, Mahadev L., "'I Am Pure, You Are Polluted!' Who Is Clean and Who Is Dirty? Humor in Ritual Behavior among Marathi Speakers in India", *Etnofloor*, Vol. 1, (1988).

Arles, J.P., "The Economic and Social Promotion of the Scheduled Castes and Scheduled Tribes in India", *International Labour Review*, Vol. 103, No. 1, (1971).

Arokiaswami, M., "The Birth of the Harijan Movement", *New Review* (Calcutta), Vol. 4, (1936).

Arora, V.N., "Special Input for the Backward", *Seminar*, No. 296, (1984).

Artal, R.C., "An Account of Dakkalgers (Dharwar District)", *Journal of the Anthropological Society of Bombay*, Vol. 8, (1908).

Ashraf, Ajaz, "Why Ambedkar is a Hero and Gandhi is Not", *The Pioneer*, (29 March 1994).

Asirvadham, E., "The Depressed Classes and Christianity", *National Council of Churches (India) Review*, (December 1935).

Assayag, Jackie, "Women-Goddess, Women-Distress:

Yellamma Goddess' Devotees in South India (Karnataka)", *Man in India*, Vol. 69, No. 4, (1989).

Atyachar Virodh Samithi, "The Marathwada Riots: A Report", *Economic and Political Weekly*, Vol. 14, No. 19, (1979).

Audi, M.J., "Ambedkar's Struggle for Untouchables: Reflections", *Indian Journal of Political Science*, Vol. 50, No.3, (July-September, 1989).

Augustin, P., "Conversion as Social Protest", *Religion and Society*, Vol. 28, No. 4, (1981).

Aurora, G.S., "Caste and the Backward Classes", *Man in India*, Vol. 48, (1968).

Awachat, A., "The Dalit Panthers and their Manifesto", *Religion and Society*, Vol. 22, No. 2, (1975).

Ayurookuzhiel, A.M.A., "How Brahmanism Enslaved Dalits: The Danger of using Religion as Identity in Kerala", *Dalit Voice*, Vol. 4, No. 14, (1985).

Ayurookuzhiel, A.M.A., "Religion and Culture in Dalits' Struggle for Liberation", *Religion and Society*, Vol. XXXIII, (1986).

Ayurookuzhiel, A.M.A., "Dalit Liberation: Some Reflections on Their Ideological Predicament", *Religion and Society*, Vol. 35, No. 2, (1988).

Ayurookuzhiel, A.M.A., "Dalit History and Culture: Its Challenges and Response", *Bangalore Theological Forum*, Vol. 30, No. 1, (1989).

Ayurookuzhiel, A.M.A., "The Ideological Nature of the Emerging Dalit Consciousness", *Religion and Society*, Vol. XXXVII, No. 3, (1990).

Ayurookuzhiel, A.M.A., "Christian Dalits in Revolt", *Jeevan Dhara*, No. 136, (1993).

Ayurookuzhiel, A.M.A., "Religious Legitimisation and Delegitimisations of Social, Relations of Power (of Caste): The Case of the Dalits in Historical Perspective", *Religion and Society*, Vol. 40, No. 4, (1993).

Ayurookuzhiel, A.M.A., "A Proposal for the Study of the Religious Heritage of the Dalits: Some Methodological Considerations", *Religion and Society,* Vol. 42, No. 1, (1995).

Ayurookuzhiel, A.M.A., "The Dalit Church's Mission: A Dalit Perspective", *Indian Missiological Review,* Vol. 18, No. 3, (1996).

Azad, J.L., "Education of Scheduled Castes and Scheduled Tribes", *Journal of Indian Education,* Vol. 1, No. 6, (1976).

Azaraiah, M., "Dalit Problem is not Poverty but Denial of Human Rights", *Dalit Voice,* Vol. 13, No. 23, (1994).

Azaraiah, V.S., "An Open Letter to our Country Men Who are Classified as Belonging to the Depressed Classes", *Indian Witness,* (17 September 1936).

Azimabadi, Reyaz, "Atrocities on Harijans: Cases and Causes", *Secular Democracy,* Vol. 13, No. 4, (1980).

Aziz, Abul, et al., "Rural Development and Scheduled Castes: Case Study of a Karnataka Village", *Journal of Rural Development,* Vol. 19, No. 2, (2000).

Baboo, B., "Cognition and Structure: Explaining the 'Exploitation' of an Untouchable Caste in Orissa", *The Eastern Anthropologist,* Vol. 39, (1986).

Babu, Jeji M., "Educational Progress of Scheduled Castes and Scheduled Tribes (1968-69 to 1977-78)", *EPA Bulletin,* No. 3, (October 1980).

Badrinath, K., "The vicious Anti-Dalit Face of the Shiv Sena", *Frontline,* Vol. 11, No. 3, (1994).

Bahuguna, S.D., "Festivals among the Rawattas (Garhwal State)", *Man in India,* Vol. 12, (1932).

Bahuguna, S.D., "Marriage and Marital Life amongst the Rawattas", *Man in India,* Vol. 12, No. 4, (1932).

Bahura, N.K., "The Nature of Authority, Structure and Judicial Machinery of the Chettiar, Kusavan and the Pallan of Villpuram", *Adivasi,* No. 1, (1964-65).

Baisantry, D.K., "Ambedkar and Conversions", *Mainstream,* (31 October 1981).

Bal, Prakash, "Driven to the Wall: Dalits under Shiv Sena–BJP Rule", *Economic and Political Weekly*, Vol. 32, No. 31, (1997).

Balagopal, K., "Dalit Literature", *Economic and Political Weekly*, Vol. 17, No. 6, (1982).

Balagopal, K., "Post-Chunduru and Other Chundurus", *Economic and Political Weekly*, Vol. 26, (1991).

Balagopal, K., "A Tangled Web: Subdivision of SC Reservations in AP", *Economic and Political Weekly*, Vol. 35, No. 13, (2000).

Balakrishnan, Rajiv, "Religious Conversion and Socio-Economic Conditions Among the Scheduled Castes: Evidence from South India", *Social Action*, Vol. 43, No. 4, (1993).

Balaram, A., "The Harijan Problem", *Mainstream*, Vol. 16, No. 39, (May 27 and July 15, 1978).

Balasundaram, F.J., "The Church in a Dalit Perspective", *Mashi Sevak*, Vol. 17, No. 3, (1993).

Balia, "Church Struggle against the Apartheid", *Bangalore Theological Forum*, Vol. 25, Nos. 2-3, (1993).

Balia, "Gospel and the Dalit Struggle for a New Identity", *International Review of Missions*, Vol. 84, No. 334, (1995).

Bandopadhyay, Sekhar, "Community Formation and Communal Conflict: Namasudra-Muslim Riot in Jessore-Khulna", *Economic and Political Weekly*, (17 November, 1990).

Bandopodhyay, Biswanath, "Ceremonial Friendship among the Bhumiji of Manbhum", *Man in India*, Vol. 35, No. 4, (1955), [The Bhumijs are categorized under the both Scheduled Caste and Scheduled Tribes in Bihar and West Bengal but only as Scheduled Tribes in Orissa].

Banerjee, Biswajit and J.B. Knight, "Caste Discrimination in Indian Urban Labour Market", *Journal of Developing Economics*, Vol. 17, (1985).

Banerjee, Hemendra Nath, "Socio-Ritual Status of the Khaira in the Ethnic Background of Manbhum", *Bulletin of the Cultural Research Institute*, Vol. 1, No. 2, (1962).

Banerjee, N.K., "A Short Note on the Haris", *Folklore*, Vol. 7, No. 3, (1966).

Banerji, Saradindu, "Untouchability", *Samiksa*, Vol. 34, (1980).

Bansal, Akhilesh, "New Classification for Harijans", *Hindustan Times*, (January 19, 1972).

Barik, S.K., "Education for Dalits: No Separate Colleges and University for Dalits", *Journal of Higher Education*, Vol. 21, No. 3, (1998).

Barnes, E., "The Bhils of Western India", *Journal of the Society of Arts*, Vol. 55, (1907), [The Bhils are noted as Scheduled Caste in Delhi but in many other states they are categorized as Scheduled Tribe].

Barnett, Marguerite Ross and Steve Barnett, "Contemporary Peasant and post-Peasant Alternatives in South India: The Ideas of the Militant Untouchable", *Annals New York Academy of Sciences*, Vol. 220, Article 6, (11 March 1974).

Baroda, His Highness the Gaekwar of, "The Depressed Classes", *The Indian Review*, (December, 1909).

Barrow, H.W., "On the Aghoris and Aghorpanthis (Bengal)", *Journal of Anthropological Society of Bombay*, Vol. 3, (1893).

Barton, W.P., "Indian Federation and the Untouchable", *Quarterly Review* (London), No. 268, (1937).

Basu, K., "Customs and Practices among the Kochs", *Journal of the Anthropological Society of Bombay*, Vol. 3, No. 2, (1888).

Basu, Kamakhya Prasad, "Notes on Bhuiyas", *Man in India*, Vol. 1, No. 2, (1921), [The Byuiyas or Bhuyans are categorized as Scheduled Castes in Bihar, Uttar Pradesh and West Bengal, but in Orissa they are categorized as Scheduled Tribes].

Basu, Kedar Nath, "Some Curious Customs among Kochs", *Journal of Asiatic Society of Bengal*, Vol. 3, (1834).

Basu, M.N., "Ethnic Position of the Pods of Bengal", *Geographical Review*, (1942).

Basu, Mahadeb P., "On the State-Wise Distribution of Scheduled Castes and Their Sex –ratio", *Journal Indian Anthropological Society,* Vol. 4, Nos., 1-2, (1969).

Basu, Minendra Nath, "An Anthropometric Study of the Bansphors", *Indian Science Congress,* (1935).

Basu, Rabindra Nath and Minendra Nath Basu, "Physical Anthropology of the Bhuiyas of Mayurbhanj", *Science and Culture,* Vol. 7, (1942), [The Byuiyas or Bhuyans are categorized as Scheduled Castes in Bihar, Uttar Pradesh and West Bengal, but in Orissa they are categorized as Scheduled Tribes].

Basu, S.K., "Agrarian Problems of Scheduled Castes and Scheduled Tribes of West Bengal", *Bulletin of Cultural Research Institute,* Vol. VII, Nos. 1 & 2, (1968).

Bathwal, C.P., "Representation of Scheduled Castes in Parliament and State Legislatures", *Economic and Political Weekly,* Vol. 4, No. 36, (1969).

Baxi, Upendra, "Operation Equality: A New Deal for Harijans", *Indian Express,* (November 3, 1977).

Baxi, Upendra, "Caste, Class and Reservation", *Economic and Political Weekly,* Vol. 20, No. 10, (1985).

Baxi, Upendra, "Historic New Law: Protecting SC/STs Human Rights", *Times of India,* (15 September 1989).

Bean, Susan S., "Toward A Semiotics of 'Purity' and 'Pollution' in India", *American Ethnologist,* Vol. 8, (1981).

Behar, S.C., "Reservation: An Insufficient Condition for Social Transformation", *The Administrator,* Vol. XLII, No. 1, (1997).

Behara, Bhajman, "Welfare Measures for Scheduled Classes", *Amrit Bazar Patrika,* (January 29, 1977).

Behari, Kamila Bana, "A Study of Attitude of Students Towards School of Harijan and Tribal Welfare Department, High School of Orissa", *Journal of Education and Psychology,* Vol. 43, Nos. 3-4, (1985-86).

Bellwinkel-Schempp, Maren, "Khatiks of Kanpur and the Bristle Trade: Towards an Anthropology of Man and Beast", *Sociological Bulletin*, Vol. 47, No. 2, (1998).

Benjamin, Joseph, "Political Participation and Sharing Power by the Scheduled Castes in Bihar", *Political Science Review*, Vol. 26, Nos. 1-4, (January-December, 1987).

Benjamin, Joseph, "Social Mobility Among the Scheduled Castes in Bihar: A Case Study of Barh Block", *Man in India*, Vol. 71, Nos. 2-3, (June-September, 1991).

Bennur, C.S., "Education and Prejudice: A Perspective", *Progress of Education*, Vol. 41, No. 9, (1967).

Bennur, C.S., "Caste Prejudice and Children", *Progress of Education*, Vol. 41, Nos. 10-11, (1967).

Berreman, Gerald D., "Caste in India and the United States", *American Journal of Sociology*, Vol. LXVI, (1960).

Berwa, Laxmi, "Anti-Dalit Alliance", *The Dalit*, (May-June 2002).

Besant, Annie, "The Depressed Classes", *The Indian Review*, (February, 1909).

Beteille, Andre, "Race and Descent as Social Categories in India", *Daedalus*, Vol. 96, (1967).

Beteille, Andre, "The Future of the Backward Classes: The Competing Demands of Status and Power", *Perspectives*, Supplement to the *Indian Journal of Public Administration*, Vol. XI, (1965), reprinted in Philip Mason (ed.), *India and Ceylon: Unity and Diversity*, (London: OUP, 1967).

Beteille, Andre, "Social Inequality in India: The Theory and Practice of Caste", *The Times of India*, (24 July 1970).

Bha Shankar, Indubhai, "Social Change in the Bhils", *Journal of the Gujarat Research Society*, Vol. 26, No. 1, (1964), [The Bhils are noted as Scheduled Caste in Delhi but in many other states they are categorized as Scheduled Tribe].

Bhadra, V. Shanti, "Bodhisattva Ambedkar", in *Milind College of Arts, College Magazine*, (Aurangabad), Vol. 4, (1966).

Bhagabati, A.C. and M.C. Goswamy, "A Typological Study of Shouldered Celts from Reehangiri (Garo Hills)", *Journal of the University of Gauhati*, Vol. 10, No. 2, (1959).

Bhagat, M.G., "The Untouchable Classes of Maharashtra", *Journal of the University of Bombay*, Vol. IV, No. 1, (July, 1935). [Later on this article was reprinted in a book form].

Bhagat, M.G., "The Untouchable Classes of the Janjira State (Konkan), *Journal of the University of Bombay*, Vol. VII, (1938).

Bhandarkar, Ramakrishna Gopal, "The Depressed Classes", *The Indian Review*, Vol. XIV, (1913).

Bharathi, Sunita Reddy, "'Dalit': A term asserting Unity", *Economic and Political Weekly*, Vol. 37, No. 42, (2002).

Bharill, Chandra, "Experiences of an Untouchable: Glimpses of Ambedkar's Early Life", *Political Science Review*, Vol. 5, (1966).

Bharthwal, C.P., "Representation of Scheduled Casts in Parliament and State Legislatures", *Economic and Political Weekly*, Vol. 4, No. 36, (1969).

Bhatia, Bela, "Massacre on the Banks of the Sone", *Economic and Political Weekly*, Vol. 32, No. 51, (1997).

Bhatt, Anil, "Caste and Politics in Akola", *Economic Weekly*, Vol. XV, (1963).

Bhatt, G.S., "The Chamars of Lucknow", *The Eastern Anthropologist*, Vol. 8, No. 1, (1954).

Bhatt, G.S., "Trends and Measures of Status Mobility among the Chamars of Dehradun", *The Eastern Anthropologist*, Vol. 14, No. 3, (1961).

Bhatt, G.S., "Urban Impact and the Trends of Intra-caste Solidarity and Dissociability as Measures of Status Mobility among the Chamars", *Journal of Social Research*, Vol. 5, (1962).

Bhatt, S.R., "What Hinduism means by Untouchability", *Hindustan Times,* (June 8, 1969).

Bhattacharya, Biswanath, "A Short Note on the Scheduled Tribes and Scheduled Castes Population of West Bengal", *Bulletin of Cultural Research Institute,* Vol. 3, No. 2, (1964).

Bhattacharya, S.K. and N.K. Das, "Marital Distance and Serological Studies among Chamars of Orissa", *Journal of Anthropological Survey of India,* Vol. 48, No. 3, (1999).

Bhatty, Kiran, "Educational Deprivation in India: A Study of Field Investigation", *Economic and Political Weekly,* (4 July 1998).

Bhaware, N.G., "The Anguished Cry: Poetry by Dalit Women", *Eve's Weekly,* (24–30 May 1980).

Bhoite, U. and A. Bhoite, "The Dalit Sahitya Movement in Maharashtra: A Sociological Analysis", *Sociological Bulletin,* Vol. 26, No. 1, (1977).

Bhole, R.R., "The Untouchables on the Move", *Asiatic Review,* Vol. XI, (1944).

Bhongle, Rangrao, "Dr. Ambedkar's Ideology on Conversion", *Indian Missiological Review,* Vol. 17, No. 1, (1995).

Bhowmik, K.L., "The Bauris: A Dominant Scheduled Caste of West Bengal", *Bulletin of Cultural Research Institute,* Vol. 4, Nos. 1 & 2, (1966).

Bhushan, Sashi, "The Belchchi Killings", *Economic and Political Weekly,* Vol. 12, No. 25, (1977).

Bhuskute, R.V., "Tribals, Dalits and Government Lands", *Economic and Political Weekly,* Vol. 24, No. 42, (1989).

Bidwai, Praful, "Relevance of Ambedkar: Modernity and Pseudo-Gandhians", *The Times of India,* (5 May 1994).

Biswas, A.R., "Human Rights and Scheduled Castes and Tribes in India", *Law Quarterly,* Vol. 15, No. 3, (July-September, 1978).

Biswas, P.C. and D.K. Bhattacharya, "A Somatometric Study

of the Bhil (Males of Rajasthan", *The Anthropologist*, Vol. 8, Nos. 1 & 2, (1961), [The Bhils are noted as Scheduled Caste in Delhi but in many other states they are categorized as Scheduled Tribe].

Biswas, S., "Dalit Vision of Gandhi", *Mainstream*, Vol. 32, No. 23, (April 23, 1994).

Biswas, Suhas Kumar, "A Hunting Ceremony of the Pauri Bhuiyas", *Folklore*, Vol. 1, No. 6, (1960), [The Byuiyas or Bhuyans are categorized as Scheduled Castes in Bihar, Uttar Pradesh and West Bengal, but in Orissa they are categorized as Scheduled Tribes].

Biswas, Suhas Kumar, "A Religious Ceremony of the Pauri Bhuiyas", *Vanyajati*, Vol. 8, No. 4, (1960).

Biswas, Suhas Kumar, "Annual Hunting Festival of the Pauri Bhuiyas and Significance of the Annual Hung Among the Tribes of Central Indian Belt", *Bulletin of the Cultural Research Institute*, Vol. 3, No. 3, (1964), [The Byuiyas or Bhuyans are categorized as Scheduled Castes in Bihar, Uttar Pradesh and West Bengal, but in Orissa they are categorized as Scheduled Tribes].

Blockmann, H., "Chero: Notes from Muhammadan Historians on Chutia Nagpur Pocket and Palamau", *Journal of the Asiatic Society of Bengal*, (1871).

Bonarji, D.N., "Untouchability and the Law", *Times of India*, (8 July 1956).

Boparai, Harinder, "India's Ex-Untouchables", *Review of International Commission of Jurists*, No. 20, (June, 1978).

Bose, A.B., "Educational Development among Scheduled Castes", *Man in India*, Vol. 50, No. 3, (1970).

Bose, A.N. and P.B.S. Bhadoria, "Caste, Class and Economic Relationship: A Case Study of Midnapore", *Social Change*, Vol. 18, (1988).

Bose, L., "Taste Sensitivity to Phenylthicarbamide in the Padmaraj (Pod) and the Bagdi of West Bengal", *Anthropologist*, Vol. 3, Nos. 1 & 2, (1956).

Bose, Nirmal K., "Scheduled Castes and Tribes: Their Present Condition", *Man in India*, Vol. 50, No. 3, (1970).

Bose, Nirmal K., "The Scheduled Caste Communities and Social Change", *Social Change,* Vol. I, No. 1, (1971).

Bose, Pradip Kumar, "Social Mobility and Caste Violence: A Study of the Gujarat Riots", *Economic and Political Weekly,* Vol. 16, No. 16, (1981).

Bose, S., "Caste –Tribe and Female Labour Participation", *Social Change,* Vol. 15, No. 2, (1985).

Bowmik, K.L., "The Bauris: A Dominant Scheduled Castes of West Bengal", *Bulletin of Cultural Research Institute,* Vol. 4, Nos. 1-2, (1966).

Bramley, B.R., "The Rawats and Merats of Rajputana", *Journal of the Asiatic Society of Bengal,* (New Series), Vol. 2, (1906).

Briggs, George W., "The Harijan and Hinduism", *Review of Religion,* Vol. II, (1937).

Brubaker, Richard L., "Barbers, Washer men and Other Priests: Servants of the South Indian Village and its Goddess", *History of Religions,* Vol. 19, No. 2, (1979).

Buragohain, Tarujyoti, "Differentials in Literacy Rate by Social Groups: An Analysis of Census Data Across States", *Margin,* Vol. 29, Nos. 3–4, (1997).

Burn, Richard, "The Thatheras as Landholders", *Journal of Asiatic Society of Bengal,* Vol. 72, No. 3, (1903).

Burra, Neera, "Was Ambedkar Just a Leader of the Mahars?", *Economic and Political Weekly,* Vol. 21, Nos. 10 & 11, (1986).

Chakrabarty, Anand, "Traditional Caste Systems: A Note on the Washer men of a Village in Rajasthan", *Economic and Political Weekly,* Vol. 1, No. 20, (1966).

Chakrabarty, G., "SCs and STs in Rural Andhra Pradesh: Their Education, Health Status and Income", *Journal of Rural Development,* Vol. 18, No. 2, (1999).

Chakrapani, C. and C.D. Deshmukh, "The Jogins of Telangana", *Eastern Anthropologist,* Vol. 45, No. 3, (1992).

Chakravarti, Manish Ranjan, "Darmatoglyphics of the Nayadis and the Paniyans of Madras", *Man in India,* Vol. 38, No. 3, (1958).

Chakravarti, N.K. and Shubhasree Subedi, "Origin of

Untouchability in Hinduism", *Man in India,* Vol. 75, (1995).

Chakravarti, Vanamali, "A Short Note on the Hinduization of the Aborigines: The Swelling of the Chandala Caste", *Indian Antiquary,* Vol. 41, (1912).

Chakravarty, Gurupada, "Income Status of Scheduled Castes in Rural Uttar Pradesh", *IASSI Quarterly,* Vol. 18, No. 3, (2000).

Chakravarty, Gurupada, "Income Status of Scheduled Castes in Rural Uttar Pradesh", *Indian Journal of Economics,* Vol. 81, No. 326, (2001).

Chalam, K.S., "Caste Reservation and Equality of Opportunity in Education", *Economic and Political Weekly,* Vol. 25, No. 41, (1990).

Chalam, K.S., "Relevance of Ambedkar's State Socialism", *Deccan Chronicle,* (7 December 1995).

Chalam, K.S., "Caste and Economic Reforms", *Seminar,* No. 471, (November 1998).

Challappan, C., "Harijan and Tribal Welfare in Tamil Nadu", *The Hindu,* (January 24, 1978).

Chanana, Dev Raj, "How Close to Equality are Scheduled Castes", *Economic and Political Weekly,* Vol. IV, No, 24, (June 14, 1969).

Chanana, Karuna, "Accessing Higher Education: The Dilemma of Schooling Women, Minorities, Scheduled Castes and Scheduled Tribes in Contemporary India", *Higher Education,* Vol. 26, No. 1, (July, 1993).

Chandana, R.C., "Distributional Pattern of Scheduled Caste population in India", *Population Geography,* Vol. 2, Nos. 1 & 2, (1980).

Chandana, R.C., "Scheduled Caste Population in Rural Haryana: A Geographic Analysis", *The National Geographical Journal of India,* Vol. 18, Nos. 3 & 4, (1972).

Chandidas, R., "How Close to Equality are Scheduled Castes?", *Economic and Political Weekly,* Vol. 4, No. 24, (1969).

Chandoke, S.K., "Caste Segregation in Villages", *The Hindustan Times,* (April 16, 1976).

Chandolia, R.N., "Enrolment of Scheduled Castes in Educational Institutions", *Yojana,* Vol. 24, No. 19, (1980).

Chandra, Bipan, "Gandhi & Ambedkar: Attitudes Towards Caste System", *The Times of India,* (13 April 1994).

Chandra, R., "Hinduism and Untouchables", *Modern Review,* Vol. 59,No. 1, (1936).

Chandra, R.C., "Distributional Pattern of Scheduled Caste Population in India", *Population Geography,* Vol. 2, (1980).

Chandra, S.C., "Harijans – Real Life Horror Stories", *Pioneer,* (November 6, 1977).

Chandra, Sekhar, "Caste War has Become a Class War", *Motherland,* Vol. 23, (1971).

Chandra, Suresh, "Harijans Need Assistance Not Pity", *Times of India,* (April 23, 1972).

Chandra, Vimal, "Constitutional Safeguards", *Seminar,* No. 177, (May 1974).

Chandramohan, P., "Popular Culture and Socio-religious Reform: Narayana Guru and the Ezhavas of Travancore", *Studies in History,* N.S. Vol. 3, No. 1, (1987).

Chandramouli, M.S., "Lip Sympathy for Harijans", *Deccan Herald,* (August 22, 1977).

Chandran, J.R., "Theologizing in the Context of the Marginalized and the Oppressed", *Bangalore Theological Forum,* Vol. 24, Nos. 3–4, (1992).

Chandrasekaran, Lalita, "Social Mobility among the Madiga of Karnataka", *Sociological Bulletin,* Vol. 41, Nos. 1 & 2, 1992.

Chandu, K., "Reservations for Scheduled Caste Christians", *Samata,* Vol. I, (1990).

Chaplin, Susan E., "Scavengers: Still Marginalised", *The Administrator,* Vol. XLII, No. 1, (1997).

Charsley, Simon, "'Untouchable': What Is in a Name?", *The Journal of the Royal Anthropological Institute* (N.S), Vol. 2, (1996).

Charsley, Simon, "Evaluating Dalit Leadership: P.R. Venkataswamy and the Hyderabad Example", *Economic and Political Weekly*, Vol. 37, No. 52, (28 December 2002 – 3 January 2003).

Chatterjee, B.K. and G.D. Kumar, "Somatometric and Somatoscopic Observations and their Affinities of the Mannans of Travancore, Cochin", *Journal of the Asiatic Society of Bengal* (Science), No. 23, (1957), [The Mannan is categorized as Scheduled Caste as well as a Scheduled Tribe in Kerala and Tamil Nadu].

Chatterjee, Bhola, "Not by Law Alone", *Amrit Bazar Patrika*, (May 24, 1977).

Chattopadhyay, Kamaladevi, "Leather Comes into its Own; But have the Mochis", *Times of India*, (3 December 1978).

Chattopadhyay, Mihir Kumar, "Quasi-Experimental Study on the Educational Backwardness of SC Secondary School Students in Some Districts of West Bengal", *Perspectives in Education*, Vol. 14, No. 2, (1998).

Chaturvedi, Arun Kumar, "Harijan Students of Uttar Pradesh", *Social Welfare*, Vol. 33, No. 1, (1986).

Chaubey, Ganesh, "The Dhangar Songs", *Folklore*, Vol. 1, No. 4, (1958).

Chaudhuri, Saroj Kanti, "Educational Progress in Rural Bengal: A Study of Four Villages", *Economic and Political Weekly*, (5 February 1970).

Chauhan, B.R., "Recent Trends among Depressed Classes in Rajasthan", *Agra University Journal of Research*, (Letters), Vol. 3, (1955).

Chauhan, Brij Raj, "Scheduled Castes and Scheduled Tribes", *Economic and Political Weekly*, Vol. 4, No. 4, (1969).

Chauhan, Brij Raj and G. Narayana, "Problems of Education Among Scheduled Caste Students in Uttar Pradesh", *Social Change*, Vol. 6, Nos. 1 & 2, (1976).

Chauhan, D.N.S. and S.L. Chopra, "A Comparative Study of the Socio-Economic Background of the Members of the Lok Sabha Elected from the Reserved and the General Constituencies", *Journal of Constitutional and Parliamentary Studies*, Vol. 3, No. 2, (1969).

Chauhan, Devraj, "Educational and Occupational Levels of Scheduled Castes and Scheduled Tribes", *Mainstream*, Vol. 28, No. 42, (August 11, 1990).

Chinna Rao, Y., "Dalits and Tribals are not Hindus", *The Hindustan Times*, (20 January 2000).

Chinna Rao, Y., "Dalits, Tribals and Conversion", *Frontier*, Vol. 32, No. 37, (2000).

Chinna Rao, Y., "Great Cultures in Little Traditions", *Social Action*, Vol. 50, No. 1, (2000).

Chinna Rao, Y., "Rise and Growth of Dalit Movement in Andhra, 1906-1946", *Indian Social Science Review*, Vol. 5, No. 1, (2003).

Chinnaiah, Jangam, "Sub-Caste Consciousness and Challenges before Dalit Intellectuals", *Mainstream*, Vol. 36, No. 12, (1998).

Chitnis, Suma, "Education for Equality: Case of Scheduled Castes in Higher Education", *Economic and Political Weekly*, Vol. 7, Nos. 31-33, (1972).

Chitnis, Suma, "Education of the Scheduled Castes", *Journal of Higher Education*, Vol. 2, No. 2, (1975).

Chittaranjan, C.M., "Beyond Caste Conflict", *Mainstream*, Vol. 16, No. 32, (April 8, 1978).

Chopra, S.L., "Changing Socio-Economic Status of Low-Caste People", *Khadi Gramodyog*, Vol. XVI, No. 12, (September, 1970).

Choudhary, B., "Forest Economy of Hill Bhuyan", *Adibasi*, No. 1, (1966-67).

Choudhary, Kameshwar, "Reservations: A Systemic Compulsion", *Mainstream*, Vol. 28, No. 19, (1990).

Choudhary, Kameshwar, "Dalits in Higher Education: Cooption or Domination", *Journal of Higher Education*, Vol. 21, No. 3, (1998).

Choudhary, Kameshwar, "The Policy of Reservation: Need to Continue and Transcend", *Social Action*, Vol. 48, No. 2, (1998).

Choudhary, Kameshwar, "Violation of Human Rights: The Case of Dalits in Gujarat", *IASSI Quarterly*, Vol. 18, No. 3, (2000).

Choudury, D.R., "Palmar Dermatoglyphics of the Rajbhanshis of Midnapur, West Bengal", *The Anthropologist*, Vol. 9, Nos. 1 & 2, (1962).

Chowdhry, B.K. Roy and B. Bhattacharya, "A Brief Records on Stagnation of Scheduled Tribes and Castes Students", *Bulletin of Cultural Research Institute*, Vol. 6, Nos. 1–2, (1967).

Chowdhury, A.K. and M. Haque, "Nutritional Status of the Pasi and the Bramhakalpit Brahman of Gaya Town", *Man in India*, Vol. 73, No. 3, (September, 1993).

Chowdhury, Neerja, "Job Reservations in Bihar sharpening the Battle Lines", *Himmat*, Vol. 15, No. 21, (1979).

Clark, Blake, "The Victory of an Untouchable", *The Reader's Digest*, Vol. 56, (1950), (reprinted from *Christian Herald*, (March 1950).

Clayton, A.C., "The Paraiyan", *Bulletin of the Madras Government Museum*, (Anthropology), Vol. 5, No. 2, (1906).

Coatman, John, "Reforms in India and the Depressed Classes", *Asiatic Review* (London), Vol. XXIX, (1933).

Cohen, Stephen P., "The Untouchable Soldier: Caste, Politics and the Indian Army", *Journal of Asian Studies*, Vol. 28, No. 3, (1969).

Cohn, Bernard S., "Changing Traditions of a Low Caste", *Journal of American Folklore*, Vol. 21, (July-September, 1958).

Cohn, Bernard S., "Madhopur Revisited", *Economic and Political Weekly*, Vol. XI, (July, 1959).

Cohn, Bernard S., "Some Notes on Law and Change in North India", *Economic Development and Cultural Change*, Vol. VIII, (1959).

Cohn, Bernard S., "Chamar Family in a North Indian Village: A Structural Contingent", *Ecnomic Weekly*, Vo. XIII,

(1961), (earlier published in *the Journal of Asian Studies*, Vol. XIX, No. 4, August, 1969).

Constable, P., "Early Dalit Literature and Culture in late Nineteenth- and early Twentieth-century Western India", *Modern Asian Studies*, Vol. 31, (May 1997).

Constable, Philip, "The Marginalization of a *Dalit* Martial Race in Late Nineteenth-and Early Twentieth-Century Western India", *Journal of Asian Studies*, Vol. 60, No. 2, (2001).

Contractor, Behram, "Dalit Homes Devastated", *Times of India*, (August 20, 1978).

Contursi, J., "Militant Hindus and Buddhist Dalits: Hegemony and Resistance in an Indian Slum", *American Ethnologist*, Vol. 16, (1989).

Corrie, B.D., "A Human Development Index for the Dalit child in India", *Social Indicators Research*, Vol.34, (1995).

Corrie, Bruce T., "Impact of the Development Process on Dalit and Tribal Children in South India", *South Asia Bulletin*, Vol. 12, No. 2, (Fall, 1992).

D'Sami, Benard, "Response to the Paper on 'Dalits In Higher Education': Need for Establishing a Counter Culture", *Journal of Higher Education*, Vol. 22, No. 1, (1999).

D'Souza, V., "Castes, Out-castes and Sociology of Stratification", *International Journal of Comparative Sociology*, Vol. 1, (1960).

D'Souza, Victor S., "Changing Status of Scheduled Castes, *Economic Weekly*, Vol. 14, No, 48, (1962).

D'Souza, Victor S., "Scheduled Castes Urbanization in Punjab: An Explanation", *Sociological Bulletin*, Vol. 35, No 1, (1975).

D'Souza, Victor S., "Does Urbanism Desegregate Scheduled Castes? Evidence from a District in Punjab", *Contributions to Indian Sociology*, Vol.11, (1977).

D'Souza, Victor S., 'The Religious Factor and the Scheduled Castes', *Social Action*, Vol. 32, No 3, (1982).

D'Souza, Victor S., "Growth and Development of Education of the Under-Privileged: The Structural Constraints", *Journal of Education and Social Change,* Vol. 3, No. 3, (1989).

Dadhich, C.L., "Farm Co-operative Credit to Scheduled Castes and Scheduled Tribes", *Economic and Political Weekly,* Vol. 12, No. 13, (1977).

Dalmia, Yashodhara, "Scheduled Castes – A View from Below", *The Times of India,* (15 December 1974).

Daly, E.J., "Helping Harijans Change: The Core Issue, Self Image", *Vidya Jyothi Journal of Theological Reflection,* No. 42, (1978).

Dandavate, Madhu, "Atrocities on Harijans and Adivasis", *Janata,* (4 June 1972).

Das, A.K. and R.N. Saha, "Post-Matric Education among the Scheduled Castes and Scheduled Tribes of West Bengal", *Bulletin of Cultural Research Institute,* Vol. 7, No. 1-2, (1968).

Das. A.K., "Comparative Assessment of Levels of Literacy amongst Scheduled Castes and Scheduled Tribes of West Bengal", *Bulletin of the Cultural Research Institute,* Vol. 8, Nos. 1-2, (1969).

Das, Amal Kumar, "A Short Note on the Kalindi Doms of West Bengal", *Folklore,* Vol. 3, No. 9, (1962).

Das, Amal Kumar, "Occupations and Literacy Among Scheduled Castes in West Bengal", *Mainstream,* Vol. 10, Nos. 1-4, (1971).

Das, B.M., "A Note on the Hira Potters of Assam", *Man in India,* Vol. 36, No. 3, (1956).

Das, Bhagwan, "Scheduled Castes and the Struggles Against Inequality", *Social Action,* Vo. 32, No. 3, (1982).

Das, Bhagwan, "Untouchability, Scheduled Castes and Nation Building", *Social Action,* Vo. 32, No. 3, (1982).

Das, Bhagwan, "Ambedkar Journey to Mass Conversion", *Manthan,* Vol. 5, No. 1, (1983).

Das, Bhagwan, "The Reservation Policy and the Mandal Judgement", *Social Action*, Vol. 43, No. 4, (1993).

Das, Bhagwan, "Moments in a History of Reservations", *Economic and Political Weekly*, Vol. 35, Nos. 43–44, (2000).

Das, Harish Chandra, "The Economic Life of the Doms of Barbaria (A Village in North Balasore)", *Orissa Historical Research Journal*, Vol. XI, (1963).

Das, K.K. and D.R. Sharma, "Study of the Utilization of Government Resources by Scheduled Caste Communities", *Indian Journal of Social Research*, Vol. XII, No. 1, (April, 1971).

Das, N., "Mobility Among the Scheduled Castes of Orissa", *Adivasi*, Vol. 8, No. 1, (1966).

Das, S.R., N. Kumar, N. Bhattacharjee and D.B. Sastry, "Blood Groups (ABO, M-N and Rh), A.B.H. Secretion, Sickle Cell, P.T.C. Taste and Colour Blindness in the Mahars of Nagpur", *Journal of Royal Anthropological Institute*, Vol. 91, Part 2, (1961).

Das, S.R., and P.N. Bhattacharjee, "Blood Groups (A, A2 Bo), ABH Secretion, Sicke-Cell, P.T.C. Taste and Colour Blindness in the Rajbanshi of Midnapur District of West Bengal", *Bulletin of the Anthropological Survey of India*, Vol. 12, Nos. 1-2, (1963).

Das, S.R., D.P. Mukherjee and P.N. Bhattacharjee, "Survey of the Blood Groups and PTC Taste Among the Rajbanshi Caste of West Bengal", *Acta Genetica* (Basel), Vol. 17, (1967).

Das, Soumitro, "Home to Suffering: Why Dalits want to Leave", *Radical Humanist*, Vol. 63, No. 10, (2000).

Das, Thakar, "Atrocities on Harijans", *Indian Express*, (August 11, 1977).

Dasgupta, Abhijit, "In the Citadel of Bhadralok Politicians: The Scheduled Castes in West Bengal", *Journal of Indian School of Political Economy*, Vol. 12, Nos. 3–4, (2000).

Dasgupta, A.K., "Gandhi on Social Conflict", *Economic and Political Weekly*, Vol. 3, No. 49, (1968).

Dasgupta, P., "Sedantary Games of Rajbansis", *Anthropological Papers No. 6,* (University of Calcutta), (1941).

Dasgupta, Probal, "Sanskrit, English and Dalits", *Economic and Political Weekly,* Vol. 35, No. 16, (2000).

Dasgupta, Satadal, "Demographic aspects of marriage among the Dule Bagdis of Jainagar", *Bulletin of the Cultural Research Institute,* West Bengal, Vol. 3, No. 1, (1964).

Dasgupta, Satadal, "Leneage & Kinship structure among the Dule Bagdis of Jainagar", *Bulletin of the Cultural Research Institute,* West Bengal, Vol. 3, No. 3, (1964).

Dasgupta, Satadal, "Locality groups among the Bagdis of Jainagar", *Bulletin of the Cultural Research Institute,* West Bengal, Vol. 2, No. 2, (1963).

Dasgupta, Satadal, "Religious concepts and ethics of Bagdi", *Bulletin of the Cultural Research Institute,* West Bengal, Vol. 2, No. 1, (1963).

Datta, B.N., "Bauriya: Ethnological Notes on Some of the Castes of West Bengal", *Man in India,* Vol. 15, No. 4, (1935), [The Byuiyas or Bhuyans are categorized as Scheduled Castes in Bihar, Uttar Pradesh and West Bengal, but in Orissa they are categorized as Scheduled Tribes].

Datta-Gupta, Jaya, "A Study of the Poundra Kshatriya of West Bengal", *Bulletin of the Department of Anthropology,* Vol. 8, No. 2, (1959).

Datta-Ray, Sunanda K., "Benefits up for grabs; Getting Harijan Problem in Focus", *Statesman,* (March 28, 1978).

Dave, P.C., "Voluntary Organizations and Welfare of Backward Classes", *Vanyajati,* Vol. XIV, (1966).

De, B., "The Depressed Classes", *The Indian Review,* (February, 1910).

De, B., "Taste Blindness among the Namsudra of West Bengal", *Science and Culture,* Vol. 32, (1966).

Deb, D., "Uplift of Scheduled Tribes and Castes", *Economic Times,* (January 5, 1979).

Deenabandhu, M., "Gospel and the Dalit Struggle for a New Identity", *International Review of Missions*, Vol. 84, (1995).

Deepankar, Rahul, "Dalits in US Decide to Fight Aryan Tyranny in India", *Dalit Voice*, Vol. 14, No. 6, (1995).

Deliege, R., "Patrilateral Cross-Cousin Marriage Among the Paraiyars of South India", *Journal of the Anthropological Society of Oxford*, Vol. 18, (1987).

Deliege, R., "Souffrance et echange: Quelques Croyances Religieuses des Intouchables Catholiques de l'Inde du Sud", *Anthropos*, Vol. 82, (1987).

Deliege, R., "A Comparison between Hindu and Christian Paraiyars of South India", *Indian Missiological Review*, Vol. 12, (1990).

Deliege, Robert, "Replication and Consensus: Untouchability, Caste and Ideology in India", *Man*, n.s. Vol. 27, (1992).

Deliege, Robert, "The Myth of Origin of the Indian Untouchables", *Man*, n.s. Vol. 28, (1993).

Den Oudenn, J., "Social Stratification as Expressed through Language: A Case Study of a South Indian Village", *Contributions to Indian Sociology*, Vol. 13, (1979).

Deo, Veena and Eleanor Zelliot, "Dalit Literature: Twenty-Five Years of Protest? Or Progress", *Journal of South Asia Literature*, Vol. 29, No.2, (1994).

Desai, B.M. and M.S. Patel, "Co-Operative Credit for Scheduled Castes and Scheduled Tribes", *Vishleshan*, Vol. 5, No. 1, (March, 1979).

Desai, C.C., "Reservation of Seats in the House of the People and State Assemblies for Scheduled Castes and Scheduled Tribes and Nominations of Anglo-Indians thereto: Case for Extension of the Period", *Journal of Constitutional and Parliamentary Studies*, Vol. 3, No. 2, (1969).

Desai, Haribhai G. and D.A. Uchat, "Self Concept of Harijan Students and Attitudes of Other Students towards them", *Indian Educational Review*, Vol. 16, No. 3, (1981).

Desai, Kiran and Parmar Rasik, "Kadi: Signs of Dalit

Assertion", *Economic and Political Weekly*, Vol. 15, No. 26, (1995).

Deshmukh, A.S., "Dr. Babasaheb Ambedkar as a Religious Reformer", *Magazine of Dr. Babasaheb College of Arts, Science and Commerce*, No 2, (Mahad: 1963-64).

Desmond, E.W., "Anti-Caste Revolution", *Time*, (April 13, 1992).

Dev Barma and Jitendra Mohan Thakur, "Origin of Tripura and its People", *Vanyajati*, Vol. 6, No. 3, (1958).

Dev, Amar and S. Banerjee-Guha, "Socio-Economic Condition of the Scheduled Castes in India: A Geographical Analysis", *National Geographical Journal of India*, Vol. 35, No. 2, (June, 1990).

Devi, Mahasveta, "Untouchability in West Bengal", *Frontier*, Vol. 24, Nos. 9-11, (October 12-26, 1991).

Dey, Shumboo Chundev, "An Account of the Garos", *Culcutta Review*, (1909).

Dhar, H., "Escalating Violence on Harijans" [UP], *Economic Political Weekly*, (19 September 1992).

Dhar, M.K., "Harijans in Punjab Disillusioned", *Hindustan Times*, (June 9, 1977).

Dharwadkar, Vinay, "Dalit Poetry in Marathi", *World Literature Today*, Vol. 68, (Spring 1994).

Dhebar, U.N., "Improving the quality of life of Harijans", *Commerce*, Vol. 132, No. 3389, (May 8, 1976).

Diwakar, D.M., "Dalit Question of Inequality, Exploitation and Mobilization: A Micro View of Ground Realities", *Journal of Indian School of Political Economy*, Vol. 10, No. 2, (1998).

DN, "Reservations and Class Structure of Castes", *Economic and Political Weekly*, (13 January 1990).

DN, "Gandhi, Ambedkar and Separate Electorates Issue", *Economic and Political Weekly*, (25 May 1991).

Dogra, Bharat, "Harijans still Suffer", *Indian Express*, (August 9, 1976).

Dogra, Bharat, "Jobs for Harijans", *Indian Express*, (February 9, 1977).

Dogra, B., "First Stirrings and Repression: A Report from Palamau" [Bihar], *Economic and Political Weekly*, Vol. XX, (1985).

Dongargoankar, G.K., "Scheduled Castes/Scheduled Tribes in Public Sector", *Yugrabodhan Weekly* (New Bombay), (September, 1991).

Drieberg, T., "How a Village is Affected by Water Problems of Caste Differences", *Indian Express*, (14 February 1971).

Du Boulay, J., "On the Bari or Panwali Caste in Khandesh District", *Journal of the Anthropological Society of Bombay*, Vol. 4, (1897).

Dua, Veena, "Elections in a Scheduled Caste Neighbourhood: A Punjab Town", *Economic and Political Weekly*, Vol. 6, No. 46, (1971).

Dube, Leela and S.C. Dube, "Chaukhutia Bhuinya: The Cult of Ancestor Spirit in Chattisgarh", *Eastern Anthropologist*, Vol. 2, No. 2, (1948), [The Bhuiyas or Bhuyans are categorized as Scheduled Castes in Bihar, Uttar Pradesh and West Bengal, but in Orissa they are categorized as Scheduled Tribes].

Dube, Saurabh, "Idioms of Authority and engendered Agendas: The Satnami Mahasabha, Chhattisgarh, 1920-50", *Indian Economic and Social History Review*, Vol. 30, No. 4, (1993).

Dube, S.C., "Educating Weaker Sections: Failure of a Strategy", *The Times of India*, (14-15 July, 1981).

Dubey, K.C., "Bhunyias", *Eastern Anthropologist*, Vol. 14, No. 1, (1961).

Dubey, S.N. and Usha Mathur, "Welfare Programmes for Scheduled Castes: Content and Administration", *Economic and Political Weekly*, Vol. 7, No. 4, (1972).

Dubey, S.N., "Welfare Schemes: Adaptation Response of Scheduled Castes", *The Economic Times*, (11 April 1975).

Dumont, L. and David Pocock, "Pure and Impure", *The Contributions to Indian Sociology*, No. 3, (1955).

Duncan, Ian, "Dalits and Politics in Rural North India: The Bahujan Samaj Party in Uttar Pradesh", *Journal of Peasant Studies*, Vol. 27, No. 1, (1999).

Dunn, D., "Gender Inequality in Education and Employment in the Scheduled Castes and Tribes of India", *Population Research and Policy Review*, Vol. 12, (1993).

Dushkin, Lelah, "The Backward Classes: Special Treatment Policy", *Economic Weekly*, Vol. XIII, [In three parts], (1961).

Dushkin, Lelah, "Scheduled Caste Policy in India: History, Problems, Prospects", *Asian Survey*, Vol. VII, No. 9, (1967).

Editorial, "Scheduled Castes and National Freedom", *Peoples War*, Vol. III, No. 45, (6 May 1945).

Editorial, "Scheduled Castes and Tribes: Commissioner Commissioned", *Economic and Political Weekly*, Vol. 13, No. 29, (1978).

Editorial, "Classes in Castes Idiom", *Economic and Political Weekly*, Vol. 14, Nos. 7–8, (1978).

Elwin, V., "Bhuiya of Bonai: An Anthology of Marriage Ceremonies", *Man in India*, Vol. 23, No. 2, (1943), [The Byuiyas or Bhuyans are categorized as Scheduled Castes in Bihar, Uttar Pradesh and West Bengal, but in Orissa they are categorized as Scheduled Tribes].

Elwin, V., "An Indian Riddle Book: The C.P. – Agarias", *Man in India*, Vo. 23, (1946).

Enthoven, R.E., "Bolas: Changes in Customs and Practices among Some Lower Agricultural Castes of Kotah State", *Eastern Anthropologist*, Vol. 21, No. 4, (1948).

Epp, Linda J., "Dalit Struggle, Nude Worship and the Chandragutti Incident", *Sociological Bulletin*, Vol. 41, Nos. 1–2, (1992).

Epstein, Scarlett, "Industrial Employment for Landless Labourers Only", *Economic Weekly*, Vol. XI, (1959).

Esme, "Three Scenes from the Life of a Garo", *Calcutta Review*, Vol. 85, (1887).

Fawcett, Fred, "Notes on the Domb of Jeypur, Madras Presidency", *Man*, Vol. 1, Article No. 29, (1901).

Felice, Sr. Anne, "Status of Harijan Students in Colleges", *The Indian Journal of Social Work*, Vol. 38, No. 1, (1977).

Fernandes, Walter, "Caste and Conversion Movements in India", *Social Action*, Vol. 31, No. 3, (1981).

Fisher, Marguerite J., "Problems of Implementation in India's Office of the Commissioner for Scheduled Castes", *Western Political Quarterly*, Vol. 23, (December, 1970).

Fiske, Adele M., "Religion and Buddhism Among India's New Buddhists", *Social Research*, Vol. 36, (1969).

Fitzgerald, T., "From Structure to Substance: Ambedkar, Dumont and Orientalism", *Contributions to Indian Sociology*, Vol. 30, No. 2, (1996).

Fitzgerald, Timothy, "Ambedkar Buddhism in Maharashtra", *Contributions to Indian Sociology*, Vo. 31, No. 2, (1997).

Foot, Isaac, "The Round Table Conference, the Future, and the Depressed Classes", *Contemporary Review*, No. 139, (1931).

Franco, Fernado and Sarvar V. Sherry Chand, "Ideology as Social Practice: The Function of Varna", *Economic and Political Weekly*, Vol. 24, No. 47, (1989).

Friends-Pereira, J.A., "Traces of the Couvade among the Hui and Mala of the Rajmahal Hills", *Journal of the Bihar and Orissa Research Society*, Vol. I, (1915).

Fuchs, Stephen, "Die hechzeits gebrauche der Balahis", *Anthropos*, Vol. 32, (1937).

Fuchs, Stephen, "Birth and Childhood among the Balahis", *Primitive Man*, Vol. 12, (1939).

Fuchs, Stephen, "Property concepts among the Nimar Balahis" *Journal of the Bombay Branch of the Royal Asiatic Society*, Vol. 18, (1942).

Fuchs, Stephen, "The cult of the Earth-Mother among the

Nimar Balahis", *Internationals Archiv fur Ethnographic,* Vol. 40, (1942).

Fuchs, Stephen, "The Matriarchal elements in the Ethnography of the Nimar Balahis" (in two parts), *New Indian Antiquary,* vol. 5, No. 4, (1942).

Fuchs, Stephen, "The Scavengers of the Nimar District in Madhya Pradesh", *Journal of the Bombay Branch of the Royal Asiatic Society,* Vol. 27, (1951).

Fuchs, Stephen, "The Religio-Ethical Concepts of the Chamars in Northern India", *Missiology: An International Review,* Vol. IV, No. 1, (1976).

Gaikwad, S.M., "Ambedkar and Indian Nationalism", *Economic and Political Weekly,* Vol. 33, No. 10, (1998).

Gajendran, A., "Transforming Dalit Politics", *Seminar,* No. 471, (November 1998).

Galanter, Marc, "'Protective Discrimination' for Backward Classes in India", *Journal of the Indian Law Institute,* Vol. III, (1961).

Galanter, Marc, "Caste Disabilities and Indian Federalism", *Journal of the Indian Law Institute,* Vol. III, No. 3, (1961).

Galanter, Marc, "Equality and 'Protective Discrimination' in India", *Rutger's Law Review,* Vol. XVI, (1961).

Galanter, Marc, "Law and Caste in Modern India", *Asian Survey,* Vol. III, (1963).

Galanter, Marc, "Temple-entry and the Untouchability Offenses", *Journal of the Indian Law Institute,* Vol. 6, (1964).

Galanter, Marc, "Equality and Preferential Treatment: Constitutional Limits and Judicial Control", *Indian Year Book of International Affairs,* Vol. XIV, (1965).

Galanter, Marc, "The Problem of Group Membership: Some Reflections on the Judicial View of Indian Society", *Journal of the Indian Law Institute,* Vol. 4, (1962). [This was reprinted in S.M. Lipset and R. Bendix (eds.), *Class, Status and Power,* (New York: Free Press, 1966), 2nd edition].

Galanter, Marc, "Group Membership and Group Preference in India", *Journal of Asian and African Studies*, Vol. II, (1967).

Galanter, Marc, "The Displacement of Traditional Law in Modern India", *Journal of Social Issues*, Vol. 24, (1968).

Galanter, Marc, "Untouchability and the Law", *Economic and Political Weekly*, (Annual Number), Vol. 4, Nos. 1-2, (1969).

Galanter, Marc, "Compensatory Discrimination in Political Representation: A Preliminary Assessment of India's Thirty-year Experience with Reserved Seats in Legislatures", *Economic and Political Weekly*, Vol. 14, Nos. 7–8, (1979).

Gandhi, Arun, "Harijans come into Their Own: Self-Help in Villages", *Times of India*, (February 16, 1979).

Gandhi, Christodas, "Assertion will Silence Oppression", *The Dalit*, (May-June 2002), [Interviewed by Punithan and Yakkan].

Gandhi, M.K., "Dr. Ambedkar's Indictment of Hinduism", *Harijan*, (18 July 1936).

Gandhi, M.K., "Untouchability, Women and Swaraj", *Indian Social Reformer*, Vol. 37, (26 March 1927).

Gandhi, P.C., "Job Reservation: Invitation to Anarchy", *Illustrated Weekly of India*, Vol. 99, No. 48, (December 24, 1978).

Gandhi, R.S., "The Practice of Untouchability: Persistence and Change", *Humboldt Journal of Social Relations*, Vol. 10, (1982-1983).

Gandhi, R.S., "The Extremes of Ethnic Violence: Some Explanations of Upper Castes – Scheduled Castes Conflicts in India, *Humboldt Journal of Social Relations*, Vol. 19, No. 2, (1993).

Gandhi, Rajmohan, "Harijans versus Caste Hindu", *Indian Express*, (August 24, 1978).

Gandhi, Sham S., "Dr. Ambedkar as a Religious Reformer", *Siddarth College of Law Magazine*, (1963-64).

Gangrade, K.D., "Social Mobility in India: A Study of Depressed Class", *Man in India,* Vol. 53, No. 3, (1975).

Gangrade, K.D., "Adult Suffrage and Social Change: Changing Status of a Depressed Caste", *Social Change,* Vol. 6, Nos. 1–2, (1976).

Gangrade, S.D. and C.G. Sanon, "Panchayat Elections in Punjab Village: Changing Political Status of a Depressed Caste", *Eastern Anthropologist,* Vol. 22, No. 1, (1969).

Ganguly, Debjani, "Can the Dalit Speak?: Caste, Postcoloniality and the New Humanities", *South Asia,* Vol. 23, (2000), [Special Issue].

Gani, H.A., "Governmental Policies to uplift the Scheduled Castes – An Eyewash", *Janata,* Vol. 31, No. 7, (1974).

Gani, H.A., "Scheduled Castes and Communal Problems", *Mainstream,* Vol. 12, (1973).

Garg, B.L., "The Commissioner of Scheduled Castes and Scheduled Tribes at Work", *Journal of the Society for Study of State Governments,* Vol. 3, Nos. 3-4, (October-December, 1970).

Gatade, Subash, "Untouchability and India's (D)Urban Elite", *Himal,* Vol. 14, No. 7, (2001).

Gaur, J.S., C.M. Thukral, V.K. Sharma and Sunita, "Values and Career Maturity of Scheduled and non-Scheduled Caste High School Boys", *Indian Educational Review,* Vol. 24, No. 2, (1989).

Gautam, M.B., 'The Untouchables Movement in Andhra Pradesh', *Souvenir,* A.P. State Harijan Conference, (10 – 12 April, 1976).

Geeta, V. and S.V. Rajdurai, "Dalits and Non-Brahmin Consciousness in Colonial Tamil Nadu", *Economic and Political Weekly,* Vol. 28, No. 39, (1993).

Geeta, V., "Who is the Third that Walks Behind You?: Dalit Critique of Modernity", *Economic and Political Weekly,* Vol. 36, No. 2, (2000).

Gehlot, N.S., "Dr. Ambedkar, Mahatma Gandhi and Dalit

Movement", *Indian Journal of Political Science,* Vol. 54, Nos. 3–4, (1993).

Gellner, D.G., "Structure and Consensus among 'Untouchables' in South Asia", *Journal of Royal Anthropological Institute,* Vol.1, (1995).

Ghandy, Kobad, "Dr. Ambedkar – Bourgeois Reformer or Revolutionary?", *Frontier,* (8 December 1979).

Ghatak, N.K., "Namsudra of Bengal through the Ages", *Bulletin of the Cultural Research Institute,* Vol. 17, (1990).

Ghorpade, K.R., "Eradication of Untouchability as a step to National Integration", *Nie Journal,* (May-July, 1971).

Ghosh, Lalita, "Taste Sensitivity to Phenylthiocarbamide in the Padmaraj (Pod) and the Bagdi of West Bengal", *The Anthropologist,* Vol. 3, (1956).

Ghosh, Partha S., "Positive Discrimination in India: A Political Analysis", *Ethnic Studies Report,* Vol. 15, No. 2, (1997).

Ghouse, Mohammad, "Judicial Control of Protective Discrimination", *Journal of the Indian Law Institute,* Vol. 11, (1969).

Gill, Raj, "Man from Garo Hills", *Social Welfare,* Vol. 6, No. 1, (1959).

Glass, Ruth, "Divided and Degraded: The Downtrodden Peoples of India", *Monthly Review,* Vol. 34, No. 3, (1982).

Goel, B.S., "Caste and Class Tensions in India", *Conspectus,* Vol. 2, (1966).

Goel, B.S., "Untouchability: An Analysis of its Causes", *National Herald,* (August 3, 1970).

Gokhale, Jayashree B., "Dr. Bhimrao Ramji Ambedkar: Rebel Against Hindu Tradition", *Journal of Asian and African Studies,* Vol. 11, (1976).

Gokhale-Turner, Jayashree B., "The Dalit Panthers and the Radicalization of the Untouchables", *The Journal of Commonwealth and Comparative Politics,* Vol. 17, No. 1, (1979).

Gokhale-Turner, Jayashree B., "Bhakti or Vidroha: Continuity and Change in Dalit Sahitya", *Journal of Asian and African Studies*, Vol. 15, (1980).

Gokhale, Jayashree B., "The Sociopolitical Effects of Ideological Change: The Buddhist Conversion of Maharashtrian Untouchables", *Journal of Asian Studies*, Vol. 14, No. 2, (1986).

Gondal, Ram Pratap, "Changes in Customs and Practices among Some Lower Agricultural Casts of Kotah State", *The Eastern Anthropologist*, Vol. 2, No. 4, (1948).

Goodwin-Austen, H.H., "On the Garo Hills", *Proceedings of the Royal Geographic Society*, Vol. 17, (1873).

Gopal, B., "National Pledge for Upliftment of Scheduled Castes and Scheduled Tribes: A Stock Taking", *Indian Journal of Political Science*, Vol. 52, No. 4, (October - December, 1991).

Gora, "The only Remedy", *Seminar*, No. 177, (May 1974).

Gore, G.M., "Socio-Economic Study of the Scheduled Castes in Rural Maharashtra", ICSSR's *Research Abstracts Quarterly*, Vol. 2, (1974).

Gosal, R.S.P., "Growth of India's Scheduled Caste Population, 1971-81: A Spatial Analysis", Population Geography", *Population Geography*, Vol. 12, Nos. 1-2, (June-December, 1990).

Gosal, R.S.P., "Scheduled Caste Population and Urbanization in India: A Spatial Analysis", *Geographical Review of India*, Vol. 55, No. 3, (1993).

Goswami, M.C., "Garo Marriage and Kinship Organisation", *Anthropologist*, Vol. 3, No. 1, (1956)

Goudie, William, "Panchama Education", *The Harvest Field*, Vol. 13, No. 3, (1902).

Gould, H., "Castes, Outcastes and the Sociology of Stratification", *International Journal of Comparative Sociology*, Vol. I, (September, 1960).

Goyal, B.R., "Education of the Under-Privileged Under the 10+2+3 Scheme", *Journal of Indian Education*, Vol. 1, No. 1, (1975).

GPD, "Dalit Literature", *Economic and Political Weekly*, Vol. 17, No. 3, (1982).

Green, Marilyn, "Voices of the Drum", *Sky*, Vol. 22, No. 11, (1993).

Gunasundari, "Dalit Literature: A Question of Identity", *The Times of India*, (April 24, 1977).

Gupta, B.C., "Spirit Worship in the Nilgiris (Pariah)", *Indian Antiquary*, Vol. 55, (1926).

Gupta, D., "Understanding the Marathawada Riots: A Repudiation of Eclectic Marxism, *Social Scientist* 7, No. 10, (1979).

Gupta, Dipankar, "Positive Discrimination and the Question of Fraternity: Contrasting Ambedkar and Mandal on Reservations", *Economic and Political Weekly*, Vol. 32, No. 31, (1997).

Gupta, Dipankar, "A Question of Quotas", *Seminar*, No. 471, (November 1998).

Gupta, Dipankar, "Caste, Race, Politics", *Seminar*, No. 508, (December 2001).

Gupta, L.P., "A Study of the Personal Characteristics and Academic Achievement of Scheduled Caste and Backward Class Students and Its Implications for Administrators", *EPA bulletin*, Vol. 2, No. 1, (1979).

Gupta, L.P., "A Study of the Personality Syndromes and Cognitive Characteristics of Scheduled Caste and Backward Class Students and non-Scheduled Caste Students", *Journal of Higher Education*, Vol. 4, No. 3, (1979).

Gupta, Meenakshi and Viney Kirpal, "Reservations: Case Study of the IITs", *IASSI Quarterly*, Vol. 16, No. 2, (1997).

Gupta, Parbita and Arabindo Bau, "Physical Characters of the Madiga of Guntur District, a Pariah caste of Andhra", *Bulletin of the Anthropological Survey of India*, Vol. 9, No. 1, (1960).

Gupta, S.C. and B.G. Prasad, "A Socio-Medical Survey of Sweepers and Their Families in Lucknow Municipal

Corporation", *Indian Journal of Social Work*, Vol. XXIV, (1964).

Gupta, S.C., "Note on Living and Working Conditions of Sweeper Community in Lucknow", *Eastern Anthropologist*, Vol. XVIII, (1965).

Gupta, Sandal Das, "Demographic Aspects of Marriage among the Dule Badgis of Jai Nagar", *Bulletin of the Cultural Research Institute*, Vol. 3, No. 1, (1964).

Gupta, Shiva K., "Harijan Legislation, Their Alienation and Activism: A Case Study of Harijan Power", *Indian Journal of Political Science*, Vol. 41, No. 3, (1980).

Gupte, G.S., "Legislation for the Improvement of the Lot of 'Depressed Classes' or 'Harijans'", *Social Reform Annual* (Bombay), (1939).

Guru, Gopal, "Reservations and the Sanskritization of Scheduled Castes–Some Theoretical Aspects", *Sociological Bulletin*, Vol. 33, Nos. 1–2, (1984).

Guru, Gopal, "Appropriating Ambedkar", *Economic and Political Weekly*, Vol. 26, No. 27-28, (1991), [Comment on S.H. Deshpande in 27th April].

Guru, Gopal, "Dalit Killings in Marathwada", *Economic and Political Weekly*, Vol. 26, No. 51, (1991).

Guru, Gopal, "The Hinduisation of Ambedkar in Maharashtra", *Economic and Political Weekly*, Vol.26, No. 7, (1991).

Guru, Gopal, "The Dalit Movement in Mainstream Sociology", *Economic and Political Weekly*, Vol. 28, No. 14, (1993).

Guru, Gopal, "Understanding Violence Against Dalits in Marathwada", *Economic and Political Weekly*, Vol. 29, No. 9 (1994).

Guru, Gopal, "Dalit Women Talk Differently", *Economic and Political Weekly*, Vol. XXX, Nos. 41-42, (1995).

Guru, Gopal, 'Human Rights and the Dalits: An Inquiry into the Human Rights Discourse in India", *Indian Journal of Human Rights*, Vol. I, No. 1, (1997).

Guru, Gopal, "Ambedkar's Idea of Social Justice", *The Administrator*, Vol. XLII, No. 1, (1997).

Guru, Gopal, "Understanding Dalit Protest in Maharashtra", *Economic and Political Weekly*, (26 July 1997).

Guru, Gopal, "Why are the Dalits Angry?", *The Hindu*, (29 July 1997).

Guru, Gopal, "The Shifting Sites of Reservation", *The Hindu*, (2 December 1997).

Guru, Gopal, "Understanding Ambedkar's Construction of National Movement", *Economic and Political Weekly*, Vol. XXXIII, No. 4, (January 24, 1998).

Guru, Gopal, "The Politics of Naming", *Seminar*, No. 471, (November 1998).

Guru, Gopal and V. Geetha, "New Phase of Dali-Bahujan Intellectual Activity", *Economic and Political Weekly*, Vol. 35, No. 3, (2000).

Guru, Gopal, "Politics of Representation", *Seminar*, No. 508, (December 2001).

Guru, Gopal, "Dalits From Margin to Margin", *IIC Quarterly*, Vol. 27, No. 2, (2002).

Haldar, A.K., "Scheduled Castes of Bihar: Their Distribution and Relative Concentration", *Journal of Social Research*, Vol. 19, No. 1, (1976).

Hantal, B., "BSP: Gaining Strength", *Economic and Political Weekly*, Vol. 31, No. 21, (1996).

Hanumanthan, K.R., 'Evolution of Untouchability in Tamil Nadu, A.D. upto 1680', *The Indian Historical Review*, Vol. XXIII, Nos. 1-2, (1997).

Hari, H.L., "A Sociological Classification of Scheduled Castes and their Socio-Political Trends", *Journal of Social Research*, Vol. 15, No. 1, (1972).

Harper, Susan Billington, "The Politics of Conversion: The Azariah–Gandhi Controversy over Christian Mission to the Depressed Classes in the 1930s", *Indo-British Review*, Vol. XV, (19??)

Hasan, Amir, "A Note on Education among the Kols of Uttar Pradesh", *Eastern Anthropologist*, Vol. 21, No.1, (1968), [Kol is a Scheduled Caste in Uttar Pradesh and Tripura; but is a Scheduled Tribe in Madhya Pradesh, Maharashtra and Orissa].

Hasan, Amir, "Harijan Welfare in Uttar Pradesh", *Social Welfare*, (January, 1972).

Hayter, O.C.G., "Conversions of Outcastes", *Asian Review*, Vol. 26, Nos. 85–88, (1930).

Hazari (pseud. of Marcus Abraham Malik), "I Was an Outcaste", *Social Welfare*, Vol. 4, (1957).

Heider, S., "Lifting the veil of Silence: Jamuna's Narrative of Pain", *Sociological Bulletin*, Vol. 44, (1995).

Henningham, Stephen, "Autonomy and Organisation: Harijans and Adivasi Protest Movements", *Economic and Political Weekly*, Vol. 16, No. 27, (1981).

Henry, Bishop of Madras, "The Outcastes of India", *The Nineteenth Century*, Vol. 66, (1909).

Hiramani, A.B., "The Place of Caste Council Among the Scheduled Castes in a Maharashtra Village", *Indian Journal of Comparative Sociology*, Vol. 2, No. 1, (1975).

Hjejle, B., "Slavery and Agricultural Bondage in South India in the 19th Century", *Scandinavian Economic History Review*, Vol. XV, Nos.1–2, (1967).

Hodgson, Brian Huaghton, "On the Origin, Location, Numbers, Creed, Customs, Character and Condition of the Koch, Bodo and Dhimal People with a General Description of the Climate they Dwell in", *Journal of the Royal Asiatic Society of Bengal*, Vol. 18, Part 2, (1849), [The *Kochs* are categorized as a Scheduled Caste in West Bengal and Tripura].

Horsey, Anita, "Conditions of Scheduled Castes and Tribes", *New Frontier Education*, Vol. 11, No. 2, (1981).

Hosten, H., "The Twelve Bhuiyas or Landlords of Bengal", *Journal of the Asiatic Society of Bengal*, Vol. 10, (N.S.),

(1913), [The Byuiyas or Bhuyans are categorized as Scheduled Castes in Bihar, Uttar Pradesh and West Bengal, but in Orissa they are categorized as Scheduled Tribes].

Hovell, Laurie, "Namdeo Dhasal: Poet and Panther", *Bulletin of Concerned Asian Scholars*, Vol. 23, No. 2, (1991).

Husain, Syed L., "Harijans: Will ever their plight Improve?", *Radiance*, (February 20, 1972).

Ilaiah, Kancha, "Scheduled Castes and Scheduled Tribes: Systemic Exploitation", *Economic and Political Weekly*, Vol. 35, No. 51, (December 22, 1990).

Ilaiah, Kancha, "Caste and Women's Sexuality: A Look at Chundur and Chelkurthi", *Mainstream*, Vol. 30, No. 31, (1992).

Ilaiah, Kancha, "BSP and Caste Ideology", *Economic and Political Weekly*, Vol. 29, No. 14, (1994).

Ilaiah, Kancha, 'Caste or Class or Caste-Class: A Study in Dalit Bahujan Consciousness in Andhra Pradesh in 1980s' Research in Progress Papers, 'History and Society', (New Delhi, NMML, 1995).

Ilaiah, Kancha, "Beef, BJP and Food Rights of People", *Economic and Political Weekly*, Vol. 31, No. 24, (1996).

Ilaiah, Kancha, "In Search of The Roots of Anti Caste Struggle: A Dalitist Reading of the Buddhist Discourse", Research in Progress Papers, 'History and Society', (New Delhi, NMML, 1996).

Ilaiah, Kancha, "Attacks on Ambedkar", *The Hindu*, (30 August 1997).

Ilaiah, Kancha, "Dalits and Globalisation", *The Hindu*, (17 November1997).

Ilaiah, Kancha, "Interview: Towards a Constructive 'Globalization'", *Seminar*, No. 508, (December 2001).

Imam, Mohammed, "Reservation of Seats for Backward Classes in Public Services and Educational Institutions", *Journal of the Indian Law Institute*, Vol. 8, (1966).

"Impact of Agricultural Development Programmes on Scheduled Castes and Scheduled Tribes Population in Maharashtra", *Journal of Indian School of Political Economy,* Vol. 12, Nos. 3–4, (2000).

Ingle, M.H., "The Touchables", *Seminar,* No. 177, (May 1974).

Ito, Shoji, "Religio-Social Movement in Modern Kerala: With Special Reference to the Ezhava Caste", (in Japanese), *Shiso,* No. 651, (1978).

Iyer, Radha, "The Dalit Panthers", *Eves Weekly,* Vol. 29, (April 1979).

Jabbi, M.K. and C. Rajyalakshmi, "Education of Scheduled Caste and Scheduled Tribe Groups in Bihar", *Social Change,* Vol. 27, Nos. 1–2, (1997).

Jacobson, Doranne, "Tea and Insults: Untouchability in Eastern India", *Bulletin of Concerned Asian Studies,* Vol. 12, No. 1, (1980).

Jadhav, S., "The Myth of Origin of the Indian Untouchables", *Man,* Vol. 29, (1994).

Jagannathan, R., "Weaker Sections of the Village Community and Panchayati Raj", *Indian Journal of Political Administration,* Vol. VIII, (1962).

Jain, Bimal Chand, "Note on Shilpakar – A Harijan Sub-Caste of Ranikhat", *Journal of the Indian Anthropological Society,* Vol. 14, (1979).

Jain, L.C., "Emancipation of Scheduled Castes and Tribes: Some Suggestions", *Economic and Political Weekly,* Vol. 16, No. 9, (1981).

Jain, M.P., "Comment: Reservation of the Posts for Scheduled Castes and Article 16 (4) - General Manager, Southern Railway Vs K. Rangachari", *Journal of the Indian Law Institute,* Vol. 3, (1961).

Jain, Pratibha, "Depressed Class Movements – The Gandhian Approach", *Gandhi Marg,* Vol. 2, No. 8, (November, 1980).

Jalali, Rita, "Preferential Policies and the Movement of the Disadvantaged: The Case of the Scheduled Castes in India", *Ethnic and Racial Studies*, Vol. 16, No. 1, (January, 1993).

James, P.A. and G. Sreenivas Reddy, "Commissioner for Scheduled Castes and Scheduled Tribes", *Economic and Political Weekly*, Vol. 14, No. 26, (1979).

James, P.A. and G. Sreenivas Reddy, "Anti-Untouchability Legislation in India", *Journal of Administration Overseas*, Vol. 19, (1980).

James, R.E., "Outcaste Progress in South India", *Asian Review*, Vol. 26, Nos. 85 – 88 (1930).

Japhet, S., "Christian Dalits: A Sociological Study on the Problem of Gaining a New Identity", *Religion and Society*, Vo.34, (1987).

Jawali, S.G., "Ambedkar and the Future of the Dalit Movement", *Olympus*, Vol. 12, No. 4, (1991).

Jaya Raju, M., "IRDP in Eliminating Poverty among the Scheduled Castes and Scheduled Tribes", *Economic Affairs*, Vol. 38, No. 2, (April – June, 1993).

Jayakumar, E.C., "Impact of Development Programme on Scheduled Castes and Scheduled Tribes: A Critical Appraisal", *IASSI Quarterly*, Vol. 17, No. 2, (1998).

Jayakumar, Samuel, "The Importance of Disciplining the Oppressed in India", *Church Planter*, (January-February 1994).

Jayaram, N., "Fresh Look at Harijan Question", *Mainstream*, Vol. 19, No. 38, (1981).

Jayaram, N., "Protective Discrimination and Education", *Mainstream*, Nos. 24-25, (1983).

Jayaram, N., "Can Law Save Scheduled Castes: A Critique of a Strategy for Change", *Mainstream*, Vol. 26, No. 37, (1986), [Republic Day special issue].

Jayaram, N., "Emancipation Through Proselytism: Some Reflections on the Marginal Status of the Depressed Castes", *Sociological Bulletin*, Vol. 41, Nos. 1 & 2, (1992).

Jebraj, D., "Exodus: A Paradigm of the Salvation and Liberation of the Oppressed", *Evangelical Review of Theology*, Vol. 16, No. 2, (1994).

Jeffrey, Robin, "Temple Entry Movement in Travancore 1860-1940", *Social Scientist*, Vol. 4, No. 3, (1976).

Jeffrey, Robin, "(Not) Being There: Dalits and India's Newspapers", *South Asia*, Vol. 24, No. 2, (2001).

Jha, Ashok Kumar, "Mahatma Gandhi's View on Harijan", *Third Concept*, Vol. 10, Nos. 116–117, (1996).

Jha, Chetkar, "Reserved Representation", *Seminar*, (November 1979).

Jha, Hetukur, "Lower-Caste Peasants and Upper-Caste Zamindars in Bihar (1921-25): An Analysis of Sanskritization and Contradiction Between the Two Groups", *The Indian Economic and Social History Review*, Vol. 9, No. 4, (1977).

Jha, Hetkur, "Promises and Lapses: Understanding the Experience of Scheduled Castes in Bihar in Historical Perspective", *Journal of Indian School of Political Economy*, Vol. 12, Nos. 3–4, (2000).

Jha, M., "Problems of Scavengers of a tribal city: a case study of Ranchi, Chotanagpur", *Man in India*, Vol. 7, No. 2, (1994).

Jha, Vivekanand, "Stages in History of Untouchables", *Indian Historical Review*, Vol. 2, No. 1, (1975).

Jha, Vivekanand, "Caste, Untouchability and Social Justice: Early North Indian Perspective", *Social Scientist*, Vol. 25, Nos. 11–12, (1977).

Jha, Vivekanand, "Chandalas and the Origin of Untouchability", *Indian Historical Review*, Vol. XIII, Nos. 1–2, (July 1986–January 1987).

Jodhka, Surinder S., "'Prejudice' without Pollution?: Scheduled Castes in Contemporary Punjab", *Journal of Indian School of Political Economy*, Vol. 12, Nos. 3–4, (2000).

Jodhka, Surinder S., "Caste and Untouchability in Rural

Punjab", *Economic and Political Weekly*, Vol. 37, No. 19, (2002).

Jodhka, Surinder S., "Nation and Village: Images of Rural India in Gandhi, Nehru and Ambedkar", *Economic and Political Weekly*, Vol. 37, No. 32, (2002).

Jogdand, P.G., "Dalit in Maharashtra: Challenges Ahead", *Economic and Political Review*, (20 December 1997).

Jogdand, P.G., "Globalisation and the Dalits", *Social Action*, Vol. 52, No. 1, (2002).

Jordens, J.T.F., "Two Giants Look at the Cosmic Man: Ambedkar and Dayananda Interpret the *Purusa-Sukta*", *Journal of the Oriental Institute* (Baroda), Vol. 33, No. 1, (1983).

Joseph, Nandi, "Dalit Reality of the Indian Catholic Church", *Dalit International Newsletter*, Vol. 5, No. 3, (2000).

Joseph, T.M., "Reservations for 'Sons of the Soil'", *Eastern Anthropologist*, Vol. 44, No. 2, (April-June, 1991).

Joseph, V.V., "A Triangle for Freedom and Equality", *Social Welfare*, (May, 1973).

Joshi, Barbara R., " 'Ex-Untouchable': Problems, Progress, and Policies in Indian Social Change", *Pacific Affairs*, Vol. 53, No.2, (1980).

Joshi, Barbara R., "Scheduled Caste Voters: New Data, New Questions", *Economic and Political Weekly*, Vol. 16, No. 33, (1981).

Joshi, Barbara R., "Whose Law, Whose Order: 'Untouchables', Social Violence, and the State in India", *Asian Survey*, Vol. 27, No. 7, (1982).

Joshi, Barbara R., "Dalit Literature – A New Sensibility", *The Indian Panorama*, (March-April 1984).

Joshi, Barbara R., "Editorial Introduction: Perspectives on the Dalit Cultural Movement", to the Section on "Perspectives on Dalit Political and Cultural Movements", *South Asia Bulletin*, Vol. VII, Nos. 1-2, (1987).

Joshi, Barbara R., "Recent Developments in Inter-Regional Mobilization of Dalit Protest in India", *South Asia Bulletin*, Vol. 7, Nos. 1–2, (1987).

Joshi, P.C., "Social and Economic Movement among the Lower Castes in U.P.", *Indian Sociologist*, Vol. 1, No. 1, (1959).

Judge, Paramjit S., "Emerging Trends in the Caste Structure of Punjab", *The Administrator*, Vol. XLII, No. 1, (1997).

Juergensmeyer, Mark, "Ad Dharm: Religion of Untouchables", *The Times of India*, (12 October 1975).

Juergensmeyer, Mark, "What If the Untouchables Don't Believe in Untouchability?", *Bulletin of Concerned Asian Scholars*, Vol. 12, No. 1, (1980).

Junghare, V., "Songs of the Mahars: An Untouchable Caste of Maharashtra India", *Ethnomusicology*, Vol. XXVII, No. 2, (1983).

Kadetotad, N.K., "Caste Hierarchy among Untouchables of Dharwar", *Eastern Anthropologist*, Vol. 19, (1966).

Kadetotad, N.K., "The Untouchables of Dharwar and Their Festivals", *Journal of Karnatak University (Dharwar), Social Sciences*, Vol. 4, (1968).

Kalam, M., "Why the Harijan Convert to Islam Views Reservations with Reservation", *South Asia Research*, Vol. 4, (1984).

Kalelkar, Kaka, "Casteism and Untouchability: An Analysis", *Indian Journal of Adult Education*, Vol. 19, No. 3, (1958).

Kamalakar Rao, P., "Socio-Economic Background and Academic Achievement of the Scheduled Caste Students in Higher Educational Institutions, Andhra University, 1960-70", *The Journal of Social Transformation*, Vol. 3, Nos. 2-3, (1979).

Kamaraju, Malyala S.S. and K.V. Ramana, "Untouchability – The Need for a New Approach", *The Indian Journal of Social Work*, Vol. 45, (1984).

Kamat, A.R., "Education and Social Change amongst the Scheduled Castes and Scheduled Tribes", *Economic and Political Weekly*, Vol. 16, No. 31, (1981).

Kamble, M.N., "Raosaheb Kasbe Yancha Dalit Chalvalicha Magova", (in Marathi), *Satyasodhak Marxwadi*, Vol. 2, No. 23, (January, 1984).

Kamble, Ramesh, "Occupation and Inherited Status", *Economic and Political Weekly*, Vol. 31, No. 40, (1996).

Kamble, Ramesh, "Dalit Interpretations of Society", *Seminar*, No. 471, (November 1998).

Kameswara Rao, N.V. and M.V.T. Raju, "Malas and Madigas: An Ethnographic Study of the Two Scheduled Castes in Telangana", *Journal of Social Research*, Vol. 18, No. 2, (1975).

Kameswara Rao, N.V., "Politics, Social Reform and Scheduled Castes in Coastal Andhra", *Journal of Social Research*, Vol. 18, No. 2, (1975).

Kamila, Banu Behari, "Occupational Status of Parents of Harijan and Tribal Welfare Department High School Students of Orissa", *National Journal of Education*, Vol. 6, No. 1, (1983).

Kananaikil, Jose, "Marginalisation of the Scheduled Castes: A Sociological Interpretation", *Social Action*, Vo. 32, (1982).

Kananaikil, Jose, "Scheduled Caste Converts in Search of Justice: In the Halls of the Supreme Court", *Social Action*, Vol. 36, No. 1, (1986).

Kananaikil, Jose, "Secular State and Religious Criterion for Reservations", *Social Action*, Vol. 36, No. 2, (1986).

Kananaikil, Jose, "The Emerging Dalit Identity in India", *Social Action*, Vol. 43, No. 4, (1993).

Kannabiran, Kalpana, "Caste, the Academy and Dalit Women", *The Hindu*, (20 June 2001).

Kannan, M. and Francois Gros, "Tamil Dalits in Search of a Literature", *South Asia Research*, Vol. 22, No. 1, (2002).

Kanungo, Sukla Deb, "Dalit Women's Search for Identity", *Social Action*, Vol. 43, No. 4, (1993).

Karar, B.R., "The Many Implications of the Dalit Question before the Government", *National Christian Council Review*, Vol. CXI, No. 4, (1991).

Karlekar, Kaka, "Casteism and Untouchability: An Analysis", *Indian Journal of Adult Education*, Vol. 19, No. 3, (1958).

Karlekar, Malavika, "Higher Education and the Scheduled Caste", *Journal of Higher Education*, Vol. 1, No. 2, (1975).

Karlekar, Malavika, "Some Perspectives on the Employment of Scheduled Caste Women", *Social Action*, Vol. 32, No. 3, (1982).

Karlekar, Malavika, "Educational Experience of Scheduled Castes and Scheduled Tribes", *Economic and Political Weekly*, Vol. 18, No. 41, (1983), [Comment on Krishna Kumar's paper in *EPW*, dated 3-10 Sept.].

Karve, Iravati and Hemalata Acharya, "Neo-Buddhism in Maharashtra", *Journal of the University of Poona*, Humanities Section, Vol. 15, (1962).

Kashyap, Subash, "Honest Efforts Needed for Social Equity", *Kurukshetra*, vol. 39, No. 1, (1990), [Ambedkar Birth Centenary Special].

Katyal, Anita, "UGC Plan for Scheduled Caste and Scheduled Tribe", *The Times of India*, (3 April 1989).

Kaul, V. et al., "Marital Distance and Serological Studies among the Balmikis and the Soods of Himachal Pradesh", *Journal of Anthropological Society of India*, Vol. 48, No. 3, (1999).

Kaur, Amit and Tarlok Singh, "Regional Education Disparity among Scheduled Castes of Punjab", *Indian Journal of Adult Education*, Vol. 46, No. 4, (1985).

Kaushik, P. Datt, "Gandhiji and Congress vis-à-vis Untouchables", *AICC Economic Review*, Vol. XV, (October 1, 1963).

Kelkar, N.C., "The Elevation of the Depressed Classes", *Mahratta*, (November 7, 1909), reprinted in *Pleasures and Privileges of the Pen*, (Poona: Kashinath N. Kelkar, 1909).

Kelkar, R.V., "The Untouchability (Offenses) Act, 1955", *Vyavahara Nirnaya* (University of Delhi, Faculty of Law), Vol. V, (1956).

Khan, M.A., "A Brief Summary of the Study on Mass Conversion of Meenakshipuram: A Sociological Enquiry", *Religion and Society*, Vol. 28, No. 4, (1981).

Khan, M. Rafiq., "Weaker Section of the Community", *Interdiscipline*, (Winter 1970).

Khan, Mumtaz Ali, "Impact of the Constitutional Protection and Safeguards on the Scheduled Castes of Satnur Village", *All-India Congress Committee Economic Review*, Vol. 20, No. 21, (1969).

Khan, Mumtaz Ali, "Social Organizations and Conversions: Case Study of Meenakshipuram", *Samata*, Vol. I, (1982).

Khan, Mumtaz Ali, "Social Conditions of the Scheduled Castes", *Journal of Dharma*, Vol. 16, (1991).

Khanna, K.C., "Promoting Harijan Welfare: Limitations of the Law", *The Times of India*, (13 February 1980).

Khare, R.S., "The Body, Sensoria and Self of the Powerless: Remembering/'Re-membering' Indian Untouchable Women", *New Literary History*, Vol. 26, (1995).

Kharwara, P.C. et al., "Comparative Adoption of Improved Technology by Female and Male Headed Scheduled Caste Families", *Journal of Rural Development*, Vol. 10, (1991).

Khobragade, Ram, "NDA Government's Economic Policy to Deprive Bahujans", *Radical Humanist*, Vol. 65, No. 5, (2001).

Khurana, G., "Education Facilities for Scheduled Castes", *Education Quarterly*, Vol. 31, Nos. 3 & 4, (1980).

Kirpal, Vijay, "Scheduled Castes and Tribes: Are They 'Government Brahmins'?", *Illustrated Weekly of India*, Vol. 97, No. 16, (1976).

Kirpal, Vinay, "Higher Education for the Scheduled Castes and Scheduled Tribes", *Economic and Political Weekly*, Vol. 13, Nos. 4–5, (1979).

Kirpal, Vinay, Nalini Swamidasan, Amitabha Gupta and Raj K. Gupta, "Scheduled Caste and Tribe Students in Higher Education: A Study of an IIT", *Economic and Political Weekly*, Vol. 20, No. 29, (1985).

Kirpal, Vinay, Nalini Swamidasan, Amitabha Gupta and Raj K. Gupta, "Wastage among Scheduled Caste and Scheduled Tribe Students", *Journal of Higher Education*, Vol. 11, Nos. 1-2, (1985-86).

Kodiyan, P.K., "Scheduled Castes and Scheduled Tribes Suffer: Directive Principle Remains on Paper", *New Age*, (March, 1972).

Kolenda, Pauline, "Changing Religious Practices of an Untouchable Caste", *Economic Development and Cultural Change*, Vol. VIII, No. 3, (1960).

Kolenda-Mahar, Pauline, "Religious Anxiety and Hindu Fate", *Journal of Asian Studies*, Vol. XXXIII, (1964).

Kolenda, Pouline, "The Functional Relations of a Bhangi Cult", *The Anthropologist*, Vol. II, (1968). (Special Issue edited by S.C. Tiwari).

Koli, G.N., "Economic Uplift of Backward Classes", *National Herald*, (24 March 1972).

Kooiman, D., "Jagjivan Ram", *India News brief*, Vol. 3, (November 1979).

Kopparty, S.N.M., "Health Status of Scheduled Castes", *Social Change*, Vol. 21, No. 1, (March, 1991).

Korthurkar, V.K. and V.V. Pendse, "A Study of Social Prejudice in Three Villages: The Problem of Neo-Buddhas", *Journal of the University of Poona*, Humanities Section, Vol. 15, (1962).

Kothari, Rajni, "Dalits of Today: Gandhi, Ambedkar Not Relevant", *The Times of India*, (16 May 1994).

Kothari, Rajni, "Rise of the Dalits and the Renewed Debate on Caste", *Economic and Political Weekly*, Vol. 29, No. 26, (1994).

Kothari, Rita, "Short Story in Gujarati Dalit Literature", *Economic and Political Weekly*, Vol. 36, No. 45, (2001).

Kriesberg, Louis, "Abolition of Untouchability in Andhra Pradesh", *Social Welfare*, Vol. 15, No. 2, (1968).

Krishna Ananth, V. (in association with Mahesh Vijapurkar, S. Annamalai and J.P. Shukla, "An Inevitable Churning...", *The Hindu*, (20 July 1997).

Krishna Reddy, B., "Conflict Between Harijans and Caste Hindus in Andhra Pradesh", *The Eastern Anthropologist*, Vol. 37, No. 2, (1984).

Krishnan, P.S., "Generation of Employment and Self Employment among the SCs of India", *National Labour Institute Bulletin*, Vol. 6, Nos. 1-2, (1980).

Krishnan, P.S., "Untouchability and Atrocities", *Social Action*, Vol. 43, No. 4, (1993).

Kuber, W.N., "Post-Ambedkar Developments", *Marxist Miscellany*, (September 1979).

Kulkarni, A.R., "Dr. Ambedkar and Buddhism", *Maha Bodhi*, Vol. 58, (1950).

Kulkarni, B. Francis, "Dalit Christian Dilemma", *Journal of Anthropological Survey of India*, Vol. 48, No. 2, (1999).

Kulkarni, M.G., "Scheduled Castes in Maharashtra: A Study in Social Change with particular reference to Mahars", *Magadh University Journal*, (July, 1969).

Kulkarni, M.G., "The Scheduled Castes in Maharashtra", *Marathwada University Journal of Humanities and Social Sciences*, Vol. 9, (1969).

Kulkarni, M.G., "Place of Weaker Sections in Rural Democracy", *Magadh University Journal*, (July 1971).

Kulkarni, Mahesh, "Pune District Leading in Violence against Women and the Higher Number of Atrocities on Scheduled Castes and Scheduled Tribes are in Kolhapur District", (in Marathi), *Daily Pudhari*, (February 13, 1997).

Kulkarni, S.D., "Scheduled Caste Elite and Social Change", *Economic and Political Weekly*, Vol. 15, No. 15, (1980).

Kulkarni, S.V., "How to Combat Untouchability", *Indian Express*, (June 8, 1969).

Kulkarni, V.B., "Fate of Harijans in Uttar Pradesh", *Link,* (March 5, 1972).

Kulkarni, V.B., "Persecuted Harijans", *Indian Express,* (June 19, 1972).

Kumar, Dharma, "Affirmative Action Debate in India", *Asian Survey,* Vol. 32, No. 3, (March, 1992).

Kumar, K. and R.C.S. Taragi, "Socially Deprived: A Case of Scheduled Caste Population in Uttar Pradesh", *Man in India,* Vol. 71, No. 1, (1991).

Kumar, K.B., "Delhi Leads in Harijan Welfare", *Indian Express,* (February 26, 1971).

Kumar, Krishna, "Educational Experience of Scheduled Castes and Scheduled Tribes", *Economic and Political Weekly,* Vol. 18, Nos. 36-37, (1983).

Kumar, Kuldeep, "Was Gandhi Anti-Dalit?", *The Pioneer,* (24 April 1994).

Kumar, Narender, "Dalit and Shudra Politics and Anti-Brahmin Movement", *Economic and Political Weekly,* Vol. 35, No. 45, (2000).

Kumar, Narender, "Grassroot Leadership among Scheduled Castes in Haryana after the 73rd Amendment Act", *Radical Humanist,* Vol. 64, No. 11, (2001).

Kumar, Narendra, "A Genetic Survey among the Tentulia Bagdi and Duley of Hooghly District in West Bengal", *Bulletin of the Department of Anthropology,* Vol. 6, No. 1, (1957).

Kumar, P.K. Sanal, "Changing Political Equations: A View on UP Politics", *Social Action,* Vol. 45, No. 3, (1995).

Kumar, Pradeep, "Dalit Politics in India: Bahujan Samaj Party Breaking Ground in Uttar Pradesh", *Mainstream,* Vol. 37, No. 19, (1999).

Kumar, Pradeep, "Dalits and the BSP in Uttar Pradesh: Issues and Challenges", *Economic and Political Weekly,* Vol. 34, No. 14, (1999).

Kumar, Pradeep, "Reservations within Reservations: Real

Dalit-Bahujans", *Economic and Political Weekly,* Vol. 36, No. 37, (2001).

Kumar, Raj, "Relevance of Ambedkarism in India", *Mainstream,* Vol. 34, No. 24, (1996).

Kumar, Raj, "Dalit Culture: A Perspective from Below", *Social Action,* Vol. 50, No. 1, (2000).

Kumar, Ravinder, "Gandhi, Ambedkar and the Poona Pact", Research in-Progress Papers *History and Society,* , No XX, (New Delhi: Teen Murti House, 1985).

Kumar, S., "Dangers of Dalit Boys Marrying Brahmin Girls", *Dalit Voice,* Vol. 9, No. 6, (1990).

Kumar, Sudeep, "Caste Mobility and Political Process: A Case of the Jatavs of Abupur", *Man in India,* Vol. 82, Nos. 1–2, (2002).

Kumar, Sudhir, "Gandhi and the *Dalit*-Question", *New Quest,* No. 121, (January–February, 1997).

Kumar, Tila, "Cultural Politics in Hindu Society and Identity Crisis among Educated Dalits", *Mainstream,* Vol. 37, No. 17, (1999).

Kumar, Vivek, "Emergence of Leadership among Dalit Women", *The Pioneer,* (23 September 1999).

Kumar, Vivek, "The Dalit Identity", *The Pioneer,* (26 January 2000).

Kumar, Vivek, "Desperately Seeking Dalits", *The Pioneer,* (7 March 2000).

Kumar, Vivek, "BSP Honeymooning with the Media", *The Pioneer,* (11 July 2000).

Kumar, Vivek, "Any Answer to Dalit Question in UP", *The Pioneer,* (20 September 2000).

Kumar, Vivek, "No Dalit Equality in Sangh Parivar", *The Pioneer,* (6 November 2000).

Kumar, Vivek, "Political Unity of Dalits", *The Pioneer,* (15 February 2001).

Kumar, Vivek, "A Blow for Dalit Dignity and Pride", *The Pioneer,* (25 September 2001).

Kumar, Vivek, "Untouchability in Uttaranchal", *Economic and Political Weekly*, Vol. 36, No. 49, (2001).

Kumar, Vivek, "Ambedkar's Vision of Social Justice: Quest for Unification, Empowerment and Differentiation", *Jagriti*, (2002), [Journal of History, Culture, Art and Social Justice, Kashi Hindu University, Varanasi].

Kumar, Vivek, "President, Dalits and Bhopal Document", *The Pioneer*, (8 February 2002).

Kumar, Vivek, "Socio-Political Mobilization and Empowerment of Dalits in Uttar Pradesh", *Journal of Contemporary Social Work*, Vol. 19, (April 2002), [This is a journal from the Department of Social Work, Lucknow University].

Kumar, Vivek, "The Power of Strategy", *The Dalit*, (May-June 2002).

Kumar, Y., "Dalit Christians Can't Claim our Share of Reservations", *Dalit Voice*, Vol. 4, No. 18, (1985).

Kumaraswami, T.J., "The Adi-Dravidas of Madras", *Man in India*, Vol. 3, No. 12, (1923).

Kurian, C.T., "Economic Conditions of Scheduled Cates", *Yojana*, Vol. 26, No. 10, (1982).

Kurian, C.T., "An Overview of the Economic Condition of Scheduled Castes in India", *Banglore Theological Forum*, Vol. 14, (1982).

Kurian, S.G., "Struggle for Survival: Experience of Christian Dalits (in Vijayapuram Diocese) in Kerala", *Religion and Society*, Vol. 42, No. 2, (1995).

Lajpat Rai, Lala, 'The Depressed Classes', *Indian Review*, March, (1910).

Lakshmanna, C., "Abolition of Untouchability in Andhra Pradesh", Social Welfare, Vol. XV, No. 2, (1968).

Lakshmanan, C., "Political Parties Blind To Dalit Concerns", *The Times of India*, (22 April 1998).

Lal, A.K., "Educational Problems of the Scheduled Communities of Bihar", *Social Welfare*, Vol. 26, No. 11, (1980).

Lal, A.K., "Fundamentalist Religious Revival: Impact on the Dalits", *Social Action*, Vol. 43, No. 4, (1993).

Lal, A.K., "Limited Participation in an Open System: A Study of Scheduled Castes in Politics", *Mainstream*, Vol. 32, No. 19, (March 26, 1994).

Lal, A.K., "Protective Discrimination and the Scheduled Castes", *Journal of Rural Development*, Vol. 19, No. 4, (2000).

Lal, Hira, "Caste Impurity in the Central Provinces", *Man in India*, Vol. 3, (1923).

Lal, Hira, "Untouchables among Animals and Plants", *Man in India*, Vol. 7, (1927).

Lal, S., "Acquiring a Dalit identity", *Sociological Bulletin*, Vol. 44, (1995).

Lal, S.K., "Scheduled Caste College Students in Rajasthan", *Journal of Higher Education*, Vol. 1, No. 2, (1975).

Lal, S.K., "Occupational Aspirations of Scheduled Caste Students", *Social Change*, Vol. 6, Nos. 1 & 2, (1976).

Lal, Shyam, "Educational Development among the Bhangis in Jodhpur City", *Tribes*, Vol. 7, No. 1, (1970).

Lal, Shyam, "Jodhpur-Ke-Bhangis", *Harijan Seva*, Vol. 27, No. 1, (1972).

Lal, Shyam, "Review: A Scheme for Bhangis Welfare in Jodhpur", *Harijan Seva*, Vol. 21, No. 6, (1972).

Lal, Shyam, "Sanskritization and Social Change among the Bhangis of Jodhpur City: A Case Study", *Indian Journal of Social Work*, Vol. XXXIV, No. 1, (1973).

Lal, Shyam, "Caste and Occupational Mobility in Jodhpur Bangi Caste", *Journal of Social Research*, Vol. 18, No. 2, (1975).

Lal, Shyam, "Social Reform Movement among the Bhangis of West Rajasthan", *Eastern Anthropologist*, Vol. 32, No. 2, (1979).

Lal, Shyam, "Caste and Political Mobilisation: The Bhangis", *Panchsheel Prakashan*, (Jaipur), (1981).

Lal, Shyam, "Origin of the Bhangis: A Hypothesis", *Eastern Anthropologist*, (1991).

Lal, Shyam, "De-Sanskritization and High Caste Converts into Bhangis", *Indian Journal of Social Work*, Vol. 2, (1992).

Lal, Shyam, "Jain Movement and Socio-Religious Transformation of the Bhangis of Jodhpur, Rajasthan", *Indian Journal of Social Work*, Vol. 53, no. 1, (January, 1992).

Lambert, R.D., "Untouchability as a Social Problem: Theory and Research", *Sociological Bulletin*, Vol. 7, No. 1, (1958).

Lanjewar, K.D., "Mahar of Maharashtra: A Study of the Process of Identity Formation", *Journal of Anthropological Survey of India*, Vol. 50, No. 3, (2001).

Lapoint, E.C. and D.N. Lapoint, "Socio-Economic Mobility among Village Harijans", *Eastern Anthropologist*, Vol. 38, No. (1985).

Laxman Rao, S., "Dalit Christians and Reservation Policy", *Third Concept*, Vol. 10, No. 114, (1996).

Laxmanan, C., "Dalits: Towards An Independent Identity", *Economic News & Views*, (16–31 January 1995).

Lederle, M.R., "The Untouchable's Claim to Human Dignity", *Journal of the University of Poona*, Humanities Section, Vol. 19, (1964).

Lele, T.P., "A Comparative Study of the Students from Different Communities", *Education and Psychology Review*, Vol. 7, No. 3, (1967).

Lobo, Lancy, "Angaliat: A Dalit Novel", *New Quest*, No. 69, (1988).

Lobo, Lancy, "Conversion, Immigration and Social Mobility of an Ex-Scheduled Caste from Central Gujarat", *Social Action*, Vol. 39, No. 4, (1989).

Lobo, Lancy, "Visions and Illusions of Dalit Converts", *Social Action*, Vol. 43, No. 4, (1993).

Loehlin, Clinton H., "The Punjab 'Ad Dharmis'", *United Church Review*, (December 1937).

Louis, Prakash, "Caste and Hatred: Violence on the Dalits", *Social Action*, Vol. 50, No. 3, (2000).

Lynch, Owen M., "Political Mobilization and Ethnicity Among Adi-Dravidas in a Bombay Slum", *Economic and Political Weekly*, Vol. 9, No. 39, (1974).

Lynch, Owen M., "Dalit Buddhism: The Liberate Both Gaya Movement", *Dalit International Newsletter*, Vol. 3, No. 1, (1998).

Macfarlane, Erlanson W. Eileen, "Blood Groups among Balahis weavers, Bhils, Korkus and Mundas with a note on Pardhi and aboriginal blood types", *Journal of the Royal Asiatic Society of Bengal*, Vol. 7, (1941).

Macwan, Martin, "(UN) Touchable in Durban", *Seminar*, No. 508, (December 2001).

Madhaviah, A., "Mathangi (A Curious Religious Institution)", *Madras Christian College Magazine*, Vol. XXIII, (New Series Vol. V), (1905–1906).

Madras, Henry, "The Out-Castes of India", *The Nineteenth Century*, No. 66, (1909).

Mahajani, V.M., "The Depressed Classes", *The Indian Review*, (February, 1911).

Mahalanobis, P.C., "Agharia", and "Chero", *Sankhya*, Vol. 9, Parts 2&3, (1949).

Mahapatra, Bishnu N. and Dwaipayan Bhattacharjee, "Tribal Dalit Conflict: Electoral Politics in Phulbani", *Economic and Political Weekly*, Vol. 31, No. 2-3, (1996).

Mahapatra, L.K., "Food Quest among the Pauri Bhuiyan", *Eastern Anthropologist*, Vol. 9, No. 1, (1955), [The Byuiyas or Bhuyans are categorized as Scheduled Castes in Bihar, Uttar Pradesh and West Bengal, but in Orissa they are categorized as Scheduled Tribes].

Mahapatra, M., "Changing Status of a Scheduled Caste (Bauri)", *Adibasi*, No. 1, (1964-65).

Mahapatra, M., "Organisation of Castes among the Bauris of Bhuwaneshwar", *Adibasi*, Vol. I, No. 3, (1966).

Mahar, Pauline Moller, "Changing Caste Ideology in a North Indian Village", *Journal of Social Issues,* Vol. 14, No.4, (1958).

Mahar, Pauline Moller, "Changing Religious Practices of an Untouchable Caste", *Economic Development and Cultural Change,* Vol. 8, No. 3, (1960).

Maheswari, S.R., "Reservation Policy in India: Theory and Practice", *Indian Journal of Public Administration,* Vol. 43, No. 3, (1997).

Majeed, A. and E.S.K. Ghosh, "Affective Syndrome Crisis in Scheduled Castes", *Social Change,* Vol. 19, No 3, (1989).

Majumdar, B.C., "Notes on the Bhuiyas of Utkala and the Jharkhanada", *Man in India,* Vol. 12, No. 4, (1932), [The Byuiyas or Bhuyans are categorized as Scheduled Castes in Bihar, Uttar Pradesh and West Bengal, but in Orissa they are categorized as Scheduled Tribes].

Majumdar, Durgadas, "Caste and the Outcaste", *Bulletin of Cultural Research Institute,* Vol. 2, No. 1, (1963).

Majumdar, D.N., "The Pollas, Bhupolias, Palias or Rajbanshis: An Instance of the Conversion of Tribes into Castes in Bengal", *Man in India,* Vol. 6, (1926).

Majumdar, D.N., "The Marriage and Rishipat Customs of the Rishis", *Man in India,* Vol. 18, (1938).

Majumdar, D.N., "The Racial Status of Nuniya Nunera, Cala, Agaria, Shargar, Kharkar and similar castes of East Manipur & Farrukabad", *Eastern Anthropologist,* Vol. 3, Nos. 2-3, (1949-50).

Malhotra, P.L., "Social Disadvantage, Education and Development in India", *Social Change,* Vol. 16, No. 2-3, (1986).

Malik, Bela, "Untouchability and Dalit Women's Oppression", *Economic and Political Weekly,* Vol. 34, No. 6, (1999).

Malkani, N.R., "Hereditary Proletariat", *Interdiscipline,* (Winter 1970).

Malkani, N.R., "Untouchability is on Way Out", *INFA Feature,* (May 12, 1970).

Mallik, B.K., "Ambedkar: His Movement for Social Equality and Buddhism", *The Great Concern,* Vol. 2, (1992).

Mallik, Basanta Kumar, "Education and Identity: Some Issues on Social Development of Dalits", *Mainstream,* Vol. 36, No. 18, (1998).

Mallik, Sima, "The Great Outsider: A Review of 'Dr. Ambedkar: Life and Mission' by Dhananjay Keer", *Quest,* Vol. 39, (1963).

Mander, Harsh, "Dalit Status and Agenda for State Intervention", *The Administrator,* Vol. 42, No. 1, (1997).

Mani, V.R., "Political Steps needed to Liberate Dalits", *The Times of India,* (14 November, 1991).

Manickvasagam, V and A.R. Alagappan, "Reservation Policy in PSUs: How Effective?", *Economic and Political Weekly,* Vol. 33, No. 15, (1998).

Manikumar, K.A., "Caste Clashes in South Tamil Nadu", *Economic and Political Weekly,* Vol. 32, No. 36, (1997).

Mankidy, A., "Scheduled Caste Entrants into Banking Industry", *Economic and Political Weekly,* Vol. 11, No. 9, (1976).

Mankidy, Aruna, "Inter-generational Occupational Mobility among the Scheduled Castes", *Social Change,* Vol. 9, Nos. 1–2, (1979).

Mann, Harold H., "The 'Mahars' of a Deccan Village (Saswad)", *Social Service Quarterly* (Bombay), Vol. II, No. 1, (1916), Reprinted in Harold H. Mann, *The Social Framework of Agriculture,* edited by Daniel Thorner, (Bombay: Vora).

Manor, J.G., 'Testing the Barrier Between Caste and Outcaste: The Andhra Evangelical Lutheran Church in Guntur District, 1920-1940', *Indian Church History Review,* Vol. V, No. 1, (1971)

Margolkar, V.S., "Removal of Untouchability – Goals Attainments", *Indian Journal of Social Work,* Vol. 30, No. 3, (1969).

Masilamani, S., "Educational Achievement of a Scheduled Caste: Sex Bias and a Case Study of Chakkiliyars of Chinnathadagam Village", *Social Action,* Vol. 36, No. 2, (1986).

Massey, James, "Christian Dalits in India: An Analysis", *Religion and Society,* Vol. 37, No. 3, (1990).

Massey, James, "Scheduled Castes: A Special Reference to Christians of Scheduled Caste Origin", *Religion and Society,* Vol. 28, No. 1, (1991).

Massey, James, "The Role of the Churches in the whole Dalit Issue", *National Christian Council Review,* Vol. CXVI, No. 5, (1996).

Massey, James, "Dalits–Tribals at the Crossroads: Faced with a new form of violence", *Dalit International Newsletter,* Vol. 5, No. 3, (October, 2000).

Mateer, Samuel, "The Pariah Caste in Travancore", *Journal of the Royal Asiatic Society of Great Britain and Ireland,* Vol. 16, (1884).

Mathew, George, "Politicisation of Religion: Conversions to Islam in Tamil Nadu", *Economic and Political Weekly,* Vol. 17, No. 25, (1982).

Mathew, George and Ramesh C. Nayak, "Panchayats at Work: What it means for the Oppressed?", *Economic and Political Weekly,* Vol. 31, No. 27, (1996).

Mathew, P.D. and Simon Stephen, "Untouchability and Law", *Social Action,* Vol. 36, No. 2, (1986).

Mathew, P.M., "Caste Reservation: A Critique", *Social Change,* Vol. 18, No. 2, (1988).

Mathew, Thomas, "Ambedkar and Marxism", *Economic and Political Weekly,* Vol. 27, Nos. 24-25, (1992), [Comment on Gopal Guru of 12 October 1992].

Mathias, Edward, "Dalit Christians and Reservation Policy", *Social Action,* Vol. 48, No. 2, (1998).

Mathias, T.A., "Social Change and Higher Education" (Editorial), *New Frontiers in Education,* Vol. 4, No. 1, (1974).

Mathias, T.A., "Perspective on Education and Social Justice: An Indian View", *New Frontiers in Education,* Vol. 4, No. 1, (1974).

Mathur, K.S., "The Festivals of the Cheroes", *Eastern Anthropologist,* Vol. 6, No. 2, (1952-53).

Mayo, Katherine, "Mahatma Gandhi and India's Untouchables", *Current History,* Vol. 32, (1930).

Mazumdar, Ambika Charan, "The Depressed Classes", *The Indian Review,* (January, 1910).

McCormack, William, "Caste and the British Administration of Hindu Law", *Journal of Asian and African Studies,* Vol. 1, (1966).

McGivray, Dennis B., "Paraiyar Drummers of Sri Lanka: Consensus and Constraint in an Untouchable Caste", *American Ethnologist,* Vol. 10, No. 1, (1983).

Meade, M.J., "On the Moghias or Baoris of Rajputana and Central India", *Journal of the Anthropological Society of Bombay,* Vol. 1, (1886) and Vol. 7, (1905).

Meenakshi, J.V., Ranjana Ray and Souvic Gupta, "Estimates of Poverty for Scheduled Caste, Scheduled Tribe and Female-Headed Households", *Economic and Political Review,* Vol. 35, No. 31, (2000).

Mehra, D.S. and I.J. Kundra, "A Study of the Scheduled Castes and Scheduled Tribes' Working Force in India", *AICC Economic Review,* Vol. 18, Nos. 391 & 392, (1966).

Mehrunnisa, "Dalits in the Muslim Community", *Dalit International Newsletter,* Vol. 8, No. 1, (2003), [An interview with Mehrunnisa].

Mehta, P.L. and Surender Singh Jaiswal, "Execution of Constitutional Safeguards for Scheduled Castes in Himachal Pradesh: A Synoptic View", *IASSI Quarterly,* Vol. 15, No. 2, (1996).

Mencher, Joan P., "Group and Self-Identification – The View from the Bottom", ICSSR's *Research Abstracts Quarterly*, Vol. 3, Nos. 2 & 3, (1974).

Mencher, Joan P., "The Caste System Upside Down, or the Not-so-Mysterious East", *Current Anthropology*, Vol. 15, No. 4, (1974).

Mendelsohn, Oliver, " 'Harijan Elite'? The Lives of Some Untouchable Politicians", *Economic and Political Weekly*, Vol. 21, No. 12, (1986).

Menon, P.S.K., "Post-Matric Scholarships for Scheduled Caste and Scheduled Tribe Students", *Journal of Higher Education*, Vol. 1, No. 2, (1975).

Michael, S.M., "The Emergence of Dalit Consciousness", *Indian Missiological Review*, Vol. 17, No. 1, (1995).

Michael, S.M., "Culture and Politics in Modern India (The Rise of Hindutva and Dalit Forces)", *Journal of the Asiatic Society*, Vol. 38, No. 1, (1996).

Michael, S.M., "The Cultural Context of the Rise of Hindutva and Dalit Forces", *Vidyajyoti*, Vol. 60, No. 5, (1996).

Michael, S.M., "Dalit Solidarity for Social Justice in India", *Indian Missiological Review*, Vol. 18, No. 3, (1996).

Miller, Robert J., "Button, Button...Great Tradition, Little Tradition, Whose Tradition?", *Anthropological Quarterly*, Vol. 39, No. 1, (1961).

Miller, Robert J., "They Will Not Die Hindus: The Buddhist Conversion of Mahar Ex-Untouchables", *Asian Survey*, Vol. 7, No. 9, (1967).

Mimrooth, P.L., "Defiance of a Taboo: Dalit Marriage Procession on Horseback", *Social Action*, Vol. 50, No. 1, (2000).

Mishra, Amaresh, "Dalit Assertion: Possibilities and Limits", *Economic and Political Weekly*, Vol. 28, No. 50, (1993).

Mishra, Amaresh, "Uttar Pradesh: Backwards and Dalits take a Back Seat", *Economic and Political Weekly*, Vol. 31, No. 39, (1996).

Mishra, N., "Economic Problems of Scheduled Castes of Bihar", *Journal of Social Research,* Vol. XVIII, No. 2, (1975).

Mishra, N., "Some Aspects of Dusadh of Darbhanga", *Journal of Social Research,* Vol. XVIII, No. 2, (1975).

Mishra, N., "Studies on the Scheduled Castes in Bihar", *Journal of Social Research,* Vol. 21, No. 2, (1978).

Mishra, R.K., "State Level Scheduled Caste Corporations in India: Promise and Performance", *Economic and Political Weekly,* Vol. 31, No. 33, (1996).

Mishra, S.N., 'Development of Scheduled Castes After Independence', *Adivasi,* Vol. 27, No. 4, (1987).

Misra, Ajay M., M.B. Gupta and Neelum Misra, "A Study of Attitude towards Learning of Science among Scheduled Caste Students", *Journal of Education and Psychology,* Vol. 41, No. 3, (1983).

Misra, B. and B.P. Mohapatra, "Socio-Economic Problems and the Level of Aspiration of Scheduled Caste People", *Adibasi,* Vol. 30, No. 4, (1990).

Misra, K.K., "Level of Literacy among Dalit Population: A Case Study of Atarra Tehsil, UP", *Geographical Review of India,* Vol. 59, No. 2, (1997).

Misra, N., "Scheduled Castes in Bihar", *Journal of Social Research,* Vol. 21, No. 2, (1978).

Misra, P.K., "Persistence of Untouchability: Analysis of Two Case Studies in a Multi-Ethnic Area of Orissa", *Manav,* Vol. 1, No. 1, (1982-1983).

Misra, P.K., "Untouchability in South India", *Eastern Anthropologist,* Vol. 52, No. 1, (1999).

Mitra Channa, Subhadra, "Dalit World View and Self Identification", *Eastern Anthropologist,* Vol. 53, No. 3–4, (2001).

Mitra Channa, Subhadra, "Right to Selfhood: The Paradox of Being a Dalit Woman", *Social Action,* Vol. 51, No. 4, (2001).

Mitra, Babu Sarada Charan, "The Depressed Classes", *The Indian Review*, (October, 1910).

Mitra, S.C., "On Ceremonies Performed by Kabirpanthi Mahants of the Saran District on their initiation as Chelas and on their Succession to the Mahantship", *Journal of the Anthropological Society of Bombay*, Vol. 3, No. 5, (1916).

Mitra, S.C., "Notes on the Goddessling Maharani Worshipped by the Bhuiyas of the Hazaribagh District in Chota Nagpur", *Journal of the Anthropological Society of Bombay*, Vol. 14, (1928), [The Byuiyas or Bhuyans are categorized as Scheduled Castes in Bihar, Uttar Pradesh and West Bengal, but in Orissa they are categorized as Scheduled Tribes].

Mitra, Sarat Chandra, "Notes on the Godling Mahakala Worshipped by the Rajbansis of the Jalpaiguri District in Northern Bengal", and "A Note on the Rain God of the Rajbansis of the Jalpaiguri District in Northern Bengal", *Journal of the Anthropological Society of Bengal*, Vol. 15, (1933).

Mitra, Vajra and Mani Sparsa, "Bhadu Ballads", *Indian Folklore*, Vol. 2, No. 2, (1957).

Mittal, J.K., "Special Representation in Legislative Bodies in India", *Indian Advocate*, Vol. 4, (1964).

Mittal, J.K., "Concept of Equality in Constituent Assembly", *Supreme Court Journal*, Vol. XXXII, No. 5, (1965).

Mittal, J.K., "Educational Equality and the Supreme Court of India", *Indian Advocate*, Vol. 5, Nos. 1-2, (1965).

Mittal, J.K., "Equal Opportunity in Matters of Public Employment and the Indian Supreme Court", *Malaya Law Review*, Vol. 7, (1965).

Mittal, J.K., "Right to Equality and the Indian Supreme Court", *American Journal of Comparative Law*, Vol. 14, (1965).

Modi, Jivanji Jamshedji, "On Dhangurs and Dhavars of Mahabaleshwar", *Journal of the Anthropological Society of Bombay*, Vol. 3, (1894), [These Dhangads or Dhangars are categorized as Scheduled Castes in Bihar, U.P. and West Bengal, where as in Madhya Pradesh and Maharashtra they are categorized as Scheduled Tribes].

Moffat, Micheal, "Untouchables and Caste System: A Tamil Case Study", *Contributions to Indian Sociology*, Vol. 9, No. 1, (1975).

Moffat, Michael, "Harijan Religion: Consensus at the Bottom of Caste", *American Ethnologist*, Vol. 6, No. 2, (1979).

Mohammad, Toha and A.L. Srivastava, "Changing Values among Untouchables through Education", *Indian Educational Review*, Vol. 6, No. 2, (1971).

Mohan, Brij, "Plight of Harijans", *Social Welfare*, (May, 1973).

Mohanty, B.B., "Land Distribution among Scheduled Castes and Tribes", *Economic and Political Weekly*, Vol. 36, No. 40, (2001).

Mohanty, P.K., "Development of Scheduled Castes and Scheduled Tribes in Independent India: Leads and Lags", *Journal of Rural Development*, Vol. 19, No. 4, (2000).

Mohanty, R.K., "Scheduled Castes as Minorities", *Mainstream*, Vol. 23, No. 18, (1984).

Mohanty, R.K., "Dynamics of Atrocities on Scheduled Castes in Rural India", *Indian Journal of Social Work*, Vol. 49, (January 1988).

Mohapatra, Bishnu N., "Understanding Indignities", *Seminar*, No. 471, (November 1998).

Mohapatra, Kulamoni and A.D. Mohanty, "Study of the Problem of Untouchability", *Adibasi*, Vol. 15, (1973-1974).

Mohapatra, Manindra Kumar, "The Scheduled Caste and the Tribal Political Elites: An Empirical Exploration of the Attributes, Ascent and Role Perceptions of 'Token

Elites' in an Indian State", *International Behavioural Scientist*, Vol. 5, No. 4, (1973).

Mohapatra, P.C., "Atrocities and Legal Provisions: A Case Study of Orissa State", *Journal of Rural Development*, Vol. 16, No. 1, (1997).

Moon, Meenakshi and Urmila Pawar, "We Made History Too: Women in the Early Untouchable Liberation Movement", *South Asia Bulletin*, Vol. 9, No. 2, (1989).

Moorthi, O.K., "Development of Scheduled Castes – An Appraisal", *Journal of Social Research*, Vol. 18, No. 2, (1975).

Morkhandikar, R.S., "Marathwada Riots: The Background", *Economic and Political Weekly*, Vol. 13, (1978).

Morkhandikar, R.S., "Marathwada Riots, 1978: Dilemmas of a Dalit Movement", *Punjab Journal of Politics*, Vol. 9, No. 1, (1985).

Morkhandikar, R.S., "Dilemmas of Dalit Movement in Maharashtra: Unity Moves and After", *Economic and Political Weekly*, Vol. 25, No. 12, (1990).

Moses, B.C., "Struggle for Panchama Lands: Dalit Assertion in Tamil Nadu", *Economic and Political Weekly*, (4 February 1995).

Mosse, D., "Idioms of Subordination and Styles of Protest among Christian and Hindu Harijan Castes in Tamil Nadu", *Contributions to Indian Sociology* (NS), Vol. 28, No. 1, (1994).

Moses, David and Robert Deliege, "Replication and Consensus among Indian Untouchable (Harijan) Castes", *Man*, Vol. 29, No. 2, (June, 1994).

Mourya, R.D., "Impact of Special Component Plan on Socio-Economic Development of Scheduled Castes in Madhya Pradesh", *Journal of Rural Development*, Vol. 20, No. 1, (2001).

"The Movement of Christian Dalit People in the CSI Madhya Kerala Diocese", *Samata*, No. 3, (1986).

Mukherjee, A.B., "Regional Contracts in Distribution Density and Relative Strength of Scheduled Caste Population in Andhra Pradesh", *Folklore*, (April & May, 1971).

Mukherjee, B.M., "A Short note on Marriage Customs of Pasi", *Journal of Social Research*, Vol. XVIII, No. 2, (1975).

Mukherjee, B.M., "The Position and Future of the Untouchables of Bihar", *Research Journal of Ranchi University*, Vols. XII & XIII, (1977).

Mukherjee, Bhabananda, "Rajbanshi Kinship System", *Bulletin of the Anthropological Survey of India*, Vol. 11, No. 1, (1962).

Mukherjee, Bhabananda, "Socio-Economic and Religious Organisation of the Rajbanshi", *Bulletin of the Anthropological Survey of India*, Vol. 12, Nos. 1 & 2, (1963).

Mukherjee, D.P., "The Mahar Handprints – A Preliminary Report", *Current Science*, Vol. 31, (1962).

Mukherjee, Prabhati, "Who Were the Indigenous People in India", *Religion and Society*, Vol. 38, Nos. 3–4, (1991).

Mukhopadhyay, Tarasish, "A Note on the Paliyas of West Dinajpur", *Man in India*, Vol. 45, No. 3, (1965).

Mukul, "Untouchable Present: Everyday Life of Musahars in North Bihar", *Economic and Political Weekly*, Vol. 34, No. 49, (1999).

Mukul, Akshaya, "I, Mr, Myself: The Dalit Writes His Story", *Hindustan Times*, (4 April 1999).

"Muktananda Saraswati on Dalits", *Mainstream*, (16 October 1993), [Muktananda Saraswati, headed the VHP appointed four-member committee to rework on rewriting the Indian Constitution, because it is "anti-Hindu"].

Mukund, Kanakalatha, "Caste Conflict in South India in Early Colonial Port Cities: 1650 – 1800", *Studies in History*, Vol. 11, No. 1, n.s. (1995).

Mungekar, B.L., "The Socio-Economic Conditions of the Dalits", *Indian Missiological Review*, Vol. 17, No. 1, (1995).

Mungekar, B.L., "Globalisation and the Dalits", *The Radical Humanist*, Vol. 65, No. 1, (2001).

Nadakarni, D.G., "No Government for Harijans in Maharashtra", *Commerce*, (June 24, 1972).

Nadakarni, M.V., "Broadbasing Process in India and Dalits", *Economic and Political Weekly*, Vol. 32, Nos. 32–34, (1997).

Nag, B.C., "Untouchability and the Sastras: Views of Gandhiji and Vivekananda", *Mail*, (April 23, 1969).

Nag, Daya Shankar, "The Agaria (Iron smelters and Blacksmiths of M.P.)", *Vanyajati*, Vol. 5, (1957).

Nagaraj, D.R., "From Political Rage to Cultural Affirmation: Notes on the Kannada Dalit Poet-Activist Siddhalingaiah", *India International Centre Querterly*, Vol. 21, No. 4, (1994).

Nagarajan, N., "Literacy Status of Scheduled Castes in Tamil Nadu: Some Issues", *Educational Review*, Vol. 100, No. 8, (1994).

Nagaraju, C.S. and B. Shashi Dhar, "The Educational System and the Educational Development of the Scheduled Castes", *Banglore Theological Forum*, No. 14, (1982).

Nagda, B.L., "Socio-Demographic Status of Scheduled Castes in Rajasthan", *Kurukshetra*, Vol. 42, No. 7, (April, 1994).

Nagel, T., "Equal Treatment and Compensatory Discrimination", *Philosophy and Public* Affairs, Vol. 2, (1973).

Nagolkar, V.S., "Removal of Untouchability – Goals and Attainments", *Indian Journal of Social Work*, Vol. 30, (1969).

Naidu, J.M. and S. Mathew, "Sickle Cell Trait in Rellis of Visakhapatnam, A.P.", *Man in India*, Vol. 58, No. 1, (1978).

Naidu, U.S., "Self-image of Scheduled Castes", *Indian Journal of Social Work*, Vol. XLII, No. 2, (1981).

Naidu, Usha S., "Socialization of Scheduled Caste Children at School", *Social Change,* Vol. 9, No. 4, (1979).

Nair, N. Gopinathan, "Spotlight on Scheduled Castes", *Link,* (26 January 1971).

Nakane, Chie, "An Ethnological Survey of the Aboriginals in the State of Tripura", *The Japanese Journal of Ethnology,* Vol. 19, No. 1, (1954).

Nambiar, K.T. Bala Krishnan, "The Depressed Classes of North Malabar", *The Dawn and Dawn Society's Magazine,* Vol. VII, No.8, (1911).

Nambissan, G.B., "Equity in Education: Schooling Dalit Children in India", *Economic and Political Weekly,* Vol. 31, Nos. 16 & 17, (1996).

Nambissan, Geeta B., "Dealing with Deprivation", *Seminar,* No. 493, (2000).

Namboodiripad, E., "Economic Backwardness of Harijans in Kerala", *Social Scientist,* Vo. 4, (1976).

Nanavathy, M.C., "Seminar on Casteism and Removal of Untouchability: A Review", *Indian Journal of Adult Education,* Vol. 16, No. 4, (1955).

Nancharaiah, G., "Political Elite Among the Scheduled Castes", *Journal of Constitutional and Parliamentary Studies,* Vol. VIII, No. 2, (April-June, 1974).

Nancharaiah, G., "The Changing Position of Scheduled Castes as Agricultural Labourers in the Labour Market", *Social Action,* No. 4, (1990).

Nancharaiah, G., "Dr. B.R. Ambedkar's Economic and Political Thought", *Journal of Social Development and Justice,* Vol. 1, (1991).

Nancharaiah, G., "The Relevance of Dr. Ambedkar views on Tax and Exchange Rate Policies", *Indian Economic Journal,* (1994), [Conference Volume].

Nanchariah, G., "New Economic Policy and Its Effects on Dalits in India", *The Fourth World,* No. 7, (April 1998).

Nanda, Meera, "Hitching Dalit Modernity to Anti-Modernist Wagon", *Economic and Political Weekly*, Vol. 36, No. 17, (2001).

Nandi, Swapan Kumar, "Impact of Christianity on the Chamars of Majhwari: A Bhojpur Village", *Journal of Social Research*, Vol. 19, No. 1, (1976).

Narayan, Badri, "Heroes, Histories and Booklets", *Economic and Political Weekly*, Vol. 36, No. 41, (2001).

Narayan, G., "The Political Elite among the Scheduled Castes", *Journal of Constitutional and Political Studies*, Vol. 8, No. 2, (1974).

Narayana, G., "Emerging Elite in Scheduled Castes", *Secular Democracy*, Vol. 7, No. 9, (1974).

Narayana, G., "Social Background of SC Lok Sabha Members 1962-71", *Economic and Political Weekly*, Vol. 13, No. 37, (1978).

Narayana, G., "Rule Making for Scheduled Castes: Analysis of Lok Sabha Debates 1962-71", *Economic and Political* Weekly, Vol. 15, No. 8, (1980).

Narayana, G., "Social Background of Scheduled Caste MPs in the Fifth Lok Sabha – A Comparative Study", *PUDR Digest*, Vol. 5, No. 2, (1972).

Narayanan, K.R., "Remembering Ambedkar", *Mainstream*, (26 January 1984).

Narayanan, R., "False Concern for Harijans", *Mainstream*, (11 February 1978).

Nariellawalla, G.E., "The Writings of Dr. B.R. Ambedkar", *Siddarth College of Commerce and Economics Annual*, Vol. 20, (1964-65).

Narula, Smita, "Caste Discrimination", *Seminar*, No. 508, (December 2001).

Nauriya, A., "Dalit-Intermediate Caste alliance. Call to Greatness", *Economic and Political* Weekly, Vol. 29, No. 29, (1994).

Nayak, V. and S. Prasad, "On levels of living of Scheduled Castes and Scheduled Tribes", *Economic and Political Weekly*, Vol. 19, No. 30, (1984).

Negi, R.S. and S. Ahmed, "The Bhatra, Muria and Mehra of Bastar: A Blood group Genetic Study", *Bulletin of the Anthropological Survey of India*, Vol. 11, Nos. 3 & 4, (1963).

Negi, R.S., "The Incidence of Sickle-Cell: Trait in Bastar, II – Muria, Mahra, Bhatra", *Man*, Vol. 63, (June 1963).

Nelson, Strart, "Panel Lists Indignities Suffered by Harijans", *The Hindustan Times*, (November 3, 1969).

Nelson, Stuart, "Caste and Untouchability and Gandhi", *Gandhi Marg*, Vol. 3, No. 50, (April, 1969).

Newell, William H., "The Comparative Study of Caste in India and Japan", *Asian Survey*, Vol. 1, 1961).

Nicholson, Sydney, "Social Organization of the Malas – an Outcaste Indian People", *Journal of the Royal Anthropological Institute of Great Britain and Ireland*, Vol. 56, (1926).

Niehaff, Arthur, "Mazbi: A Study of Matrimonial Advertisement in North India", *Eastern Anthropologist*, Vol. 12, No. 2, (1959).

Nigam, Aditya, "Secularism, Modernity, Nation: Epistemology of the Dalit Critique", *Economic and Political Weekly*, Vol. 35, No. 48, (2000).

Nigam, Aditya, "In Search of a Bourgeoisie: Dalit Politics Enters a New Phase", *Economic and Political Weekly*, Vol. 37, No. 13, (2002).

Nigam, S.S., "Equality and the Representation of the Scheduled Classes in Parliament", *Journal of the Indian Law Institute*, Vol. 2, (1960).

Nihila, Millie, "Marginalisation of Women Workers: Leather Tanning Industry in Tamil Nadu", *Economic and Political Weekly*, Vol. 34, No. 16-17, (1999).

Nirmal, A.P., "Doing Theology from a Dalit Perspective", *Sathri Journal*, No. 1, (1991).

Niyogi, M.B., "Problem of Nava Buddha in Maharashtra", *Social Service Quarterly*, Vol. 48, (1963).

Novetzke, Christian, "Twice Dalit: The Poetry of Hira Bansode", *Journal of South Asian Literature*, Vol. 28, Nos. 1 & 2, (1998).

Omvedt, Gail, "Jotirao Phule and the Ideology of Social Revolution in India", *Economic and Political Weekly*, Vol. 6, No. 37, (1971).

Omvedt, Gail, "Class Struggle or Caste War", *Frontier*, (30 September 1978).

Omvedt, Gail and Bharat Patankar, "The Dalit-Liberation Movement in Colonial Period", *Economic and Political Weekly*, Vol. 14, Nos. 7 &8, (Annual Number), (1979).

Omvedt, Gail, "Who Should Dalits Ally With?", *Economic and Political Weekly*, Vol. 15, No. 32, (1980).

Omvedt, Gail and Eleanor Zelliot, "Introduction to Dalit Poems", *Bulletin of Concerned Asian Scholars*, Vol. 10, No. 3, 1987).

Omvedt, Gail, "Dalit Literature in Maharashtra: Literature of Social Protest and Revolt in Western India", *South Asia Bulletin*, Vol. 7, Nos. 1–2, (1987).

Omvedt, Gail, "Ambedkar and Dalit Labor Radicalism: Maharashtra, 1936-1942", *South Asian Bulletin*, Vol. 10, No. 1, (1990).

Omvedt, Gail, "Anti-Caste Movement and the Discourse of Power", *Race and Class*, Vol. 33, No. 2, (October-December, 1991).

Omvedt, Gail, "Ambedkarism: The Theory of Dalit Liberation", (in Two parts), *Frontier*, Vol. 25, No. 12, (October 31, 1992).

Omvedt, Gail, "Peasants, Dalits and Women: Democracy and India's New Social Movements", *Journal of Contemporary Asia*, Vol. 24, No. 1, (1994).

Omvedt, Gail, "Ambedkar and Economics", *Fourth World*, Vol. 3, No. 1, (1996).

Omvedt, Gail, "Dalit Politics", *The Hindu*, (1 April 1999).

Omvedt, Gail, "Dalit Suicides?", *The Hindu*, (24 April 1999).

Omvedt, Gail, "Why Dalits dislike Environmentalists", *The Hindu*, (24 June 1999).

Omvedt, Gail, "Water as a Human Right", *The Hindu*, (6 July1999).

Omvedt, Gail, "Reservations", *Dalit International Newsletter*, Vol. 5, No. 3, (October, 2000).

Oommen, Philip P., "The Harijan Movement in India in relation to Christianity", *International Review of Missions*, 24, (1935).

Oommen, T.K., "Strategy for Social Change: A Reply", *Economic and Political Weekly*, Vol. 4, No. 4, (1969).

Oommen, T.K., "Strategy for Social Change: A Study of Untouchability", *Economic Political Weekly*, Vol. 3, No. 25, (1969).

Oommen, T.K., "Sources of Deprivation and Styles of Protest: The Case of the Dalits in India", *Contributions to Indian Sociology* (NS), Vol. 18, No. 1, (1984).

Oommen, T.K., 'Panchama to Dalits: The Context and Content of Identity', *The Times of India*, (11 May 1994).

Oza, M.A., "Survey of the Economic Conditions and State of Health and Nutrition of Harijan Families of Baroda", (abstract), *Journal of the Gujarat Research Society*, Vol. 20, (1958).

Pachaury, A.C., "Cardinal Invariance: Cognitive Ability of Second Grade Scheduled Tribe/Scheduled Caste Children of multi Grade School", *Indian Educational Review*, Vol. 36, No. 1, (2000).

Padgoankar, Dilip, "Dalit Literature", *Times of India*, (25 November 1973).

Padgoankar, Dilip, "Plight of Harijans", *Times of India*, (12 August 1978).

Pai, A. Vasudeva, "The Depressed Classes: Their education by the higher classes of Hindus with a few suggestions for their elevation", *The Indian Review*, (October, 1911).

Pai, Sudha and Jagpal Singh, "Politicisation of Dalits and Most Backward Castes: Social Conflict and Political Preferences in Four Villages of Meerut District", *Economic and Political Weekly*, Vol. 32, No. 23, (1997).

Pai, Sudha, "Dalit Assertion in UP: Implications for Politics", *Economic and Political Weekly*, Vol. 32, No. 37, (1997).

Pai, Sudha, "The BSP in Uttar Pradesh", *Seminar*, No. 471, (November 1998).

Pai, Sudha, "BSP's New Electoral Strategy Pays off", *Economic and Political Weekly*, Vol. 34, No. 44, (1999).

Pai, Sudha, "New Social and Political Movements of Dalits: A Study of Meerut District", *Contributions to Indian Sociology*, Vol. 34, No. 2, (2000).

Pai, Sudha, "Changing Socio-Economic and Political Profile of Scheduled Castes in Uttar Pradesh", *Journal of Indian School of Political Economy*, Vol. 12, Nos. 3–4, (2000).

Pai, Sudha, "Social Capital, Panchayats and Grass Roots Democracy: Politics of Dalit Assertion in Uttar Pradesh", *Economic and Political Weekly*, Vol. 36, No. 8, (2001).

Painter, A.F., "The Untouchables of India and Christ", *East and West*, Vol. 9, (April 1912).

Pakhiddey, B., "Dalit Panther – A Story of Fight for Emancipation", *Buniyadi Sangharsh*, (March 1985).

Pal, N.K., "An Assessment of Progress of Post-Matric Education among the Scheduled Castes and Scheduled Tribes of West Bengal", *Bulletin of the Cultural Research Institute*, Vol. 12, No. 1-2, (1976).

Pal, R.M., "Police Firing in a Mumbai Suburb: A Larger Issue of Human Rights of Dalits and Not a mere a Law and Order Problem", *Radical Humanist*, Vol. 61, No. 6, (1997).

Pal, R.M., "Durban: A Victims' Conference", *Mainstream*, Vol. 39, No. 40, (2001).

Pal, R.M., "Human Rights of Dalits on the Agenda of UN", *The Radical Humanist*, (April, 2001).

Palshikar, S., "Gandhi–Ambedkar interface ... When shall the Twain Meet?", *Economic and Political Weekly*, Vol. 31, (1996).

Palshikar, Sanjay and Arun Kumar Patnaik, "Violence in a University: Defending the Indefensible", *Economic and Political Weekly*, Vol. 37, No. 16, (2002).

Palshikar, Vasant, "Gandhi and Ambedkar", *New Quest*, Vol. 53, (September – October 1985).

Panchbhai, S.C., "The Levels of Regional and National Identification and Inter group Relations Among Harijans and Adivasis", *Journal of Indian Anthropological Society Journal*, Vo. 2, (March 1967).

Pande, N., "Irregular Attendance at School: Climate Support for Scheduled Caste Students", *Social Change*, Vol. 10, Nos. 1 & 2, (1980).

Pande, S.V., "The Politicisation: The Special Constitutional Provision and Perpetuation of Casteism", *Indian Political Science Review*, Vol. 14, No. 1, (1980).

Pandey, Balaji, "Educational Development Among Scheduled Castes", *Social Scientist*, Vol. 14, Nos. 2-3, (1986).

Pandey, Nisha and V.K. Tandon, "A Comparative Study of Palmar Dermatoglyphics on Pasi and Chamar", *Florida Anthropologist*, Vol. 29, (1976).

Pandian, M.S.S., "State, Christianity and Scheduled Castes", *Economic and Political Weekly*, Vol. 20, No. 42, (1985).

Pandian, M.S.S., "On A Dalit Woman's Testimonio", *Seminar*, No. 471, (November 1998).

Pandian, M.S.S., "Dalit Assertion in Tamil Nadu: An Exploratory Note", *Journal of Indian School of Political Economy*, Vol. 12, Nos. 3–4, (2000).

Pandit, Nalini, "Ambedkar and the Dalits", *Seminar*, No. 461, (Annual Issue), (1998).

Pandya, B.V., "Occupations Pattern of Scheduled Castes in

Ahmedabad District", *Journal of the Gujarat Research Society*, Vol. 19, (1957).

Pandya, B.V., "Trends and Patterns of Indebtedness among Harijans", *Journal of the Gujarat Research Society*, Vol. 21, (1959).

Paranjape, K., "Educational Reservations: Results of a Survey", *Mainstream*, Vol. 28, No. 23, (1990).

Parikh, N.P., A.J. Baxi, H.I. Jhola and K.V. Kulkarni, "Blood Group and other Genetical Characters in Mahars: A Socially Low Caste from Maharashtra", *Indian Journal of Medical Research*, Vol. 57, No. 8, (1969).

Parmar, Y.A., "Occupational Change Among Mahyavanshisa–Scheduled Caste", *Indian Journal of Social Work*, Vol. 39, (October 1978).

Parmer, F., "Untouchability", *Jeevandhara*, No. 63, (1981).

Parui, Sasanka Sekhar, "Untouchability in the Early Indian Society", *Journal of Indian History*, Vol. 39, (April, 1961).

Parvathamma, C., "The Case for Untouchables", *United Asia*, Vol. 20, No. 5, (1968).

Parvathamma, C. and R.T. Jangam, "India's Scheduled Caste M.Ps: A Socio-Economic Profile", *Journal of the Karnatak University*, Vol. 5, (April 1969).

Parvathamma, C. and R.T. Jangam, "India's Scheduled Castes M.Ps.: A Socio-Economic Profile", *The Journal of Karnataka University (Social Sciences)*, Vol. 5, (1969).

Parvathamma, C., "Ambedkar and After: The position and future of Indian Scheduled Caste Masses", *Eastern Anthropologist*, Vol. 26, No. 3, (1973).

Passin, Herbert, "Untouchability in the Far East", *Monumenta Nipponica*, Vol. 11, (1955).

Patankar, Bharat, and Gail Omvedt, "The Dalit Liberation Movement in Colonial Period", *Economic and Political Weekly*, Vol. 14, (1979), [Special Issue and Caste and Class].

Pathak, A.B., "A Study of Aspirations and Achievement

Motivation of Scheduled Caste Student Teachers", *Journal of Education and Psychology*, Vol. 42, No. 4, (1985).

Pathy, Jaganath, "Political of Reservation in India: Case study of Political Agitation in Bihar and Gujarat", *Philosophy and Social Action*, Vo. 8, No. 2, (1982).

Pathy, Suguna, "The Untouchables–Protectors Fail", *State and Society*, Vol. 5, No. 3, (1985).

Patil, Gajanan M., "Harijans in Mehesana District", (abstract), *Journal of Gujarat Research Society*, Vol. 21, (1958).

Patil, Leela, "Changing Status of Low Castes", *Economic Times*, (May 26, 1972).

Patil, Ravindra, "Search for Identity among Dalit Middle Class in Maharashtra", *Social Action*, Vol. 50, No. 1, (2000).

Patil, Sharad, "In Defense of Marxism and Ambedkarism", *Frontier*, Vol. 23, No. 46, (1991).

Patil, Sharad, "Mobilizing Scheduled Castes and Scheduled Tribes", *Economic and Political Weekly*, Vol. 24, Nos. 35-36, (1989).

Patnaik, Arun Kumar, "Dalit common sense against Hindutva", *Economic and Political Weekly*, Vol. 31, No. 40, (1996).

Patnaik, Nityananda, "A Survey of the Economic and Social Condition of the Chamars of Barpali in Orissa and Proposal for a Development Programme", *Economic Weekly*, (12 and 19 September 1953).

Patnaik, Paravanshu and S. Das, "Crisis in the Life of the Tamudias and the Impact of Hinduism", *Adibasi*, Vol. 8, No. 1, (1966).

Patrudu, B.V.S., "Scheduled Castes in India: Social Progress and Social Legislation", *Social Welfare*, (January, 1971).

Pattanaik, N., "Offering to the manes (sradha) among the Agarias of Sundargarh, Orissa", *Man in India*, Vol. 32, No. 3, (1952).

Patwardhan, Sunanda, "Changing Religious Practices and

Traditions of Scheduled Castes", *Deccan College Research Institute (Centenary) Bulletin*, No. 2, (September, 1967-68).

Patwardhan, Sunanda, "Social Mobility and Conversion of Mahars", *Sociological Bulletin*, Vol. 17, No. 2, (1968).

Perelia, C., "Prayer Cure amongst the Kaibarttas of West Bengal", *Journal of the Asiatic Society of Bengal*, Vol. 72, No. 3, (1903).

Phadnis, U., "Neo Buddhists in India and Ceylon", *Economic and Political Weekly*, (December 6, 1969).

Philip, P.O., "The Harijan Movement in India in Relation to Christianity", *International Review of Mission*, Vol. 24, (1935).

Phillips, W.S.K., "Social Distance: A Study of the Attitudes of the Upper Castes Towards Lower Castes of Bengal", *Eastern Anthropologist*, Vol. 20, No. 2, (1967).

Pillai, K.G., "Equality of Opportunity in Public Employment", *Supreme Court Journal*, Vol. 34, (1966).

Pimpley, P.N., "Educational Problems of Scheduled Caste Students of Punjab", *Social Change*, Vol. 6, (September–December, 1976).

Pimpley, P.N., "Politicization among the Scheduled Castes Students of Punjab", *Social Change*, Vol. 6, Nos. 3 & 4, (1976).

Pimpley, P.N., "Social Characteristics of the Scheduled Caste Students in Punjab", *Indian Journal of Social Work*, Vol. 37, No. 2, (1976).

Pimpley, P.N. and Bushan Lal Kapoor, "Educational Problems of Female Scheduled Caste Students in Punjab", *Interdiscipline*, Vol. 12, No. 283, (1975).

Pinto, A., "Judiciary's Approach to Reservation: Not Progressive Enough", *Deccan Herald*, (13 October 1990).

Pinto, A., "Reservation and the Constitute: A Struggle towards Equality", *Deccan Herald*, (13 September 1990).

Pinto, A., "Caste Conflict in Karnataka", *Economic and Political Weekly*, (11 July 1992).

Pinto, A., "Politics of Reservation", *Economic and Political Weekly*, (27 August 1994).

Pinto, A., "Atrocities on Dalits in Gulbarga", *Economic and Political Weekly*, Vol. 29, Nos. 16–17, (1994).

Pinto, A., "The Birth of a Dalit Regime", *Social Action*, Vol. 45, No. 3, (1995).

Pinto, A., "Dalits in Higher Education: Need for Establishing a Counter Culture", *Journal of Higher Education*, Vol. 21, No. 3, 1998).

Pinto, A., "Reservation for Dalit Christians: Reflections", *Indian Currents*, (26–31 October 1998).

Pinto, A., "Reservations and Law", *Vidyajyothi*, Vol. 62, No. 7, (1998).

Pinto, A., "Not a Call for Conversions", *The Hindustan Times*, (14 December1999).

Pinto, A., "Saffronisation and Affirmative Action", *Economic and Political Weekly*, Vol. 34, No. 52, (1999).

Pinto, A., "Conversions Are Acts of Protest", *The Hindustan Times*, (21 January 1999).

Pinto, A., "Hindutva Vs Ambedkarism: Views on Conversions", *Economic and Political Weekly*, Vol. 35, No. 41, (2000).

Pinto, A., "Is Reservation the Answer for Dalit Empowerment?", *Journal of Rural Development*, Vol. 19, No. 4, (2000).

Pinto, A., "Conversion Are Acts of Protest", *Integral Liberation*, Vol. 4, No. 4, (2000).

Pinto, A., "Caste is a variety of Race", *The Hindu*, (27 March 2001).

Pounde, Nigel, "Not Dalit, Not Brahmin", *Mashi Sevak*, Vol. 17, Nos. 1 & 2, (1993).

Prabhakar, M.E., "Caste-Class and Status in Andhra Churches and Implications for Mission Today: Some Reflections", *Religion and Society*, Vol. 28, (September 1981).

Prabhakar, M.E., "Caste in Andhra Churches: A Case Study

of Guntur District", *Religion and Society*, Vol. 34, (September 1987).

Prabhakar, M.E., "The Indian Christian Dalits", *Saplings* (UTC Magazine), (1988).

Prabhakar, M.E., "Developing A Common Ideology for Dalits of Christian and Other Faiths", *Religion and Society*, Vol. 37, No. 3, (1990).

Prabhakar, M.E., "Christian Dalits Want to with Scheduled Castes – Not Backward Classes", *Dalit Voice*, Vol. 10, No. 18, (1990).

Prabhakar, M.E., "Relevance of Dr. Ambedkar", *National Christian Council Review*, Vol. CXI, (1991).

Prabhakar, M.E., "Dalit Education and Youth", *National Christian Council Review*, No. 123, (1993).

Prabhakar, M.E., "Beginning and Growth of Dalit Studies in the CISRS and its Joint Programmes", *Religion and Society*, Vol. XL, Nos. 1–2, (1993).

Prabhakar, M.E., "In Search of Roots: Dalit Aspirations and the Christian Dalit Question (Perceptions of the Andhra Poet Laureate, Joshua)", *Religion and Society*, Vol. XLI, No. 1, (1994).

Prabhakar, M.E., "Human Rights' Violations: With Particular Reference to Dalits and Tribals", *National Christian Council Review*, (1995).

Prabhakar, Chaman Lal, "When 'Chamars' Speak out", *Frontier*, Vol. 23, No. 50, (July, 27, 1991).

Pradhan, Atul Chandra, "Depressed Classes Uplift in the Gandhian Era: A Critique of three Approaches", *Indian Historical Review*, Vol. 19, Nos. 1 & 2, (July 1992 January 1993).

Pradhan, R. Gopinath, "Bombay Workers of Untouchable Classes", *Bombay University Journal*, Vol. 4, (January, 1936).

Prakash, Om, "Educational Attainment of Children in the Sweeper Community at AIIMS Campus: An Exploratory Study", *Indian Educational Review*, Vol. 15, No. 4, (1980).

Prasad, Chandra Bhan, "Alternative Strategy for Scheduled Castes and Scheduled Tribes in Education", *Mainstream*, Vol. 28, No. 49, (September 29, 1990).

Prasad, L.M., "Educational Policy for Scheduled Caste Scheduled Tribes", *Indian Journal of Public Administration*, Vol. 32, No. 4, (1986).

Prasad, P.R., "Untouchability and Measures for its Eradication", *Gandhi Marg*, vol. 8, (November 1986).

Prasada Rao, C.R. and K. Radhakrishna Murty, "Dalit Consciousness and Brahmanism: A Multiplex Question", *Eastern Anthropologist*, Vol. 46, No. 1, (January-March, 1993).

Prashad, V., "The Untouchable Question", *Economic and Political Weekly*, Vol. 32, No. 9, (1996).

Pratap, Vijay, "Dalit Consciousness, Voluntary Work and Social Change", *Janata*, Vol. 50, Nos. 1–4, (Annual Number), (1995).

Pratt, B., "A Plea for Mission Work among Low-Caste Hindus", *Harvest Field*, Vol. 1, No. 3, (1890).

Premi, Kusum K., "Educational Opportunities for the Scheduled Castes: Role of Protective Discrimination in Equalization", *Economic and Political Weekly*, Vol. 9, Nos. 45–46, (1974).

Premi, Kusum K., "Educational Problems of the Scheduled Castes in Punjab", *Journal of Indian Education*, Vol. 1, No. 6, (1976).

Premi, Kusum K., "Scheduled Castes and Educational Opportunities", *The Indian Journal of Social Work*, Vol. 37, No. 3, (1976).

Premi Kusum K., "Educational Equality and Economic Opportunities: A Comparative Study of Scheduled Castes and non-Scheduled Castes", *Journal of Higher Education*, Vol. 9, (Spring 1984).

Premi, Kusum K., "Industrial Training for Scheduled Castes and Scheduled Tribes", *Social Change*, Vol. 18, No. 1, (1988).

Premi, Kusum K., "Education of Disadvantaged Children: Issues in Universalisation of Elementary Education in India", *Perspective in Education*, Vol. 5, No. 1, (1989).

Pressler, Henry H., "The Neo-Buddhist Stir in India", *India Cultures Quarterly*, Vol. 21, No. 4, (Leonard Theological College, Jabalpur, Madhya Pradesh).

Pullapilly, Cyriac K., "The Ezhavas of Kerala and the Historic Struggle for Acceptance in the Hindu Society", *Journal of Asian and African Studies*, Vol. XI, Nos.1-2, (1976).

Punalekar, S.P., "Harijans of Eastern U.P. Region: A Profile on Marginality", *The North-Eastern Research Bulletin*, Vol. 6, (1975).

Punalekar, S.P., "Farewell to Schooling: Harijan Dropouts – A Sociological Explanation", *Philosophy and Social Action*, Nos. 1-2, (1978).

Punalekar, S.P., "Caste, Class and Reaction: An Overview of Marathwada Riots", *Society and Change*, Vol. 3, No. 1, (1982).

Punalekar, S.P., "Untouchability and Social Change: A Maharashtra Study", *Mainstream*, Vol. 21, (January, 1983), (Republic Day Special Issue).

Punalekar, S.P. "Identities and Consciousness: An Overview of Dalit Literature in Maharashtra", *Man and Development*, Vol. 10, No. 4, (1988).

Punalekar, S.P., "Prison without Walls: Social Situation of Sweepers and Scavengers in Western India", *IASSI Quarterly / Social Change* Vol. 9, Nos. 1-2, (July-December, 1990).

Punalekar, S.P., "Dalitism and Gender", *Third Concept*, Vol. 8, No. 90, (1994).

Pundir, J.K., "Social Change among Scheduled Castes in North India", *Social Change*, Vol. 25, No. 4, (1995).

Puniyani, Ram, "Dalits and Adivasis Hindutva's Foot-Soldiers", *The Dalit*, (May-June 2002).

Punwani, Jyoti, "The Fire Dims with Age", *The Times of India*, (7 January 1996).

Pushpendra, "Dalit Assertion through Electoral Politics", *Economic and Political Weekly*, Vol. 36, No. 35, (2001).

Radetotad, N.K., "Caste Hierarchy among the Untouchables of Dharwar", *Eastern Anthropologist*, Vol. 19, No. 3, (1966).

Radha Devi, D., "Note on the Education of Scheduled Caste Population in Urban Trivandrum", *Man and Development*, Vol. 12, No. 4, (1990).

Radhakrishnan, N., "Reservation to the Backward Classes", in *Indian Yearbook of International Affairs, 1964*, (University of Madras), Vol. XIII (Part I), (1964).

Radhakrishnan, N., "Chitralekha Vs State of Mysore: Art. 15(4) – Meaning of Socially and Educationally Backward Classes", *Jaipur Law Journal*, Vol. 6, (1966).

Radhakrishnan, N., "Units of Social, Economic and Educational Backwardness: Caste and Individual", *Journal of the Indian Law Institute*, Vol. 7, (1965).

Radhakrishnan, P., "Ambedkar's Legacy to Dalits: Has the Nation Reneged on its Promises?", *Economic and Political Weekly*, Vol. 26, No. 33, (1991).

Radhakrishnan, P., "Ambedkar's Legacy", *The Hindu*, (20 January 1991).

Radhakrishnan, P., "Reservations in Theory and Practice", *MIDS Bulletin*, Vol. 20, No. 4, (1990).

Radhakrishnan, P., "Sensitising Officials on Dalits and Reservations", *Economic and Political Weekly*, Vol. 37, No. 7, (2002).

Rae, Joginder Nath, "Baisware folk songs", *Journal of the Asiatic Society of Bengal*, Vol. 53, No.1, (1884).

Raghavendra Rao, J.S. and H.S. Verma, "Weaker Sections: Concept, Research and Social Policy", *Interdiscipline*, (Winter 1970).

Raha, Manis Kumar, "The Khairas of Bankura", *Bulletin of the Cultural Research Institute*, Vol. 3, No. 1, (1964).

Rai, Lala Lajpat, "The Depressed Classes", *The Indian Review*, (May, 1909).

Rai, Lala Lajpat, "The Depressed Classes", *The Modern Review,* (July, 1909).

Rai, Lala Lajpat, "The Depressed Classes", *The Indian Review,* (May, 1910).

Rai, Lala Lajpat, "The Depressed Classes", *The Indian Review,* Vol. XIV, (1913).

Rai, P. Shivprasad, "Bali Chakravarti: The Great Dalit Emperor, Killed by the Wily Vaman", *Dalit Voice,* (January 6-21), (1989).

Raina, B.L., "Responses of Scheduled Caste and Scheduled Tribe Students to Schooling in Rural India", *Progress of Education,* Vol. 66, No. 7, (February, 1992).

Raj Kumar, "Relevance of Ambedkarism in India", *Mainstream,* Vol. 34, No. 24, (May 18, 1996).

Raj, Anony, "The Dalit Christian Reality in Tamil Nadu", *Jeevandhara,* Vol. 22, No. 128, (1992).

Raj, S. Albones, "Mass Religious Conversion as Protest Movement: A Frame Work", *Religion and Society,* Vo. 28, (December 1981).

Raja, A.M.A., "Some Reflections on a Dalit Reading of the Bible", *Indian Theological Studies,* Vol. 33, No. 3, (1996).

Raja, A.M.A., "Exorcism and the Dalit Self-Affirmation", *Vidyajyothi Journal for Theological Research,* Vol. 60, No. 12, (1996).

Raja, D., "Dr. Ambedkar Remembered – But How?", *New Age,* (11 – 17 December 1994).

Rajabhoj, P.N., "Harijans", *Journal of Social Psychology,* Vol. 51, (1960).

Rajabhoj, P.N., "Harijans", *Illustrated Weekly of India,* (3 October 1971).

Rajaiah, B., "Reservation in Higher Education and Jobs", *Educational Review,* Vol. 88, No. 3, (1982).

Rajan, S. Irudaya and P. Mohana Chandran, "Infant and Child Mortality estimates for Scheduled Castes and

Scheduled Tribes: Based on the 1991 Census", *Economic and Political Weekly*, Vol. 36, No. 48, (2001).

Rajghatta, Chidanand, " The angry Balladeer", *The Times of India,* (9 December 1990).

Rajghatta, Chidanand, "Madiga Malliah Inherits the Earth", *The Times of India,* (9 December 1990).

Rajpramukh, R.E., "The Harijan Ambivalence in Andhra: Case Studies of a Village and a Town in Guntur District", *Indian Anthropologist,* Vol. 10, No. 1, (1980).

Raju, B.R.K. and M.R.B. Narasimha Rao, "Weaker Sections: Problems and Prospects", *Voluntary Action,* (March – April, 1972).

Raju, C.S., "Don't divide Dalits on the Bases of Religion: They are all one", *Dalit Voice,* Vol. 14, No. 4, (1995).

Rakshit, H.K., "The Mahars of Maharashtra: An Anthropometric Appraisal", *Bulletin of Department of Anthropology* (Government of India), Vol. 9, No. 1, (1960).

Ram, Jagjivan, "Casteism and Untouchability: An Analysis", *Indian Journal of Adult Education,* Vol. 19, No. 3, (1958).

Ram, Nandu, "Social Mobility and Social Conflict in Rural Uttar Pradesh", *Indian Anthropologist,* Vol. 7, No. 2, (1977).

Ram, Nandu, "Atrocities and Segregation in an Urban Social Structure: Views from the Bottom", *Journal of Social and Economic Studies,* (N.S.), Vol. I, No. 4, (1984).

Ram, Nandu, "Socio-Structural Variants and Higher Education among the Scheduled Castes and Scheduled Tribes", *Social Action,* Vol. 36, No. 2, (1986).

Ram, Nandu, "Marginalised Groups and the State of Human Rights in India", *Journal of Peace Studies,* (April 1997).

Ram, Nandu, "Dalit Movements in India: A Perspective from the Below", *The Indian Journal of Social Work,* Vol. 59, (1998).

Ram, Ratan, "Bangi: A Study in Magic and Medicine", *Vanyajati,* Vol. 3, No. 2, (1955).

Ram, Ratan, "The Changing Religion of the Bhangis of Delhi: A Caste of Sanskritisation", *Journal of Social Research*, Vol. 4, Nos. 1-2, (1961).

Rama Swamy, B. et.al., "Distribution of some Genetic Markers among Two Scheduled Caste Groups of Andhra Pradesh (South India)", *Acta Anthropogentica*, Vol. 3, Nos. 1 & 2, (1979).

Ramagundam, Rahul, "Gandhi and Ambedkar: Titans in Collisions", *The Concept*, (December 1996).

Raman, Kannamma S., "Dynamics of the Reservation Policy: An Overview", *Social Action*, Vol. 45, No. 4, (1995).

Raman, M. and Z. Agha, "Dalits: A new Assertiveness", *India Today*, (30 April 1994).

Ramanamma, A., "A Comparative Analysis of Education of Scheduled Castes and Scheduled Tribes in Maharashtra", *Journal of University of Patna (Humanities)*, Vol. 43, (1978).

Ramanamma, A. and Usha Bambvala, "Social Implications of School Dropouts in Maharashtra", *Social Change*, Vol. 8, No. 2, (1978).

Ramanathan, S., "Profile Study on Economic Problems of Scheduled Castes in Tamil Nadu", ICSSR's *Research Abstracts Quarterly*, Vol. 3, Nos. 2-3, (1974).

Ramanathan, Sugana, "Impact of Conversions on Dalit Identity", *Social Action*, Vol. 50, No. 1, (2000).

Ramaseshan, Radika, "Dalit Politics in Uttar Pradesh", *Seminar*, No. 425, (Annual Number), (1995).

Ramaswamy, Uma, "Scheduled Castes in Andhra: Some Aspects of Social Change", *Economic and Political Weekly*, Vol. 9, No. 29, (1974).

Ramaswamy, Uma, "Self-identity Among Scheduled Castes: A Study of Andhra", *Economic and Political Weekly*, Vol. 9, No. 47, (1974).

Ramaswamy, Uma, "Preference and Progress: The Scheduled Castes", *Economic and Political Weekly*, Vol. 19, No. 30, (1984).

Ramaswamy, Uma, "Education and Inequality", *Economic and Political Weekly*, Vol. 20, No. 36, (1985).

Ramaswamy, Uma, "Protection and Inequality among Backward Groups", *Economic and Political Weekly*, Vol. 21, No. 9, (1986).

Ramderia, Shalini, "Carrion and Corpses: Conflict in Categorizing Untouchability in Gujarat", *European Journal of Sociology*, Vol. 30, No. 2, (1989).

Rami Reddy, V. and G. Padmanabha Naidu, "Blood Groups and Dental Caries in the Madiga of Chittoor District, A.P.", *Heredity*, Vol. 12, (1980).

Rami Reddy, V. and K. Rajasekhara Reddy, "A1 A2 B O and Rh Blood Groups in the Madiga: A Scheduled Caste Population of Andhra Pradesh", *Indian Journal of Physical Anthropology and Human Genetics*, Vol. 8, (1982).

Ramotra, K.C., "Scheduled Castes Literacy in the North Western India: A Spatial Perspective", *National Geographer*, Vol. 23, No. 2, (1988).

Ramu, G.N., "Untouchability in Rural Areas", *Indian Journal of Social Work*, Vol. 29, No. 2, (1968).

Ranade, Prabha Shastri, "Spatial Distribution of the Scheduled Caste Population in Vidarbha", *Geographical Review of India*, Vol. 51, No. 2, (1989).

Ranadive, B.T., "Six Crore Untouchables: Their Place in Freedom's Battle", *People's War*, Vol. III, No. 23, (1944).

Randeria, S., "Carrion and Corpses: Conflict in Categorizing Untouchability in Gujarat", *European Journal of Sociology*, Vol. 30, (1989).

Ranga Rao, C.V., "Classification of Scheduled Castes: A Study in Public Policy Making", *Third Concept*, No. 142, (1998).

Ranganatham, N., "The Depressed Classes", *The Indian Review*, (November-December, 1911).

Ranjan, Sudhanshu, "Reservation for Minority Dalits", *Mainstream*, Vol. 38, No. 51, (2000).

Rao, Amba, "Higher Education and Occupational Mobility among the Scheduled Castes Youth", *Journal of Higher Education*, Vol. 1, No. 3, (1976).

Rao, C.R.P. and K.R. Murty, "Dalit-Consciousness and Brahmanism: A Multiplex Question", *Eastern Anthropologist*, Vol. 46, (1993).

Rao, D.M., "Disparities of Representation Among Direct Recruits to the I.A.S.", *Indian Journal of Public Administration*, Vol. 9, (1963).

Rao, Gopinath, "Residential Schools for Weaker Sections: A Study", *ASCI Journal of Management*, Vol. 15, No. 2, (1986).

Rao, P.B., "Karamchedu Massacre: Games Played by Political Parties", *Samata*, No. 2, (1985).

Rao, Prasad and R.K. Murty, "Dalit Consciousness and Brahmanism", *The Eastern Anthropologist*, Vol. 46, No. 1, (1993).

Rao, R., "Dalit Movements in Contemporary India", *Kerala Sociologist*, Vol. 17, No. 1, (1989).

Rao, V.K.R.V., "Employment of Scheduled Castes and Scheduled Tribes", *Tribal Research Institute Bulletin*, Vol. I, No. 1, (1964).

Rastogi, S.P., "Attitudes and Beliefs of Harijan Students", *Journal of Higher Education*, Vol. 4, No. 2, (1978).

Rastogi, S.P., "The Impact of Constitutional Provision upon the Uplift of Harijans", *Indian Educational Review*, Vol. 15, No. 4, (1980).

Ratan, Ram, "A Study in Magic and Medicine: Treatment by Poison-Sucking Among the Bhangis", *Vanyajati*, Vol. 3, (1955).

Rath, R. and N.C. Sircar, "The Cognitive Background of Six Hindu Caste Groups Regarding the Low Caste Untouchables", *Journal of Social Psychology*, Vol. 51, (1960).

Rath, Rajlaxmi, "Social Implications of Reservation in Public Services for Scheduled Castes in Bihar", *Third Concept*, Vol. 10, Nos. 116–117, (1996).

Rath, Sharada, "Welfare of Scheduled Castes and Scheduled Tribes: A Study of Cooperative Federalism in India", *Journal of State Politics and Administration*, Vol. 5, Nos. 1-2, (1982).

Rathod, P.B., "Dalit Bahujans and the Politics of Alliance", *Radical Humanist,* Vol. 64, No. 6, (2000).

Rathod, P.V. and Vijay Kumar, "The Working of the Scheduled Castes and Schedled Tribes (Prevention of Atrocities) Act 1989 in Gujarat", *The Administrator,* Vol.XLII, No. 1, (1997).

Ravinder, D., "Andhra Pradesh: Victimising Dalits – 'Encounter' in Palakurthy", *Economic and Political Weekly,* Vol. 31, No. 9, (1996).

Ravindranath, M.N., "Educational Problems of Scheduled Castes", *Educational Review,* Vol. 87, No. 4, (1981).

Ray, Baren, "Gandhiji and the Dalit Question: Then and Now", *Mainstream,* Vol. 33, No. 22, (1995).

Ray, Gautam Sankar, "A Study of the Physical Characteristics of Rajbansis", *Journal of the Royal Asiatic Society of Bengal,* Vol. 12, (Letter), (1945).

Ray, Manmohan, "Some Notes on the Rajvanci Caste", *Journal of Asiatic Society of Bengal,* Vol. 71, Part 3, (1902).

Ray, S., "Categorisation of Scheduled Castes", *Andhra Pradesh,* (July 1998).

Rayappa, P. Hanumantha and Deepak Grover, "Employment Planning for Scheduled Castes and Scheduled Tribes", *Economic and Political Weekly,* Vol. 14, No. 24, (1979).

Rayappa, P. Hanumantha and R. Mutharayappa, "Scheduled Castes and Tribes: In the Deep South", *State and Society,* Vol. 5, No. 3, (1985).

Reddy, M.M. Krishna, "Population Characteristics of Scheduled Castes and Scheduled Tribes in Andhra Pradesh", *Social Change,* Vol. 21, No. 2, (June, 1991).

Reddy, N.S., "Community-Conflict among Depressed Castes of Andhra", *Man in India,* Vol. 30, No. 4, (1950).

Reddy, P.C. and D.P. Mukherjee, "A1 A2 B O Blood Groups Among the Malas of Andhra Pradesh", *Journal of Indian Anthropological Society,* Vol. 17, (1982).

Rege, Sharmila, "A Dalit Feminist Standpoint", *Seminar,* No. 471, (November 1998).

Rege, Sharmila, "'Real Feminism' and Dalit Women: Scripts of Denial and Accusation", *Economic and Political Weekly*, Vol. 35, No. 16, (2000).

Reidy, M., "Solidarity: India's Dalits", *One World*, (May 1992).

Rice, Marion J., "Harijan Wasti", *Progress of Education*, Vol. 55, No. 2, (1981-82).

Rice, Stanley, "The Indian Untouchables", *World Unity Magazine*, Vol. XIV, (1934).

Richards, F.J., "From Paraiah to Brahman in South India", *Man*, Vol. 32, No. 17, (1932).

Richedson, David, "An Account of Bazeegurs: A Sect commondly dominated the Nuts", *Asiatic Researches (Asiatic Society of Bengal)*, Vol. 7, Art. 19, (19??).

Rodrigues, Valerian, "Dalits and Cultural Identity: Ambedkar's Prevarications on the Question of Culture", *Social Action*, Vol. 50, No. 1, (2000).

Rothermund, Indira, "Mahatma Gandhi's Harijans", *Gandhi Marg*, Vol. I, No. 5, (August, 1979).

Rout, S.P., "Hunting among the Pauri Bhuiya of Kuira Sundergarh", *Adibasi*, No. 2, (1964-65).

Roy Burman, B.K., "A Note on the Scheduled Castes and Scheduled Tribes of West Bengal", *Vanyajati*, Vol. 4, (1954).

Roy Burman, B.K., "The Problems of Untouchables", *Seminar*, No. 177, (May 1974).

Roy Choudhary, B.K., "Progress of Secondary Education among Scheduled Caste and Scheduled Tribes of West Bengal", *Bulletin of Cultural Research Institute*, Vol. II, No. 1, (1963).

Roy Choudhury, B.K., "A Note on the Progress of Secondary Education among Scheduled Castes and Scheduled Tribes of West Bengal", *Bulletin of the Cultural Research Institute*, Vol. 5, No. 162, (1966).

Roy Choudhry, Dibyender, "Palmar Dermatoglyphics of the Rajbanshis of Midnapur, West Bengal", *The Anthropologist*, Vol. 9, Nos. 1 & 2, (1962).

Roy Chowdhry, B.K., "Bagadis: The Racial Problem of Bengal", *Man in India*, Vol. 32, No. 2, (1952).

Roy Chowdhry, B.K. and B. Bhattacharya, "A Brief Record on Stagnation of Scheduled Tribe and Scheduled Caste Students", *Bulletin of the Cultural Research Institute*, Vol. 6, Nos. 1 & 2, (1967).

Roy Chowdhury, T.C., "The Racial Problem of Bengal", *Man in India*, Vol. 32, No. 2, (1952).

Roy, Biren, "A.K. Roy Yanchi Nav Dalit Kranti", (in Marathi), *Tatparya*, (August, 1984).

Roy, S.C., "A General Account of the Pahris or Hill Bhuiyas of Bonai", *Journal of the Bihar and Orissa Research Society*, Vol. 5, (1919), [The Byuiyas or Bhuyans are categorized as Scheduled Castes in Bihar, Uttar Pradesh and West Bengal, but in Orissa they are categorized as Scheduled Tribes].

Roy, S.C., "Birth, Childhood and Puberty and Death Customs of the Pahri Bhuiyas", *Journal of the Bihar and Orissa Research Society*, Vol. 5, (1919).

Roy, S.C., "Kinship Organisation, Marriage and Inheritance among the Pahri Bhuiyas", *Journal of the Bihar and Orissa Research Society*, Vol. 5, (1920).

Roy, S.C., "An Indian Riddle Book Orissa (Bhuiya)", *Man in India*, Vol. 23, (1943).

Roy, S.N., "A Few Notes on the Sabakhias or Swalgiti Tribes of Orissa", *Man in India*, Vol. 2, No. 3, (1922).

Roy, Thirthankar, "Foreign Trade and the Artisans in Colonial India: A Study of Leather", *Indian Economic and Social History Review*, Vol. 31, No. 4, (1994).

Roy, U.N. and K. Gopal Iyer, "Status of Dalits in Shivalik Region of Punjab: Case Study of Watershed Development Villages", *Journal of Rural Development*, Vol. 21, No. 1, (2001).

Rudolph, Lloyd and Susanne H. Rudolph, "The Political Role of India's Caste Associations", *Pacific Affairs*, Vol. XXXIII, No. 1, (March, 1960).

Saberwal, Satish, "The Reserved Constituency: Candidates and Consequences", *Economic and Political Weekly*, Vo. 7, No. 2, (1972).

Saberwal, S., "Receding Pollution: Intercaste Relations in Urban Punjab", *Sociological Bulletin*, Vol. 22, (1973).

Saberwal, Satish, "Blacks, Harijans and Muslims", *Economic and Political Weekly*, Vol. 8, No. 41, (1973).

Sachchidananda, "Emergent of Scheduled Castes Elite in Bihar", *Religion and Society*, Vo. 21, No. 3, (1974).

Sachchidananda, "Untouchability and Gandhi", *Interdiscipline*, (Winter, 1970).

Sadhu, Arun, "Neo-Buddhists in Maharashtra: Conversion has Helped", *Times of India*, (15 November, 1975).

Sadhu, Arun, "The Dalits", *Seminar*, No. 177, (May 1974).

Saggar, M. and I. Pan, "SCs and STs in Eastern India: Inequality and Poverty Estimates", *Economic and Political Weekly*, (5 March 1994).

Saha, Ramendra Nath, "An Assessment of Progress of Secondary Education amongst the Scheduled Castes and Scheduled Tribes of West Bengal During 1961-71", *Bulletin of Cultural Research Institute*, Vol. 13, Nos. 1-2, (1978).

Sahay, Balkrishna, "The Depressed Classes", *The Indian Review*, (May, 1911).

Sahay, K.N., "Eradication of Untouchability and Caste System", *Journal of Social Research*, (Vol. XVIII, No. 2, (1975).

Sahu, L.N., "Bhuiya Marriages", *Man In India*, Vol. 23, (1943), [The Byuiyas or Bhuyans are categorized as Scheduled Castes in Bihar, Uttar Pradesh and West Bengal, but in Orissa they are categorized as Scheduled Tribes].

Sahu, L.N., "The Amanatyas", *New Review*, Vol. 18, (1943).

Sainath, P., "Glass Struggle in Telangana", (in two parts), *The Hindu*, (8 & 15 November 1998).

Sainath, P., "When the Alphabet Ends with ABCD", *The Hindu*, (13 December 1998).

Sainath, P., "After the Meenakshipuram Conversions: One People, Many Identities", *The Hindu*, (31 January 1999).

Saldomha, J.A., "On the right of taking the Hides of Dead Cattle Exercised by Chamar and Mahars of the Kolaba District", *Journal of the Anthropological Society of Bombay*, Vol. 7, No. 8, (1938).

Samata Sanghatana, "Upper Caste Violence: Study of Chanduru Carnage", *Economic and Political Weekly*, Vol. 26, No. 36, (1991).

Sami, Bernard D., "Reponse to the Paper on 'Dalits in Higher Education': Need for Establishing a Counter Culture", *Journal of Higher Education*, Vol. 22, No. 1, (1999).

Sanadhya, Ghanshyam, "Aparthied in India", *Young Age*, (December 30, 1970).

Sangarakshita, Stavira, "Dr. Babasaheb Ambedkar and Buddhism", *Bodhisattva*, Vol. I, (1965).

Sangarakshita, Stavira, "Mass Civil Disobedience in India by Ex-Untouchable Buddhists", *Institute of Race Relations News Letter* (London), (March 1965).

Sankaran, S.R., "The Administration and the Poor", *The Administrator*, Vol. XLII, No. 1, (1997).

Sankaran, S.R., "Development of Scheduled Castes in Andhra Pradesh", *Economic and Political Weekly*, Vol. 33, No. 5, (1998).

Sankaran, S.R., "Mala, Madiga Controversy – An Appeal to Scheduled Castes", *Sanghika Sankshema Smacharam*, (June-July 1998).

Sankaran, S.R., "Welfare of Scheduled Castes and Scheduled Tribes in Independent India – An Overview of State Policies and Programmes", *Journal of Rural Development*, Vol. 19, No. 4, (2000).

Sarana, Gopala, "Kinship among the Chamars of Dhanaura", *Agra University Journal of Research*, Vol. III, (1955).

Saraswati, Baidyanath, "Untouchability in Hindu Society: An Interpretation", *Journal of Social Research*, Vol. 14, No. 2, (1971).

Sardesai, Rajdeep, "Ambedkar's Frayed Legacy: Dalits Must Resist Hindu Militancy", *The Times of India*, (9 September 1993).

Sardesai, S.G., "Ambedkar and the Emanicipation of the Scheduled Castes", *Mainstream*, Vol. 35, No. 19, (1997).

Sarkar, Benoy Kumar, "The Sociology of the Poor and the Pariah", *Man in India*, Vol. 15, No. 1, (1940).

Sarkar, Chanda, "A Study of Stagnation in the Field of Secondary Education among the Scheduled Castes, Scheduled Tribes and Other Communities", *Bulletin of the Cultural Research Institute*, Vol. 12, Nos. 1-2, (1976).

Sarkar, N.C., "Fringer Dermatoglyphics of the Namasudras of Nadia, West Bengal, India: Quantitative Genetics", *Journal of the Anthropological Survey of India*, Vol. 49, No. 2, (2000).

Sarkar, R.M., "The Religious Activities of the Bauris and their Modern Trends", *Vanyajati*, Vol. XII, No. 1, (1964).

Sarkar, R.M., "Bahubir Sammelan: A Case of Social Mobility Movement", *Eastern Anthropologist*, Vol. XIX, (1966).

Sarkar, R.M., "Profession of Midwife and the Bauri Women", *Vanyajati*, Vol. 15, No. 2, (1967).

Sarkar, Sumit, "The System of Caste: Gandhi, Ambedkar & Hindutva", *The Times of India*, (11 June 1994).

Sathe, S.P., "Reservations and the Constitution", *Mainstream*, Vol. 28, No. 14, (1990).

Satpathy, Gopinath, "Bhuiyan", *Adibasi*, No. 3, (1963-64), [The Byuiyas or Bhuyans are categorized as Scheduled Castes in Bihar, Uttar Pradesh and West Bengal, but in Orissa they are categorized as Scheduled Tribes].

Satyanarayana, A., "Dalit Protest Literature in Telugu: A Historical Perspective", *Economic and Political Weekly*, Vol. 30, No. 3, (1995).

Satyanarayana, A., "Dalit Identity and Consciousness in Colonial Andhra, 1904–1947", *Vikalp,* Vol. 6, No. 2, (1998).

Satyanarayaṇa, B.S., "Educational Problems of Scheduled Caste College Students in Karnataka", *Journal of Higher Education,* Vol. 7, No. 3, (1982).

Sayee Sekhar, A., "Unique form of Protest to get Justice", *The Hindu,* (7 May 1997).

Schermerhorn, R.A., "Scheduled Caste Welfare: Public Priorities in the States", *Economic and Political Weekly,* Vol. 4, No. 8, (1969).

Schermerhorn, R.A., "The Indian Constitution and the Untouchability Offences Act", *Indian Journal of Politics,* Vol. 9, (1975).

Schwartz, Michael B., "Indian Untouchable Texts of Resistance: Symbolic Domination and Historical Knowledge", *Social Analysis,* Vol. 25 (September, 1989).

SD, "Children of God Become Panther", *Economic and Political Weekly,* (August 1973), [Special Issue].

Searle-Chatterjee, M., "Kinship in an Urban Low Caste Locality", *Eastern Anthropologist,* Vol. 27, No. 4, (1974).

Searle-Chatterjee, M., "Urban Untouchables and Hindu Nationalism", *Immigrants and Minorities,* Vol. 13, (1994).

Searle-Chatterjee, M., "In the Skin of an Untouchable?", *Anthropology Today,* Vol. 14, (1998).

Sehgal, K.C., "Harijans in India – the Salient Suffers", *Economic Times,* (February 28, 1969).

Seshan, Radhika Rama, "Dalit Politics in U.P.", *Seminar,* No. 425, (January 1995).

Sethi, Sunil, "When Dalit Women will find Voice", *The Times of India,* (28 July 1997).

Setty, E.D., M. Palanisami and R. Subrahmanyam, "A Study of Social Relations in a South Indian Village", *Social Change,* Vol. 2, No. 3, (1972).

Shah, A.B., Dalit Movement and Its Historical Background", *Bulletin of the Indian Institute of Education*, Vol. 2, No. 1, (1981).

Shah, A.M., "Job Reservations and Efficiency", *Economic and Political Weekly*, Vol. 26, No. 29, (1991).

Shah, A.M., "'Dalit' Category and its Differentiation", *Economic and Political Weekly*, Vol. 37, No. 14, (2002).

Shah, Ghanshyam, "Stratification and Reservation: Case of Scheduled Castes and Tribes", *Mainstream*, Vol. 19, No 41, (1981).

Shah, Ghanshyam, "Caste, Class and Reservation", *Economic and Political Weekly*, Vol. 20, No. 3, (1985).

Shah, Ghanshyam, "Dalit Movements and the Search for Identity", *Social Action*, Vol. 40, No. 4, (1990).

Shah, Ghanshyam, "Social Backwardness and Politics of Reservation", *Economic and Political Weekly*, (Annual Number, (March 1991).

Shah, Ghanshyam, "Panchayat Raj and the Dalits: A Study of Social Justice Committee in Gujarat", *The Administrator*, Vol. 42, No. 1, (1997).

Shah, Ghanshyam, "Hope and Despair: A Study of Untouchability and Atrocities in Gujarat", *Journal of Indian School of Political Economy*, Vol. 12, Nos. 3–4, (2000).

Shah, Ghanshyam, "Caste, Hindutva and Hideousness", *Economic and Political Weekly*, Vol. 37, No. 15, (2002).

Shahabuddin, Syed, "Universal Reservation: High Road to Social Justice", *Mainstream*, Vol. 39, No. 33, (2001).

Shaket, Mishima, "Scheduled Castes: Beyond the System", *Economic and Political Weekly*, (April, 1974).

Shakir, Moin, "Dalit Panthers: A Study of Young Movement in Maharashtra", *Parivartan*, (1974), [Marathwada Vidyapeeth Yuvak Kalyan Vibhag].

Shankar, Prem, "Education and Rorschach Affective Factors of the Harijans", *Indian Psychological Review*, Vol. 4, No. 2, (1968).

Sharan, Ramesh and Hariswar Dayal, "Migration and Occupational Changes of a Scheduled Caste Community: A Case Study of Ghasis of Ranchi", *Indian Journal of Labour Economics,* Vol. 39, No. 4, (October – December, 1996).

Sharma, B.D., "Scheduled Castes and Tribes: A Status Report", *Lokayan Bulletin,* Vol. 8 No.6 (1990).

Sharma, G.B., "Enforcement of the Untouchability Offences Act in India", *Political Science Review,* Vol. 13, (1974).

Sharma, G.B., "Law as an Instrument for Abolition of Untouchability: Case of Rajasthan", *Economic and Political Weekly,* Vol. 10, No. 15, (1975).

Sharma, Govind P., "Trends in Study of Scheduled Castes", *Indian Anthropologist,* Vol.14, No. 2, (1984).

Sharma, H.R., "Distribution of Landholdings in Rural India: A Comparative Study of Scheduled Castes, Tribes and Non-Scheduled Castes and Tribes", *Artha Vijnana,* Vol. 40, No. 2, (1998).

Sharma, K.C., D.S. Thakar and Jasminder Kaur, "Socio-Economic Conditions of Scavengers in Himachal Pradesh", *Social Change,* Vol. 19, No. 3, (1989).

Sharma, K.L., "Educational Inequalities among Rajasthan's Scheduled Castes", *Economic and Political Weekly,* Vol. 9, No. 37, (1974).

Sharma, K.L., "Caste and Class: Factors Affecting Social Mobility Among the Scheduled Castes", *Journal of Sociological Studies,* Vol. 3, (1983).

Sharma, K.L., "Caste and Class in the Emergence of Dalit Identity and Movement", *The Administrator,* Vol. XLII, No. 1, (1997).

Sharma, Rajendra, "Constructing Dalit Identity", *Link,* Vol. 37, No. 1, (August 14, 1994).

Sharma, R.S., "Developing Educational Technology for Deprived Sections of the Indian Society", *Bulletin of Non-Formal Education,* Vol. 3, No. 3, (1985).

Sharma, S.S., "Untouchability: A Myth or a Reality", *Sociological Bulletin*, Vol. 35, (1986).

Shasmal, Kartick Chandra, "The Worship of Bahadu and Barabhum among the Bauris of Hooghly District", *Folklore*, Vol. 5, No. 9, (1964).

Shasmal, Kartick Chandra, "Thumur and Khomta songs the Baurees of Hooghly District, West Bental", *Folklore*, Vol. 6, (July 1965).

Shasmal, Kartick Chandra, "Bauri: The Role of artificial relationship towards growth of Social Solidarity", *Vanyajati*, Vol. 14, No. 1, (1966).

Shasmal, Kartick Chandra, "Divorce and Its Causes among the Bauris of West Bengal", *Bulletin of the Cultural Research Institute*, Vol. 6, (1967).

Shasmal, Kartick Chandra, "Economic Conditions of Bauris of West Bengal", *Khadi Gramodyog*, Vol. 13, No. 5, (1967).

Shastri, Chandra Hans, "Hinduism and Untouchability", *Free Press Journal*, (April 20, 1969).

Shastri, Sankarananda, "A Report on the Conversion Movement", *Maha Bodhi*, No. 65, (1957).

Shatrugna, M., "Road to 'Raktakshetram': Report from Chundur", *Economic and Political Weekly*, Vol. 26, No. 36, (1991).

Shenoy, G.T.L., "Indian Constitutional and the Removal of Socio-economic Inequalities", *Journal of the University of Bombay*, (October, 1970).

Sheth, D.L., "The Problems of Reservations: Economic Backwardness or Social Injustice", *Indian Journal of Adult Education*, Vol. 47, No. 5, (1986).

Sheth, Jyotsna, "The Neo-Buddhists", *The Illustrated Weekly of India*, (May 24, 1970).

Sheth, Surabhi, "Origins of Untouchability in India", *The Indian Journal of Social Science*, Vol. 3, (1990).

Shetye, Madhu, "Dalit Panthers Aim at Total Chance", *Free Press Journal*, (12 February 1974).

Shiri, Godwin, "The wide prevalence of Traditional Occupations among Christian Dalits – A Sign of Continued Oppression", *Religion and Society*, Vol. 42, No. 2, (1995).

Shivram, K. and M.B. Chennagowda, "Perceived Problems of Members of Mandal Panchayats", *Journal of Rural Development*, Vol. 11, No. 1, (January, 1992).

Shrikant, L.M., "Scheduled Castes and Their Welfare", in M.S. Gore (ed.), *Encyclopaedia of Social Work in India*, vol. II, (Delhi: Director of Publication, Government of India, 1968).

Shrivastava, V.K., "Development of Scheduled Castes Intention Realities and Task Ahead in Madhya Pradesh", *Madhya Pradesh Journal of Social Sciences*, Vol. 4, No. 1, (1999).

Shukla, S., "Strategy for Social Change: A Comment", *Economic and Political Weekly*, Vol. Vol. 3, No. 50, (1968).

Shukla, S., "Strategy for Social Change: A Rejoinder", *Economic and Political Weekly*, Vol. 4, No. 20, (1969).

Sigrist, Christian, "The Problem of 'Pariahs'", in Otto Stammer (ed.), *Max Weber and Sociology Today*, (New York: Harper & Row, 1971).

Simha, Hari Mohan, "Notes on Koch, Poliya, Rajvamsi in Dinapur", *Journal of the Asiatic Society of Bengal*, Vol. 12, (Part 3), (1902).

Singh, Abha, "Scheduled Caste Working Population in the Urban Centres of Varanasi City Region: A Geographical Analysis", *Geographical Review of India*, Vol. 54, No. 3, (September, 1992).

Singh, Bhupender, "Constitutional and Statutory Provision for the Weaker Sections of the Society", *Indian Journal of Public Administration*, Vol. 29, No. 2, (1983).

Singh, Charan, "Harijan Welfare", *Akashvani*, Vol. 33, No. 1, (January 1, 1978).

Singh, Hari, "Scheduled Castes and Tribes in India", *New Age*, Vol. VIII, No. 6, (1959).

Singh, Hoshiar and Ajmer Singh Malik, "Scheduled Castes and Development: Structure, Process and Performance", *Kurukshetra University Research Journal*, Vols. 2-3, (1989).

Singh, Jagpal, "Dalits in Haryana Politics", *Economic and Political Weekly*, Vol. 32, No. 43, (1997).

Singh, Jagpal, "Ambedkarisation and Assertion of Dalit Identity: Socio-Cultural Protest in Meerut District of Western Uttar Pradesh", *Economic and Political Weekly*, Vol. 33, No. 40, (1998).

Singh, Madhu, "How Equal are the Scheduled Castes?: Some aspects of their Educational Development", *Bulletin of the Indian Institute of Education*, Vol. 11, (1981).

Singh, Maheep, "Sikhism: A Religio-Social Haven for Dalits", *Sikh Reivew*, Vol. 46, No. 10, (1998).

Singh, Nihal, "India's Untouchables", *Contemporary Review* (New York), No. 103, (March, 1913).

Singh, P., "Equal Opportunity and 'Compensatory Discrimination': Constitutional Policy and Judicial Control", *Journal of the Indian Law Institute*, Vol. 18, (1976).

Singh, P., "Social Justice for the Harijans: Some Socio-Legal Problems of Identification, Conversion and Judicial Review", *Journal of the Indian Law Institute*, Vol. 20, (1978).

Singh, P., "*Bakke* and *Thomas*: A Comparative Legal Analysis of the Emerging Judicial Responses to the Problem of Equality and Compensatory Discrimination in U.S.A. and India", *Delhi Law Review*, Vols. 6–7, (1978–79).

Singh, S. and P.S. Jammu, "Untouchability in Rural Punjab: An Analysis", *Man in India*, Vol. 76, (1996), [This was published earlier in *EASSI Quaraterly*, Vol. 13, No. 4, (1995)].

Singh, Saint Nihal, "The Depressed Classes", *The Indian Review*, (September, 1910).

Singh, Saint Nihal, "India's Untouchables", *Contemporary Review*, Vol. 103, (1913).

Singh, Shyama Nand, "Ambedkar and Reservation Policy in India", *Third Concept*, Vol. 10, No. 118, (1996).

Singh, Soran, "Occupational Mobility among Scheduled Castes", *Indian Journal of Social Work*, Vol. 37, No. 3, (1976).

Singh, Soran, "The Scheduled Castes and New Dimension of Social Change", *Indian Journal of Comparative Sociology*, Vol. III, No. 1, (1977).

Singh, Surender, "Reservations: Issued Involved", *Mainstreami*, Vol. 28, No. 16, (1990).

Singh, T.P., "Removal of Inequalities of Opportunity in Education", *Maharashtra Educational Journal*, Vol. 20, No. 1, (1971).

Singh, T.P., B.P Pandey, G.S. Dubey and D.R. Yadava, "Educational Aspirations of Scheduled Caste Students in Eastern Uttar Pradesh", *Social Change*, Vol. 6, Nos. 1 & 2, (1976).

Singh, T.R., "The Harijan Leather Workers – Some Aspects of Untouchability in Andhra Pradesh", *Voluntary Action*, Vol. IX, No. 2, (1967).

Sinha, Ajay, "A Profile of Poorest among Poor: Missing Link in the Development Strategy", *The Administrator*, Vol. 42, No. 1, (1997).

Sinha, Arun, "Class War, Not 'Atrocities on Harijans'", *Economic and Political Weekly*, Vol. 12, No. 50, (1977).

Sinha, Arun, "The Bishrampur Carnage", *Economic and Political Weekly*, (1 April 1978).

Sinha, D.N., "Cognitive and Motivational Correlates of Deprivation and Their Implications for the Education of Scheduled Caste Children", *Journal of Personality and Clinical Studies*, Vol. I, No. 1, (1985).

Sinha, R.K., "Changing Identity of Mala of Madhya Pradesh", *Journal of the Anthropological Survey of India*, Vol. 48, No. 4, (1999).

Sinha, Rakesh, "Dalit Movement", *The Times of India*, (22 October 1993).

Sinha, Rita, "Equalization of Educational Opportunities, Scheduled Castes and Scheduled Tribes: Problems and Future Strategies", *Man in India*, Vol. 76, No. 2, (1996).

Sinha, S., "Scheduled Caste Students at College", *Journal of Social Research*, (1975).

Sirkar, R.M., "Bahubir Sammelan: A Case of Social Mobility Movement - a Study of Bouri Caste", *Eastern Anthropologist*, Vol. 19, No. 3, (1966).

Sivanandan, P., "Economic Backwardness of Harijans in Kerala", *Social Scientist*, Vol. 4, (1976).

Snatak, B.D., "Untouchables Remember Their Crusader", *Social Welfare*, Vol. XV, No. 2, (1969).

Solanki, B.R., R.R. Shukla and J.J. Sood, "Study of Blood Groups of Mahars and Marathas Showing Presence of Sickle Cell Trait in Nagpur", *Indian Journal of Medical Research*, Vol. 48, No. 2, (1960).

Sood, Renu, "Role of Achievement Anxiety, Alienation and Value Discrepancy in Academic Achievement of Scheduled Caste Students", *Journal of Higher Education*, Vol. 6, Nos. 1–3, (1980-81).

Sorabji, Cornelia, "Temple Entry and Untouchability", *Nineteenth Century and After* (London), No. 113, (1933).

Sreedevi, P.L., "Welfare of Scheduled Castes and Scheduled Tribes in Kerala", *Social Welfare*, (January, 1971).

Srinivas, M.N., and A. Beteille, "The 'Untouchables' of India", *Scientific American*, No. 213, (December, 1965).

Srinivasan, R., "Dalit Buddhists Before Dr. Ambedkar", *New Quest*, No. 121, (January–February, 1997).

Srinivasulu, K., "Andhra Pradesh: BSP and Caste Politics", *Economic and Political Weekly*, Vol. 29, No. 40, (1992).

Srivastava, Arun, "The Bishrampur Carnage", *Frontier*, (22 April 1978).

Srivastava, B.N., "Working of the Constitutional Safeguards and Protective Measures for the Scheduled Castes and Scheduled Tribes", *Journal of Rural Development*, Vol. 19, No 4, (2000).

Srivastava, Jai Prakash, "Aggressiveness in Scheduled Caste Children", *Education*, Vol. 33, Nos. 4 and 5 (1954), [in two parts].

Srivastava, Prem et al., "Education of Under-Privileged", *The Indian Journal of Social Work*, Vol. 13, No. 3, (1952).

Srivastava, R.K., "Gandhi and the Problem of Caste and Untouchability", *Indian Political Science Review*, Vol. 4, No. 1, (October 1969–March 1970).

Subba Reddy, N., "Community Conflict among the Depressed Castes of Andhra Pradesh", *Man in India*, Vol. 30, No. 4, (October-December, 1950).

Subedar, M.B., 'The Elevation of the Depressed Classes', *Indian Review*, October, (1909).

Subramanian, K.S., "Caste Violence Against the Scheduled Caste", *Social Science Probing*, Vol. 3, No. 4, (1986).

Subramanyam, S., "Problems of School Dropouts: A Study with a special reference to Scheduled Castes and Scheduled Tribes in Andhra Pradesh", *Educational Quarterly*, Vol. 38, No. 3, (1986).

Sudame, G.R. and A.P. Thiagarajan, "Enrolment of the Scheduled Castes in General Colleges: A Case Study of Tamil Nadu", *Experiments in Education*, Vol. 9, No. 4, (1981).

Sudame, G.R. and A.P. Thiagarajan, "Academic Difficultues of College Youth: A Case Study of the Scheduled Castes", *Indian Education*, Vol. 12, Nos. 5-6, (1982).

Sudhakar Rao, N., "Ideology, Power and Resistance in a South Indian Village", *Sociological Bulletin*, Vol. 45, No. 2, (1996).

Sudhakar Rao, N., "Religion of Endavur Untouchables", *Eastern Anthropologist*, Vol. 44, No. 2, (April – June, 1991).

Sujatha, V., "Leather Processing: Role of Indegeneous Technology", *Economic and Political Weekly*, (23 November 2002).

Suman Chandra, K. and S.N. Pradhan, "Crime Against Scheduled Castes/Scheduled Tribes in Rural Areas: A Study of Causes and Remedies", *Journal of Rural Development*, Vol. 20, No. 1, (2001).

Sundar Rajan, K.R., "Harijans: The Great Betrayal – 200 killed every year by Caste Hindus", *The Illustrated Weekly*, Vol. XCIV, No. 30, (30 September, 1973).

Sundaresh, Aruna, "Constitutional Law and Reservations", *New Frontiers in Education*, Vol. 16, No. 2, (1986).

Suri, Surindar, "New Perspectives", *Seminar*, No. 177, (May 1974).

Suryanarayana Rao, R., "House Sites for Depressed Classes", *Servant of India*, Vol. 19, No. 190, (1936).

Swaminathan, M.S., "Educational Development of the Scheeduled Castes", *Journal of Indian Education*, Vol. 8, No. 1, (1982).

Swaroopa Rani, Challapalli, "Dalit Women's Writing in Telugu", *Economic and Political Weekly*, Vol. 33, No. 17, (1998).

Tamrakar, Tek, "Rights Against Untouchability", *Dalit Solidarity*, Vol. 4, (February 2003).

Tarakam, Bojja and K.G. Kannabiran "What Happened in Tsundur", *Olympus*, Vol. 12, No. 4, (1991).

Teltumbde, Anand, "Impact of New Economic Policy on Dalits in India", *Occasional Paper Series 1*, (Pune: Department of Sociology, University of Pune, 1997).

Tewari, Badri Narayan, "Semiology of Dalit Consciousness: A North Indian Experience", *Eastern Anthropologist*, Vol. 51, No. 2, (1998).

Thakkar, K.K., "The Problem of Casteism and Untouchability", *Indian Journal of Social Work*, Vol. XVII, No. 2, (1956).

Thakur, Laxmi, "IQ of Scheduled Caste Children: The Effect of Environment", *Journal of Indian Education*, Vol. 7, No. 4, (1992).

Thaliath, Joseph, "Notes on the Scavenger Caste of Northern Madhya Pradesh, India", *Anthropos*, Vol. 56, (1961).

Thangaraj, M., "Access to Land by Scheduled Castes and Scheduled Tribes in India", *The Administrator*, Vol. XLII, No. 1, (1997).

Thiagarajan, A.P., "A Study of the Scheduled Caste Students in Some Secondary Schools of Tamil Nadu", *Indian Education*, Vol. 11, No. 5, (1981).

Thiagarajan, A.P., "Educational Progress of Scheduled Castes", *Experiments in Education*, Vol. 15, No. 5, (1987).

Thorat, S.K., "Economic Status of Scheduled Castes Under Five Year Plans", *Ambedkar Journal of Social Development and Justice*, Vol. 5, (1978).

Thorat, S.K., "Dalits and the New Economic Policy", *Dalit International Newsletter*, Vol. 1, No. 1, (1996).

Thorat, S.K., "New Economic Policy and Its Impact on Employment and Poverty of the Scheduled Castes", *Occasional Paper Series* 2, (Pune: Department of Sociology, University of Pune, 1997).

Thorat, S.K., "Scheduled Caste after India's Independence – Where do they Stand?", *Dalit News International*, (October 1999).

Thorat, S.K., "Social Security in Unorganised Sector in India: How Secure are the Scheduled Castes?", *Indian Journal of Labour Economics*, Vol. 42, No. 3, (1999).

Thorat, S.K., "Dr. Babasaheb Ambedkar: Film as a Lost Opportunity", *Economic and Political Weekly*, (1-14 April 2000).

Thorat, S.K., "Programmes for Empowerment and Reducing Inequality: Long Way to Go for Untouchables", *Journal of Rural Development*, Vol. 19, No. 4, (2000).

Thorat, S.K., "Oppression and Denial: Dalit Discrimination in the 1990s", *Economic and Political Weekly*, Vol. 37, No. 6, (2002).

Thorat, Vimal, "Dalit Women", *Dalit International Newsletter*, Vol. 2, No. 1 and 10, (1997).

Thripathi, B.D., "On Minimising Social Distance Existing Between the Upper Castes and Harijans", *Interdiscipline*, Vol. 4, No. 1, (1967).

Thripathy, R.M., "Socio-Economic Profile of Scheduled Caste Population in India", *Geographical Review of India*, Vol. 61, No. 1, (1999).

Thurston, Edgar, "The Brahmans, Kammalans, Pallis and Pariahs of Madras City", *Bulletin of the Madras Government Museum*, Vol. 1, No. 4, (1896).

Thurston, Edgar, "Note on a Cheruman Skull", *Bulletin of the Madras Government Museum*, Vol. 2, No. 1, (1897).

Tilak, B.G., "The Emancipation of the Untouchables", *The Hindu Missionary*, Vol. 42, (15 April, 1918), (Bombay).

Tilak, J.B.J., "A Note on Equality of Education in India", *Indian Journal of Economics*, Vol. 56, No. 221, (1975).

Tilak, J.B.J., "A New Criteria", *Seminar*, No. 268, (1981).

Tripathi, Chandra Bhal, "Dalit Christians: Vested Interests are at Work", *Statesman*, (2 August 1996).

Trivedi, S.R., "Experiences and Problems about Education of Scheduled Caste Hostellers in Sagar", *Vanyajati*, Vol. 24, No. 4, (1977).

U Nu, "The Late Dr. B.R. Ambedkar", *Maha Bodhi*, No. 66, (1958).

Uniyal, B.N., "In Search of a Dalit Journalist", *The Pioneer*, (16 November 1996).

Uniyal, N.P. and B. Shah, "Caste and Academic Achievement", *Social Change*, Vol. 14, No. 1, (1984).

Uplaonkar, A.T., "Protective Discrimination and the Equality of Opportunity", *Journal of Higher Education*, Vol. 11, No. 1-2, (1985-86)

Uplaonkar, A.T., "Protective Discrimination and the Equality of Opportunity", *Social Change*, Vol. 19, No. 3, (1989).

Uplaonkar, A.T., "Scheduled Castes and Social Justice: A Karnataka Case in Point", *Indian Journal of Social Work*, Vol. 53, No. 1, (1992).

Varghese, Alexander V., "Education, Earning and Occupation of Weaker Caste", *Journal of Higher Education*, Vol. 9, No. 3, (1984).

Varma, R.P., "Educating the Disadvantaged: A Few Suggestions", *National Journal of Education*, Vol. 6, No. 2, (1984).

Vaudeville, Charlotte, "Chokhamela: An Untouchable Saint of Maharashtra", *South Asian Digest of Regional Writing*, Vol. 6, (1977).

Velaskar, Padma, "Politics of Untouchability and Social Change: A Astudy of the Scheduled Castes of Maharashtra", *Journal of Indian School of Political Economy*, Vol. 12, Nos. 3–4, (2000).

Venkateswarlu, D., "Socio-Economic Differences between Harijans, Middle-Castes and Upper-Castes: A Comparative Study of Six Villages in Andhra Pradesh", *The Eastern Anthropologist*, Vol. 39, No. 3, (1986).

Venkateswarlu, D., "Psychological Conflict between Harijans and Upper Class/Middle Class Caste Hindus: A Study in Andhra Pradesh", *Sociological Bulletin*, Vol. 36, No. 1, (1987).

Venkateswarlu, D., "Gandhi and the Scheduled Castes", *Mainstream*, Vol. 32, No. 50, (1994).

Venkateswarlu, D., "Malas resent Madiga bid to Divide A.P. Dalits", *Dalit Voice*, Vol. 15, No. 21, (1996).

Venktraman, S.R., "Review of Seminar on Casteism and Removal of Untouchability", *Indian Journal of Social Work*, Vol. XVI, (1956).

Verma, B.P., Keshar Sharma and A.N. Sinha, "A Comparative Study of Locus of Control and Self-Concept of Higher, Backward and Scheduled Caste Students", *Progress of Education*, Vol. 63, No. 9, (1989)

Victus, Solomon, "Dalits, Development and Ecology", *Gandhi Marg*, Vol. 19, No. 2, (1997).

Vidyarthi, L.P. and M. Mishra, "Economic Problems of Scheduled Castes of Bihar: Some Preliminary Observations", *Journal of Social Research*, (February 18, 1978).

Vidyarthi, L.P., "Economic Problems of the Scheduled Castes of Bihar", *Journal of Social Research*, Vol. XVIII, No. 2, (1975).

Vidyarthi, L.P., "Thinking About the Problems of the Scheduled Castes", *Indian Anthropologist*, Vol. 6, No. 1, (1976).

Vijayan, O.V., "Concept of the Brahmin: Dalits should not repudiate India's preserved wisdom", *Indian Express*, (4 June 1994).

Vincentnathan, L. Nandanar, "Untouchable Saint and Caste Hindu Anomaly", *Ethos*, Vol. 21, 1993).

Vincentnathan, Lynn, "Untouchable Concepts of Person and Society", *Contributions To Indians Sociology* (N S) Vol. 27, No. 1, (1993).

Vincentnathan, S.G. and L. Vincentnathan, "Equality and Hierarchy in Untouchable Intergenerational Relations and Conflict Resolution", *Journal of Cross-cultural Gerontology*, Vol. 9, (1994).

Vishwakarma, S.R., "Opportunities for non-Farm Employment and Economic Progress of a Depressed Caste: A Case Study", *AICC Economic Review*, Vol. XV, (July 15, 1963).

Visvanathan, Shiv, "Durban and Dalit Discourse", *Economic and Political Weekly*, Vil. 36, No. 33, (2001).

Wadia, A.R., "The Casteism and Untouchability: An Analysis", *Indian Journal of Adult Education*, Vol. 14, No.

3, (1958), [Excerpts from the Paper read at the Seminar on "Casteism and Removal of Untouchability", held in 1955 at Delhi].

Waghmare, Janardan, "Nigro Wangmay va Dalit Wangmay", *Asmitadarsh*, Vol. VII, No. 1, (1974).

Waldman, Peter, "Reforms bring Little Change for India's 'Untouchables'", *Wall Street Journal*, (20 June 96).

Wankhede, G.G., "Social and Educational Problems of Scheduled Castes: Some Critical Insights", *Indian Journal of Social Work*, Vol. 60, No. 3, (1999).

Webster, John C.B., "A Historic Rally for Dalit Christians", *The Christian Century*, (27 February 1991).

Webster, John C.B., "The Rise of Dalit Consciousness and the Ministry of the Local Congregation", *Puthu Valvu*, Vol. 3, No. 9, (1995).

Webster, John C.B., "Understanding the Modern Dalit Movement", *Sociological Bulletin*, Vol. 45, No. 2, (1996).

Webster, John C.B., "Dalits and Anti-Conversion Legislation in Tamil Nadu", *Dalit International Newsletter*, Vol. 8, No. 1, (2003).

Weitbrecht-Stanton, H.U., "The Untouchables of India and their Enumeration", *Asiatic Review*, Vol. XVI (1920).

West Bengal State, Government of Tribal Welfare Department, *Backward Classes Welfare in West Bengal, 1952-56*, (Calcutta: 1957).

Whitehouse, Bishop, The Gospel for Pariahs, *Missionary Review*, (1903).

Wiebe, P.D. and G.N. Ramu, "Christian and Hindu Harijans", *The Eastern Anthropologist*, Vol. 28, No. 3, 1975).

Wiebe, Paul D. and G.N. Ramu, "Christian and Hindu Harijans: Study of the effects of Christian Programmes in India", *The Eastern Anthropologist*, Vol. 28, (July–September 1975).

Wilson, K., "Political Perspectives of Dalits in Contemporary India", *National Christian Council Review*, Vol. CXV, No. 11, (1991).

Wingate, Andrew, "A Study of Conversion from Christianity to Islam in Two Tamil Villages", *Religion and Society*, Vol. 28, (December 1981).

Wyatt, Andrew K.J., "Dalit Christians and Identity Politics in India", *Bulletin of Concerned Asian Scholars*, Vol. 30, No. 4, (1998).

Xaxa, Virginius, "Protective Discrimination: Why Scheduled Tribes lag behind Scheduled Castes", *Economic Political Weekly*, Vol. 36, No. 29, (2001).

Xaxa, Virginius, "Ethnography of Reservation in Delhi University", *Economic and Political Weekly*, Vol. 37, No. 32, (2002).

Yadav, S.K., "Education of Scheduled Castes: Problems and Solutions", *Avaghana*, Vol. 3, No. 1, (1979).

Yadav, S.K., "Intelligence, Motivational Tendencies of Scheduled Caste and Non-Scheduled Caste Secondary Students", *Journal of Education and Psychology*, Vol. 37, No. 2, (1979).

Yadav, S.K., "A Study of the Scheduled Castes Awareness about the Schemes for their Educational Progress", *Indian Educational Review*, Vol. 17, No. 1, (1982).

Yadav, S.K., "Research Review on Implementation of the Educational Schemes of Scheduled Castes", *Indian Educational Review*, Vol. 18, No. 3, (1983).

Yadav, S.K., "Awareness Studies about Educational Schemes amongst Scheduled Castes: A Research Review", *Indian Educational Review*, Vol. 19, No. 4, (1984).

Yadu Bhushana Reddy, P. and A. Papa Rao, "Anthropometric Variation among the Madiga and Mala: Two Scheduled Caste Groups", *Man in India*, Vol. 79, Nos. 3–4, (2000).

Yagnik, Achut and Anil Bhatt, "The Anti-Dalit Agitation in Gujarat", *South Asia Bulletin*, Vol. R, No. 1, (1984).

Youngson, John W., "Chuhras", *The Indian Antiquary*, Vol. 35, (March, November and December 1906); and Vol. 36, (January, March, April and May 1907).

Youth, Cast, "Effect of Socio-Economic Status on the Modernity attitude of Scheduled Castes", *Indian Psychological Review*, Vol. 36, Nos. 7 – 8, (1991).

Yurlova, Yevgenia, "Political Ememrgence of the Scheduled Caste Ethnocommunity", *Mainstream*, Vol. 29, No. 51, (1991).

Zachariah, Mathew, "Positive Discrimination in Education for India's Scheduled Castes: A Review of the Problems, 1950-1970", *Comparative Education Review*, Vol. 16, No. 1, (1972).

Zelliot, Eleanor, "The Revival of Buddhism in India", *Asia*, Vol. 10, (Winter 1968).

Zelliot, Eleanor, "The Nineteenth Century Background of the Mahar and Non-Brahman Movements in Maharashtra", *The Indian Economic and Social History Review*, Vol. 7, No. 3, (1970).

Zelliot, Eleanor, "Dalit Sahitya: The Historical Background", *Vagartha*, (January 1975).

Zelliot, Eleanor and Vidyut Bhagwat, "Dalita Sahitya – The Historical Background", *Vagartha*, Vo. 12, (1976).

Zelliot, Eleanor and Gail Omvedt, "Introduction to Dalit Poems", *Bulletin of Concerned Asian Scholars*, Vol. 10, No. 3, (1978).

Zelliot, Eleanor, "Dalit – New Cultural Context for an Old Marathi Word", *Contributions to Asian Studies*, Vol. IX, (1978).

Zelliot, Eleanor, "Dalit Poetry", *Illustrateed Weekly*, Vol. C, No. 33, (1979), [A page of translations, with others, from the Marathi].

Zelliot, Eleanor, "Chokhamela and Eknath: Two Bhakti Modes of Legitimacy for modern Change", *Journal of Asian and African Studies*, Vol. XIV, Nos. 3&4, (July-October, 1980), [this issue also appeared as a book, *Tradition and Modernity in Bhakti Movements*, edited by Jayant Lele, (Leiden: E.J. Brill, 1981)].

Zelliot, Eleanor and Philip Engblom (eds.), "A Marathi Sampler", a special issue of *Journal of South Asian Literature,* Vol. 17, No. 1, (1982). [This collection includes introductory notes and translations of Dalit short stories by Shankarrao Kharat and Baburao Bagul and Dalit poets Dhasal, Pawar and Sapkale].

Zelliot, Eleanor, "The Varied Voices of Dalit Poets from Maharashtra", *South Asia Bulletin,* Vol. VII, Nos. 1–2, (1987).

Zelliot, Eleanor, "Dalit – New Perspectives on India's Ex-Untouchables", *India Briefing* (New York: The Asia Society), (1991).

Zelliot, Eleanor, "Dalit Culture and Social Action" (Interviewed by JNU Students), *Frontier,* (21 November 1992).

Zelliot, Eleanor and Veena Deo, "Dalit Literature – Twenty Five Years of Protest? Or Progress?", *Journal of South Asian Literature,* Vol. 29, No. 2, (1994).

Zelliot, Eleanor, "Stri Dalita Sahitya" (The Literature of Dalit Women), *The Downtrodden India,* Vol. I, No. 1, (1994).

Zelliot, Eleanor, "The Dalit Movement", *Dalit International Newsletter,* Vol. 1, No. 1, (1996).

Zelliot, Eleanor, "The Roots of Dalit Consciousness", *Seminar,* No. 471, (November, 1998).

Zelliot, Eleanor, "History of Untouchables in Pune", *The Journal of the Asiatic Society of Bombay,* N.S. Vol. 74, (1999).

Zelliot, Eleanor, "New Books on Dalits", *Dalit International News Letter,* Vol. 4, No. 2, (June, 1999).

Zelliot, Eleanor, "Self Critical Honesty: The Writing of Urmilla Pawar", *Manushi,* No. 122, (2001).

Zelliot, Eleanor, "Immortalizing Babasaheb", *The Dalit,* (May-June 2002).

3

Reports of Various Commissions/Committees

Ambedkar Chair, Centre for Study in Social Systems, *Report of National Seminar on Implementation and Impact of Scheduled Castes/ Scheduled Tribes (Prevention of Atrocities) Act, 1989, on the Scheduled* Castes, (New Delhi: Jawaharlal Nehru University, 2000).

Bajaj, Jamnalal (Chairman), Indian National Congress; Anti-Untouchability Sub-Committee, *Report of the Work Done by the Anti-Untouchability Sub-Committee,* (April-December, 1929).

Bombay Presidency, Depressed Classes and Aboriginal Tribes Committee, *Report of the Depressed Classes and Aboriginal Tribes Committee,* (Chairman: O.H.B. Starte), (Bombay: Government Central Press, 1930).

Census of India, 1921, "The Depressed Classes of the Kumaun Hills", in Appendix C, Vol. XVI, *United Provinces of Agra and Oudh,* Part I, *Report,* (Allahabad: Superintendent of Government Press, 1923).

Census of India, 1931, "Ad-Dharmi", Section 4, Chapter XI, "Depressed Classes", Appendix III, Vol. XVII, *Punjab,* Part I, *Report,* (Lahore: Government Printing Press, 1933).

Census of India, 1931, "Depressed Classes", in Appendix II, Vol. XXI, *Cochin,* Part I, *Report,* (Ernakulum: Superintendent of Cochin Government Press, 1933).

Census of India, 1931, "Depressed Classes", in Chapter XII, Vol. XIV, *Madras*, Part I, *Report*, (Calcutta: Government of India, Central Publishing Branch, 1932).

Census of India, 1931, "Depressed Classes", in Chapter XII, Vol. XXV, *Mysore*, Part I, *Report*, (Bangalore: Government Press, 1932).

Census of India, 1931, "Exterior Castes", (By J.H. Hutton), Appendix I, in Vol. I, *India*, Part I, *Report*, (Delhi: Manager of Publications, 1933).

Census of India, 1931, "Notes on (i) Untouchables, (ii) Depressed Classes, and (iii) Backward Classes", in Appendix No. 2, Vol. XVIII, *United Provinces of Agra and Oudh*, Part I, *Report*, (Allahabad: Superintendent of Printing and Stationery, U.P., 1933).

Census of India, 1931, "The Depressed and Backward Classes of Assam", in Appendix to Chapter XII, Vol. III, *Assam*, Part I, *Report*, (Shillong: Superintendent of Assam Government Press, 1932).

Census of India, 1931, "The Depressed and Backward Classes", in Appendix II, Vol. XXVII, *Travancore*, Part I, *Report*, (Trivandrum: Superintendent of Government Press, 1932).

Census of India, 1931, "The Depressed Classes of the Central Provinces and Berar", in Appendix II of Vol. XII, *Central Provinces and Berar*, Part I, *Report*, (Nagpur: Government Printing, Central Provinces, 1933).

Census of India, 1931, "The Depressed Classes", in Appendix I, Vol. V, *Bengal and Sikkim*, Part I, *Report*, (Calcutta: Central Publishing Branch, 1933).

Census of India, 1931, "The Depressed Classes", in Appendix III, Vol. VII, *Bihar and Orissa*, Part I, *Report*, (Patna: Superintendent of Government Printing, 1933).

Census of India, 1931, "The Depressed Classes", in Appendix, III, Vol. XX, *Central India Agency*, Part I, *Report*, (Calcutta: Government of India, Central Publication Branch, 1933).

Census of India, 1931, "The Depressed Classes", in Section V of Vol. VIII, *Bombay Province,* Part I, *General Report,* (Bombay: Government Central Press, 1933).

Census of India, 1931, "The Depressed Classes", in Vol. XXIII, *The Nizam's Dominions (Hyderabad State),* Part I, *Report,* (Hyderabad: Government Central Press, 1933).

Census of India, 1951, *Papers, 1960, No. 2, Scheduled Castes and Scheduled Tribes,* (New Delhi: 1960).

Census of India, 1961, (U.B. Mathur), *Ethnographic Atlas of Rajasthan (With reference to Scheduled Castes and Scheduled Tribes),* Vol. 14, Part 9, (New Delhi: Manager of Publications, 1969).

Census of India, 1961, "Special Tables for Scheduled Castes and Scheduled Tribes", in Vol. XVIII, *Dodhra and Nagar Haveli,* Part V, (Dodhra and Nagar Haveli: Superintendent of Census Operations, 1967).

Census of India, 1961, "Tables on Scheduled Castes", Vol. XVI, *West Bengal and Sikkim,* Part V-A(i), (Delhi: Manager of Publications, 1966).

Census of India, 1961, *Consolidated Statement Showing Scheduled Castes, Scheduled Tribes: Denotified Communities and Other Communities of Similar Status in Different Statutes and Censuses Starting from 1921,* Vol. I, *India,* Parts V-B (ii) and (iii), (New Delhi: 1966).

Census of India, 1961, *Ethnographic Notes on Dom, Dombara, Paidi or Pano Ghasi, Chachati, Relli, Sapru and Matangi, Andhra Pradesh,* Vol. II, Part V-B (9), (Delhi: Manager of Publications, 1964).

Census of India, 1961, *Ethnographic Notes on Madiga, Jambuvulu, Jaggali, Arundhatiya, Chalavadi, Chamar, Mochi or Muchi, Samagara and Chambhar in Andhra Pradesh,* Vol. II, Part V-B (12), (Hyderabad: Office of the Director of Census Operations, 1967).

Census of India, 1961, *Ethnographic Notes on Mala Jangam, Andhra Pradesh,* Vol. 2, Part 5-B(10), (Delhi: Manager of Publication, 1964).

Census of India, 1961, *Mallah of Delhi*, Monograph Series, Part V-B (iv), (Delhi: Manager of Publications, 1969).

Census of India, 1961, *Report on Scheduled Castes and Scheduled Tribes: A Study of Gaddi Scheduled Tribe and Affiliated Castes*, (By William H. Nawell), Vol. XX, *Himachal Pradesh*, Part V-B, (Delhi: Manager of Publications, 1967).

Census of India, 1961, *Scheduled Castes – Tables*, Vol. XXV, *Pondicherry State*, Part III-C, (Madras and Pondicherry: Superintendent of Census Operations, 1964).

Census of India, 1961, *Scheduled Castes and Scheduled Tribes in Maharashtra – Tables*, Vol. X, *Maharashtra*, Part V-A, (Delhi: Manager of Publications, 1964).

Census of India, 1961, *Scheduled Castes and Tribes (Report and Tables)*, Vol. IX, *Madras*, Part V-A(i), (Madras: Superintendent of Census Operations, 1964).

Census of India, 1961, *Scheduled Castes and Tribes (Tables)*, Vol. IX, *Madras*, Part V-A(ii), (Madras: Superintendent of Census Operations, 1965).

Census of India, 1961, *Scheduled Tribes and Scheduled Castes: Reprints from Old Census Reports and Special Tables*, Vol. III, *Assam*, Part V-A, (Delhi: Manager of Publications, 1964).

Census of India, 1961, *Social Mobility Movements Among Scheduled Castes and Scheduled Tribes of India*, (Delhi: Manager of Publications, 1968).

Census of India, 1961, *Special Tables for Scheduled Castes and Scheduled Tribes*, Vol. II, *Andhra Pradesh*, Part V-A, (Delhi: Manager of Publications, 1964).

Census of India, 1961, *Special Tables for Scheduled Castes and Scheduled Tribes*, Vol. IV, *Bihar*, Part V-A, (Patna, Bihar: Superintendent of Census Operation, 1965).

Census of India, 1961, *Special Tables for Scheduled Castes and Scheduled Tribes*, Vol. VII, *Kerala*, Part V (A), (Delhi: Manager of Publications, 1967).

Census of India, 1961, *Special Tables for Scheduled Castes and Scheduled Tribes*, Vol. 8, *Madhya Pradesh*, Part V (A-1), (Delhi: Manager of Publications, 1965).

Census of India, 1961, *Special Tables for Scheduled Castes and Scheduled Tribes*, Vol. 9, *Madras*, Part V (A-1 and 2), (Delhi: Manager of Publications, 1965).

Census of India, 1961, *Special Tables for Scheduled Castes and Scheduled Tribes*, Vol. XIV, *Rajasthan*, Part V-A, (Superintendent of Census Operations, Rajasthan, 1965).

Census of India, 1961, *Special Tables for Scheduled Castes and Scheduled Tribes*, Vol. XXVI, *Tripura*, Part V-A, (Superintendent of Census Operations, Tripura, 1967).

Census of India, 1961, *Special Tables for Scheduled Castes*, Vol. I, *India*, Part V-A (i), (New Delhi: 1966).

Census of India, 1961, *Special Tables for Scheduled Castes*, Vol. VIII, *Madhya Pradesh*, Part V-A (i), (Superintendent of Census Operations, Madhya Pradesh, 1965).

Census of India, 1961, *Special Tables for Scheduled Castes*, Vol. XV, *Uttar Pradesh*, Part V-A(i) and (ii), (Delhi: Manager of Publications, 1965).

Census of India, 1961, *Special Tables of Scheduled Castes and Scheduled Tribes, (Including Reprints)*, Vol. XX, *Himachal Pradesh*, Part V-A, (Superintendent of Census Operations, Himachal Pradesh, 1965).

Census of India, 1961, *Special Tables on Scheduled Castes and Scheduled Tribes*, Vol. XI, *Mysore*, Part V-A, (Delhi: Manager of Publications, 1966).

Census of India, 1961, *Special Tables on Scheduled Castes and Scheduled Tribes*, Vol. XIII, *Punjab*, Part V-A, (Superintendent of Census Operations, Punjab, 1965).

Census of India, 1961, *Study of Customary Rights and Living and Working Conditions of Scavengers in Two Towns (Haryana and UP)*, Monograph Series, Vol. I, Part XI, D, (Delhi: Manager of Publications, 1966).

Census of India, 1961, *Study of Customary Rights and Living and Working Conditions of Scavengers*, Vol. I, Monograph Series, Part XI-D, (Delhi: Manager of Publications, 1969).

Census of India, 1961, *Tables on Scheduled Castes and Scheduled Tribes, Orissa*, Vol. 12, Part 5 (A), (Delhi: Manager of Publications, 1965).

Census of India, 1961, *Tables on Scheduled Castes and Scheduled Tribes*, Vol. XIX, Delhi, Part V-A, (Delhi: Superintendent of Census Operations, 1968).

Census of India, 1961, *Tables on Scheduled Castes and Scheduled Tribes*, Vol. V, *Gujarat*, Part V-A, (Delhi: Manager of Publications, 1964).

Census of India, 1961, *Tables on Scheduled Castes and Scheduled Tribes*, Vol. XXII, *Manipur*, Part V, (Manipur: Superintendent of Census of Operations, 1964).

Census of India, 1961, *Tables on Scheduled Castes and Scheduled Tribes*, Vol. XII, *Orissa*, Part V-A, (Delhi: Manager of Publications, 1965).

Census of India, 1961, *Vannan – A Scheduled Caste Community of Madras*, Vol. I, Monograph Series, Part V-B (iv), (Delhi: Manager of Publications, 1970).

Census of India, 1971, (A. Singh), "Social and Cultural Tables; Himachal Pradesh", in *Himachal Pradesh Series 7*, (Delhi: Manager of Publications, 1973).

Census of India, 1971, (K. Chokkalingam), *Ethnographic Notes: Scheduled Castes of Tamil Nadu*, Tamil Nadu, Series 19, Part v-B, (Delhi: Controller of Publication, 1976).

Census of India, 1971, (R.V. Pandya), *Special Tables on S.C. and S.T.*, Social Cultural Tables v, Series 10, Madhya Pradesh, Part II-C(i), (Delhi: Controller of Publications, 1975).

Census of India, 1971, *Scheduled Castes and Scheduled Tribes, (Table C VIII, Parts A & B)*, (Delhi: Government of India Press, 1975).

Census of India, 1981, *Gujarat, Tables on Scheduled Castes and Scheduled Tribes*, (New Delhi: 1944).

Census of India, 1981, *Primary Census Abstract of Scheduled Castes and Scheduled Tribes*, Paper 1, Series, 2, *Andhra Pradesh*, (Hyderabad: Director of Census Operations, 1982).

Census of India, 1981, *Special Tables for Scheduled Castes*, (New Delhi: 1988).

Cochin, State Government of, *Report of the Temple Entry Enquiry Committee, 1934*, (Trivandrum: Superintendent, Government Press, 1935).

Government of Assam, *Report of the Study Committee for Scheduled Castes*, (Assam, 1972).

Government of Bombay, *Report of the Depressed Classes and Aboriginal Tribes Committee*, (Bombay: 1950), (First Published in 1930).

Government of Bombay, *Report of the Committee (Tanneries and Leather Manufactory) Appointed by the Government of Bombay Under the Minimum Wages Act, 1948*, (Bombay: 1951).

Government of Bombay, *Report of the Scavenger's Living Conditions Enquiry Committee, State of Bombay*, (Bombay: 1952).

Government of Gujarat State, Directorate of Social Welfare, *Annual Administration Report on the Working of the Social Welfare Department*, (Ahmedabad: Government Printing, Publications and Stationery, 1963-64).

Government of Gujarat, *Social Welfare Schemes for the Socially and Educationally Backward Castes in Gujarat*, (Gandhinagar: 1998).

Government of Haryana State, Legislative Assembly, Committee on the Welfare of Scheduled Castes and Scheduled Tribes, *Report, Ist January*, (Chandigarh: Vidhan Sabha Secretariat, 1975).

Government of India, (Fifth Lok Sabha), *First Report on Action Taken by Government on the Recommendations for Scheduled Castes and Scheduled Tribes in India*, (New Delhi: Lok Sabha Secretariat, 1971–1973).

Government of India, (Fifth Lok Sabha), *Twentieth Report on Plan Allocations for Scheduled Castes and Scheduled Tribes in India*, (New Delhi: Lok Sabha Secretariat, 1973).

Government of India, *Brochure on Reservation for Scheduled Castes and Scheduled Tribes*, (Delhi: Government of India Press, 1978).

Government of India, Commissioner for Scheduled Castes and Scheduled Tribes, *Handbook on Scheduled Castes and Scheduled Tribes*, (Compiled by Vimal Chandra, Deputy Commissioner), (Delhi: 1968).

Government of India, Commissioner for Scheduled Castes and Scheduled Tribes, *Annual Report*, (Delhi: Manager of Publications, 1956). [First report was published in 1956 for the period 1950-55, supposed to be issued annually thereafter but very irregular].

Government of India, Committee on Plan Projects, *Report of the Study Team on Social Welfare and Welfare of Backward Classes* (Chairman: Renuka Ray), Vol. I, (Delhi: Manager of Publications, 1951).

Government of India, Committee on the Welfare of Scheduled Castes and Scheduled Tribes, *First Report on Reorganization of Offices*, (New Delhi: Lok Sabha Secretariat, 1969).

Government of India, Committee on the Welfare of Scheduled Castes and Scheduled Tribes, *Second Report on Reservations for Scheduled Castes and Scheduled Tribes in Public Undertakings*, (New Delhi: Lok Sabha Secretariat, 1969).

Government of India, Committee on the Welfare of Scheduled Castes and Scheduled Tribes, *Third Report on Post-Matric Scholarship Scheme for Scheduled Castes and Scheduled Tribes Students for Studies in India*, (New Delhi: Lok Sabha Secretariat, 1969).

Government of India, Committee on the Welfare of Scheduled Castes and Scheduled Tribes, *Fourth Report on Reservations for Scheduled Castes and Scheduled Tribes in Public Services*, (New Delhi: Lok Sabha Secretariat, 1970).

Government of India, Committee on the Welfare of Scheduled Castes and Scheduled Tribes, *Fifth Report on Employment for Scheduled Castes and Scheduled Tribes in Services*, (New Delhi: Lok Sabha Secretariat, 1970).

Government of India, Committee on the Welfare of Scheduled Castes and Scheduled Tribes, *Sixth Report on Action Taken by Government on the Recommendations contained in the First Report – On the Department of Social Welfare – Reorganization of the Office of the Commissioner for Scheduled Castes and Scheduled Tribes and Director General, Backward Class Welfare,* (New Delhi: Lok Sabha Secretariat, 1970).

Government of India, Committee on the Welfare of Scheduled Castes and Scheduled Tribes, *Seventh Report on Action Taken by Government on the Recommendations Contained in the Second Report – On the Ministry of Finance (Bureau of Public Enterprises) and Ministry of Home Affairs – Reservations for Scheduled Castes and Scheduled Tribes in Public Undertakings,* (New Delhi: Lok Sabha Secretariat, 1970).

Government of India, Committee on the Welfare of Scheduled Castes and Scheduled Tribes, *Eighth Report on Action Taken by Government on the Recommendations Contained in the Third Report – On the Department of Social Welfare – Post-Matric Scholarship Scheme for Scheduled Castes and Scheduled Tribes Students for Studies in India,* (New Delhi: Lok Sabha Secretariat, 1970).

Government of India, Committee on the Welfare of Scheduled Castes and Scheduled Tribes, *Ninth Report on Reservations for Scheduled Castes and Scheduled Tribes in Air India,* (New Delhi: Lok Sabha Secretariat, 1970).

Government of India, Committee on the Welfare of Scheduled Castes and Scheduled Tribes, *Tenth Report on Reservations for Scheduled Castes and Scheduled Tribes in Indian Airlines,* (New Delhi: Lok Sabha Secretariat, 1970).

Government of India, Committee on the Welfare of Scheduled Castes and Scheduled Tribes, *Eleventh Report on Action Taken by Government on the Recommendations contained in the Fifth Report – On the Ministry of Labour, Employment and Rehabilitation (Department of Labour and Employment) Directorate General of Employment and Training – Employment of Scheduled Castes and Scheduled Tribes in Service,* (New Delhi: Lok Sabha Secretariat, 1970).

Government of India, Committee on the Welfare of Scheduled Castes and Scheduled Tribes, *Twelfth Report on Reservation for Scheduled Castes and Scheduled Tribes in Gauhati Oil Refinery*, (New Delhi: Lok Sabha Secretariat, 1970).

Government of India, Committee on the Welfare of Scheduled Castes and Scheduled Tribes, *Thirteenth Report on Reservations for Scheduled Castes and Scheduled Tribes in Heavy Engineering Corporation Limited*, (New Delhi: Lok Sabha Secretariat, 1970).

Government of India, Committee on the Welfare of Scheduled Castes and Scheduled Tribes, *Fourteenth Report on Admission Facilities for Scheduled Castes and Scheduled Tribes in Educational Institutions, Technical and Non-Technical*, (New Delhi: Lok Sabha Secretariat, 1970).

Government of India, Committee on the Welfare of Scheduled Castes and Scheduled Tribes, *Fifteenth Report on Reservation for Scheduled Castes and Scheduled Tribes*, (New Delhi: Lok Sabha Secretariat, 1970).

Government of India, Committee on the Welfare of Scheduled Castes and Scheduled Tribes, *Sixteenth Report on Housing Facilities for Scheduled Castes and Scheduled Tribes Students*, (New Delhi: Lok Sabha Secretariat, 1970).

Government of India, Committee on the Welfare of Scheduled Castes and Scheduled Tribes, *Seventeenth Report on Hotel Facilities for Scheduled Castes and Scheduled Tribes Students*, (New Delhi: Lok Sabha Secretariat, 1970).

Government of India, Committee on the Welfare of Scheduled Castes and Scheduled Tribes, Eighteenth Report on Action Taken by Government on the Recommendations contained in the Fourth Report – On the Ministry of Home Affairs and Department of Social Welfare – Reservations *for Scheduled Castes and Scheduled Tribes in Public Services*, (New Delhi: Lok Sabha Secretariat, 1970).

Government of India, Committee on the Welfare of Scheduled Castes and Scheduled Tribes, *Nineteenth Report on Complaints/Representations received by the Committee on the Welfare of Scheduled Castes and Scheduled Tribes*, (New Delhi: Lok Sabha Secretariat, 1970).

Government of India, Department of Personal, *Brochure on Reservation for Scheduled Castes and Scheduled Tribes in Services*, (Delhi: Manager of Publications, 1972), (3rd edition).

Government of India, Department of Social Security, *The Report of the Advisory Committee on the Revision of Lists of Scheduled Castes and Scheduled Tribes* (Chairman: B.N. Lokur), Delhi: 1965).

Government of India, Department of Social Welfare, *Report of Committee on Untouchability, Economic and Educational Development of Scheduled Castes and Connected Documents*, (Delhi: Manager of Publications, 1969).

Government of India, Department of Social Welfare, *Report of the Committee on Untouchability, Economic and Educational Development of the Scheduled Castes*, (The Elayaperumal Report), (1969).

Government of India, Department of Social Welfare, *Report of the Committee on Customary Rights to Scavenging*, (Chairman: N.R. Malkani), (Faridabad: (Government of India Press, 1966)

Government of India, *Enquiry Committee on Scavenging Conditions, 1960, Report*, (Delhi: Manager of Publication, 1960).

Government of India, Harijan Welfare Board, *Rehabilitation of Displaced Harijans: Nine Year's Report, 1948-57*, (Delhi: n.d.).

Government of India, House of the People Parliament (Fifth Lok Sabha), Committee on the Welfare of Scheduled Castes and Scheduled Tribes, *Reports 1–14, 16–38, 40–51*, (New Delhi: Lok Sabha Secretariat, 1971-76).

Government of India, House of the People Parliament (Fourth Lok Sabha), Committee on the Welfare of Scheduled Castes and Scheduled Tribes, *Reports 1–19*, (New Delhi: Lok Sabha Secretariat, 1969-70).

Government of India, Ministry of Community Development and Cooperation, *Report of the Study Group on the Welfare of the Weaker Sections of the Village Community* (Chairman: Jayaprakash Narayan), (Delhi: Manager, Government of India Press, 1961).

Government of India, Ministry of Education and Scientific Research, *Progress of Scholarships for Scheduled Castes and Scheduled Tribes and Other Backward Classes*, (Delhi: Manager, Government of India Press, 1957), (4th edition).

Government of India, Ministry of Education and Social Welfare, *Education in India, 1951-52*, (Delhi: Manager of Publications, 1955).

Government of India, Ministry of Education and Social Welfare, *Education in India, 1961-62*, (Delhi: Manager of Publications, 1968).

Government of India, Ministry of Education and Social Welfare, *Report, 1972-73*, (Delhi: Manager of Publications, 1973).

Government of India, Ministry of Home Affairs, *Brochure on Reservations for Scheduled Castes and Scheduled Tribes in Services*, (Delhi: Manager of Publications, 1972), (Third edition).

Government of India, Ministry of Home Affairs, *Report of the Scavenging Conditions Enquiry Committee*, (New Delhi: Manager of Publications, 1960), (Chairman: N.R. Malkani).

Government of India, Ministry of Home Affairs, *Report of the Working Group to Study the Progress of Measures for Land Allotment to Scheduled Castes and their Representation in Services*, (Delhi: Manager, Government of India Press, 1968).

Government of India, Ministry of Home Affairs, *Report on the Working Group to Study the Progress of Measures for Land Allotment to Scheduled Castes and Their Representations in Services*, (Delhi: Manager of Publications, 1968).

Government of India, Ministry of Information and Broadcasting, *Harijans Today*, (Delhi: Director, Publications Division, 1952).

Government of India, Ministry of Social Welfare, *Report of the Study Group Appointed during the VII Five Year Plan to Look into the Progress of the SCs and STs*, (New Delhi: Ministry of Social Welfare, 1990).

Government of India, Ministry of Welfare, *Report of the National Scheme of Liberation and Rehabilitation of Scavengers and Their Dependents*, (New Delhi: 1991-92).

Government of India, National Commission on Labour, (Chairman: P.B. Gajendragadkar), *Report of the Committee on to Study the Working and Service Conditions of Sweepers and Scavengers*, (Delhi: Manager of Publications, 1969).

Government of India, National Commission on Labour, *Report of the Committee to Study the Working and Service Conditions of Sweepers and Scavengers*, (Delhi: Manager of Publications, 1969), (Chairman: P.B. Gajendragadkar).

Government of India, Planning Commission, *Report of the Seminar on Employment of Scheduled Castes and Scheduled Tribes*, (Delhi: Manager, Government of India Press, 1963).

Government of India, Planning Commission, *Social Welfare in India*, (Delhi: Publications Division, Ministry of Information and Broadcasting, 1960), (Forwarded by Jawaharlal Nehru, revised and abridged edition).

Government of India, Planning Commission, Programme Evaluation Division, *Study of Post-Matric Scholarship Scheme for Scheduled Castes and Scheduled Tribes: Report Survey (July-August 1980)*, (New Delhi: Planning Commission, 1982).

Government of India, Police Research and Development Bureau, *The Problem of Atrocities on Harijans in Bihar: A Sample Survey in the District of Rohtas, Bhogpur and Begusavai*, (New Delhi: The Bureau, 1979).

Government of India, *Report of the Seminar on Employment of Scheduled Castes and Scheduled Tribes*, (Delhi: The Manager, Government of India Press, 1963).

Government of India, Scavenging Conditions Enquiry Committee, *Report of the Scavenging Conditions Enquiry Committee*, (New Delhi: Central Advisory Board for Harijan Welfare, Ministry of Home Affairs, 1961).

Government of India, Scheduled Castes and Scheduled Tribes Commission, *Report on the Atrocities on Scheduled Castes and Scheduled Tribes: Causes and Remedies*, (New Delhi: Government Press, 1990).

Government of Karnataka, *Report of the Committee on Improvement of Living and Working Conditions of Sweepers and Scavengers*, (Bangalore: 1976).

Government of Karnataka, *The Third Report of the Legislature Committee (Armugam Committee) Reservations for the Scheduled Castes and Scheduled Tribes in the Universities of Karnataka*, (Bangalore: Legislature Secretariat, (1980).

Government of Kerala State, Commission for Reservation of Seats in Educational Institutions, (Chairman: G. Kumara Pillai), *Report*, (Trivandrum: Printed at the Government Press, 1966),

Government of Kerala State, Harijan Welfare Department, *Administrative Report*, 1956–57 to 1963–64; 1967–68 to 1971–72, (Ernakulam: Printed at the Government Press, n.d.).

Government of Kerala State, Harijan Welfare Department, *First Supplement to the Hand Book of the Department of Harijan Welfare: Departments Rules and Standing Orders as on 30th September 1965*, (Shoranur: Government Press, 1967).

Government of Kerala State, Legislative Assembly, Committee on the Welfare of Scheduled Castes and Scheduled Tribes, *Second Report on the Representation of Scheduled Castes and Scheduled Tribes in the Services of Various Departments under the Government of Kerala*, (Trivadandrum: Secretariat of the Kerala Legislature, 1974).

Government of Kerala State, Revenue Department, *A Handbook of the Department of Harijan Welfare (as on 31*

August 1962), (Trivandrum: The Government Press, 1964).

Government of Madras State, *Report of the Harijan Welfare in Madras State*, (Madras: 1948).

Government of Madras, *Harijan Welfare in Madras State*, (Madras: Director of Information and Publicity, 1952).

Government of Maharashtra State, Social Welfare Department, *Annual Administration Report of Scheduled Areas in Maharashtra State*, (Bombay: Director, Government Printing, Publications and Stationery, 1962), [Annually from 1960-61 onwards].

Government of Maharashtra, *Report of the Scavengers' Living Conditions Enquiry Committee*, (Bombay: 1958).

Government of Mysore State, Commissioner for Depressed Classes, *Summary Record and Main Recommendations of the Mysore State Depressed Class Seminar Held at Kengeri, February 11th to 14th, 1956*, (Mysore: Deputy Director, Government Branch Press, 1957).

Government of Mysore State, General Administrative Department, *Scheduled Castes and Scheduled Tribes Appointments Committee Report*, (Coorg: Manager, Government Branch Press, 1962).

Government of Mysore State, Legislature, Committee on the Welfare of Scheduled Castes and Scheduled Tribes, *First Report: Education of Scheduled Castes and Scheduled Tribes*, (Bangalore: Mysore Legislature Secretariat, 1973).

Government of Mysore State, Planning, Housing and Social Welfare Department, *The Welfare of Scheduled Castes in Mysore State*, (Bangalore: The Government Press, 1962).

Government of Mysore State, Social Welfare Department, *Detailed Administration Report, 1958-59*, (Bangalore: The Government Press, 1961).

Government of Punjab State, Welfare Department, *Report of the Evaluation Committee on Welfare Regarding the Welfare of Scheduled Castes, Backward Classes and Denotified Tribes in Punjab State for the Period Commencing from 15 August*

1947 (December 1965–August 1966), (Chandigarh: Controller of Printing and Stationery, 1966).

Government of Tamil Nadu State, Harijan Welfare Department, *Administrative Report*, (Madras: Government Press, n.d.), [Annually from 1955-56 onwards].

Harijan Sevak Sangh, *Report of the Committee Appointed by the Cawnpore Harijan Sevak Sangh in May 1933 to make a Survey of the Social and Religious Disabilities, Working Conditions and the Standard of Life of the Harijans of Cawnpore*, (Cawnpore: Harijan Sevak Sangh, Cawnpore Branch, 1934).

Indian Franchise Committee, 1932, Report of the Indian Franchise Committee, 1932, (Chairman: Marquess of Lothian), 5 vols., (London: H.M.S.O., 1932). Vol. I: *Report*, Cmd. 4086. [This includes Dr. B.R. Ambedkar's note on the Depressed Classes and a Chapter on the Depressed Classes]. Vols. IV and V: *Selections from Memoranda Submitted by Individuals and Oral Evidence*, [This contains testimony of various Depressed Class groups].

Indian National Congress, Anti-Untouchability Sub-Committee, *Report of the Work Done by the Anti-Untouchability Sub-Committee, April-December 1929*, (Secretary: Jamnalal Bajaj), Reported in the Indian Annual Register, Part II, (1929). [Pamphlet].

Indian Statutory Commission (1928), *Report of the Indian Statutory Commission* (Chairman: Lord Simon), 17 vols., (London: H.M.S.O., 1929-30), Vol. I: *Survey*, Cmd. 3568, [includes report on Depressed Classes]. Vol. III: *Reports of the Committees Appointed by the Provincial Legislative Councils to Cooperate with the Indian Statutory Commission*, Cmd. 3572. [Includes the report of Dr. B.R. Ambedkar as adjunct to Bombay Report]. Vols. XVI, XVII: *Selections from Memoranda and Oral Evidence by Non-Officials*. [Includes testimony from twenty Depressed Class groups / individuals.

Karnataka University, *Educational Problems of Scheduled Castes in Dharwar and Neighbouring Villages*, (Dharwar: Karnataka University, n.d.), (mimeograph).

Malkani, N.R., *Report of the Scavenging Conditions Enquiry Committee*, (Delhi: Ministry of Home Affairs, Central Advisory Board for Harijan Welfare, Government of India, 1961).

Maurya, R.L., *A Study of the Impact of the Planned Process on the Life of the Scheduled Castes of Kumaon*, (Kumaon: Kumaon University, 1986), [Unpublished Report].

Mysore Government, *Report of the Committee on Scheduled Caste and Scheduled Tribes*, (Mysore: 1962).

Mysore State, Government of, *Scheduled Castes and Scheduled Tribes Appointment Committee Report*, (Mercara: General Administration Department, 1962).

Mysore State, Government of, Scheduled Castes and Scheduled Tribes Appointments Committee, 1960, *Report*, (Chairman: B. Birappa), (Bangalore: General Administration Department, 1962).

Official Report, *Ad Dharm Mandal, 1926–1931*, (Jullundur: Kisan Steam Press, 1931).

Pandya, B.P., *Committee on Conditions of Sweepers and Scavengers*, ((New Delhi: National Commission on Labour, 1969).

Proceedings of the Federal Structure Committee and Minorities Committee, (London: H.M.S.O., 1932).

Punjab State, Government of, Evaluation Committee on Welfare, *Report: Regarding the Welfare of Scheduled Castes, Backward Classes and Denotified Tribes in Punjab State* (Chairman: Brish Bhan), (for the period commencing from 15 August, 1947, (Chandigarh: 1966).

Rajagopalan, C., *Social Mobility Among the Scheduled Castes*, (Unpublished Report of a Research Project), (Bangalore: Department of Sociology, Bangalore University, 1978).

Report on the Reservation of Teaching Posts for Scheduled Castes and Tribes, (Delhi: Delhi University, 1979), (Chairman: M.V. Mathur).

Report of "Seminar on Casteism and the Removal of Untouchability", Delhi, 26 September – 2 October 1955, (Bombay: Indian Conference of Social Work, 1955).

Report of the Committee Appointed to Inquire into the Educational, Economic and Social Conditions of the Depressed Classes (Untouchables) and the Aboriginal Tribes in the Bombay Presidency, (London: 1930), (Chairman: O.H.B Starte).

Report of the Depressed Class Conference, (Nagpur: G.T. Meshram, 1942).[Formation meeting of the Scheduled Castes Federation].

Report of the Depressed Class Conferences, Nagpur Sessions, (Nagpur: G.T. Meshram, 1942).

Report, Education Commission Report, *Facilities to Scheduled Castes and Scheduled Tribes in Universities and Colleges,* (New Delhi: University Grants Commission, 1982).

Report, Progress of Education of Scheduled Castes and Scheduled Tribes, 1964-65 – 1977-78, (New Delhi: Ministry of Education and Culture, Government of India, 1980).

Roy Burman, B.K., *Report on the Practice of Untouchability and Other Social Disability in West Bengal,* (Calcutta: Cultural Research Institute, 1957), [Booklet].

Slappa, I.P.D., *Committee on Improvement of Living and Working Conditions of Sweepers and Scavengers,* (Bangalore: Government of Karnataka, 1976).

Starte, O.H.B., (Chairman), *Bombay (Presidency) Depressed Classes and Aboriginal Tribes Committee Report,* (Bombay, 1930).

Statutory Commission, 1929, *Review of growth of Education in British India: Auxiliary Committee of India Statutory Commission,* (London: H.M.S.O., CMB 3407, 1930), (Chairman: Sir Phillip Hartog), [Chapter X deals with the Education of the Depressed Classes].

Temple Entry Enquiry Committee, *Report of the Committee,* 1934, (Trivandrum: Superintendent of Government Press, 1935).

The Reforms Committee (Franchise, 1918), *Evidence Taken Before the Reforms Committee* (Chairman: Lord Southborough), 2 vols., (Calcutta: Government of India, 1919). [The earliest record of Depressed Classes representations on the idea of separate electorates].

Upadhyaya, Arun Kumar, *Scheduled Caste Leaders in a Rural Setting in Eastern U.P.*, (Un published Project Report), (Meerut: Meerut University, 1992).

Weekly Round Table, "Special Report on Treatment on Harijans", (September 30, 1973).

4

Journals/Magazines/Periodicals

Adi Danka [Newspaper of the Ad Dharm Mandal, an Association of Untouchables of Punjab].

Ambedkar Journal of Social Development and Justice is an annual Journal Published every March by Dr. Babasaheb Ambedkar National Institute of Social Sciences, Mhow, (Madhya Pradesh).

Atrocities on Dalit, Centre for Rural Studies, Lal Bahadur Shastri National Academy of Administration, Mussourie, (U.P).

Bheem Patrika, [Ambedkar Weekly Periodical, edited by L.R. Balley, Jullundhur, in Punjabi. It's English version/ edition, edited by Bhagwan Das, Jullundur].

The Dalit: exploring alternatives expanding possibilities, (Published by Dalit Media Network, Chennai, Editor: Meena Kandasamy).

Dalit Bandhu [Depressed classes mouthpiece in Poona, 1930]

Dalit International Newsletter, P.O. Box 932, Waterford, CT 06385, USA, [Editor John C.B. Webster].

Dalit Solidarity, (Quarterly Bulletin of Jan Utthan Pratisthan; Executive Editors: Bronwyn Hudson and Kamla Bishwakarma).

Dalit Voice, Fortnightly Magazine, C/o. Dalit Sahitya Akademy, Bangalore.

Depressed Class Awakenings, Appeared from Lucknow, [Newspaper, no further issues known except the issue dated June 24, 1936].

The Downtrodden India, Journal of Dalit and Bahujan Studies, [Ed. Kashinath Ranveer].

Ezhuchi Dalit Murasu (Tamil), (Chennai, Editor: Punitha Pandian).

Ham Dalit (Hindi), Quarterly Journal from Indian Social Institute, New Delhi.

Harijan was edited successively by Mahadev Desai, Pyarelal Nayyar and K.G. Mashruwala was published in Poona or Madras from 1933 to 1941, then in Ahmedabad by Navajivan. [Many views and ideas of M.K. Gandhi were published earlier in this periodical, some of them later published in the form of books or pamphlets].

Mulnivasi Times: Voice of Liberation of Indigenous People and their Motherland from Aryan Invaders, (Monthly magazine, Editor: Waman Meshram, Delhi).

Ravidas Patrika, (Weekly Newspaper of the new Ad Dharm Movement, edited by Chanan Lal 'Manik'; Proprietor: Mangu Ram 'Jaspal'; from Jullundur, Punjab).

Social Justice, (Fortnightly Newsletter of the Ambedkar Foundation, New Delhi, Editor in Chief: Dr. Bindeshwar Pathak).

Thai Mann, (Tamil), Monthly Journal of Dalit Panthers of India – Viduthalai Chiruthaigal, (Chennai, Editor: Thirumavalvan)

Thamukku, [Bi-monthly Newsletter of the Dalit Resource Centre, Madurai, Editor: V. Abraham Ponnudurai].

Valmik Sundesh, (Monthly journal of the Punjab Valmik Sabha, edited by Nahal Chand Chetta; from Amritsar).

Voice of Dalits, (The Newsletter of Dalit NGO Federation, Nepal), (Editor: Tej Sunar).

Young India was edited by M.K. Gandhi from 1919-1932, and others during his absence and published by Navajivan of Ahmedabad. [Many views and ideas of M.K. Gandhi were published earlier in this periodical, some of them later published in the forms of books or pamphlets].

5

Unpublished Dissertations/ Theses

Abbasayalu, Y.B., **A Study of Scheduled Caste Elite in Andhra Pradesh**, Ph. D. Thesis, (Osmania University, 1977).

Agrawal, Kamlesh, **Social Mobility among Chamar and Bhangis in Shergarhi**, M. Phil. Dissertation, (Meerut University, 1987).

Ahmad, N., **Educational Opportunities and Socio-Economic Changes among the Muslim Backward Classes, Non-Muslim Backward Classes and Scheduled Castes of Faizabad District During the Post-Independence Period: A Comparative Study**, Ph.D. Thesis, (Aligarh Muslim University, 1980).

Alexander, K.C., **A Study of the Changing Pattern of Behaviour of the Pulaya Untouchables of Kerala**, Ph.D. Thesis, (University of Poona, 1966).

Arjunan, P., **Temple Entry Movement in Tamil Nadu, 1924-47**, M. Phil. Dissertation, (University of M dras, 1979).

Arya, Subedar Singh, **Politics in Scheduled Caste Constituency: A Study of Legislative Assembly Elections in Jalesar, U.P. 1962-85**, M. Phil. Dissertation, (Jawaharlal Nehru University, 1987).

Bagat, M.G., **The Untouchables Classes of Maharashtra,** M.A. Dissertation, (Bombay University, 1935).

Behari, Kamila Bana, **An Evaluative Study of Harijan and Tribal Welfare Department High Schools in Orissa in Respect of Student Achievement,** Ph.D. Dissertation, (Visva Bharti University, 1985).

Behere, Suman, **The Process of Urbanization and Status Equilibration among Neo-Buddhists in Bombay,** Ph.D. Thesis, (Poona University, 1975).

Bharill, Chandra, **Social and Political Ideas and Contribution of Ambedkar,** Ph.D. Dissertation, (University of Rajasthan, 1969).

Bhaskaramma, K., **Political Participation of Scheduled Castes: A Case Study of Khammam District in Andhra Pradesh,** M. Phil. Dissertation, (Jawaharlal Nehru University, 1980).

Bhatt, Bharat L., **The Scheduled Castes and Tribes of India: A Geographical Analysis,** Dissertation, (Syracuse University, 1972).

Bhatt, G.S., **The Chamars of Lucknow,** M.A. Dissertation, (University of Lucknow, 1952).

Chand, Krishan, **Regional Disparities in the Levels of Educational Development among Scheduled Castes of Northwestern India,** M. Phil. Dissertation, (Jawaharlal Nehru University, 1984).

Chandrasekaran, Lalita, **Social Mobility of the Scheduled Castes of Karnataka: A Case Study of the Madiga,** Ph.D. Thesis, (Jawaharlal Nehru University, 1989).

Chaudhary, Vandana, **Social Mobility Among the Scheduled Castes in Harodui,** M. Phil. Dissertation, (Meerut University, 1987).

Chauhan, Anita, **Scheduled Castes and their Leadership in a Western Uttar Pradesh Village,** (in Hindi), M. Phil. Dissertation, (Meerut University, 1992).

Chinna Rao, Yagati, **Dalit Movement in Andhra: 1900–1950,** Doctoral Dissertation, (Jawaharlal Nehru University, 1999).

Chinnaiah, Jangam, **Dalit Intellectual Discourse in Modern Andhra: A Study of Gurram Jashua (1895-1971),** M. Phil. Dissertation, (Jawaharlal Nehru University, 1997).

Cohn, Bernard S., **The Chamars of Senapur: A Study of the Changing Status of a Depressed Caste,** Doctoral Dissertation, (Cornell University, 1954).

Darokar, Sailesh Kumar, **Dr. Ambedkar's Thought on New Social Order in India,** M. Phil. Dissertation, (Jawaharlal Nehru University, 1998).

Das, Surendra Prasad, **Electoral Participation of Scheduled Castes: A Study of Nayakhandi Gram Panchayat 1984 Election, Orissa,** M. Phil. Dissertation, (Jawaharlal Nehru University, 1986).

Dolbeer, Martin Luther, **The Movement for Emancipation of Untouchable Classes in South India,** M.A. Thesis, (University of Chicago, 1929).

Dube, Saurabh, **Social History of Satnamis of Chhattisgarh,** M. Phil. Dissertation, (University of Delhi, 1988).

Dube, Saurabh, **Religion, Identity: An Authority among the Satnamis in Colonial Central India,** Ph.D. Thesis, (University of Cambridge, 1992).

Dube, S.N., **Reaction of Frustration as a Function of Personality Factors and Need Patterns of Scheduled Caste Adolescents and Young Adults,** Ph.D. Thesis, (Jodhpur University, 1982).

Dushkin, Lelah, **The Policy of the Indian National Congress Toward the Depressed Classes – An Historical Study,** M.A. Thesis, (University of Pennsylvania, 1957).

Dutta, D.N., **Social Structure of Scheduled Caste – Kaivartas Living in Dinjyostra,** Dissertation, (Dibrugarh University, 1970).

Fiske, Adele M. **The Use of Buddhist Scriptures in Dr. B.R. Ambedkar's 'The Buddha and His Dhamma',** M.A. Thesis, (Columbia University, 1966).

Ganguly, N., **Namasudras,** M. Sc. Dissertation, (University of Calcutta, 1944).

Gawarguru, G.N., **The Party Politics in Reserved Constituencies: A Case Study of Pandharpur Parliamentary Reserved Constituency for the Scheduled Castes in Maharashtra**, Ph.D. Thesis, (Jawaharlal Nehru University, 1985).

Ghosh, S.K., **Study the Position of Employment of Scheduled Castes and Scheduled Tribes on Teaching Post of Secondary Schools in 24-Parganas (South) Districts**, Dissertation, (National Institute of Educational Planning and Administration, 1989).

Gokhale-Turner, Jayashree, **From Concessions to Confrontation–The Politics of the Mahar Community in Maharashtra**, Ph.D. Thesis, (McGill University, 1980).

Goyal, Prem Prakash, **An Inquiry into the Impact of Urbanism on the Magico-Religious Beliefs and Practices of Raidas Chamars of Dehra Dun**, M.A. Thesis, (D.A.V. College, Dehra Dun, 1961).

Gupta, Laxman Prakash, **A Study of the Personal Characteristics and Academic Achievement of Scheduled Caste and Backward Class Students of Meerut University**, Ph.D. Dissertation, (Meerut University, 1978).

Guru, Gopal, **SC Politics in the Reserved Constituencies: Assembly Segment in Maharashtra**, M. Phil. Dissertation, (Jawaharlal Nehru University, 1980).

Houska, W., **Religious Belief and Practice in an Urban Scheduled Caste Community**, Doctoral Dissertation, (Syracuse University, 1981).

Jadhav, R.K., **Scheduled Caste in Maharashtra: A Study in their Socio-Economic Disabilities**, (Shivaji University, Kolhapur, 1980).

Jain, N.P., **Culture Status and Personality Factors as Correlates of Parenting (fathering) in High, Backward and Scheduled Caste People of Mainpuri District (Uttar Pradesh)**, Ph.D. Dissertation, (Meerut University, 1984).

Japhet, S., **Christian Dalits: A Sociological Study of Post-Conversion Experience**, M. Phil. Thesis, (Bangalore University 1987).

Jhali, Naresh Kumar, **A Study of the Life and Work of the Great Peaceful Revolutionary of Modern Times and Father of the Indian Constitution Dr. B.R. Ambedar,** B.A. (Hons) Dissertation, (Coventry University, 1994).

Jogdand, P.G., **From Discrimination to Movement: A Study of Dalit Movement in Maharashtra,** M. Phil. Dissertation, Jawaharlal Nehru University, 1981).

Joshi, Shriniwas D., **Educational Problems of the Scheduled Castes and Scheduled Tribes of Baroda District,** Ph.D. Dissertation, (Maharaja Sayajirao University of Baroda, 1979).

Juergensmeyer, Mark, **Political Hope: The Social Movements of North India's Untouchables, 1900–1970,** Ph.D. Dissertation, (University of California, Berkeley, 1974).

Kakade, Suresh, **The Study of Integration of Scheduled Castes in Indian Society: A Case Study in Marathwada,** (Poona University, 1979).

Kananaikil, Jose, **The Experience of Scheduled Castes,** Ph.D. Thesis, (University of Chicago, 1981).

Kantha Mani, Narla, **Self-esteem and the Extent of Modernisation Among Harijan Women in Two Urban Slum Areas of Tirupati,** M. Sc. Thesis, (Sri Venkateswara University, 1952).

Kapoor, Anju Sood, **Education, Social Mobility and Social Change: A Comparative Study of the American Blacks and Scheduled Castes,** M. Phil. Dissertation, (Jawaharlal Nehru University, 1985).

Konchole, D.D., **Mang Community in Transition,** (Marathwada University, 1975).

Kuber, Waman Narayan, **Critical Study of the Social and Political Thought of Ambedkar,** Ph.D. Dissertation, (Poona University, 1968).

Kumar, Anoop, **Rural Development Programmes and Scheduled Castes in Kishtwar,** Ph.D. Thesis, (Chaudhary Charan Singh University, Meerut, 1995).

Kumar, Narender, **Political Participation of Scheduled Castes: A Case Study of Three Gram Panchayat Elections, 1994**

in Haryana, M. Phil. Dissertation, (Jawaharlal Nehru University, 1996).

Kumar, Narender, **Policy Formulation in Parliament for Dalits: Analysis of Lok Sabha Debates and Questions During 1985-95**, Ph. D. Thesis, (Jawaharlal Nehru University, 2001).

Kumar, Rabindra, **Differential Impact of Development on Scheduled Castes: A Study of Rural Central Bihar**, Ph. D. Thesis, (Jawaharlal Nehru University, 2000).

Kumar, Tila, **Dalit Protest Movement: A Study in Hegemony Equality and Identity**, M. Phil. Dissertation, (Jawaharlal Nehru University, 2000).

Kumar, Vivek, **Nature and Crises of Dalit Leadership in India: A Macro Sociological Analysis**, M. Phil. Dissertation, (Jawaharlal Nehru University, 1994).

Kumar, Vivek, **Nature and Dynamics of Dalit Leadership in Northern India: A Sociological Study of Selected Regions of Uttar Pradesh**, Ph.D. Thesis, (Jawaharlal Nehru University, 2000).

Lal, L., **A Study of Adjustment Problems of Scheduled Caste Students in Schools of Haryana with Reference to Some Personality Variables"**, Ph. D. Dissertation, (University of Delhi, 1985).

Lal, Shyam, **The Bhangi: A Sweeper Caste and its Socio-economic Portraits (With Special reference to Jodhpur City)**, Ph.D. Thesis, (University of Rajasthan, 1978).

Lavanya, K., **Scheduled Castes in Medical Profession: A Sociological Study**, Ph.D. Thesis, (Jawaharlal Nehru University, 1997).

Lynch, Owen, **The Politics of Untouchability: Social Structure and Social Change in a City of India**, Ph.D. Thesis, (Columbia University, 1966).

Mahapatra, L.K., **A Hill Byuiyan Village: An Empirical Socio-Economic Study**, Doctoral Dissertation, (Humburg University, 1959-60), [The Byuiyas or Bhuyans are categorized as Scheduled Castes in Bihar, Uttar Pradesh and West Bengal, but in Orissa they are categorized as Scheduled Tribes].

Malik, Suneila, **Social Consequences of Social Mobility Among Scheduled Castes**, Ph.D. Dissertation, (Punjab University, Chandigarh, 1971).

Mehta, C.P., **An Investigation into the Effect of Some Psychological Factors on School Achievement of Scheduled Caste and Scheduled Tribe Students and the Students as Identified by the Baxi Commission in Saurashtra**, Ph.D. Dissertation, (Sardar Patel University, 1987).

Mehta, B.H., **The Social and Economic Conditions of the Meghwal Untouchables in Bombay City**, Ph.D. Dissertation, (University of Bombay, 1937).

Merchant, R.D., **Leather Industry in India**, Ph.D. Thesis, (University of Bombay, 1950).

Mishra, Keshav Narayan, **Gandhian Approach to the Question of Dalit in the Context of Gandhi-Ambedkar Debate**, M. Phil. Dissertation, (Jawaharlal Nehru University, 1998).

Mitra, G.R., **Education among the Backward Classes in Howrah District, West Bengal**, Ph.D. Dissertation, (Calcutta University, 1981).

Moffatt, Michael, **Untouchables in a Region of South India**, M.A. Thesis, (University of Chicago, 1969).

Mohanty, R.K., **Factors affecting Social Mobility among Scheduled Castes: Survey of Literature Published from 1972-1984**, M. Phil. Dissertation, (Institute of Advanced Studies, Meerut, 1985).

Mohapatra, Samir Kumar, **Ambedkarism and Contemporary Indian Sociology: An Analysis**, M. Phil. Dissertation, (Jawaharlal Nehru University, 1999).

Moses Samuel, Injeti, **A Study of Physical Growth and Development of Valmiki and Bagatha Boys of Visakhapatnam District**, Ph. D. Thesis, (Andhra University, 1980).

Mukherjee, B.M., **A Comparative Study of Scheduled Castes of Bihar**, M.A. Dissertation, (University of Patna,)

Murugkar, Lata, **Dalit Panther Movement of Maharashtra: A Sociological Appraisal**, Ph.D. Thesis, (University of Bombay, 1987).

Nagaraju, C.S., **A Study of a Few Social Factors affecting Scholastic achievement of Scheduled Caste Students Studying in Secondary Schools of Karnataka**, Ph.D. Thesis, (Banaras Hindu University, 1977).

Naik, D. Ramalu, **M V Bhagya Reddi Varma's Life and Mission: A Study**, M Phil. Dissertation, (Osmania University, 1992).

Nanda, Bimal Chandra, **Social Exclusion, Education and Social Movements: A Study of Dalit and Backward Class Movements in Maharashtra**, M. Phil. Dissertation, (Jawaharlal Nehru University, 2000).

Pal, R., **A Comparative Study of Personality Patterns of Scheduled Caste and High Caste Students in the State of Haryana**, Ph.D. Thesis, (Kurukshetra University, 1984).

Panda, Minati, **Perceived Equality in Education, Employment Prospects and Self-Esteem: A Case Study of SC, ST and General Category College Students of Orissa**, M. Phil. Dissertation, (Jawaharlal Nehru University, 1990).

Pandey, P.N., **Education and Social Mobility Among Scheduled Castes**, Ph.D. Thesis, (Banaras Hindu University, 1978).

Pasayat, Chitrasen, **Purity and Pollution in Indian Society: A Sociological Analysis**, M. Phil. Dissertation, (Jawaharlal Nehru University, 1986).

Paswan, Birendra Kumar, **Levels of Education, Occupation among Urban Scheduled Castes of Selected States, 1971: A Geographical Analysis**, M. Phil. Dissertation, (Jawaharlal Nehru University, 1986).

Pathak, T., **Occupational Structure of Scheduled Caste in a Village**, Dissertation, (Dibrugarh University, 1970).

Patel, D., **Academic Achievement in Relation to Cognitive and Personality Differentials of Socially Disadvantaged and Advantaged Secondary School Children of Orissa,** Ph.D. Thesis, (Punjab University, 1987).

Pathak, K.D., **Anusuchit Jati Awam Jana Jati Ke Vidyarthiyon Ki Akanksha Aur Abhivrittyatmak Unmukhata Main Pariwartan: Changes in Attitudinal Orientation and Aspiration of Scheduled Caste and Scheduled Tribe Students,** Ph.D. Thesis, (Banaras Hindu University, 1981).

Patil, Ravindra Ramesh, **Social Formation of New Middle Classes: A Study of Dalits in Maharashtra,** M. Phil. Dissertation, (Jawaharlal Nehru University, 1999).

Patwardhan, S., **A Study of Scheduled Caste in an Urban Setting,** Dissertation, (Poona University, 1965).

Phulmali, P.M., **Charmkars of Maharashtra: Social and Cultural Study,** (Pune University, 1974).

Pichandi, D., **Diwan Bahadur R. Srinivasan: A Study,** M. Phil. Dissertation, (University of Madras, 1986).

Prajapati, G.K., **Impact of Education on Social, Economic and Political Changes among Scheduled Castes: A Case Study of Danapore Sub-Division,** Ph.D. Thesis, (Patna University, 1982).

Prakash, M.S., **Caste and Social Conflicts in Rural Andhra,** M. Phil. Dissertation, (Jawaharlal Nehru University, 1991).

Prakash, Om, **A Study of some Psycho-Social Variables among Caste Hindu and Scheduled Caste Children in the Rural Set-Up,** Ph.D. Thesis, (Delhi University, 1981).

Prashad, V., **Revolting Labour: The Making of the Balmiki Community,** Ph.D. Dissertation, (University of Chicago 1994).

Premala Bai, D., **A Study of the Extent and Problems of Educational Facilities Offered by the Government of Karnataka to the SCs at the Primary School with**

Special Reference to Bangalore District, Ph.D. Thesis, (Banaras Hindu University, 1986).

Premi, Kusum K., **Protective Legislation and Equality of Education Opportunity: A Study of Scheduled Castes in Punjab**, Ph.D. Thesis, (Jawaharlal Nehru University, 1977).

Pulla Rao, Y., **Dalit Ideology: An Examination of Some Issues**, M. Phil. Dissertation, (Jawaharlal Nehru University, 1990).

Punditrao, C.D., **Holer and Madar Women in the Gifted Women System: A Study of the Savadatti Yellamma Devi with special reference to Vijapur and Dharward Districts in Karnataka**, M. Phil. Dissertation, (Jawaharlal Nehru University, 2001).

Raghunath, G.N., **Study into the Management of Incentives for Children of Scheduled Castes and Scheduled Tribes in Chitradurga District, Karnataka State**, Doctoral Dissertation, (New Delhi: DPEP, NIEPA, 1987).

Rahate, J.V., **Modernization among Scheduled Castes with Special Reference to Mahars, Weavers and Sweepers of Nagpur City**, Ph. D. Thesis [Marathi], (Aurangabad: Marathwada University, 1985).

Raj, A.P.M.J., **The Social Bases of Obedience of the Untouchables in India**, Ph.D. Dissertation, (University of Chicago, Chicago, 1987).

Rajalakshmi, V., **The Administration Setup and Programmes of the Department of Social Welfare in the State of Tamil Nadu**, M. Litt. Thesis, (University of Madras, 1974).

Rajpramukh, K.E., **Harijan and Harijan Christians of Andhra: A Study in Social Mobility and Change**, Ph. D. Thesis, (Andhra University, 1978).

Ram, B., **An Analytical Survey of Living and Study Conditions of Scheduled Caste Students Studying in the Banaras Hindu University**, Ph.D. Dissertation, (Banaras Hindu University, 1987).

Ram, Nandu, **Social Mobility and Status Identification Among Scheduled Castes: A Study of SC Employees in Kanpur City**, Ph.D. Thesis, (I.I.T., Kanpur, 1976).

Ram Palat, Bindu, **Progress of Education of Scheduled Castes in Uttar Pradesh**, Ph.D. Thesis, (Banaras Hindu University, 1974).

Rama Murthy, B., **The Changing Socio-Economic Conditions of Harijans in Chittoor District**, Ph. D. Thesis, (Sri Venkateswara University, 1981).

Ramaiah, A., **Identity and Protest Movements among the Scheduled Castes: Consequences of the Constitutional Provisions in Six Villages in Tamil Nadu**, Ph. D. Thesis, (Jawaharlal Nehru University, 1998).

Ramotra, Krishan Chand, **Impact of Developmental Process on the Scheduled Castes of Maharashtra: A Spatial Perspective**, Ph. D. Thesis, (Jawaharlal Nehru University, 2000).

Rangari, A.D., **Comparative Study of the Scheduled Caste and Non-Scheduled Caste College Students of Aurangabad**, Ph.D. Thesis, (Poona University, 1981).

Rani, Vibha, **Self-Concept and Other Non-Cognitive Factors Affectiing the Academic Achievement of the Scheduled Caste Students in Institutions for Higher Technical Education**, Ph.D. Thesis, (Jawaharlal Nehru University, 1980).

Ravenell, Barbara J., **The Scheduled Castes and Panchayati Raj**, M.A. Thesis, (University of Chicago, 1965).

Reddy, N.S., **Transition in Caste Structure in Andhra Pradesh with Particular Reference to Depressed Classes**, Ph.D. Dissertation, (University of Lucknow, 1954).

Rowe, William L., **Social and Economic Mobility in a Low-Caste North Indian Community**, Ph.D. Dissertation, (Cornell University, 1960).

Sekine, Y., **Pollution Theory and Harijan Strategies among South Indian Tamils**, Doctoral Dissertation, (University of London, School of Oriental and African Studies, 1993).

Sethy, Bijaya Nanda, **Political Participation of Scheduled Castes in Orissa: The Case Study of two Reserved Parliamentary Constituencies**, M. Phil. Dissertation, (Jawaharlal University, 1999).

Sharma, J.P., **A Study of Scheduled Caste Students in Patna University**, Ph.D. Thesis, (Patna University, 1982).

Sharma, M.C., **A Psychological Study of Adjustment Problems of Harijans, Scheduled Caste and Backward Class Students of Agra District**, Ph.D. Thesis, (Agra University, 1979).

Shashidhar, B., **A Study of the Relationship Between a Few School Variables and the Achievement of Scheduled Caste Students Studying in Secondary Schools of Karnataka**, Ph.D. Thesis, (Banaras Hindu University, 1981).

Shastree, Uttara Suhas, **Neo-Buddhists as a Marginal Group in India**, (Pune University, 1981).

Shridhar, Balan, **Dalit Panther Movement in Maharashtra: Problems and Prospects**, M. Phil. Dissertation, (Jawaharlal Nehru University, ??).

Simmons, Ruth, **The Berwas of Delhi: Social and Political Mobility in a Caste of Ex-Untouchables**, Ph.D. Dissertation, (University of California, Berkeley, 1971).

Singh, Hridaya Narain, **Power and Privilege: A Sociological Analysis (A Study of Dobhi Block in Jaunpur District of U.P)**, Ph. D. Thesis, (Jawaharlal Nehru University, 1987).

Singh, Madhu, **Social Origins, Educational Attainments and Occupational Mobility among Scheduled Castes in Delhi**, Ph.D. Thesis, (Jawaharlal Nehru University, 1980).

Singh, P., **A Comparative Study of Achievement, Adjustment, Attitudes and Problems of First and Subsequent Generation Learners Belonging to Scheduled Castes at Higher Secondary Level**, Ph.D. Thesis, (Meerut University, 1987).

Singh, S.D., **The Education of the Scheduled Castes and Their Development Needs Since Independence (1947)**

in the Varanasi Educational Region, Ph.D. Thesis, (Gorakhpur University, 1981).

Singh, S.P., **Harijan Students: Their Values, Problems and Level of Frustration**, Ph.D. Thesis, (Bhagalpur University, 1986).

Singh, Shruti, **Dalit Ethnography – Doms in Eastern Uttar Pradesh**, M. Phil. Dissertation, (Jawaharlal Nehru University, 1997).

Singh, Trilochan, **A Study of the Educational Problems of Scheduled Caste and Scheduled Tribe Students Studying in the Colleges Affiliated to the Avadh University**, Ph.D. Thesis, (Avadh University, 1987).

Sisodia, Meena, **Social Mobility among Scheduled Castes in Kundeshwari Village**, M.Phil. Dissertation, (Meerut University, 1987).

Sivarajan, M.K., **Facilities and Constraints in providing non-Formal Education for Harijans**, Ph. D. Thesis, (Calicut University, 1983).

Srinivas Reddy, G., **Administration of Harijan Welfare Programmes: Case Study of a District in Andhra Pradesh**, Ph. D. Thesis, (Kakatiya University, 1981).

Strickler, J.H., **The Religion and Customs of the Chuhra in the Punjab Province, India**, M.A. Thesis, (University of Kansas, Lawrence, 1926).

Sudhakaran, K.M., **Political Participation of SCs and STs: A Comparative Study of Two Panchayats in Kerala**, M. Phil. Dissertation, (Jawaharlal Nehru University, 1998).

Suresh Babu, N.R., **Sociological Analysis of Caste Conflicts in Tamil Nadu**, M. Phil. Dissertation, (Jawaharlal Nehru University, 2000).

Thakral, M.M.S., **A Comparative Study of Locus of Control, General Intelligence and Level of Vocational Aspiration of Scheduled Castes and non-Scheduled Castes High School Students**, Ph.D. Thesis, (Kurukshetra University, 1977).

Thakur, Rakesh, **Competing Perspective on Caste: A Dialogue Between Gandhi and Ambedkar,** M. Phil. Dissertation, (Jawaharlal Nehru University, 1998).

Thangavelu, G., **Depressed Classes in the Composite State of Madras, 1909-1947 (A Socio-Political Study),** Ph.D. Thesis, (Karnatak University, 1979).

Thiagarajan, A.P., **A Study of the Scheduled Caste Students in the Madurai Kamaraj University,** Ph.D. Thesis, (Maharaja Sayajirao University, 1983).

Thribhuvan, U.D., **A Study of Educated Scheduled Caste Women in an Urban Setting,** Ph.D. Thesis, (Poona University, 1977).

Topal, Y.P.S., **The Scheduled Caste Elites in an Urbanized Village in Meerut,** M.Phil. Dissertation, (Meerut University, 1991).

Tuinmin, H., **The Political Economy of Untouchability,** Thesis, (University of New South Wales, Sydney, 1984).

Umakant, **Human Rights of Dalits: A Case Study of Bihar (1977-1997),** Ph. D. Thesis, (Jawaharlal Nehru University, 2000).

Upadhyay, H.C., **The Problems of Scheduled Castes in the Kumaun Hills: A Sociological Study,** Ph.D. Thesis, (Kumaon University, 1981).

Upadhyaya, Arun Kumar, **Scheduled Caste Leaders in a Rural Setting in Eastern Uttar Pradesh,** M. Phil. Dissertation, (Meerut University, 1992).

Usha, P., **Leather Industry of Tamil Nadu: Study of Structural Change with Special Reference to the 1973 Export Trade Control Policy,** Ph. D. Thesis, (Madras University of Development Studies, 1984).

Vaishnav, B.S., **A Study of Educational and Occupational Experiences of the Scheduled Caste Post-Matric Scholars of Ahmedabad City,** Ph.D. Dissertation, (Gujarat University, 1983).

Vidya Sagar, Kasi, **Politics of Reserved Constituencies: A Study of Ibrahimpatnam Constituency, Ranga Reddy**

District, A.P. 1978-83, M. Phil. Dissertation, (Jawaharlal Nehru University, 1984).

Vijaisri, K. Priyadarshini, **Patterns of Sacred Prostitution in Colonial South India: A Comparative Study of Andhra and Karnataka,** Ph.D., Thesis, (Jawaharlal Nehru University, 2002).

Vincentnathan, Lynn, **Harijan Subculture and Self-esteem Management in a South Indian Community,** Ph.D. Dissertation, (University of Wisconsin – Madison, 1988).

Vyas, K.B., **The Untouchables of Kathiawar,** M.A. Thesis, (University of Bombay, 1938).

Wadhwani, Nanak, **The Bhangis of Lucknow,** M.A. Dissertation, (University of Lucknow, 1952).

Waghaye, V.S., **A Comparative Study of Attitudes of Scheduled Caste and Scheduled Tribe Pupils Towards Education,** Ph.D. Dissertation, (Nagpur University, 1983).

Wahi, L.N., **The Bhantus: A Criminal Tribe of Uttar Pradesh,** Ph. D. Dissertation, (University of Lucknow, 1945), [These Bhantus are also a Scheduled Caste in Uttar Pradesh].

Woodruffe, Gertrude M., **An Adi-dravida Settlement in Bangalore, India: A Case Study of Urbanization,** Ph.D. Dissertation, (Radcliffe College, 1959).

Yadav, S.K., **Study of the Scheduled Castes' Awareness about the Schemes for their Educational Progress,** Ph.D. Thesis, (Maharaja Sayajirao University, 1981).

Zelliot, Eleanor, **Dr. Ambedkar and the Mahar Movement,** Ph.D. Dissertation, (University of Pennsylvania, 1969).

6

Special Issues and Bibliographies

Dr. B.R. Ambedkar Souvenir, London School of Economics, (London: Dr. Ambedkar Memorial Committee, 1972).

Economic and Political Weekly, Vol. 14, Nos. 7 and 8, (1979), Special Issue (Annual Number) on "Class and Caste in India".

Interdiscipline, Special Issue on "Weaker Sections", (Winter 1970).

Janata, Special Number on "Ambedkar", (14 April 1942).

Journal of Indian School of Political Economy, Special Issue on "Scheduled Castes: An Inter-Regional Perspective", Vol. 12, Nos. 3-4, (2000).

Journal of Rural Development, Special Issue on "Welfare of Scheduled Castes and Scheduled Tribes in Independent India, (A Quarterly of NIRD), Vol. 19, No. 4, (2000).

Journal of Rural Development, Special Issue on "Welfare of Scheduled Castes and Scheduled Tribes in Independent India, (A Quarterly of NIRD), Vol. 20, No. 1, (2001).

Kurukshetra (Ambedkar Birth Centenary Special), Vol. 39, No. 1, (1990).

Mainstream, Special Issue on "Reservations: Issues Involved", Vol. 28, No. 16, (1990).

The Administrator, Special Issue on "Dalits", Vol. XLII, No. 1, (1997), [This is a Journal of the Lal Bahadur Shastri National Academy of Administration, Mussorie, and the Theme Editor: Ghanshyam Shah].

Monthly Public Opinion Surveys, "Harijans: Thirty Years Later", Vol. 22, No. 9 (19??).

Pioneer, Special [12 page] Edition on "Dalit Millennium" (30 January 2000), [probably the only English Daily in India so far which published those many pages in a single issue and been contributed by the experts on the subject of their respective fields, including Eleanor Zelliot, Gail Omvedt, T.K. Oommen and many others; there is also been a Weekly Column on "Dalit Dairy" in the Pioneer].

Seminar, No. 177, (May 1974), a special issue on *The Untouchables*, a symposium on the most deprived section of our society.

Seminar, No. 243, (November 1979), a special issue on the *Harijans*, a symposium on some aspects of the problem of Untouchability.

Seminar, No. 471, (November 1998), a special issue on the *Dalit*, a symposium on the Voices, Visions and Political Assertions of Dalits.

Seminar, No. 508, (December 2001), a special issue on *Exclusion*: A symposium on Caste, Race and the Dalit Question.

Social Action, Special Issue on "Emerging Dalit Identity", Vol. 43, No. 4, (1993).

Social Action, Special Issue on "Policy of Reservation", Vol. 48, No. 2, (1998).

Social Action, Special Issue on "Dalit Identity and Culture", Vol. 50, No. 1, (2000).

Social Change, Special Issue on "Scheduled Castes in India", Vol. 19, No. 3, (1989).

Times Weekly Supplement, Special Issue on "Dalit Literature", (25 November, 1973).

Weekly Round Table, Special Report on "Treatment of Harijans", (30 September 1973).

*   *   *   *   *

Malhotra, Nirmal and Najma Rizvi, *Source Material on Education of Scheduled Castes and Scheduled Tribes*, (Delhi: Anamika, 1997).

Roy Burman, B.K. (Compiler), *Bibliography on Scheduled Castes, Scheduled Tribes and Selected Marginal Communities of India*, (New Delhi: Registrar-General of India, 1961), 2 Vols., [This collection was a part of *Census of India, 1961*, Part XI (IV-A) A–K and L–Z series].

Zelliot, Eleanor, "Bibliography on Untouchability", in Michael J. Mahar (ed.), *The Untouchables in Contemporary India*, (Tucson: University of Arizona Press, 1972), [Perhaps this was the first ever systematically compiled 'bibliography' on Dalits].

APPENDIX

Major Dalit Communities: Brief Notes on their Location and Status

Ad Dharmi, Adi-Dharmi: In the early decades of the twentieth century some of the 'untouchable' communities (particularly Chamars and Chuhras) claimed that they belonged to a quom, which is a first or primeval (Adi) faith (Dharm); later Ad Dharma recognized as a religious faith and enumerated as a separate caste during the 1931 census. They are now prevalent in Chandigarh, Himachal Pradesh, Punjab and Rajasthan.

Adi Andhra: Adi Andhra means the oldest people or settlers of Andhra. This caste appeared only in 1931 Census, drawn heavily from Mala and Madiga communities of Andhra Pradesh, thanks to Adi-Andhra /Dalit movement of Andhra Pradesh, which fought for their self-identity and compelled the then government to use "adi" prefix to their regional identity, justifying their claim that they were the original inhabitants and 'sons of the soil'. Information available about these communities in *Census of India, 1931, Vol. XXIII: H.E.H.*

The Nizam's Dominion, Hyderabad, Part I: Report, (Hyderabad Deccan, 1933); *Census of India, 1931, Vol. XIV: Madras, Part I: Report,* (Madras: 1932). This caste is found in Andhra Pradesh, Kerala, Madras, Mysore, Orissa and Pondicherry.

Adi Dravida: On the same line of the above, these Adi-Dravidas (were) are "untouchables" of Tamil speaking areas of erstwhile Madras Presidency. This caste is found in Andhra Pradesh, Kerala, Madras, Mysore and Pondicherry. Information is available about this community in *Census of India, 1931, Vol. XXVIII, Travancore, Part I: Report,* (Trivandrum: 1932).

Adi Karnataka: are mostly drawn from Holeya and Balagai communities of ex-untouchables. Adi Karnatakas are devided into six subgroups, namely the Kula Sale, the Muri, the Magga (weaving), the Hagga (rope making), the Morasu and the Gangadikar.

Adiya, Adiyan: This caste is termed as Scheduled Caste in Mysore and as Scheduled Tribe in Kerala, Madras and Mysore. Information about this caste found in *Census of India 1901, Vol. XV, Madras, Part I: Report,* (Madras: 1902).

Agariya, Agaria: This caste is Scheduled Caste in Uttar Pradesh and Scheduled Tribe in Madhya Pradesh and Maharashtra. Information about this caste found in R.E. Enthoven, *The Tribes and Castes of Bombay,* Vol. I, (Bombay: 1920); J.H. Hutton, *Caste in India,* (Bombay: 1951); and H.H. Risley, *The Tribes and Castes of Bengal,* Vol I, (Calcutta: 1891).

Ager: This Community name is derived from the word 'agara' means a salt pan. This caste is Scheduled Caste in Gujarat, Maharashtra, Mysore (i.e., Karnataka) and Rajasthan. For details see the Castes and Tribes volume of the state concerned and census reports of 1911, and see H.A. Rose, *A Glossary of the Tribes and Castes of Punjab and North West Frontier Provinces,* Vol. II, (Lahore, 1911).

Aheria, Aheri: Popularly known as 'Shikari'. This caste is a Scheduled Caste in Rajasthan and Delhi; and denotified Tribe in Punjab and Uttar Pradesh.

Ahirwar: is a Scheduled Caste in Madhya Pradesh. For details see Enthoven and Russel's volumes.

Amant, Amat: is a Scheduled Caste in Orissa. They also have known as the 'Amanat'. For details see Risley's volume on Bengal castes and census reports of 1891, and 1901.

Anamuk: is a Scheduled Caste in Andhra Pradesh, Karnataka and Maharashtra.

Aray (Mala): is a Scheduled Caste in Andhra Pradesh, and cultivators in Mysore; is considered to be the subdivision of Malas, who perhaps the second largest community among the "untouchables" of Andhra.

Arunthatiyar, Arundhatiya, Arunthathiyar, Arundhatiyar: is a Scheduled Caste in Andhra Pradesh, Karnataka, Maharashtra, Tamil Nadu and Kerala. The Madigas, the Madaris and the Pagadais are also occasionally describes themselves as Arundhatiyas, or Arundhateyulu. Because the Madigas of Andhra Pradesh believe that Arundhati (the mythical Hindu character) took birth in this community and there fore they associate themselves with her name.

Arwa Mala, Arwamala: is a Scheduled Caste in Tamil Nadu and Andhra Pradesh. The Arwamala are also known as Tamil Malas and Dher. The Telugu people call the Tamil language as 'Aravam', so the Malas of Tamil speaking are known as Arwamalas.

Asadaru: is a Scheduled Caste in Gujarat, Maharashtra, Karnataka and Rajasthan.

Asodi: is a Scheduled Caste in Gujarat, Maharashtra, Karnataka and Rajasthan.

Audhelia: is a Scheduled Caste in Madhya Pradesh and Orissa.

Ayyanavar: is a Scheduled Caste in Kerala and Tamil Nadu.

Badhik, Baraik, Badaik: is a Scheduled Caste in Orissa and Uttar Pradesh.

Badi, Badhi: is a Scheduled Caste in Rajasthan and Uttar Pradesh and nomadic tribe in Gujarat and Uttar Pradesh.

Bagdi, Bagri: is a Scheduled Caste in Madhya Pradesh, Rajasthan, West Bengal and Tripura and denotified tribe in Rajasthan. They are also known as Byagra Kshatriya. A legend has it that the Bagri migrated from Bagradesh, hence their name. For more details of this caste see *Bengal District Gazetteers* and the *Census Reports* of the State concerned.

Bagheti /Baghuti: is Scheduled Caste in Orissa. The Bagheti are also known Baguiti, Bagti, Bogti, Bongti.

Baheliya/Bahelia/Bhellia: is a Scheduled Caste is Uttar Pradesh, Scheduled Tribe in Madhya Pradesh and Maharashtra and Nomadic Tribe in Madhya Pradesh Uttar Pradesh and West Bengal.

Bahna, Bahana: is a Scheduled Caste in Madhya Pradesh and Maharashtra.

Baiga: is Scheduled Caste in Uttar Pradesh and Scheduled Tribe in Bihar, Madhya Pradesh, Maharashtra, Orissa and West Bengal.

Baira: is a Scheduled Caste in Karnataka. The Baira are various known as Bhaira and Bhairavar.

Bairwa, Berwa: is a Scheduled Caste in Rajasthan.

Baiswar: is a Scheduled Caste in Uttar Pradesh.

Baiti: is a Scheduled Caste in West Bengal and Tripura.

Bajania, Bajaniya: is a Scheduled Caste in Uttar Pradesh, they are called the Parnewala or the Karnat and are returned as the Bajania.

Bajgar: is a Scheduled Caste in Rajasthan.

Bajgi: is a Scheduled Caste in Uttar Pradesh. Their community name is derived from their traditional profession of beating drums, for the word baj means playing music.

Bajikar: is a Scheduled Caste in Orissa.

Bakad: is a Scheduled Caste in Gujarat, Maharashtra, Karnataka and Rajasthan.

Bakuda: is a Scheduled Caste in Kerala, Tamil Nadu and Karnataka. They are also called Bayalu Bakuda. The bayalu means 'open land' or 'the agricultural field'.

Balagai: is a Scheduled Caste in Karnataka. The Balagai are also known as Adi Karnataka.

Balahar: is a Scheduled Caste in Uttar Pradesh. Variously known as Vargi, Chobdar or Thakur, the Balahar are traditionally a community of summoners and guards.

Balahi, Bali: is a Scheduled Caste in Gujarat, Madhya Pradesh, Maharashtra, Rajasthan, Uttar Pradesh and Delhi. Their community name is derived from the Hindi term bulahi, meaning 'the one who calls' or 'a messenger'.

Balmiki, Balmik, Valmiki, Valamiki: is a Scheduled Caste in Gujarat, Madhya Pradesh, Maharashtra, Mysore, Orissa, Punjab, Rajasthan, Uttar Pradesh, Delhi and Himachal Pradesh. Some sections of a cluster of communities such as the Bhangi, Mehtar, Lalbegi and many other castes who were associated with scavenging in the past, are now commonly claims descent from the legendary saint Balmiki.

Banchada: is a Scheduled Caste in Madhya Pradesh.

Bandhela: is a Scheduled Caste in Himachal Pradesh, and for details see H.A. Rose's volume.

Bandi, Bandhi, Badhi: is a Scheduled Caste in Kerala, Tamil Nadu and Karnataka. In Himachal Pradesh they are notified as Bandhi and Nagalu. In addition to the Volumes of Crooke, Enthoven, Risely, Thurston, also see Census of India, 1911, Vol. VII, Bombay Report.

Bangali: is a Scheduled Caste in Punjab, Uttar Pradesh and Himachal Pradesh and Denotified Tribe in Punjab. They are also known as Singhiwala, because they use a kind of horn (sing) for cupping. Now Bangalis are a community of snake charmers, medicinemen and beggars. For details see the above-mentioned volumes for the respective region.

Banjara, Banjari, Lambani, Laban, Lambana: is Scheduled Caste in Karnataka, Delhi and Himachal Pradesh; Scheduled Tribe in Bihar, Orissa and West Bengal; Denotified Tribe in Madhya Pradesh, Rajasthan and Uttar Pradesh; and Nomadic Tribe in Gujarat, Karnataka and Rajasthan. They are also referred to as Lamani, Lambadi, Ladhari, Sugali, Vanjara, and Labhan and are identified at the national level.

Banmanus: is Scheduled Caste in Uttar Pradesh. For details see Census of 1911and 1931 of U.P. Banmanu is a synonym for Musahar.

Bansi: is Scheduled Caste in Himachal Pradesh. For details see volumes of H.A. Rose and R.V. Russel and Hira Lal.

Bansor, Basod, Basor, Bansodi: is a Scheduled Caste in Madhya Pradesh, Maharashtra, Orissa, Rajasthan and Uttar Pradesh.

Bansphod, Bansphor: is a Scheduled Caste in Assam, Madhya Pradesh, Rajasthan and Uttar Pradesh. Also known as the Benbansi Bansphor, they consider themselves one of the subgroups of the Dom. The term Bansphor is derived from the Hindi word bans meaning bamboo and phorna meaning to split.

Bant: is a Scheduled Caste in Gujarat, Maharashtra, Mysore and Rajasthan. For details, in addition to the volumes on Caste and Tribes, also see Madras Census of 1881.

Bantar: is a Scheduled Caste in Bihar and West Bengal. A community whose traditional craft is basket-making, using bamboo.

Baori, Bauri, Bavuri, Bauria, Bawaria, Bawariya: is a Scheduled Caste in Andhra Pradesh, Bihar, Orissa, Punjab, Rajasthan, Uttar Pradesh, West Bengal, Delhi and Himachal Pradesh; Denotified Tribe in Punjab, Rajasthan, Uttar Pradesh and Delhi; and Nomadic Tribe in Madhya Pradesh, Rajasthan and Himachal Pradesh.

Barad: is a Scheduled Caste in Himachal Pradesh. For more details see the journal *Vanyajati* of early 1960s, particularly volumes 9-11, where innumerable articles published in these issues.

Barar, Burar, Berar: is a Scheduled Caste in Punjab and Himachal Pradesh; and denotified Tribe in Punjab. For details see the volumes of Rose, Sherring and Risley; and Punjab Census Reports of 1881, 1891, 1911 and 1931.

Bargi, Vargi, Birgi: is a Scheduled Caste in Rajasthan. For details see the Caste volumes of Crooke and Enthoven.

Bargunda: is a Scheduled Caste in Madhya Pradesh and Rajasthan.

Barhi, Barai, Barhai, Badhi or Nagalu: is a Scheduled Caste in Himachal Pradesh.

Bari: is a Scheduled Caste in Orissa.

Bariki: is a Scheduled Caste in Andhra Pradesh and Orissa. Village Servant is also called Bariki in Andhra Pradesh, either the profession became a caste or only this caste men are engaged in this profession is not known. For details see Edgar Thurston & C Rangachari and Russel & Hira Lal.

Barud: is a Scheduled Caste in Gujarat, Madhya Pradesh, Maharashtra and Orissa.

Barwala: is a Scheduled Caste in Jammu and Kashmir. Also known as the Doom or the Dum Bantwals.

Barwar: is a Scheduled Caste and also codified under Denotified Tribe in Uttar Pradesh.

Basith: is a Scheduled Caste in Jammu and Kashmir. Also known as the Basithe, the Basmishth or the Bashishth Rajput. More details are available in Census of Kashmir, 1911 and 1931.

Basor: is a Scheduled Caste in Madhya Pradesh, Maharashtra and Uttar Pradesh. An occupational community of bamboo workers, they are known by various names, such as the Bansor, Basar, Bansphor, Bansodi, Baskar and Burud.

Bathada: is a Scheduled Caste in Karnataka.

Batwal, Barwala: is a Scheduled Caste in Jammu and Kashmir, Punjab and Himachal Pradesh.

Bauri: is a Scheduled Caste in Orissa, Bihar and West Bengal.

Bauti: is a Scheduled Caste in Orissa.

Bawa (Dedh), Dhed Bawa, Dhedh-Sadhu: is a Scheduled Caste in Gujarat.

Bawaria, Bauria, Bawariya: is a Scheduled Caste in Haryana, Uttar Pradesh, Delhi, Rajasthan and Punjab. Their community name is derived from the word bawar meaning a 'noose' which is used to snare wild animals.

Bazigar: is a Scheduled Caste in Punjab, Rajasthan, Delhi and Himachal Pradesh; Nomadic Tribe in Gujarat, Jammu and Kashmir, Madhya Pradesh, Karnataka and Himachal Pradesh.

Beda Jangam: is a Scheduled Caste in Maharashtra, Andhra Pradesh and Karnataka.

Bedar, Berad: is a Scheduled Caste and Denotified Tribe in Gujarat, Maharashtra, Karnataka and Andhra Pradesh. In Maharashtra, the Bedar were also known previously as the Pindaries and were infamous for their vocation of free-booting.

Bedia, Bediya, Beria, Bariya, Bejia: is a Scheduled Caste in Madhya Pradesh, Orissa, Rajasthan, Uttar Pradesh and West Bengal; Scheduled Tribe in Bihar and West Bengal; and Nomadic Tribe in Gujarat, Madhya Pradesh, Maharashtra, Mysore, Uttar Pradesh and Tripura. They are also known as the Bedia Kudmi, Aad Kudmi, Choto Kudmi or San Kudmi in Orissa. In Madhya Pradesh they identify themselves with the Kshatriya Rajputs and are also known as the Berani and the Berai.

Beldar: is a Scheduled Caste in Madhya Pradesh, Orissa, Uttar Pradesh and West Bengal. Also known as Lonia, the Beldar's existence as a distinct community. The word Beldar is derived from the word bel, meaning a digging implement, and dar refers to the person who handles it.

Bellara: is a Scheduled Caste in Kerala, Tamil Nadu and Karnataka. The term bellara is derived from bilu hari, meaning 'tearing the fibre of a plant'.

Bhambhi, Bhambi, Bambhi: is a Scheduled Caste in Gujarat, Madhya Pradesh, Maharashtra, Karnataka and Rajasthan.

Bhand: is a Scheduled Caste in Rajasthan; Nomadic Tribe in Gujarat, Maharashtra and Rajasthan.

Bhangi: is one of the major community among Scheduled Castes in northern, central and western India, particularly in Assam, Bihar, Gujarat, Madhya Pradesh, Maharashtra, Mysore, Orissa, Punjab, Rajasthan, West Bengal, Delhi and Himachal Pradesh. The term Bhangi has been derived from the Sanskrit word bhangi meaning hemp. The Bhangi was described as a representative of the Chandala of Manu, who is said to have descended from the union of a Sudra and a Brahman woman.

Bhanjra, Bhanjre: is a Scheduled Caste in Punjab and Himachal Pradesh.

Bhantu: is a Scheduled Caste and also a Denotified Tribe in Uttar Pradesh. Popularly known as Bhatu among the local people, they are also known as Sahaisi or Sahasi, meaning brave.

Bhanumati: is a Scheduled Caste in Madhya Pradesh and Rajasthan. Also known as Banmata, they are traditionally a professional group of magicians and fumnabulists.

Bharatar: is a Scheduled Caste in Kerala and Tamil Nadu. Also known as Paravan, Chavalakkaran and Padaiachy.

Bhata: is a Scheduled Caste in Orissa. Also referred to as Raj Bhat or Bhat and are believed to have migrated from Khallary in Chattisgarh.

Bhedkut: is a Scheduled Caste in Punjab and Delhi; Denotified Tribe in Punjab.

Bhil: is a Scheduled Caste in Delhi; and Scheduled Tribe in Andhra Pradesh, Gujarat, Madhya Pradesh, Maharashtra, Karnataka, Rajasthan and Tripura.

Bhogta: is a Scheduled Caste in Bihar and West Bengal. They are also called Pradhan.

Bhoi, Bhovi: is a Scheduled Caste in Gujarat, Karnataka and Orissa. Also known as Basuri Skandakara, the Bhoi (one who carries litters or palanquins) is a synonym of Dhimar and Kahar.

Bhuinmali or Mali: is a Scheduled Caste in Assam, West Bengal and Tripura. Also known as Bhuisundar Siddhiputra and Hari. Bhuimali means a care-taker of the soil. Bhuinmali means a person who makes malas, meaning garlands.

Bhuiya, Bhuyan: is a Scheduled Caste in Bihar, Uttar Pradesh and West Bengal; Scheduled Tribe in Orissa. Also known as Manjhi and Rikhiasan, and they trace their mytholocial origin to the legendary Sabri.

Bhumij: is a Scheduled Caste in Bihar and West Bengal; a Scheduled Tribe in Bihar, Orissa and West Bengal.

Bhunar: is a Scheduled Caste in Tripura.

Bidakia: is a Scheduled Caste in Rajasthan.

Bijikar: is a Scheduled Caste in Orissa.

Bind: is a Scheduled Caste in West Bengal; Nomadic Tribe in Tripura.

Bindla: is a Scheduled Caste in Andhra Pradesh. They discharge the functions of priests for the Madiga caste and perform their religious rites to the music of the jamadika, a musical instrument characteristic of their profession.

Bola: is a Scheduled Caste in Rajasthan.

Boria, Boriya: is a Scheduled Caste and also a Denotified Tribe in Uttar Pradesh.

Boyan: is a Scheduled Caste in Kerala and Tamil Nadu.

Brittialbania: is a Scheduled Caste in Assam. Also known as the Sonari (goldsmith), the Brittial Bania are variously notified as the Brittial Bania and Bania.

Byagara: is a Scheduled Caste in Andhra Pradesh, Gujarat, Maharashtra and Karnataka. Also called Begari, Begarolu and Begara. Their community name is a derivative of the word beggar, meaning service.

Chachati: is a Scheduled Caste in Andhra Pradesh and Orissa.

Chadar: is a Scheduled Caste in Madhya Pradesh and Maharashtra. They are also known as Athia and Pawar.

Chakali, Chakkoli: is a Scheduled Caste in Orissa and a Backward Class in Andhra Pradesh.

Chakkiliyan: is a Scheduled Caste in Kerala, Tamil Nadu, Karnataka and Pondicherry. Also referred to as Pagadai, Arundhatiyar, Madari and Toti.

Chalavadi, Chalvadi: is a Scheduled Caste in Andhra Pradesh, Gujarat, Tamil Nadu, Maharashtra, Karnataka and Rajasthan. They are also known as Channayya in Maharashtra.

Chamadia: is a Scheduled Caste in Gujarat, Maharashtra, Karnataka and Rajasthan.

Chanal: is a Scheduled Caste in Haryana, Chandigarh, Punjab and Himachal Pradesh. The Chanals are akin to the Hali Community, they are otherwise treated as a synonymous with the Halis both occupational and social terms.

Chandal, Chandala: is a Scheduled Caste in Andhra Pradesh, Kerala, Tamil Nadu, Karnataka, Orissa and Rajasthan.

Chandhai Maru, Charaimar: is a Scheduled Caste in Orissa. Also known as Sikari Jara and Satara or Savara, Chariamar means 'those who kill birds'.

Charmakar, Chamari, Chambhar, Chamgar, Charamkar: is a Scheduled Caste in Andhra Pradesh, Bihar, Gujarat, Jammu and Kashmir, Kerala, Madhya Pradesh, Tamil Nadu, Maharashtra, Karnataka, Orissa, Punjab, Rajasthan, Uttar Pradesh, West Bengal, Delhi, Himachal Pradesh, Tripura and Dadra and Nagar Haveli. Their community name is derived from the Sanskrit word

Charmakara, meaning leather worker. In Uttar Pradesh and Himachal Pradesh, the Chamar are also known as the Raidas. In Bihar, they are also known as the Charmkar, Harijan and Ravidas. In Chandigarh, they are also called the Joatia Chamar, Reghar, Raigar, Ramdasi and Ravidasi. In Tripura, the Chamar are also known as the Rishidas and Muchi. In Goa, they are known as the Chambhars and Hadis.

Chaupal, Choupal: is a Scheduled Caste in Bihar. Also known as Basak and Tanti. Originally, their mother tounge is Surajpuri, which belongs to the eastern group of the Indo-Aryan family of languages.

Chenna Dasar, Dandiga Dasar: is a Scheduled Caste in Gujarat, Maharashtra, Karnataka and Rajasthan. They also called Jambu Dasar and Hari Dasar.

Chero: is a Scheduled Caste in Uttar Pradesh; Scheduled Tribe in Bihar and West Bengal. The Chero kingdom (Chero-raj) was once reported spread all over the Gangetic plain from Chunar to Girid.

Cherua, Chhelia: is a Scheduled Caste in Orissa. They also called Chhelia Gola.

Cheruman, Cheramar: is a Scheduled Caste in Kerala, Tamil Nadu and Karnataka. Also known as Cherumakkal.

Chhimbre: is a Scheduled Caste in Himachal Pradesh. Also known as Chhippa, Chimbe and Chhimba, and they are almost synonymously identified with the washermen (Dhobis).

Chidar: is a Scheduled Caste in Madhya Pradesh, and also known as Athia and Chadar.

Chikwa, Chaikwa, Chikva: is a Scheduled Caste in Gujarat, Madhya Pradesh and Maharashtra. They also referred to as Suthbansi Chouhan.

Chitar, Chidar: is a Scheduled Caste in Madhya Pradesh and Rajasthan.

Chuhra, Chura, Chohra, Chuhre: is a Scheduled Caste in Jammu and Kashmir, Punjab, Rajasthan, Delhi and

Himachal Pradesh. They also have known as Bhangi, Chaamri, Jemadar and Khakrobe.

Dabgar: is a Scheduled Caste in Bihar, Rajasthan, Uttar Pradesh and West Bengal. They often called Dhalgar and Chamars, because of their occupation of making dhals (shield) out of leather.

Dagi: is a Scheduled Caste in Punjab and Himachal Pradesh. Also known as Dagee or Bethu.

Dahait, Dahayat, Dahat: is a Scheduled Caste in Madhya Pradesh.

Dakkala, Dakkalwar: is a Scheduled Caste in Andhra Pradesh, Gujarat, Maharashtra and Karnataka. Also called the Dokkala and Dakkals.

Dakkaliga: is a Scheduled Caste in Karnataka.

Damai (Nepali): is a Scheduled Caste in West Bengal. Also known as the Darjee or Dorjee. Their community name Damai has been derived from the word Damaha meaning a drum which is skillfully played by them.

Dandasi: is a Scheduled Caste in Andhra Pradesh, Orissa and Tripura; Denotified Tribe in Orissa. The Dandasis are traditionally village watchmen or guarding villages at night.. Their community name, Dandasi, comes from the danda (stick) and asi (sword) that were carried by their men.

Daole, Daule: is a Scheduled Caste in Himachal Pradesh. They are known for their traditional occupation of washing gold particles collected from the alluvial soils of rivers. Daule might be a derivative of the word dhul, meaning dust, as they search for gold dust in sand.

Darai, Daryai, Darain: is a Scheduled Caste in Punjab and Himachal Pradesh.

Deha, Dhaya, Dhea: is a Scheduled Caste in Punjab.

Devandra Kulathan: is a Scheduled Caste in Tamil Nadu and Karnataka. Also called Devendran, Ponnadi, Pallan and Kudumban, as mentioned in their *Devendrakula Stalapurana*.

Dewar: is a Scheduled Caste in Madhya Pradesh and Orissa. The Dewar of Orissa are also known as Keuta, Kaibarta, Dhibara, Kevta, Kalbarta and Dhubar.

Dhaki: is a Scheduled Caste in Himachal Pradesh. Basically a community of musicians, they are also known as Toori, Turi and Bajgi.

Dhanak, Dhanuk, Dhankia: is a Scheduled Caste in Madhya Pradesh, Haryana, Punjab, Rajasthan, Uttar Pradesh and Delhi. The Dhanuk of Uttar Pradesh considers them an offshoot of the Ahit, who adopted the occupation of reading pigs. The Dhanak in Haryana are known as Kabirpanthi and Julaha and claim their descent from Dhanusamuni.

Dhangad, Dhangar: is a Scheduled Caste in Bihar, Uttar Pradesh and West Bengal; Scheduled Tribe in Madhya Pradesh and Maharashtra. Considered the original inhabitants of Mirzapur and the adjoining districts of Bihar, they are also known as Oraon.

Dhanwar, Dhenuar: is a Scheduled Caste in Orissa and Tripura; Scheduled Tribe in Madhya Pradesh and Maharashtra.

Dhari, Dharhi: is a Scheduled Caste in Bihar and West Bengal; also Denotified Tribe in Bihar.

Dharkar: is a Scheduled Caste in Madhya Pradesh and Uttar Pradesh. They believe that Dharkar comes from dhar, meaning rope or cane making.

Dhed, Dheda, Dher: is a Scheduled Caste in Gujarat, Madhya Pradesh, Maharashtra, Karnataka, Rajasthan and Dadra and Nagar Haveli.

Dhenuar: is a Scheduled Caste in Tripura.

Dhobi, Dhupi, Dhoba: is a Scheduled Caste in Assam, Bihar, Madhya Pradesh, Orissa, Rajasthan, Uttar Pradesh, West Bengal, Delhi, Himachal Pradesh, Manipur and Tripura, but in Andhra Pradesh the Dhobi is categorized as 'Backward Caste' and not under S.C. The Dhoba are also known as Rajak and Suklavaidya.

Dhogri, Dhangri: is a Scheduled Caste in Punjab and Himachal Pradesh. Also known as Siggi and they are ironsmiths, miners and charcoal-burners.

Dholi: is a Scheduled Caste in Assam and Rajasthan. In Rajasthan they also known as Nagarchi, as they community name is derived from the word dhol, meaning a drum, Nagarchi could be a reference to a particular kind of drum.

Dhor, Dohor: is a Scheduled Caste in Andhra Pradesh, Gujarat, Madhya Pradesh, Maharashtra, Karnataka and Rajasthan. A community of tanners, their community name derived from dhor, meaning cattle. In Karnataka, they are synonymously called Dhor Kakayya or Kankayya. In Maharashtra they are notified as the Dhor Kakkayya and Kankayya.

Dhusia: is a Scheduled Caste in Uttar Pradesh.

Dhyar: is a Scheduled Caste in Jammu and Kashmir.

Doai: is a Scheduled Caste in West Bengal. They were known as the Behars in the past. Behara is a title reported to have been bestowed on them by erstwhile rulers as they were palanquin bearers and load carriers.

Dom, Dome, Doom, Dum, Dumna, Dumne: is a Scheduled Caste in Andhra Pradesh, Bihar, Gujarat, Jammu and Kashmir, Madhya Pradesh, Tamil Nadu, Maharashtra, Karnataka, Orissa, Punjab, Rajasthan, Uttar Pradesh, West Bengal, Delhi and Himachal Pradesh; and also a Denotified Tribe in Andhra Pradesh, Tamil Nadu and Orissa.

Domar, Domban, Dombar, Dombara, Dommar, Dumar, Dommara, Dombari, Dombo: is a Scheduled Caste in Andhra Pradesh, Gujarat, Kerala, Orissa, Madhya Pradesh, Tamil Nadu, Maharashtra, Karnataka and Uttar Pradesh; a Nomadic Tribe in Andhra Pradesh, Gujarat, Maharashtra and Mysore.

Dosad, Dusad, Dusadh: is a Scheduled Caste in Bihar, Uttar Pradesh and West Bengal.

Dugla: is a Scheduled Caste in Assam.

Duley: is a Scheduled Caste in West Bengal.

Dumna, Mahasha: is a Scheduled Caste in Punjab.

Gagra: is a Scheduled Caste in Punjab. Also called Jukera or Jonkawale, the word Jonkawala is derived from jonk, meaning leech as they used to catch and apply leeches to remove impure blood from the body.

Gancha, Garancha: is a Scheduled Caste in Rajasthan.

Ganda: is a Scheduled Caste in Madhya Pradesh, Maharashtra and Orissa.

Gandhila, Gandhiel, Gandil, Gondola: are a Scheduled Caste in Punjab; and Denotified Tribe in Punjab and Uttar Pradesh. They claim descent from Sabal Singh Rajput who was killed in a war in Delhi.

Gandia: is a Scheduled Caste in Rajasthan.

Ganti Chore: are a Scheduled Caste in Karnataka; and a Denotified Tribe in Gujarat, Maharashtra and Mysore. They are also known as Uchillian, Bhamta, Pathrut, Takari and Kamati.

Gardi: is a Scheduled Caste in Jammu and Kashmir, A group of professional musicians who performs at both social and religious functions.

Garmatang: is a Scheduled Caste in Gujarat. They claim to be descendants of the great monk, Matang, and consider themselves religious priests (gor) to the Maheswari Meghwal and other Dalit communities.

Garo, Garoda, Garura, Gurda: is a Scheduled Caste in Gujarat, Maharashtra, Karnataka and Rajasthan. Also known as Guru, Gurwa and Pandiya, they trace their descent to saint Gargacharya, the brother of Sukracharya who was the guru of the Asurs.

Garudi Mang: is a Scheduled Caste in Gujarat, Madhya Pradesh and Maharashtra.

Gavara: is a Scheduled Caste in Kerala.

Gavaria: is a Scheduled Caste in Rajasthan. Also known as Gowaria and Gavar Banjara, they derive their name from the term gowal, meaning cowshed.

Ghantarghada, Ghantra: is a Scheduled Caste in Orissa.

Gharami, Gharrami: is a Scheduled Caste in Uttar Pradesh and Delhi.

Ghasi, Ghasia, Ghasiya: is a Scheduled Caste in Andhra Pradesh, Bihar, Gujarat, Madhya Pradesh, Maharashtra, Orissa, Uttar Pradesh, West Bengal and Tripura; and a Denotified Tribe in Bihar, Tamil Nadu and Orissa. The word Ghasi means, fish killer.

Ghogia: is a Scheduled Caste in Orissa. The name Ghogia has been derived from the word godna, meaning tattooing.

Ghusuria: is a Scheduled Caste in Orissa.

Godagali: is a Scheduled Caste in Andhra Pradesh, Kerala, Tamil Nadu, Karnataka and Orissa. The word Godagali is derived from the Telugu word godugu, meaning umbrella. They were umbrella-makers.

Godari: is a Scheduled Caste in Andhra Pradesh and Orissa.

Godda: is a Scheduled Caste in Karnataka and Tamil Nadu. Also known as Goddar, Avular, Oddar, Avulavaru and Dravidar. Their community name is derived from the word goddu meaning cattle.

Godhi: is a Scheduled Caste in Rajasthan.

Godra: is a Scheduled Caste in Orissa, claimed to be an offshoot of the Mahar.

Gokha: is a Scheduled Caste in Orissa. The word Gokha has been derived from the words go and kha, meaning a cow eater.

Gond: is a Scheduled Caste in Uttar Pradesh; but most of the states, such as Andhra Pradesh, Bihar, Gujarat, Madhya Pradesh, Maharashtra, Karnataka, Orissa, Rajasthan and West Bengal, it is categorized as a Scheduled Tribe.

Gonrhi: is a Scheduled Caste in West Bengal. Also known as Gurshi, Mollah and Machhuar.

Gorait or Karai: is a Scheduled Caste in Orissa; but in Bihar and West Bengal they are Scheduled Tribes.

Gosangi: is a Scheduled Caste in Andhra Pradesh, Kerala and Karnataka. Also referred to as the Gosika, Gosikollu, Gosangollu or Gostika. It is believed that they are called Gosangi because of their occupation as caretakers of cattle.

Gual, Gour: is a Scheduled Caste in Uttar Pradesh, Bihar andTripura.

Gur: is a Scheduled Caste in Tripura.

Hadi, Haddi, Hari: is a Scheduled Caste in Andhra Pradesh, Bihar, Gujarat, Maharashtra, Karnataka, Orissa, Rajasthan, Uttar Pradesh and West Bengal.

Halalkhor: is a Scheduled Caste in Bihar, Gujarat, Maharashtra, Karnataka, Rajasthan and West Bengal.

Hali: is a Scheduled Caste in Himachal Pradesh. The Hali are also known as Arya or Dhingra.

Halleer: is a Scheduled Caste in Gujarat, Maharashtra, Karnataka and Rajasthan.

Halsar, Halsar Hulasvar, Halasvar: is a Scheduled Caste in Gujarat, Maharashtra, Karnataka and Rajasthan.

Halsar, Hulasvar, Hulsavar: is a Scheduled Caste in Karnataka. Also referred as to Hasalaru and Murger.

Handi Jogi: is a Scheduled Caste and a Denotified Tribe and also a Nomadic Tribe in Karnataka. They also known as Handi Golla and Handi Chickka and they are a pig-rearing community.

Harali: is a Scheduled Caste in Gujarat, Maharashtra, Karnataka and Rajasthan.

Hari: is a Scheduled Caste in West Bengal. Also known as Hadi or Haddi, they were traditionally engaged in collecting the earthen pots used in burial grounds for death rituals. Hari means an earthen pot used for death rituals.

Hasala, Hasla: is a Scheduled Caste in Kerala and Karnataka.

Hela, Mehtar: is a Scheduled Caste in Uttar Pradesh. They also referred to under the generic term, Mehtar, their community name is derived from the word hela, meaning a cry.

Hesi: is a Scheduled Caste in Himachal Pradesh. They also pronounced as Hensi in Kangra, they are considered the eighteenth caste or an odd caste. The inauspicious month of Chaitra (March-April) is called the Hesi's month (Hesion ka mahina) because the Hesi marry within that month, whereas other caste Hindus in the area do not conduct marriages or social ceremonies during that month. They identify themselves with the Sanhai (those who play the Shahnai).

Hira: is a Scheduled Caste in Assam.

Holar: is a Scheduled Caste in Gujarat, Maharashtra, Karnataka and Rajasthan. They also known as Valhar, they were mentioned as a subdivision of the Mahars and a synonym for the Holeya.

Holaya: is a Scheduled Caste in Gujarat, Maharashtra, Karnataka and Rajasthan.

Holer: is a Scheduled Caste in Gujarat, Maharashtra, Karnataka and Rajasthan.

Holeya Dasari: is a Scheduled Caste in Karnataka. The word Holeya Dasari is derived from the Kannada words hola, meaning dry-crop field, and dasari, meaning servant.

Holeya: is a Scheduled Caste in Andhra Pradesh, Kerala, Tamil Nadu, Maharashtra and Karnataka.

Holiya, Holia: is a Scheduled Caste in Madhya Pradesh and Maharashtra.

Hubura: is a Scheduled Caste as well as a Denotified Tribe in Uttar Pradesh.

Irika: is a Scheduled Caste in Orissa.

Jaggali: is a Scheduled Caste in Andhra Pradesh, Tamil Nadu, Karnataka and Orissa. Also known as Joggali, and they are referred to differently in different languages such as Madiga in Telugu, Muchi in Oriya, Godari in the rural dialect and also as Chamar. They sometimes also call themselves Jambava and claim descent from Jambuvan of Ramayana fame.

Jalia, Jaliya, Kaibartta, Kaibarta: is a Scheduled Caste in Assam, West Bengal and Tripura. This caste is also referred to as Jele, Jalo, Jali etc. Many are of the opinion that their name has been derived from the word jal, meaning a fishing net, whereas others maintain that it is derived from jal, meaning water.

Jalkeot: is a Scheduled Caste in Assam. They are also known as the Joluwa, Jalua, Jaluwai or Jolu Wai Keot.

Jambuvulu, Jambavulu, Adi Jambavulu: is a Scheduled Caste in Tamil Nadu and Andhra Pradesh. They are also known as Chakkiliyan, Arundhatiyar, and they prefer to be referred to as Adi Jambavulu after the name of their deity, Jambavamurthi.

Jatav, Jatava, Jatia, Jatya, Jatya Chamar: is a Scheduled Caste in Madhya Pradesh, Punjab, Rajasthan, Uttar Pradesh and Delhi.

Jhala: is a Scheduled Caste in Orissa.

Jhalo Malo, Jhalo-Malo: is a Scheduled Caste in Arunachal Pradesh, Meghalaya, Mezoram, West Bengal and Tripura. They also referred to as Malo or Malo patni. Jhalo Malo, perhaps be a composite of two words, Jhalo and Malo; the former may be the corrupt form of the word jaal meaning net or jal meaning water, and the latter may be a derivative of the Arabic word mallah, which means a boatman. These also probably refer to their occupation of fishing.

Jhalo: is a Scheduled Caste in Assam.

Jhusia: is a Scheduled Caste in Uttar Pradesh.

Jingar: is a Scheduled Caste in Rajasthan. Their name is derived from their occupation of making jins (saddle) for horses and camels.

Jogi: is a Scheduled Caste in Himachal Pradesh; a Denotified Tribe in Tamil Nadu; and a Nomadic Tribe in Gujarat.

Usually referred to as Nath or Kanphata Jogi, and they claim their descent from Baba Gorakhnath.

Jolaha, Julaha, Julahe: is a Scheduled Caste in Jammu and Kashmir, Punjab, Delhi and Himachal Pradesh. They are a community of weavers. The etymology of the word julaha, perhaps derived from the Persian word julah, meaning a ball of thread.

Kabirpanthi: is a Scheduled Caste in Jammu and Kashmir, Punjab, Rajasthan, Delhi and Himachal Pradesh. The Julahas are grouped with the Kabir Panthi in the notification of the Scheduled Castes in Punjab. By profession they are weavers in Punjab.

Kachhanda: is a Scheduled Caste in Delhi.

Kadaiyan: is a Scheduled Caste in Karnataka, Tamil Nadu and Kerala. Their community name, Kadaiyan, is derived from the word kadai, meaning lower caste, as they are the last in the social hierarchy.

Kadar: is a Scheduled Caste in West Bengal.

Kahar: is a Scheduled Caste in Tripura. Kahar is derived from the words Kandh and Bhar, i.e., one who bears a burden on his shoulders and they are traditional palanquin-bearers. They claim their descent from Jarasandha, King of Magadh.

Kaibartta, Jalia Kaibartta, Jalia Kaibarta: is a Scheduled Caste in Assam, West Bengal and Tripura. The word Kaibarta is derived from ka, meaning water, and varta, meaning livelihood. Before 1912 they were known as Nadial or Jalia.

Kaikadi: is a Scheduled Caste, a Denotified Tribe and a Nomadic Tribe in Maharashtra; and a Denotified Tribe in Andhra Pradesh. In some parts of Maharashtra they are also referred to as Godhwe Sonar, and professionally, they are basket makers.

Kakkalan: is a Scheduled Caste in Kerala and Tamil Nadu; and a Nomadic Tribe in Tamil Nadu. Also known as Kakka Kuravan, Kuravan, Koravan and Kakkan.

Kalabaz: is a Scheduled Caste in Uttar Pradesh. They trace their origion to Rajputana and they are now acrobats.

Kalebelia: is a Scheduled Caste in Madhya Pradesh, Rajasthan and Delhi. They also have known as Gattiwala, from their occupation of manufacturing grinding stones (gatti).

Kalindi: is a Scheduled Caste in Tripura.

Kalladi: is a Scheduled Caste in Kerala, Tamil Nadu and Karnataka.

Kamad, Kamadia: is a Scheduled Caste in Rajasthan. This community is known for their Terathali dance.

Kami (Nepali): is a Scheduled Caste in West Bengal and Sikkim. The Kamis are basically a Nepali blacksmith community, who claim descent from the mythical architect, Visvakarma.

Kamoh, Dagoli: is a Scheduled Caste in Himachal Pradesh.

Kan: is a Scheduled Caste in Tripura.

Kanakkan: is a Scheduled Caste in Kerala and Tamil Nadu. They also referred to as Padanan.

Kanda: is a Scheduled Caste in Tripura.

Kandra, Kandara, Kondara: is a Scheduled Caste in Orissa and West Bengal; but a Scheduled Tribe in Madhya Pradesh and Maharashtra as a sub-tribe of Gond.

Kanera: is a Scheduled Caste in Madhya Pradesh and Maharashtra.

Kanjar or Giarah: is a Scheduled Caste in Bihar, Madhya Pradesh, Rajasthan, Uttar Pradeh, West Bengal and Delhi; is a Denotified Tribe in Tamil Nadu, Madhya Pradesh, Punjab, Rajasthan and Uttar Pradesh; and is a Nomadic Tribe in Andhra Pradesh, Madhya Pradesh, Maharashtra, Karnataka, Rajasthan and Uttar Pradesh. They are also known as Kanjar Kuchbandhiya (Kuchbandne), Patharkute, Pachyeye, Kanmaelia Sirkipal and Siriband.

Kanugh: is a Scheduled Caste in Tripura.

Kaora, Koera: is a Scheduled Caste in West Bengal.

Kapadia Sansi: is a Scheduled Caste in Rajasthan. They are an offshoot of the Sansi and re also referred to as the Kapadia.

Kapariya, Kaparia: is a Scheduled Caste as well as a Nomadic Tribe in Uttar Pradesh. They derive their name from the Hindi word kapra, meaning cloth.

Karenga, Koranga, Kurunga: is a Scheduled Caste in Orissa and West Bengal. The term Karanga or Koranga refers to those people who castrate goats and bullocks and are also called Chhutar.

Karim Pallan: is a Scheduled Caste in Kerala, Tamil Nadu and Karnataka.

Karoack: is a Scheduled Caste in Himachal Pradesh.

Karua: is a Scheduled Caste in Orissa.

Karwal: is a Scheduled Caste in Uttar Pradesh. Karwal is derived from the word karol, meaning a sickle, which is associated with their occupation of hunting, and they are also known as Karual.

Katia: is a Scheduled Caste in Madhya Pradesh, Maharashtra and Orissa. They are also referred to Kotia Kaibarta and Keuta. They are tradition occupation is fishing and weaving and spinning. The word Kalibarta is derived from ka, meaning water and vrta, meaning livelihood.

Kaur: is a Scheduled Caste in West Bengal. The Kela is a generic group, and they encompass various acrobatic communities like the Bajikar, Matia, Patharia, Naik, Nalua, Malikota, Dum Duma and Mundapotta.

Kavara: is a Scheduled Caste as well as a Nomadic Tribe in Kerala and Tamil Nadu.

Kela: is a Scheduled Caste in Orissa.

Keot, Kewat, Keyot: is a Scheduled Caste in West Bengal and Tripura. They are also referred to as Kevot, meaning fishermen.

Kepmari: is a Scheduled Caste in Karnataka.

Khadala: is a Scheduled Caste in Orissa.

Khadit: is a Scheduled Caste in Tripura.

Khaira: is a Scheduled Caste in West Bengal and the Khaira are also known as Roy. They received the title Roy from the zamindars.

Khairaha: is a Scheduled Caste in Uttar Pradesh.

Khalpa: is a Scheduled Caste in Gujarat, Maharashtra, Karnataka and Rajasthan.

Khangar: is a Scheduled Caste in Uttar Pradesh, Madhya Pradesh, Bihar, Maharashtra and Rajasthan. The word Khangar means a sword bearer or a warrior. They are called Khangar Thakur in Uttar Pradesh, Raj thakur in Bihar and Gohenja in Rajasthan. They are also known as Kehngar, Kharal, Khara, Rawat and Kharwal.

Kharia, Kharian, Kheria: is a Scheduled Caste in Tripura; but is a Scheduled Tribe in Bihar, Madhya Pradesh, Maharashtra, Orissa and West Bengal.

Kharwar: is a Scheduled Caste in Uttar Pradesh; but is Scheduled Tribe in Bihar, Orissa and West Bengal. Their community name is derived either from their occupation as makers of catechu (khair) from a tree, Acacia catechu, or from their emigration from a place called Khairgarh.

Khatik: is a Scheduled Caste in Uttar Pradesh, West Bengal, Rajasthan, Punjab, Chandigarh, Himachal Pradesh, Haryana, Delhi, Maharashtra and Madhya Pradesh. The word Khatik is derived from the Sanskrit word, Khatika, meaning a butcher or a hunter.

Khorot: is a Scheduled Caste in Uttar Pradesh.

Koch: is a Scheduled Caste in West Bengal and Tripura.

Kodaiyan: is a Scheduled Caste in Kerala, Tamil Nadu and Karnataka.

Kodalo, Khodalo: is a Scheduled Caste in Orissa. They are also referred to as Bhoi and Bauri.

Koir: is a Scheduled Caste in Tripura.

Kol: is a Scheduled Caste in Uttar Pradesh and Tripura; but is a Scheduled Tribe in Madhya Pradesh, Maharashtra and Orissa.

Koli, Kori: is a Scheduled Caste in Madhya Pradesh, Maharashtra, Punjab, Orissa, Rajasthan, Uttar Pradesh, Delhi and Himachal Pradesh.

Koliyan: is a Scheduled Caste in Tamil Nadu. They are also called Vadiriyan or Vathiriyan.

Kolupulvandlu: is a Scheduled Caste in Andhra Pradesh, Maharashtra and Karnataka.

Komah: is a Scheduled Caste in Himachal Pradesh.

Konai: is a Scheduled Caste in West Bengal. The Konai are also referred to as the Chasi Konai. The word chasi means cultivator.

Konwar: is a Scheduled Caste in West Bengal.

Koochband, Kuchband, Kuchbandhia: is a Scheduled Caste in Rajasthan; and is a Scheduled Caste as well as a Nomadic Tribe in Madhya Pradesh.

Koosa: is a Scheduled Caste in Karnataka, Kerala and Tamil Nadu.

Kootan, Koodan: is a Scheduled Caste in Kerala and Tamil Nadu.

Kora: is a Scheduled Caste in Tripura; and a Scheduled Tribe in Bihar, Orissa and West Bengal.

Koracha: is a Scheduled Caste in Karnataka; and a Scheduled Tribe in Andhra Pradesh and Maharashtra.

Korama, Korma, Kunchi Korava: is a Scheduled Caste as well as a Scheduled Tribe in Karnataka.

Korar: is a Scheduled Caste in Gujarat, Maharashtra, Karnataka and Rajasthan.

Kori: is a Scheduled Caste in Uttar Pradesh, Rajasthan, Delhi, Haryana, Madhya Pradesh and Maharashtra

Korwa, Korua: is a Scheduled Caste in Uttar Pradesh; and a Scheduled Tribe in Bihar, Madhya Pradesh, Maharashtra, Orissa and West Bengal.

Kotal: is a Scheduled Caste in West Bengal and Tripura. They are also referred to as Kotwal, meaning watchman, the Kotwal are a caste that are employed as watchman.

Kotegar: is a Scheduled Caste in Karnataka. The word Kotegar is derived from the word kottai, meaning fort, as once they were the guards of forts.

Kotwal: is a Scheduled Caste in Madhya Pradesh and Rajasthan.

Kuchbandhia, Kuchbandhiya: is a Scheduled Caste in Madhya Pradesh.

Kudumban: is a Scheduled Caste in Kerala, Tamil Nadu and Karnataka. They are also known as Pallar, Pallan, Devendra Kulattan, Kaladi, Muppan, Kadaiyan, Pannaiyadi or Pannadi, Mannadi, Pattakkaran and Mambattikkaran.

Kuli: is a Scheduled Caste as well as a Scheduled Tribe in Orissa.

Kumhar: is a Scheduled Caste in Madhya Pradesh.

Kummari, Kummeri: is a Scheduled Caste in Orissa; but a Backward Class (OBC) in Andhra Pradesh. They are known by different names such as Kummari in Telugu, Kumbhara in Oriya and Kumba in Canarese, all of which have been derived from the Sanskrit word Kumbhakara, meaning the pot maker.

Kurariar, Kureri: is a Scheduled Caste in Bihar and West Bengal.

Kuravan, Sidhanar: is a Scheduled Caste in Kerala, Tamil Nadu, Karnataka and Pondicherry.

Kurunga: is a Scheduled Caste in Orissa.

Laheri: is a Scheduled Caste in Orissa.

Lalbegi: is a Scheduled Caste in Assam, Bihar, Gujarat, Madhya Pradesh, Maharashtra, Karnataka, Rajasthan, Uttar Pradesh, West Bengal and Delhi.

Lambadi, Lambani, Lamani, Laban: is a Scheduled Caste in Karnataka and Orissa; Scheduled Tribe in Andhra Pradesh; Denotified Tribe in Gujarat, Tamil Nadu and

Maharashtra and a Nomadic Tribe in Andhra Pradesh, Gujarat, Maharashtra and Karnataka.

Lingader: is a Scheduled Caste in Maharashtra, Karnataka and Gujarat. The name Lingader is referent to all those who wear the phallic emblem symbolizing Shiva (lingam).

Lohar: is a Scheduled Caste in West Bengal and Himachal Pradesh. The word lohar is derived from loha, meaning iron, and they are a traditional ironsmith community. The lohar is also known as the Nar, Nar Bagdi and Lohar Bagdi in West Benga.

Loi, Lois: is a Scheduled Caste in Manipur.

Machala: is a Scheduled Caste in Karnataka.

Madari: is a Scheduled Caste in Gujarat, Madhya Pradesh, Tamil Nadu, Maharashtra, Karnataka, Orissa, Rajasthan and Delhi; a Nomadic Tribe in Andhra Pradesh, Assam, Gujarat, Jammu and Kashmir, Kerala, Madhya Pradesh, Tamil Nadu, Maharashra, Karnataka, Rajasthan, Uttar Pradesh, Himachal Pradesh and Tripura.

Madasi Kuruva, Madari Kuruva: is a Scheduled Caste in Andhra Pradesh.

Madiga Dasu, Mashteen: is a Scheduled Caste in Andhra Pradesh.

Madiga, Madgi: is a Scheduled Caste (also the largest community amongst the SCs in A.P.) in Andhra Pradesh, Tamil Nadu, Madhya Pradesh, Maharashtra, Karnataka, Orissa and Pondicherry. The Madiga of Andhra Pradesh are also referred to as Arundhatiya, Jambavalu, Jambhavanthulu and Adi Andhra.

Mahar, Mehar, Mahara, Mehara: is a Scheduled Caste in Andhra Pradesh, Assam, Gujarat, Madhya Pradesh, Maharashtra, Karnataka, Orissa, Rajasthan, West Bengal and Dadra and Nagar Haveli. In Maharashtra they also notified as Taral, Dhegu and Megu, and call themselves Neo-Buddhist or Buddhist, after their conversion to Bhuddhism in 1956 under the leadership of Dr. B.R. Ambedkar.

Mahisyadas: is a Scheduled Caste in Tripura. They are also referred to as Matsyadas, Haluadas and Halladas.

Mahuria: is a Scheduled Caste in Orissa. They are also known as Muhuri and Mahurbais.

Mahyavanshi, Mahya Banshi: is a Scheduled Caste in Gujarat, Maharashtra, Karnataka, Rajasthan and Dadra and Nagar Haveli. In Maharashtra they are notified as Mahyavanshi, Dhed, Vankar and Maru Vankar. In Gujarat they are also known as Meghawal, Vankar, Vankor Mahya Vanshi Vankar, Goneshya and Harijan.

Maila: is a Scheduled Caste in Karnataka. They ae also known as Dikka Nakalu. The word maila might have been derived from its meaning – unclean or pollution.

Majhi, Majhwar: is a Scheduled Caste in Uttar Pradesh; but a Scheduled Tribe in Madhya Pradesh and Maharashtra.

Mal: is a Scheduled Caste in West Bengal.

Mala Dasari, Mala Dasu: is a Scheduled Caste in Andhra Pradesh, Tamil Nadu, Maharashtra and Karnataka. The Mala Dasaris are priests to the Vaishnavite Mala.

Mala Hannai: is a Scheduled Caste in Andhra Pradesh, Karnataka and Maharashtra.

Mala Jangam: is a Scheduled Caste in Andhra Pradesh, Maharashtra and Karnataka. The Mala Jangam offer priestly services to the Saivite Malas (due to heavy influence of Vira Shaivism of Basavesvara). The Malas who converted to Lingayat sect or opted to be a Jangam, became mala jangam.

Mala Masti: is a Scheduled Caste in Andhra Pradesh, Maharashtra, Karnataka and Pondicherry. They are known variously as Mala Machachathi, Mala Machachatiollu and Mastiollu.

Mala Sale (Netkani, Netkani): is a Scheduled Caste in Andhra Pradesh and Karnataka. In Andhra Pradesh, they are a community of weaving.

Mala Sanyasi: is a Scheduled Caste in Karnataka, Maharashtra and Andhra Pradesh.

Mala: is a Scheduled Caste in Andhra Pradesh, Tamil Nadu, Kerala, Maharashtra, Karnataka, Orissa and Pondicherry.

Malayan: is a Scheduled Caste in Tamil Nadu; but in Kerala it is categorized both as Scheduled Tribe and Scheduled Caste.

Mali, Malakar: is a Scheduled Caste in Assam and Tripura.

Malkana: is a Scheduled Caste in Gujarat, Maharashtra, Karnataka and Rajasthan.

Mallah: is a Scheduled Caste in West Bengal and Delhi; but a Denotified Tribe in Uttar Pradesh.

Malo: is a Scheduled Caste in Assam, Orissa and West Bengal.

Manesh: is a Scheduled Caste in Punjab.

Mang: is a Scheduled Caste in Andhra Pradesh, Gujarat, Madhya Pradesh, Maharashtra, Karnataka, Orissa and Rajasthan.

Mangan: is a Scheduled Caste in Orissa.

Mang-Garodi, Mang-Garudi: is a Scheduled Caste in Andhra Pradesh, Gujarat, Madhya Pradesh, Maharashtra, Karnataka and Rajasthan; also a Denotified Tribe in Gujarat and Maharashtra.

Mannan: is a Scheduled Caste as well as a Scheduled Tribe in Kerala and Tamil Nadu. They are also referred to as Neriyan, Pathiyan, Velan, Vannan, Perumannan and Peruvannan.

Manne: is a Scheduled Caste in Andhra Pradesh, Maharashtra and Karnataka.

Marija or Mareecha: is a Scheduled Caste in Punjab.

Maruvankar: is a Scheduled Caste in Gujarat, Maharashtra, Karnataka and Rajasthan.

Mashti, Masthi: is a Scheduled Caste in Andhra Pradesh, Maharashtra and Karnataka.

Matang: is a Scheduled Caste in Gujarat, Maharashtra, Karnataka and Rajasthan.

Matangi: is a Scheduled Caste in Andhra Pradesh. They are also known as Madiga Bhogam Vallu, Basavi, Basavirandru, Matammavallu and Yellamma vandlu. They claim to be the descendants of Matanga Maharishi, the son of Adi Jambava.

Mavilan, Mavillon: is a Scheduled Caste in Kerala, Tamil Nadu and Karnataka. Etymologically Mavilan is derived from the word mavilavu, a local herb, which they used to collect and sell.

Mazhabi, Majhabi: is a Scheduled Caste in Punjab, Haryana, Rajasthan, Uttar Pradesh, Delhi and Himachal Pradesh. They are also referred to as Mazbi or Mazzhabi and Rangretta or Rangretha. The word Mazbi means faithful.

Megh, Maghwal, Meghval, Menghvar: is a Scheduled Caste in Andhra Pradesh, Gujarat, Jammu and Kashmir, Madhya Pradesh, Maharashtra, Karnataka, Punjab, Rajasthan, Delhi and Himachal Pradesh.

Mehar: is a Scheduled Caste in Rajasthan. They are also spelt as Meher, and they call themselves Nandavanshi and claim a Rajput descent.

Mehtar, Mehtor: is a Scheduled Caste in Assam, Andhra Pradesh, Bihar, Gujarat, Madhya Pradesh, Maharashtra, Karnataka, Orissa, Rajasthan, West Bengal and Tripura. The term Mehtar, meaning a prince or a leader, is an ironic title given to the people who are traditionally engaged as sweepers and scavengers and are known by different names in different parts of the country, like Bhangi, Hari, Lalbegi (those who are the followers of the patron-saint Lalbeg) and so on.

Metri: is a Scheduled Caste in Karnataka.

Mewar: is a Scheduled Caste in Orissa.

Minimadig: is a Scheduled Caste in Maharashtra, Gujarat, Karnataka and Rajasthan.

Mirdha: is a Scheduled Caste in Madhya Pradesh and Maharashtra; but a Scheduled Tribe in Orissa.

Mitha Ayyalvar, Mithulu Ayyavaru: is a Scheduled Caste in Andhra Pradesh. They are a community of priests and spiritual guides (gurus) to the Dalit communities in Telangana region of Andhra Pradesh. They are also known as Nithya Ayyavar.

Mochi, Muchi, Mochigar, Machigar: is a Scheduled Caste in Bihar, Andhra Pradesh, Gujarat, Madhya Pradesh, Karnataka, Maharashtra, Orissa, West Bengal, Rjasthan, Himachal Pradesh and Delhi.

Moger, Mugger: is a Scheduled Caste in Kerala, Tamil Nadu and Karnataka. The word Mugger, derived from the Tulu word, mugela, meaning rabbit, and it is believed that they were rat hunters in the olden days.

Moghia, Moghya, Mogia, Monghya: is a Scheduled Caste in Maharashtra; but it is a Scheduled Caste as well as a Scheduled Tribe in Madhya Pradesh.

Mukri: is a Scheduled Caste in Maharashtra, Gujarat, Karnataka and Rajasthan. They are also known as the Ganji.

Mundala: is a Scheduled Caste in Karnataka, Tamil Nadu, Kerala and Andhra Pradesh.

Mundapotta: is a Scheduled Caste in Orissa. They are also known as Anadari.

Musahar: is a Scheduled Caste in Tripura, Bihar, Orissa, Uttar Pradesh and West Bengal.

Mushkan: is a Scheduled Caste in Madhya Pradesh. Mushkan seems to be a corrupt form of Musahar or Mushar that is derived from musa (flesh) and hera (seeker); and another derivation is that it is from musa and har, meaning rat-eaters.

Nadia: is a Scheduled Caste in Rajasthan, Maharashtra, Gujarat and Karnataka. They are also known as Hadi, and the community name Nadia is derived from their traditional occupation of making narda ornardi, a leather strip used to tie the bullocks with the plough.

Nagarchi: is a Scheduled Caste in Orissa.

Naikda, Nayakada Nyaka, Nayak, Naik: is a Scheduled Caste in Rajasthan; a Scheduled Tribe in Andhra Pradesh,

Gujarat, Maharashtra, Mysore, Rajasthan and Dadra and Nagar Haveli; also a Nomadic Tribe in Madhya Pradesh, Rajasthan.

Nalakedava, Nalkedaya: is a Scheduled Caste in Karnataka, Tamil Nadu and Kerala. They also referred to as Paner, Ajila, Nalke and Nalkadaya and they are well known for their ritual dance, which forms part of spirit (bhuta) worshipping.

Namsudra, Namsaudra: is a Scheduled Caste in Assam, Arunachal Pradesh, Meghalaya, Orissa, West Bengal, Manipur and Tripura. The other synonymous of the Namasudra are Chandal, Chanral, Namasud and Nama. Their community name is derived from Namasa or Lomasa Muni.

Naribut, Naribat: is a Scheduled Caste in Delhi. The word naribat is derived from the Hindi words nari, meaning chord and bat which means to knit, whereas their synonym Bawari is derived from the word bavar, meaning a noose, which is used for trapping animals.

Nat, Nut: is a Scheduled Caste in Bihar, Madhya Pradesh, Rajasthan, Uttar Pradesh, Punjab, West Bengal, Chandigarh, Delhi and Himachal Pradesh; a Scheduled Tribe Madhya Pradesh; and a Denotified Tribe in Madhya Pradesh, Rajasthan and Uttar Pradesh; and a Nomadic Tribe in Gujarat, Madhya Pradesh, Maharashtra, Karnataka, Rajasthan, Uttar Pradesh and West Bengal. They are a community of professional dancers, singers and acrobats of Rajasthan. They prefer to call themselves Raj Nat because of their traditional linkages with the erstwhile Rajput rulers. Their community name is derived from the Sanskrit word nata, meaning a dancer, a term popularly associated with their acrobatic skills.

Nayadi: is a Scheduled Caste in Kerala, Karnataka and Tamil Nadu. The term Nayadi is derived from the word nayattu, meaning hunting, which is their traditional occupation.

Neo-Buddhist: is a Scheduled Caste in Maharashtra, Uttar

Pradesh, Andhra Pradesh, Gujarat, Karnataka, Punjab, Delhi and many other places across the country. They also referred to as Nav Buddhist, as they are the new converts to Buddhism. Dr. B.R. Ambedkar initiated these conversions to the Buddhist faith and the first mass-level conversions took place in 1956 at Nagpur in Maharashtra.

Nona: is a Scheduled Caste in Gujarat, Madhya Pradesh and Maharashtra.

Nuniya: is a Scheduled Caste in West Bengal. They are also known as Chauhan.

Od: is a Scheduled Caste in Himachal Pradesh, Haryana and Punjab. In Haryana these were also known as Beldar Rajputs.

Olgana: is a Scheduled Caste in Maharashtra, Gujarat, Karnataka and Rajasthan.

Padannan: is a Scheduled Caste in Kerala and Tamil Nadu. These were also known as Kankkan Padannan or Padanna Vettuvan.

Pagadai: is a Scheduled Caste in Tamil Nadu and Karnataka. They are also known as Chakkiliyan and Arundhatiyar. The Pagadai claim their descent from sage Adi Jambavadu.

Paidi: is a Scheduled Caste in Andhra Pradesh, Karnataka, Orissa and Tamil Nadu.

Painda: is a Scheduled Caste in Orissa.

Paky, Paki: is a Scheduled Caste in Andhra Pradesh and Pondicherry. They are also called Thoti and Moti. The name Paky is derived from paki, meaning a bird.

Pale: is a Scheduled Caste in Karnataka.

Paliya: is a Scheduled Caste in West Bengal.

Pallan: is a Scheduled Caste in Tamil Nadu, Karnataka, Kerala and Pondicherry.

Palluvan, Pulluvan: is a Scheduled Caste in Tamil Nadu and Kerala. These are a community of medicinemen and singers who sing songs in praise of snakes.

Pambada, Pambala, Pambanda: is a Scheduled Caste in Orissa, Karnataka, Kerala, Tamil Nadu and Andhra Pradesh.

Pamidi: is a Scheduled Caste in Andhra Pradesh.

Pan, Pano: is a Scheduled Caste in West Bengal, Bihar and Orissa. These are also known as the Sawasi.

Panan: is a Scheduled Caste in Tamil Nadu and Kerala, and professionally they are umbrella makers.

Panchama: is a Scheduled Caste in Andhra Pradesh, Tamil Nadu, Karnataka, Kerala and Orissa. This is an another generic term, used by the caste-Hindus under the scheme of Chaturvarna scheme of social stratification. A number of endogamous communities like the Mala, Madiga, Paky, Chachoti, Relli, Thoti, Mala Masteen, and many others are encompassed in the generic category of Panchama.

Panika, Panka, Punkah, Pankhia: is a Scheduled Caste in Orissa and Uttar Pradesh; and a Scheduled Tribe in Madhya Pradesh. There are also various synonyms like Ponka, Manikpuri Panka, Kabir Das Panka or Das Panka. They are traditional weaving and basket making community.

Pannadi, Pannadai: is a Scheduled Caste in Karnataka and Tamil Nadu. They are often known as Pallar and Devendrakulathan, and are belived to be the original inhabitants of Tamil Nadu.

Pannan, Panans, Panan: is a Scheduled Caste in Kerala and Tamil Nadu.

Panniandi: is a Scheduled Caste in Tamil Nadu.Their community name is derived from their traditional occupation of piggery – Panni means pig and andi denotes a wanderer.

Pano: is a Scheduled Caste in Andhra Pradesh, Orissa, Karnataka and Tamil Nadu.

Pantanti, Patartanti: is a Scheduled Caste in Orissa.

Pap: is a Scheduled Caste in Orissa.This is a little known community, and they believe that they are called Pap because of a sinful act committed by their ancestors. The word Pap means sin.

Parahiya, Parhaiya, Parheya: is a Scheduled Caste in Uttar Pradesh; and a Scheduled Tribe in Bihar and West Bengal.

Paravan, Parvar: is a Scheduled Caste in Kerala, Karnataka and Tamil Nadu. This is a community of shell collectors and lime burners, and they distinguish themselves from the Tamil Paravan who are fishermen and the Canarese Paravan who are devil-dancers.

Paraya, Parayan, Paraiyan: is a Scheduled Caste in Karnataka, Kerala, Pondicherry and Tamil Nadu. The name of the community Paraiyan derived from the Tamil word parai, a drum, as they are professional drummers and musicians.

Pardhi, Paradhi: is a Scheduled Caste and as well as Scheduled Tribe in Madhya Pradesh and Rajasthan; and only a Scheduled Tribe in Gujarat, Maharashtra and Karnataka. They are also known as Mogia and Bagri.

Pariah: is a Scheduled Caste in Andhra Pradesh.

Pasi: is a Scheduled Caste in Bihar, Gujarat, Karnataka, Maharashtra, Orissa, Punjab, Rajasthan, West Bengal, Himachal Pradesh and Delhi; and a Scheduled Caste as well as a Denotified Tribe in Madhya Pradesh and Uttar Pradesh. Many of them trace their origin to the sage, Bhrigu. In Bihar they are toddy-tappers.

Patari, Pathari: is a Scheduled Caste in Uttar Pradesh; and a Scheduled Tribe in Madhya Pradesh and Maharashtra.

Patharia: is a Scheduled Caste in Maharashtra and Madhya Pradesh.

Pathiyan: is a Scheduled Caste in Tamil Nadu and Kerala. They are also described as Varnavar and Mannan.

Patial, Patikar: is a Scheduled Caste in Orissa.

Patni: is a Scheduled Caste in West Bengal, Assam, Manipur and Tripura.

Patratanti, Patrachandri, Pataar Tanti: is a Scheduled Caste in Orissa.

Patua: is a Scheduled Caste in Orissa.

Perna: is a Scheduled Caste in Delhi and Punjab.

Perumannan, Peruvannan: is a Scheduled Caste in Tamil Nadu and Kerala.

Pherera, Phrera, Pharera: is a Scheduled Caste in Himachal Pradesh and Punjab. They pursue the same occupation as the Rangrez and Rangsaz, who are dyers.

Pod, Poundra: is a Scheduled Caste in West Bengal. They were also known as Poundra Kshatriya.

Pulaya, Pulayan: is a Scheduled Caste as well as a Scheduled Tribe in Kerala and Tamil Nadu, but only a Scheduled Tribe in Karnataka.

Puthirai Vannan, Puthurai Vannan: is a Scheduled Caste in Tamil Nadu and Kerala.

Radhe-Mang: is a Scheduled Caste in Maharashtra and Madhya Pradesh.

Raigar, Regar, Rehgar, Rehgarh: is a Scheduled Caste in Madhya Pradesh, Punjab, Rajasthan and Delhi.

Rajbanshi, Rajbasi: is a Scheduled Caste in West Bengal. They are known as Desi, Bahey and Rajbansi Kshatriya.

Rajna: is a Scheduled Caste in Orissa.

Rajuar, Rajwar: is a Scheduled Caste in Bihar and West Bengal; and a Scheduled Tribe in Orissa.

Ramdasi, Ramdasia, Ramdeshi: is a Scheduled Caste in Jammu and Kashmir, Punjab, Rajasthan, Delhi and Himachal Pradesh.

Rana, Ranah: is a Scheduled Caste in Delhi.

Raneyar: is a Scheduled Caste in Karnataka, Kerala and Tamil Nadu.

Ratal: is a Scheduled Caste in Jammu and Kashmir.

Ravidasi, Raidasi, Raidas, Raidass, Rohidas, Ruidas: is a Scheduled Caste in Gujarat, Madhya Pradesh,

Maharashtra, Karnataka, Punjab, Rajasthan, West Bengal, Delhi, Himachal Pradesh and Manipur.

Rawal, Rawalia: is a Scheduled Caste in Rajasthan.

Rawat, Ravat, Rawatta: is a Scheduled Caste in Gujarat, Karnataka, Maharashtra, Rajasthan and Uttar Pradesh.

Rehar, Rehara: is a Scheduled Caste in Himachal Pradesh.

Relli: is a Scheduled Caste in Andhra Pradesh and Orissa. They are also known as Sachcharis, Chachatis, Relli Chachadis, Spris and Sapru.

Rishi: is a Scheduled Caste in Assam and West Bengal.

Rujjhar, Rujjar: is a Scheduled Caste in Madhya Pradesh. They claim their descent from Bhimsen and Darui Thakur.

Sabakhia: is a Scheduled Caste in Orissa. They also have known as Swalgiri.

Sabar: is a Scheduled Caste in Tripura.

Saharia, Shariya, Seharia, Sehria: is a Scheduled Caste in Uttar Pradesh; and a Scheduled Tribe in Madhya Pradesh and Rajasthan. They are also known as Rawat, Sahoria, Sohariya, Bamrawat, Banrakha, Soonrain and Sororain.

Salvi, Halvi: is a Scheduled Caste in Rajasthan.

Samagara, Samgar: is a Scheduled Caste in Andhra Pradesh, Karnataka, Kerala, Tamil Nadu, Gujarat and Rajasthan. They are also known as the Chamgars and Chambar.

Samasi: is a Scheduled Caste in Orissa. There are called Swasi.

Samban: is a Scheduled Caste in Andhra Pradesh, Karnataka, Tamil Nadu, Kerala and Pondicherry.

Sambavar, Sambavan (Pavan): is a Scheduled Caste in Tamil Nadu, Kerala and Pondicherry.

Sanaurhiya, Sanauria, Sanoria: is a Scheduled Caste in Uttar Pradesh.

Sanei: is a Scheduled Caste in Orissa. The community name Sanei might be derived from sind, meaning a hole under the floor, an allusion to those who stole things by making holes.

Sanhai, Sanahai: is a Scheduled Caste in Himachal Pradesh, Haryana and Punjab. Their community name is derived from the musical instrument called sehnai (clarionet) as they are traditionally enganged in sehnai playing.

Sanhal: is a Scheduled Caste in Punjab, Haryana, Chandigarh and Himachal Pradesh.

Sansi, Sansia, Sansiya: is a Scheduled Caste in Gujarat, Maharashtra, Madhya Pradesh, Himachal Pradesh, Punjab, Rajasthan, Haryana, Chandigarh, Uttar Pradesh and Delhi. They are also known as Bhedkut and Manesh.

Sansoi, Sansoe: is a Scheduled Caste in Himachal Pradesh.

Santia: is a Scheduled Caste in Rajasthan.

Sapari, Sapru: is a Scheduled Caste in Andhra Pradesh, Karnataka, Tamil Nadu and Orissa.

Sapera, Sapela: is a Scheduled Caste in Madhya Pradesh, Punjab, Rajasthan, Himachal Pradesh and Delhi. The word Sapera is derived from the Hindi word sap, meaning sname. They are snake charmers.

Sarbhangi, Sarbanggi, Sharbhange, Sar Bhangi: is a Scheduled Caste in Rajasthan.

Sarde, Sardi: is a Scheduled Caste in Himachal Pradesh.

Sarera, Sarare, Siryare, Sorehra, Sarde: is a Scheduled Caste in Jammu and Kashmir, Punjab and Himachal Pradesh.

Sargara: is a Scheduled Caste in Rajasthan. They are localled Harhgada.

Sarki (Nepali): is a Scheduled Caste in West Bengal. They are also referred to as Mistri, Karighar and Kanikar.

Saryara: is a Scheduled Caste in Jammu and Kashmir.

Satnami: is a Scheduled Caste in Madhya Pradesh, Maharashtra and Orissa.

Sauntia, Santia, Sauntiya: is a Scheduled Caste in Orissa. The community name derived from saman tiba, meaning to pick up scattered things or gathered in.

Semalia: is a Scheduled Caste in Gujarat.

Semman, Chemman: is a Scheduled Caste in Karnataka, Kerala and Tamil Nadu. They are also known as Tol Mestri, Tondaman and Semmaravan.

Shenva, Senva, Senava: is a Scheduled Caste in Karnataka, Gujarat, Maharashtra and Rajasthan. They are also referred to as Chenva, Senwa, Sindhva, Sedma or Rawat.

Shilpkar: is a Scheduled Caste in Uttar Pradesh. They are also referred to as Darji, Damai, Dhoni, Dhaloti, Kolai, Telia, Hurkiya, Dhunar, Koli, Kolta, Lapor, Mour, Lohar, Okhera, Orh, Pauri, Parki, Tamta, Rudia, Tirwa, Chuniyara and Chanyal.

Sidhria: is a Scheduled Caste in Orissa.

Sidugadu Siddha, Sudugadusidda: is a Scheduled Caste in Karnataka.

Sikligar: is a Scheduled Caste in Haryana, Chandigarh, Himachal Pradesh, Punjab and Delhi. They are also referred to as Saiqalgar and Siqligar, and locally they are called Tala-Chabi wala.

Silawat, Silavant: is a Scheduled Caste in Madhya Pradesh. The term Silawat originated from the word sila, meaning stone, i.e., those who work on stone.

Sillekyatha, Sillakyata: is a Scheduled Caste in Karnataka. They are also known by different names such as Killekyata, Marathi, Killiket and Gokmbe Ramaru.

Sindhollu, Sindhuvallu: is a Scheduled Caste in Andhra Pradesh, Karnataka and Maharashtra.

Sinduria: is a Scheduled Caste in Orissa. They are also known as Sidhiria.

Singiwala, Singhiwala: is a Scheduled Caste in Rajasthan and Delhi. They are known for their indigenous surgical practices. The name Singiwala is a combination of two words, singi (a colonial brass pipe with a wide mouth at one end and a narrow hole at the other) and wala (holder), i.e., a person with a singi; a singi is used to such impure blood from the infected woulds of the body. They are also called Kalebelia and Jheewar Bengalee (because this knowledge was supposed to have come to them from Bengal).

Sipi, Chhipi, Sippi: is a Scheduled Caste in Himachal Pradesh.

Sirkiband: is a Scheduled Caste in Punjab, Haryana, Himachal Pradesh and Delhi. The community name derived from the words sirki and band and the combined meaning of these words refer to those who make mats (sirkis).

Siyal, Siols, Siyalgir: is a Scheduled Caste in Orissa. They are also known as Khajuria.

Sudugadu Siddha: is a Scheduled Caste in Karnataka. They are also called Telugu Jangama, Gombeyatadavaru, Pakanti Golla, Kadupapa, Adike Sidda and Siddaru. The term sudugadu means a crematorium or burial ground and sidha connotes mystic powers.

Sunkar, Sungar, Sonkar: is a Scheduled Caste in Madhya Pradesh.

Sunri, Sunti, Sundhi, Saundika: is a Scheduled Caste in West Bengal. They are also known as Saundika, Sundika and Shaha.

Surjyabanshi, Surajbans, Suraj-bansi: is a Scheduled Caste in Maharashtra and Madhya Pradesh.

Sutradhar, Chhutar: is a Scheduled Caste in Arunachal Pradesh, Manipur, Meghalaya, Assam and Manipur.

Tamadia, Tamudia: is a Scheduled Caste in Orissa.

Tanla, Taonla: is a Scheduled Caste in Orissa.

Taral: is a Scheduled Caste in Karnataka, Gujarat, Maharashtra and Rajasthan.

Tarmali, Tirmalis: is a Scheduled Caste in Uttar Pradesh.

Teli: is a Scheduled Caste in Himachal Pradesh. They are traditionally oil pressers.

Thandan, Tandan Thantan: is a Scheduled Caste in Tamil Nadu and Kerala.

Thathera, Thathiar: is a Scheduled Caste in Himachal Pradesh.

Thori: is a Scheduled Caste in Gujarat, Maharashtra and Rajasthan. They are also known as Utlari-wala Thori, Harijan Suthar, Batwala Thori and Batwala Suthar. There is a (Scheduled Caste) community Thori Nayak available in Rajasthan.

Thoti, Toti: is a Scheduled Caste in Andhra Pradesh, Tamil Nadu, Kerala, Karnataka and Pondicherry; and a Scheduled Tribe in Andhra Pradesh, Karnataka and Maharashtra.

Tippera, Tipperah, Tripura, Tripur: is a Scheduled Caste in Tripura.

Tirgar: is a Scheduled Caste in Karnataka, Rajasthan, Gujarat and Maharashtra. There are also known as Tirbanda, Tirkar, Tidgad, Banwati, Tirwar, Tirmali and Tridar.

Tiruvalluvar, Tiruvalluvan: is a Scheduled Caste in Karnataka and Tamil Nadu.

Tiyar, Tiar, Tior: is a Scheduled Caste in Orissa and West Bengal. They are known as Rajbanshi and Muchhua.

Turaiha, Turaha: is a Scheduled Caste in Uttar Pradesh.

Turi Barot: is a Scheduled Caste in Gujarat. They are a community that keeps the genealogies of the Vankar and are also known as Dhedh Barot and Harijat Barot.

Turi Betra: is a Scheduled Caste in Orissa. They are popularly known as Turi and Patikar.

Turi, Tooree, Toori: is a Scheduled Caste in Bihar, Gujarat, Maharashtra, Karnataka, Himachal Pradesh, West Bengal, Orissa and Rajasthan. They are known as Dom and Domra. Etymologically, the name Turi is derived from the word tokri, meaning basked, as they are of community of basket makers. In Gujarat, they are a community of genealogists and mythographers, who are also known as Turi Barot.

Ujia: is a Scheduled Caste in Orissa.

Ulladan: is a Scheduled Caste as well as a Scheduled Tribe in Tamil Nadu and Kerala.

Uraly: is a Scheduled Caste as well as a Scheduled Tribe in Tamil Nadu and Kerala.

Valhar: is a Scheduled Caste in Karnataka, Gujarat, Maharashtra and Rajasthan.

Vallan, Valan: is a Scheduled Caste in Kerala and Tamil Nadu.

Valluvan: is a Scheduled Caste in Kerala, Karnataka, Tamil Nadu and Pondicherry. They also have number of synonyms in Kerala and Tamil Nadu, namely Thiruvalluvar, Vallon, Parayasathi, Jyoshiar, Vidiyar, Dadar, Viniar, Nainar, Iyyer, Pandaram, Vinji, Alwar and Jyotidar.

Valmiki, Valamiki: is a Scheduled Caste in Orissa.

Vankar: is a Scheduled Caste in Gujarat, Karnataka, Maharashtra and Rajasthan.

Vannan: is a Scheduled Caste in Tamil Nadu and Kerala.

Vathiriyan: is a Scheduled Caste in Tamil Nadu.

Vavuri, Bavuri: is a Scheduled Caste in Andhra Pradesh. They are known as Khodalo.

Velan, Velar: is a Scheduled Caste in Kerala and Tamil Nadu.

Vetan, Vetar: is a Scheduled Caste in Kerala and Tamil Nadu.

Vettiyan: is a Scheduled Caste in Tamil Nadu and Pondicherry.

Vettuvan: is a Scheduled Caste in Kerala and Tamil Nadu.

Watal: is a Scheduled Caste in Jammu and Kashmir.

Yellamalawar, Ellamalwar, Yellammalawandlu: is a Scheduled Caste in in Andhra Pradesh, Karnataka and Maharashtra.

Zamral: is a Scheduled Caste in Madhya Pradesh and Rajasthan.

Author Index

Subject Index